First published in Great Britain in 2013
by Wymer Publishing, Bedford, England
www.wymerpublishing.co.uk
Tel: 01234 326691
Wymer Publishing is a trading name of Wymer (UK) Ltd.

Second edition, 2017. Copyright © 2013 Peter Overend Watts / Wymer Publishing.

ISBN: 978-1-908724-72-4

Edited by Phil Syphe at Grammar Eyes

Typeset by Wymer (UK) Ltd.
Printed and bound in Great Britain by
Clays Ltd, Bungay, Suffolk

A catalogue record for this book is available from the British Library.

Cover design by Wymer UK.
Front cover photo © P. O Watts

The Man Who Hated Walking
The South West Coast Path

Overend Watts

*This book is dedicated to my Mum - Joan Watts,
my late father Ron Watts,
and my sister Jane Johnstone.
Family just don't come any better than them!*

The Man Who Hated Walking

The South West Coast Path

Overend Watts

WP
WYMER
PUBLISHING
Bedford, England

CORNWALL

CIT
PLYM

ISLES OF
SCILLY

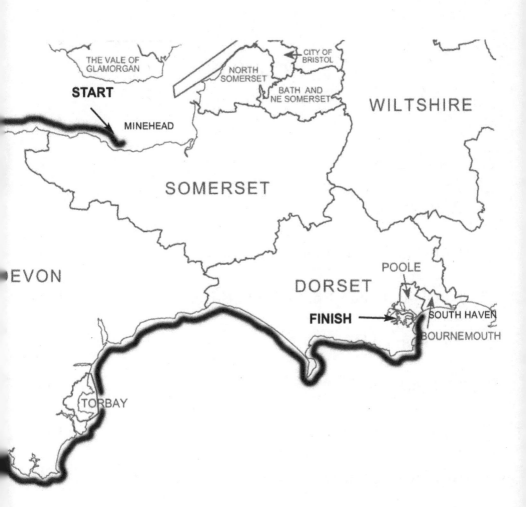

Contents

PREFACE

This is the story of my 2003 attempt to walk the whole 630.4 miles of the South West Coast Path in one go, from a standing start, having never walked a single inch previously in my life. In retrospect the journey was rather like banging my head against a brick wall - in other words it was great when I stopped!

Anyway, I kept a rough journal throughout the backpacking trip and that formed the basis of this book along with my thoughts, observations, and the various adventures that happened to me while on that long and arduous journey. I also used the trip as a bridge from my old safe familiar life into a new and uncertain one. I needed to sort myself out both mentally and physically, and it certainly worked.

It was strange that I decided to go for it at all as I'd never done any walking or even thought about it. It had always seemed a pointless pastime, and besides that, also the most long-winded and boring way of getting from A to B - why spend a whole boring hour walking 3 miles when it would only take 3 minutes in the car?

The only positive memories I had of walking and camping were my childhood fascination for good old-fashioned tramps and camping in dad's old tent in our back garden in Birmingham as a 7-year old.

It possibly all began back in the early 1950s when there were still quite a few "gentlemen of the road" about, complete with threadbare rags, full tousled beards, red and white spotted handkerchiefs on a stick, and the remainder of their meagre belongings slung over their shoulders in an old Hessian sack. I would stand and stare openly at them in wonderment. Where did they walk to - and why? Where did they sleep at night - in a barn, a haystack, or simply under the stars? These wild, scary and offbeat characters grabbed my imagination and it all seemed very enticing and exciting to a young lad. My parents would usually have to drag me away before I got sworn at and chased off by the said tramps! Maybe this was what originally awakened that romantic ideal of "FREEDOM" within me, which I've craved as long as I can remember. Some deep-rooted sense of adventure and wanderlust that was not able, due to life's turgid yet necessary commitments, to blossom until my mid-fifties and inspire me to take to "the road" myself - albeit rather like a posh and clean shaven tramp! However, had I been a bit younger it could've been worse: I may have taken it to extremes and opted for wilder places still, and taken up mountaineering or Antarctic exploration. I'm so glad I was too old to start that caper! A blessing in disguise.

Anyway, all this aside - if you are expecting lurid tales of "Sex and Drugs and Rock and Roll" within these pages you'd better put this book down now and pick up something raunchier like "50 Shades of Filth"! There again, on the other hand, if you are expecting light hearted tales of "Celibacy, Tea, and Light Classical" (albeit with the odd tantrum thrown in), you could well be barking up the right tree after all - but proceed with caution as there are a few well chosen words along the way!

Many of the names within these pages have been changed for various reasons but some are real, and I would like to thank all those people who may recognise themselves for their kindness and help throughout my journey. You will not find a great deal of controversial material within these pages however. For example you won't find me droning on about politics, football, terrorism, war, dieting, reality TV (only when I couldn't avoid it)), global warming and climate change - unless it directly affected me on the walk. Nor the credit crunch or recession - apart from my own personal one that it is! Immediately prior to my trip I had given up my slowly failing business, and as a result of this I no longer had any income - nothing - nowt - zilch! I had some meagre savings but really didn't know where the next penny was coming from, hence my reluctance to spend any money whatsoever when it wasn't absolutely necessary - so if I appear to be a pitiful miser you'll know the reason why. I allowed myself a budget of £1000 for the entire 2 months for food, accommodation, fares, repairs, "luxuries", and everything else. I almost did it but not quite - that expensive CF card for my camera's what did it!

Finally, I must also warn you that the following pages are littered with spoonerisms, malapropisms, and even more horrible word travesties which I've shoe-horned and hauled, kicking and screaming, into the English language. It's something I've done since I was about 3 and have no control over - so I'm afraid you'll either have to decipher it or miss those bits out completely. N.B. A grim thought - maybe I'm the closet Richard Stilgoe of rock?

Anyway, that's it in a bombshell, and now it's all over I never intend to walk another single step, and so, for that reason, I've pledged to reduce my carbon footprint by having both feet amputated forthwith!

INTRODUCTION

I first heard about the SW Coast Path one Saturday evening in September 2002. I'd been reading the *TV Times* after another mind-numbing stint in my department store. I hate the public! I hate myself too though, if that's any consolation to anyone reading this who happens to be a member of the aforementioned public. The strains of *Who Wants to be a Millionaire?* could be heard in the background. As I didn't want to be one, the volume was turned down low, so I could plan my evening of relaxation and fun on the telly. I was thinking, whilst eating another large bar of Cadbury's Fruit and Nut, what a couch potato I was becoming. I was working longer and longer hours at home as well as at the shop, to stand still in a business which, after ten years, I knew was doomed, owing to changing times. This was inevitable, simply a matter of "When?" By the time I sat down in the evenings I was too exhausted to do anything. Things were grim. Something had to give.

While pondering on my non-too pleasant plight, I was brought back to reality upon hearing Chris Tarrant say to a new contestant, "I understand you have an unusual interest."

I glanced at the gent he was talking to, noticed his sturdy physique, and thought, It has to be pigeon wrestling or digital gardening. Perhaps even barbed wire origami or maybe playing Mozart on the chainsaw. I wasn't even close. When he said, "I've walked the whole of the South West Coast Path, which is Great Britain's longest National Trail," my ears pricked up. Discarding the paper, I turned up the volume. It sounded interesting, even though I'd never heard of it. He explained that the path ran from Minehead to Poole Harbour, along the *whole* of the coastline, starting by going west at the Bristol Channel, South West down the Atlantic coast to Land's End, and finally east along the English Channel to Poole Harbour. The path itself was really a conglomeration of numerous old paths that'd been trodden for centuries by coastguards, lookouts, smugglers, farmers, miners, fishermen, and anyone who might find them useful. These paths had now been linked together to form this mammoth National Trail. The total length is 630.4 miles – not "as the fly crows", but measured exactly by GPS and computers. The walk also makes Land's End to John o'Groats seem like an easy Sunday afternoon stroll in the park. The *Millionaire* contestant said it'd been an incredible life-changing experience, during which he'd lost two and a half stones, becoming supremely fit. Unfortunately, I forgot to see how much he actually won – that could've been even more life changing.

I've had several cheapo yet joyous holidays in Somerset, Devon, Cornwall, and Dorset over the years and always loved the spectacular coastal scenery. I had a few strolls and pottered about on various beaches, gawping and prodding at things. Once I even climbed a low cliff – at least 30 feet! At the top, however, I needed to lie down for fifteen minutes because I went "all funny." I wasn't used to that kind of thing – exercise and all that – and I'd overdone it. I learned from my mistake to never attempt anything like this again.

Anyway, this grey-haired chap in his mid-fifties was extolling the virtues of walking this 630.4 mile path and immediately I was drawn in. I hadn't even known it existed, despite realising I'd stood on it, looking at the sea from various parts of it. One of the things that frustrated me on those holidays was the amount of coast I didn't see. The short sections I'd observed were great, but I'd always wondered what was round that next headland – the one that couldn't be reached by any form of transport. What was I missing? It would be great to see "the lot" in one go like this chap had done.

I checked my road maps, looked on the internet, forgot about the TV – it's all rubbish anyway, except for *Emmerdale Farm*. I still can't bring myself to call it "*Emmerdale*." I got quite interested in this South West Coast Path "thingy." I thought of the views, the unspoilt fishing villages and coves, rivers and streams, mining and maritime history, pirates and smugglers, geology and rock formations, the people, camping under the stars, the remoteness and getting back to nature – not to mention all the gorgeous blondes probably hanging out on the cliffs looking for action – and all this could only be achieved on foot. Yes, this was the life. I was hooked on the idea. Of course, I was overlooking the practical reality of it. Regardless of this, I lay in bed that night thinking it would be nice to have a bash at it.

I had trouble sleeping, feeling excited by the thought of "the big walk". I needed a change, maybe a new challenge too. I was still fired up at 3 a.m. the next morning, when I woke up to go to Gloucester car boot sale to buy stock for my shop. I needed to get down to brass tacks and work out *if* I could really attempt this huge feat or whether it was going to remain a pipe dream.

After the car boot I went for lunch with my parents. They were walkers and were much fitter than I, despite being in their eighties. When I mentioned the walk they looked at me strangely. This is not the son they'd come to know and love. What's wrong with him? Is he ill? They asked me nervously which section I intended to try walking – there are seventy-nine in total. I told them I might try "the lot". They recoiled in horror, then in disbelief, and finally into fits of hysterical laughter.

"You'll *never* do it! We've got lots of friends who've been lifelong walkers and even they wouldn't attempt it. Have you any idea what the terrain is like? It's all up and down. The entire path; no respite at all – almost impossible, even for ultra-fit people. There're hundreds of dangerous cliff-edge paths with sheer drops to the sea and rocks. And the weather on those isolated Atlantic coasts! Oh, dreadful! *Absolutely dreadful!*"

I hadn't thought that far ahead. I'm not good with heights – or widths, wind, rain, or gales, think about it. I'd pictured myself strolling across the top of gently rolling downs on a sunny day with a little rucksack – red and not too heavy – stopping for a pint or a cream tea every so often, chatting to the locals, never over-exerting myself. My parents painted a different picture that was similar to one known as *The Scream*, by Edvard Munch. I wanted to go on a pleasant walking holiday, not risk my life scaling Everest, or its Cornish equivalent!

I wondered if I was cut-out for this sort of thing after all. Perhaps I should stick to what I know, like a bit of fishing, ambling on a beach or round the car boot, or pottering round town. Even that hill up Broad Street finishes me off each time I scale it and that's only 50 yards long. I was so unfit and overweight at fifty-five. I get an asthma-thing, not to mention chronic hay fever, and a bad foot from kicking a cupboard in temper three years earlier. I couldn't walk for three months but was too scared to go to the doctor in case I needed an operation. Apart from that I'm also a bit of a renegade, extremely anti-social, and can't bear going anywhere unless I have to. I hate pubs, clubs, parties, showbiz and celebrity bullshit, small talk, and the majority of the human race. I cross the road to avoid most of them, keeping my hat pulled down when shopping in case anyone tries talking to me. I have no social skills and am not a good communicator either. In short, I prefer being alone, whereas a lot of people strive for and eagerly look forward to their allotted "fifteen minutes of fame". Since my mid-thirties I would've given my eye teeth for "fifteen minutes of peace and quiet". This, however, could be difficult on a trip of this nature. I'd have to mix with people and communicate in order to survive.

There was my lovely old bulstrode – BB the cat – what could I do with her for two months? In the cold light of day it's an ill wind that blows nobody any good and none of it boded too well. Yet I still really wanted to do the South West Coast Path. I put it down to either yet another mid-life crisis or maybe some kind of mental breakdown.

PREPARATIONS

After mentioning my now slightly diminishing intentions to friends and people in the various "outdoor" shops that I started to frequent, it was dawning on me that if I were to attempt this walk I'd have to prepare myself very thoroughly indeed. In one shop a super-fit young lady, who did Triathlons and loads of other extreme sports, winced when I related my plans.

"Wow, that's the longest and toughest National Trail there is! You'll need to train hard by doing army-style route marches and camping out in the Brecon Beacons for a few months first."

A few *months*! I was getting scared now. It's cold and grim up there, teeming with wolves, huge beasties, and ghosts everywhere you look.

To make matters worse, the manager chipped in with, "I had two mountaineer friends who attempted that trail. They packed it in after a week. It was too tough for them. You do realise that if you completed it you'll have climbed over four times the height of Everest in total."

I skulked sideways out of that shop a broken man, but after ten minutes of soul-searching I was a mended man again. I would not give up on my idea without a fight. This usually applies to anything I decide to do in life. For one thing, I'm too darn stubborn to be beaten by most challenges. If I do decide to undertake a project I tend to throw myself into it 111 per cent with drive, passion, and commitment. I don't like to fail. Besides, I felt I was already too far in to back out. After the sobering outdoor shop experience, however, it became obvious that I'd have to get fit somehow – fitter than I'd ever been if I was stupid enough to proceed with this epic trek. That shouldn't be too difficult to achieve, as I'd never been fit before – ever! I'd have to practice the walking itself. How's it done? I believe that feet come into the equation somewhere but I could be wrong. I'd never done any more than 3 miles in one go, but sod those dangerous army-style route marches in the Brecons for a game of soldiers. My logic told me that the best way to get fit for "The Big Walk" was to actually do "The Big Walk"! I'd have to lose weight first though. At over 14 stone I couldn't possibly lug all that lard around with me as well as tons of equipment.

I also had to consider *when* to do it. Logic told me that sometime in the spring of 2003 would be the best time to start as this would give me six much-needed months to prepare everything and train. Besides which, only a complete pranny would undertake a walk of that nature and magnitude in winter anyway. Apart from the cold vile weather there'd only be eight short hours of daylight. I'd no wish to spend fourteen hours a day in a tiny tent on the cliffs in snow and blizzards. So winter was ruled out in one split second. On the other hand, the summer could prove too hot for all the climbing. Millions of tourists could be milling about, causing me grief, leaving no peace and quiet. Everything would be double the price plus my hay fever may lay me out by June. Anyway, it didn't take me long to narrow it down to mid-April, shortly after the clocks had "sprung" forward, allowing maximum daylight hours at the start.

Not being able to afford accommodation, I'd need to buy all the basic camping equipment, otherwise I'd have to keep walking for seven weeks non-stop without sleeping. But what if I bought all the gear only to pack it in and come home beaten into submission and humiliated after two days? Frightening thoughts!

Despite all warnings, worries, and drawbacks, I decided in October that I *was* going to attempt the walk in spring. From that day onwards nothing would stand in my way. I started making long lists. I'm a list person. I used to make lots of "fishing lists" in the old days. The only trouble was, it didn't matter if it took five years to write a list, there was always something vital missing, like when I arrived at the lake with every piece of ingenious tackle ever invented, except I'd left my rods at home. These new lists were exciting, containing hundreds of inventive items of camping gear, not to mention rations, emergency rations, emergency-emergency rations, medicines for every ailment imaginable, guidebooks, maps, emergency maps, clothing, emergency clothing, special UV and IR shades, a state-of-the-art walking pole, rucksack, and special headgear for all the different types of weather. The lists were infinitive. I bought things immediately, thus committing myself to doing the walk. If I bought the gear I'd have to use it, for I couldn't afford not to.

The first thing I bought was a fire-new maroon Puffer waterproof jacket, costing £70. I never took it on the walk, as it turned out to be too hot and heavy after the first training session in the rain. I purchased another special lightweight Gore-Tex one for £140, causing me to weep. Thank God I bought it cos it was worth its "goat in whaled" in the long run (change it round). I'd only worn the Puffer jacket once. As it'd been in the rain I couldn't exchange it – B******s! It's now all runkled up and covered in oil in the back of the old van. The other pricier items were a small one-man, or one-and-a-half-woman tent. A Vango Micro 100 at £79 seemed about the best value for money, only weighing 4 lbs. – or 1.9 kg. for you Euro lovers. It was easy to erect, though I wasn't keen on the bright blue colour. I wanted to blend into the background rather than stick out like a sore thumb at a wedding. A 65-litre Tracpac "Airjet" camouflage lightweight rucksack not only looked great and felt comfortable but cost a mere £42 by the time I'd beaten the salesman into the ground on price. With my background in antiques and junk, this came as second nature. My self-inflating mattress, which turned out to be a self-deflating mattress after two weeks, was almost the only piece of equipment that let me down. It was a "Therm-a-Rest" and at £65 wasn't cheap, but sleep would be vital if I was to stand any chance. I chose a "Snugpak" lightweight synthetic sleeping bag for £55 after another violent beating down. At less than 2 lbs. it'd take up a small space in the rucksack once crushed in a compression sack.

Smaller items included a lightweight digital camera/camcorder. I bought a cheap one in case I fell on it or lost it. This proved to be one of my best buys at £69. The memories it provided me with are irreplaceable. It was a Nisis DV2, working on 2 x AA batteries – a fantastic little gadget – with 1,000 pictures and video clips on one 512 mb. compact flash card. I got some brilliant mini torches too – "Guardian" lights at £15 each, but tiny with miniscule lithium batteries. A minute Sony radio – from Argos, £29 – measuring 2 x 1 and a half inches sounded great with micro headphones. I needed a fix of Vaughan Williams and Warren Zevon in my system to inspire me whilst camping in the wilds. A Coleman Pocket stove cost £18 including a gas cylinder. Another fantastic buy was my Tilley hat, costing £47, proving virtually indestructible, never shrinking or losing its great shape, despite being crushed and suffering numerous douses in water. I'd fill it with cold water and wear it soaking wet during the heatwaves. Clothing was difficult with April ranging from sub-zero temperatures to heatwaves. Luckily it proved to be mainly the latter, allowing me to post my navy thermal vests, long johns, and other winter-wear home after a week or two, thus lightening my pack-weight considerably. I only retained my army camo fleece, which was worth its "gate in wold" on the trip.

The other item that proved to be crucial was my Leki walking pole. Being right-handed meant I could push myself *away* from the sheer-drops – I suffer terrible vertigo. Thank goodness I didn't decide to do the walk in reverse – I would've fallen over the edge! I couldn't have descended the steep cliffs without using my stick as a "brake". Despite all my efforts and omitting more and more important gear, my rucksack still weighed a crippling 56 lbs. at the start of my journey. I also needed the basic South West Coast Path Association Guidebook, a small notebook/journal, plus a map of the whole SW peninsular. I refused to carry loads of maps, as it'd take forever to organise them and would cost a small fortune, weighing a ton to boot. Instead I took the calculated risk of getting lost, which I successfully managed to do at least ten times a day. This seems insane, as in reality all I needed to do was ensure the sea was on my right and the land was on my left for the whole 630.4 miles. This was not as simple as it sounds, what with inland diversions, bad signposting, horrid dunes, estuaries – don't remind me, fresh land-slips, fans constantly bothering me, asking for autographs and photographs – I jest, I jest. This is why I actually walked more like 680 miles in total. I don't mind telling you there was a lot of cursing during those seven weeks. My estimation is that I swore somewhere between 5,750,000 and 6 million times. I'm afraid I can't be any more accurate than that.

By Christmas 2002 I was doing well with my preparations but the lists were getting forever huger. Would I really need to take a guitar, a comfy chair, a gigantic machete-style blade, plus some groovy outfits for the evenings to impress any women I may happen to meet? I'd abandoned the idea of taking floral wallpaper, stilts, and a petrol lawnmower early on. They all had to go in the "no" pile. Despite this I still managed to get through the best part of a grand on gear before finishing.

As I was getting more determined to walk I kept wondering what to do about the shop. I'd never been away for more than five days at a time in the last twelve years. That had only been twice a year, so this presented a real dilemma. The answer suddenly became apparent during mid-October when I decided – after yet another pile of collectable records had been stolen in my absence – to leave the shop for good as soon as possible. *That* would definitely solve the problem of how to manage the business while I was away – dead simple – so I did! Mum and Dad offered to look after BB the "bulstrode", which was terrific of them.

Something else happened that really clinched it, making me desperate to do the walk. My good friends Trevor and Dawn Berry came over from Cheltenham for a Christmas drink, bringing me a present too. It was a great book called *500 Mile Walkies*, by Mark Wallington. The walk had been much shorter when he'd done it in 1981, but thanks to the SW Coast Path Association and the National Trust, more sections had become available over the years. Most of the coast was now accessible to walkers. The book contains Mark's own experiences of his 1981 walk with his amazing dog, Boogie. It's a warm, witty, informative account of his trip, which inspired me tremendously. I wish I could thank him for one of the best walking books I've ever read. Thanks too to Trev and Dawn for discovering it and giving me a copy. I read it three times before undertaking the walk and twice more upon my return, by which time I could relate to his wonderful stories even more. I now had many of my own stories, which maybe one day I'll get round to relating – like *now*!

Determined and fired up, I started walking locally, including gentle hill walking that almost crippled me with the weight of the pack being horrendous from the word go. The longest training walk I managed was a mere eight miles. I suffered so much shoulder pain during this that I decided not to do any more. From then on I only did about 20 miles a week, not wanting to injure myself or wear out my new boots before the big walk. These boots were made by Hawkins & Co., the famous old footwear company, and were still new in their box when I got them at Gloucester Car Boot for only £3! I'd like to say they were "secondfoot", but can't, as they were new. Anyway, they turned out to be my worst purchase, possibly of all time. I was virtually crippled by those bloody boots for the first 400 miles – they were agony. In retrospect I should've ditched them after a couple of days, but not being an experienced walker I didn't understand the position clearly because I was in too much pain to think straight. I thought this was normal and I'd soon "wear them in", thus they'd be as comfortable as an old pair of slippers. This was never to happen. When they finally fell apart halfway round Cornwall they were still killing me! I found out after my 680 miles that Hawkins & Co. had gone out of business fifteen years previously. I wasn't in the least bit surprised. My boots, although "new" in theory, had probably been in somebody's loft for thirty years before being palmed off on "some mug" – namely me – for three quid!

Back to the preparations: I camped in my garden in temperatures below -6 degrees. No problems. Snug as a bug in a bag. I felt confident my gear was up to it. My main worry was that of serious equipment failure during the trip. If you're camping out in the wild at night and your tent gets wrecked or blows away in a gale you're buggered. The preparations also entailed me religiously soaking my feet in surgical spirit every morning and evening for two months. That cost another fiver, not to mention the countless wasted hours.

The seminal moment arrived in mid-March. After five months' preparation the time arrived to pick up the phone and book my rail ticket to Minehead. I'd decided to travel on a Sunday, partly because I knew there'd be no commuters, therefore it'd be less crowded, and partly because it seemed logical to begin the walk "proper" at the start of a new week. I needed to book at least a month ahead to save a pile of money on the fare, but it felt weird, as I knew this was the real turning point. Although I'd been going through the motions, ticking all the boxes for months, up till that moment I hadn't made a total commitment. Uttering those words into the receiver, "I'd like to purchase a one-way ticket to Minehead, please, for Sunday 13 April," made me realise this was really it – no going back now!

PART ONE
Minehead to Land's End

Day Zero: Sunday 13 April, 4.50 p.m.

Istepped off the bus with my rucksack onto Minehead seafront. It was
4.45 p.m. on Sunday 13 April 2003. It was raining, cold, and deserted.
Not exactly an auspicious beginning to what was supposed to be one of
the greatest experiences of my life. I ducked into the nearest promenade
beach shelter to dig out my waterproof jacket. I'd hoped I wouldn't need it
for a few days at least, but this wasn't to be. I donned it before staggering
out under the enormous weight of my load. By the time I'd walked 50 yards
I felt exhausted. I crawled westwards at a snail's pace, towards the large
sculpture marking the start of "The South West Coast Path" 400 yards
further west along the prom. I rested in another shelter near the
magnificent monument, as it was raining so hard that the dogs in the street
were unable to wizzle!

I sat on the uncomfortable slatted bench out of the wind and rain,
wondering what I was doing there and was this ordeal I was about to put
myself through really necessary? If I did walk this evening I'd definitely get
soaked and would need to make camp in a couple of hours, as it'd be dusk
around 7.30. It wouldn't be easy pitching the tent in the driving rain and
wind, however far I may get, which given the way I felt was probably going
to be somewhere in the region of another 200 yards by nightfall.

As the rain persisted down I reflected on the events of the day. It'd been
a long, difficult one, beginning at 7 a.m. after a frantic couple of days
making final preparations with little sleep. Excitement mixed with anxiety.
Mum and Dad picked me up at 10 a.m. to run me to Gloucester Railway
Station. The weather had been sunny in the morning and remained good as
we drank our tea in the station café. The train was due at noon, but we went
out onto the platform fifteen minutes early. I needed to travel through
Bristol to Taunton to get a connecting bus on to Minehead. Everything
needed to run like clockwork without any hitches. I should arrive at
Minehead at 2.45 p.m., allowing around five hours of walking before dark.
Several trains came and went. Mine was due any moment. Dad had
disappeared inside the station for some reason, but suddenly came rushing
out exclaiming that *my* train was leaving right now from a different

platform! He'd spotted the digital signboard inside, displaying this new absurd information. Apparently there'd been an announcement over the PA, but no passengers heard it because a train had been standing beside us making one hell of a racket, drowning out any voice announcing train information. No prizes for guessing – yep, all twenty-two of us missed it, despite running like idiots for a good 400 yards, in time to see the back end drifting away from us – b******s! We went berserk at the station master who, fearing for his life, ran into his office, locking himself in.

The next train for Taunton was due to leave at 3 p.m. – three hours away and too late to get the connecting bus in Taunton. I wouldn't get there until at least 7.30 p.m. Apart from that my cheapo £9 ticket was only valid for that one single train. If I had to catch another it'd cost the full non-discount price of £40! The prospects had become gloomy.

The disgraced station master reappeared, bravely but cautiously, in an desperate attempt to restore his previously untarnished reputation by telling us that *he* personally had organised us a "special" train that would leave at 2 p.m. at no extra cost. I suppose it was marginally better than 3 p.m., creating a glimmer of hope after all. The special train did come on time and all of us caught it. It was good to be off at last. I waved goodbye to Mum and Dad, secretly wondering if I'd ever see them again – a strange feeling.

Ten minutes out of Gloucester it started raining and continued all afternoon. The journey to Taunton was uneventful. The train was packed, which I thought was strange for a Sunday afternoon in April, though I hadn't travelled by train since 1970, so how would I know? It seemed ironic that I hadn't been on a train for thirty years and missed the first one I tried to catch.

At Taunton I had an hour-long wait for the Minehead bus through missing the earlier connection. The Station café was the only option, as there was no sign of Taunton anywhere, despite me scanning the horizon in all directions with my new monocular – a brainwave of a purchase – half the weight and half the price of a pair of binoculars, but unfortunately only half the vision too.

In the station café I had my first conversation of the trip. It was rather one-sided though. The chap was Irish, about sixty, and had flown over that morning for a religious music festival at Butlin's in Minehead – I think! I'd seen him on the train. Now he was waiting for my bus. His lilting Irish accent was so strong I had to try deciphering the odd word and piece them together to make sense of it. He spoke, I nodded, saying words like, "Really," or "Yes" and "No" occasionally so I wouldn't seem impolite. After half an hour or so I became quite adept at it, even improvising with the odd, "No, that *is* incredible," or "Well, that must be a first," without having a clue what he was talking about. I think I got away with it.

We caught the bus and headed for Minehead with him chatting away in a foreign language like a good 'un, while I gazed out of the window at the rainy Somerset afternoon, wondering what lay ahead, answering him monosyllabically by now, having grown bored and run out of steam with the nifty ad-libs. I began worrying about the weather too. Only ten minutes later and I'd be on the streets in Minehead, alone, cold, and old. I contemplated what I was about to attempt and how it'd all come to take place.

After six months of planning and preparation the time at last arrived to begin my epic adventure – "*The Big Walk*" in heavy rain! Not a soul was in sight as I donned my black Berghaus Extreme Paclite jacket and black rucksack cover, but oddly enough not my waterproof trousers – guess what colour though – yep, light black. I don't know why I didn't bother with them. Maybe my mind was already befuddled. I slithered over to study the impressive ten-foot-high "Big-Hands-Holding-a-Map" sculpture, signifying the official start of the SW C. Path. It was sculpted by Owen Cunningham, from a design by local art student Sarah Ward, and is a fitting symbol for Great Britain's longest National Trail. I took some miserable photos for posterity and went to sit in yet another shelter weighing it all up.

After weighing it all up I realised I didn't feel like walking today after all. With the rain beating on the roof I took out the guidebook to read up on Minehead – anything rather than make that dreaded first step that would clearly commit me to leaving the safety of the town behind once and for all.

With the weather now looking worse, I began toying with the idea of getting a cosy B & B for the night, as the idea of walking in the rain now seemed an even grimmer prospect. It also appeared impossible to comprehend the magnitude of what I was about to undertake. Surely I couldn't really be climbing four times the height of Everest carrying a 65 lb. pack, could I? Yep, I could, so I thought, Best not think about it anymore. After a couple more minutes of reasoning with myself my head tried bullying my body into action by yelling aloud, "*Walk! Get on with it*, you fool!" My body ignored it. Luckily nobody was about to hear me arguing inanely with myself, before my head finally got the better of my body and set off alone, followed reluctantly and inevitably, by the still un-enthusiastic latter. This is *it*! I thought. Best foot forward, worst foot backward! Before having chance to dwell upon it I crossed the road and strode up the alleyway in between the old pink and white stone cottages where I spotted my first National Trail emblem, set into a wooden post It was a black medallion with a 3-inch central white acorn. I would see thousands of these identical markers during the coming weeks. They were most reassuring – when you could bloody well find them.

30 yards further on I realised I was lost! I've never been great at directions but this was ridiculous. Completely baffled, I took a wild guess before setting off up the hill in the rain. My legs got soaked owing to the lack of waterproof trousers. After 400 hundred yards a car passed me, stopped, reversed, and offered me a lift. It was a man with his teenage son. They said I looked dead on my feet, making me feel great. I was tempted to

get in but heroically declined. I wasn't about to cheat (yet), despite feeling desperate to get out of the rain to rest. Afterwards I wondered why they'd offer a lift to a total stranger who wasn't even hitching. I decided they were serial killers looking for their umpteenth victim. I'd unwittingly foiled their evil plot by nobly refusing their cunning invitation. My courage, sheer doggedness, and grim determination to succeed alone had saved my life, like a mini version of Scott of the Antarctic, except he didn't survive his journey. Surely it was my destiny to complete this walk now. It never occurred to me that they could've been kind people who felt sorry for this soaked old bloke struggling up a vertical hill, and that it was an act of true altruism.

Onwards and up the steep North Hill the walking was *not* like Ross at all. It was much harder, higher, and horrible. On to the top and through the Exmoor gorse and bracken, blackened and charred by fires in many areas. It was still dull but the rain had eased. I began to feel, for no particular reason, abnormally cheerful, despite not knowing where I was or where was I'd sleep that night. I passed a deserted forlorn-looking campsite with shuttered log cabins, which had yet to come out of hibernation to greet the approaching season. So that was out. I'd realised that the directions in the guidebook were going to be lacking in the common sense department – not a good omen at this early stage. This wasn't aided by my deciding against bringing any maps. I would've needed a wheelbarrow for the 100 or so Explorer maps required to cover the whole walk. My one tiny map gave me a rough idea of my progress between major landmarks or towns.

I met my first humans – a brave local couple – who advised me not to bother with the "Rugged Cliff Walk" as it'd be too dangerous in these conditions. I wasn't going to bother with it anyway. I was walking parallel a further inland on the official path – not cheating – where it was less rugged. There was some flatter walking for a while. A kind of euphoric feeling swept over me in giant waves as other equally giant white waves crashed against the cliffs below. I felt ecstatic and quite emotional too. I couldn't figure out why as I hadn't even taken anything or been drinking. I put it down to the sudden sensation of complete freedom, something I hadn't experienced for some time – not since 1989, in fact. I knew I didn't need to be anywhere in particular, at any particular time for the foreseeable future. What a tremendous feeling it was, too.

The terrain became a wave-like series of valleys and steep hogs-backs rolling towards the sea with sheer drops of 300 feet or so to the Bristol Channel. I stayed on this path 100 yards inland to stay on the safe side. I couldn't avoid the dizzy heights for long though. I got lost again but after passing Selworthy Beacon I somehow arrived at Bossington Hill where I had to walk a terrifying ledge path for half a mile in the fading light. I couldn't look down. The walking pole proved invaluable. I depended upon it to aid my balance, thus lessening the awful vertigo. Thankfully, I eventually started to descend, but immediately panicked about another issue – where to camp? Dusk was fast approaching. I needed to find a spot quickly or endure walking through the night.

Whilst climbing another hillside through some woods, I miraculously found a nice one – unknowingly in someone's garden! It was a small meadow over a low wire fence, off the path by a stream, high up, overlooking Porlock, visible about 2 miles below. A house was some 200 yards lower down to my left but I didn't see it until I was lying in the tent holding a steaming cuppa when it was too late to move. I hoped nobody spotted the tent.

It was 7.45 p.m. when I camped and by 8.15 p.m. I phoned Mum and Dad, informing them of my location, assuring them I was safe. It was a short call to save my phone battery. I couldn't carry luxuries like a heavy charger. It'd been a long day but I felt optimistic. At least I'd begun, completing about 7 miles without losing or breaking anything. As I lay there in the twilight looking at the distant twinkling lights of Porlock, I realised that after all the months of planning and preparation the torch had been lit and my big adventure was truly underway.

Day 1: Monday 14 April

I woke at 6 a.m. after a bad night's sleep. I couldn't get off until after midnight, being too anxious and hyper. I brewed some strong tea and ate a protein bar before packing everything away and leaving the meadow at 8.40 a.m., feeling better. Nobody had caught me, which was a bonus, and it was a warm day, though somewhat muggy.

It was a lovely walk down the hill to a shallow gurgling river. I followed its course towards the sea. I met a friendly farmer – Somerset *is* different to Herefordshire – who said the unofficial coast route was even nicer – the b****** – I hadn't taken that path! Still, this was a pleasant enough route, until I realised I was lost again, heading back east towards Minehead. In the end I climbed over a 6-foot-high barbed wire fence, risking everything before being able to aim for Porlock. I found a little home-made cardboard memorial plaque lying in the sand, with an inscription from the poor lad's family. I stuck it back on the fence from where it had fallen. It was to be the first of many along the way, normally placed where someone had died in an accident or because they'd loved a particular spot on the coast. I always liked to read them but hoped my name wasn't going to end up on one in the near future!

Many paths were closed for various reasons, leading to several tricky detours. By the time I entered Porlock I felt pretty rough. Before reaching the town I stopped at another out-of-season campsite to "camel-up" and wash (i.e. drink gallons of water). I chatted with the site owner for five minutes; a helpful cove, preparing for the anticipated coming seasonal onslaught. He helped me with directions into Porlock. I walked on feeling nauseous and faint, not a good sign, as I'd only walked a couple of miles. I put it down to the pain in my shoulders from the weight of my rucksack – 60 lbs. now– plus the 6 lb. shoulder bag. They were starting to cause me problems.

In Porlock I bought supplies in Londis, including bread, fruit, chocolate bars, and a bunch of sausages from the local butchers. You can't beat a good sausage ... or can you? I walked past the Visitors' Centre only to find myself horribly lost *again*. This was becoming a habit I could do well without. Bloody guidebook! Have the authors actually done these walks themselves?

There was some road walking for a mile or so followed by a nasty shale beach to Porlock Weir, before which I stopped to eat some sandwiches and chocolate, with coke, on some concrete beach steps where I was sheltered from the cold breeze. Less nauseous now, I rubbed some Ibuleve double-strength pain-killing gel into my shoulders, which were really giving me jip. NB: why would anyone in their right mind *ever* decide to buy single-strength Ibuleve when both single and double are the same size and, more to the point, the same price? Why do they even make single-strength Ibuleve? If you've got pain you want to shift it *immediately*, not at some time in the future.

I sat on a low stone wall opposite The Ship Inn at Porlock Weir and finished my drink. The sun began to shine. Several tourists were about. I pondered on the notorious, yet unknown figure in literary history who hailed from this area. The story goes that as the legendary romantic poet - Samuel Taylor Coleridge, who lived nearby at Nether Stowey for three years, was impulsively scrawling out his freshly conceived masterpiece the epic tale of "Kubla Khan," which had just come to him in an opium induced dream, someone knocked on his door and detained him on "some trivial business matter." By the time Coleridge was able to return to his desk some time later, the final two or three hundred crucial lines of the poem had escaped him - never to be recaptured - ever ! As a result he was then forced to curtail the yarn limply as his inspiration had totally deserted him. He then proceeded to place all the blame on this inconsiderate untimely visitor who was from then on referred to by Coleridge, with immense frustration, as "The Person From Porlock." This purportedly happened at Ash Farm around 1798 and the "Person" was reputed to be his opium dealer. See, it can happen to anyone! The wooded bluffs above Minehead also feature in Coleridge's other works such as the hermit's abode "in that wood which slopes down to the sea" from "The Rime of the Ancient Mariner." Coleridge's statue can also be seen at the nearby harbour at Watchet. He and Wordsworth,who lived nearby at Alfoxton House, would often roam the hills and the coast on long night walks which led to local gossip that they were "spies" for the French. The Government even sent an agent to investigate their suspicious forays, but he found out that they were indeed "mere poets!"

After a ten-minute rest by the picturesque old harbour I left for Culbone Church and Woods. As I walked past a row of old stables that now contained small businesses. I stuck my head inside a blacksmith's forge to have a quick shufti and saw all the guys beating the hell out of a punch bag, training for something or other, with the huge furnace blazing away behind them. Then it was time for my first really serious zigzag ascent that would take me up the tree-lined cliffs to Exmoor and Culbone Church. A couple of eighty-three-year-olds overtook me halfway up and were sitting at the top when I arrived fifteen minutes later – knackered. We chatted for several minutes. Turned out they lived in Weston-Super-Mare, up the road. They took some photos before continuing on whilst I was left floundering in their wake.

I finally staggered up the final incline, sweating like a pig, before arriving at the incredible twelfth-century miniature Culbone Church. The shoulder pain was excruciating again and it was only lunchtime on "Day 1". A self-made cup of tea refreshed me in the hut where "they" provide all the accoutrements, i.e. kettle, water, teabags, milk, sugar, for which I left the princely sum of 9p. in the money box, which was all the change I had on me. As I rested outside the hut with my 9p. cuppa, I made the mistake of picking up a leaflet on the history of Culbone, which immediately informed me that there'd been a leper colony here in 1544. I wasn't too happy about that in case there were any germs still hanging round looking for an unsuspecting victim to latch on to – like me. When I rose I gave myself a thorough brushing down with my Tilley hat to be on the safe side, followed by doing the church, reputedly the tiniest one in England. It stands in a minute wooded valley with a few unusual houses nearby. The entire setting was reminiscent of fairyland. In other words it's enchanting and magical, seeming like elves and pixies may appear at any moment to dance among the graves.

One grave bore the name of the historian Joan Cooper who died in 1982. She'd lived in the charming house next to the stream for many years with her husband, Waistel, a potter. When she died, her funeral was held in the church, which was packed for the service. Mind you, any more than a congregation of three and this minuscule church would be packed. I don't know if she died of leprosy but it was time I was moving on. Many of the remaining graves bore the family name of Richards but, there was no mention of the causes of death.

Feeling rather freaked out now, I reflected that I was in spooky *Lorna Doone* territory. The book of the same name was what really put Exmoor on the map. A murderous romantic blood and guts yarn of feuding families. The novel was written by R. D. Blackmore, better known to the layman as Ritchie Blackmore, legendary Deep Purple guitarist – wow, that guy is so versatile.

As I was about to leave Culbone I met a posh young fellow emerging from his posh old house. He said the route to Lynmouth was "hell on earth" and meant it. I shivered at the prospect, but had no alternative other than giving up and going home, which I couldn't possibly do. He was certainly correct. It was tough from the word go, and the word "go" was tough enough in itself! Even more worrying was my decision to take the lower and supposedly easier of the two paths. I climbed higher through woodland, encountering elusive red deer, which seemed to fade silently into the trees as I approached. Tantalising glimpses of the sea were visible way below through the trees to my right. Legend has it that this area beyond Culbone Church towards Lynmouth, where Glenthorne is now situated, is where Jesus may have landed on a trip with Joseph of Arimathea. This supposed event is said to have inspired the words to William Blake's famous poem, *Jerusalem.* I had a go at singing it at the top of my voice to see if he'd materialise – Jesus, not William Blake, you fools! After five minutes nothing happened. I was too exhausted to continue, so contented myself with "imagining" the tune instead, all to no avail.

The afternoon was humid. As I kept climbing I became even hotter with the effort. Sweat poured down my face. Several woodland streams trickled down into mossy pools from the sheer rock face to my left. I continually soaked my towel in the cool waters and spread it over my face, eventually abandoning all caution by filling my Tilley hat before replacing it. The water cascaded down me, providing temporary relief. Who cares about cholera? This was no time to be acting like a big girl's blouse. I'd probably contracted leprosy back in Culbone anyway, so in for a penny, what the hell?

The directions by Boar's Head seemed all wrong but I pressed on towards Caddow Combe, eventually descending from the woods in shock at the sudden dramatic change of landscape. Not a tree in sight now. I was on a narrow tarmac road with dusk approaching, looking for somewhere to camp. I felt stunned, as everything appeared different, scary, barren, and exposed to the elements. I walked down the open flat valley surrounded by huge rounded hills, resembling massive dormant dinosaurs. I suddenly felt tiny, insignificant, and alone amongst this *mighty* landscape, with not another soul for miles. I hadn't met anyone since the posh young fellow in Culbone that morning – suddenly a cold shiver ran right through me.

The sea was visible a mile ahead by Fore Point Lighthouse and it was very gusty. I needed to make camp somewhere sheltered, which was easier said than done. I tried several spots without success. They were either too exposed or the ground was too bumpy or hard for pegs. I settled for a tiny area adjacent to the road, big enough for my one-man tent. It took a while to pitch in the wind. When I'd done it I couldn't find my new knife. After a ten-minute tantrum, during which I ran back and forth between all the places I'd tried to camp, shouting and cursing, and searching in vain. I eventually found the offending article in my camera case, exactly where I had packed it on Saturday afternoon! I pitched about 30 yards from a stone bridge over a stream, discovering that this was the only spot where I could cook my sausages without the now ferocious wind blowing out my stove. The scene was slightly ridiculous, lying in my tent watching the sausages cooking 30 yards away through my monocular, ensuring they didn't burn. Every five minutes I ran to the bridge with my fork to turn them and then scurry back to the tent. This was a frustrating twenty minutes. This wasn't an ideal cooking situation. Within a few more days I abandoned the idea of cooking whilst camping, apart from simple cup-a-soups or tea that only entailed boiling a kettle.

It was 8 p.m. by the time I'd eaten the superb black sausages, with hunks of crusty bread and brown sauce. I lay inside the cosy bag, watching the spooky light fade among those overpowering hills. I would be glad to get out of here tomorrow. I fell into a troubled sleep, waking at midnight, but slept again from 3-6 a.m. Not good, but better than nothing. I'm not a good sleeper at home but hoped to get into a regular pattern. This hadn't happened yet. As a result I felt tired most of the time.

Day 2: Tuesday 15 April

At 6.30 a.m. I was aware that it was still chilly but an hour later the sun rose. I felt its instant warmth through the nylon walls, which quickly turned into blazing heat. All of a sudden it became so unbearable that I was forced to exit the tent in a blind panic for fear of being roasted alive. By 8 a.m. I was washing myself, my hair, and clothes in the refreshing stream under the bridge in the shade. I'd never do this if I was inland, as the soap may pollute the water, but this close to the sea I felt comfortable about it. It'd hardly matter if I polluted the Bristol Channel. I felt better after my ablutions but apprehensive about the walk to Lynmouth and Combe Martin as the guidebook summed up this section as "Strenuous." This would sort the men out from the boys. I kind of knew which category I'd fall into: the one with the gobstoppers, short trousers, a satchel, and a little round cap. If my prior walking was classed as "moderate", I dreaded to imagine what the next bit would be like.

When entering the valley the previous evening, I'd wondered how I was going to leave it when the time came. I'd only seen one path zigzagging its way up a steep hill – Countisbury – which didn't look humanly possible.

The next morning, studying the terrain again, I ruled that impossible path out and set off at 9.30 a.m. downhill, passed some disused mine workings towards the sea and Fore Point Lighthouse a mile away. An hour later I was back at my camping spot sweating profusely in the stifling heat, looking at the impossible path again, realising it had to become "possible", as I'd no option but to take it. No other way out of the valley was available unless I scaled the dangerous overhang above the lighthouse. I'd tried crawling 30 yards along it on my hands and knees but it was too awful for words with my vertigo. I gave up and retraced my steps, walked the mile uphill, back to square one.

The intense sun burned into every part of me as I took the long hill incredibly slow, stopping every 30 yards or so to rest I was also running low on drinking water, which wasn't a sensible thing to do on a day like this. The climb seemed endless but after an energy-sapping hour I reached the top where I met a couple who announced I was still on the official route. This amazed me. They recommended a product called Compede for my feet, which I could sense were blistering. I soon saw Lynton and Lynmouth 2 miles distant, far down below. The old water-powered lift that carries passengers up and down the cliff face from one to the other was visible even from this distance. I wished I was on it. I continued round the hillside, across some open fields, down to the A39, along the main road, and down into Lynmouth at noon. It was beautiful weather for non-walkers, feeling more like August than April, though way too hot for me. Before I did anything else I sat on the old harbour wall in the shade for a quick breather.

On a gorgeous day like today it was difficult to imagine how this beautiful coastal town had been devastated in August 1952 when during a freak storm the deluge of rainwater caused the rivers Lyn and Bray, plus the many streams above the town, to swell to enormous proportions. With nowhere else to go, the waters, along with all the debris, poured into Lynmouth with terrible consequences. Over 100 buildings were destroyed or damaged. Thirty-four people died. A museum in Lynmouth tells the story of the tragedy.

Today it looked perfect. I took some pictures of the lovely town, the harbour, and shops, before my thoughts turned to food. The last time I was in Lynmouth was five years ago and the kitchen staff in the big hotel had never heard of plaice and chips. It's the truth, I tell you! I didn't risk going there again. Instead I chose an outdoor café for my superb plaice, chips, and peas, also getting my water bottles filled too. It was wonderful sitting there with a cold beer chatting with four happy tourists on the next table. It already seemed hard to imagine the misery and torment I'd been going through all morning. I wrote up the journal and finished off with a huge Toffee Sundae priced £1.95. The whole meal cost £8 and was great value. I'd needed a proper meal after all the energy I'd expended during the last three days. I pottered around Lynmouth a while, looking in shops, not wanting to get back to the grindstone, but knowing I'd have to in due course.

Before I could feel any more guilty for skiving off I took the Victorian Water Powered Lift, built in 1888, the year of London's notorious serial killer "Rick the Japper", up to Lynton with difficulty and much jocularity among the other passengers owing to the size and awkwardness of my rucksack. We were like sardines but nevertheless I managed to squeeze in among them. I bought fruit bars, chocolate, and drinks, and found a chemists to buy the mysterious miracle cure – Compede – and at a quid a plaster it'd better be miraculous. My right heel was now extremely painful from a huge blister. After a quick wash and brush-up in the Town Hall gents' it was on to Tourist Information to check my route. With nobody on duty after me waiting five minutes, with my weighty rucksack killing me, I tapped on a door that read, "Private". A minute later a disinterested bloke came out, looking like a grumpy Ken Dodd with specs, disgruntled that I'd disturbed him. He deliberately avoided giving me any useful information, no matter what tack I took with him. I wondered why he'd been given a job working with the public whom he obviously regarded as a nuisance and an intrusion upon his privacy. What an awful ambassador he was for Lynton. I decided to write a letter of complaint to the town council when I arrived home, but didn't of course.

It was about 2.30 p.m. when I took the splendid "North Walk" out of Lynton towards Combe Martin. This is a Victorian-metalled walkway about 6 feet wide but frighteningly near to the edge of the steep cliff. I hugged the left side of it, forcing oncoming walkers to move outwards towards the edge in order to pass me – very considerate of me, I must say – only half a dozen or so went over. Quite a few people were enjoying the sun and there were many a cheery "Good Afternoon!" not to mention the odd, "Nice day for it!" or even, "How's it gaping?" on the way to The Valley of the Rocks. When I arrived it was reminiscent of the Grand Canyon, being red hot and rocky, only smaller. I didn't see one goat, which was disappointing, as I'd heard they were famous round here. I was hoping to get a few autographs. I soon felt weary again. My right heel was grimmer than grim. The shoulders were in agony too after only a couple of miles. The heat was becoming unbearable.

I trudged on through the valley, on to Lee Bay (No.1), where I took a picture of the honey-coloured Lee Abbey and a strange sign, which was plonked on some grass: "On 1 April 1780, nothing happened here." Odd!

Next I took the way-marked Woodland Walk to try finding some shade. I filled my hat with water from every stream available and replaced it like that but it still dried out completely within twenty minutes in the extreme heat. I eventually saw the beautiful Woody Bay through the trees, arriving there around 6 p.m. I spotted most of the houses mentioned in Mum's book of the area: Red House, Hawks Cottage, and the Woody Bay Hotel.

I saw the lovely singer Elkie Brooks, the region's most famous resident. She passed by me slowly with her husband after I'd held them up by walking on the lane in front of their car, but they smiled anyway as they went by, only shaking their fists a little. I felt like flagging them down and reminding her I used to chat to her at the Speakeasy Club in the 1970s. So how about putting me up for the night at their lovely house, the aforementioned ex-Woody Bay Hotel? While she was at it, I wouldn't mind some of that heady lilac wine to help me get to sleep too. (Groan, groan.) Needless to say I didn't do anything, and so had to start looking for somewhere to pitch the tent. I couldn't find anywhere as Woody Bay is an exclusive area. The residents probably wouldn't take kindly to bedraggled semi-vagrants camping anywhere in their upper-class proximity. I walked out of the area, feeling slightly panic-stricken about where I was going to sleep. This became a familiar feeling throughout much of the walk as dusk approached. I would always see a perfect spot at 6 p.m., which was far too early a time to pitch. Of course by 8 p.m., when it *was* time, I'd either be on a cliff ledge, in the middle of a town, in a 45 per cent sloping jungle, or on strictly private farmland – Sod's Law.

After climbing out of Woody bay I came to a gate half a mile out of the residential area, discovering a small patch of grass under some trees beyond it. It was some distance from the village. No other people were around now anyway. As I finished pitching the tent I was aware of someone approaching in the fading light.

As he drew level he said, "I was going to camp there."

For a moment I thought he was serious, until he started laughing, as did I. His name was Clive Parkinson. We chatted for a good half-hour into the twilight. Clive was the first proper walker/backpacker I'd ever encountered in my short "career". He looked to be in his forties, small but sturdy, ultra-fit, an hilarious guy, and extremely informative. He also shared loads of great advice about walking and explained how to pack my rucksack correctly, with weight at the top. We discussed foot treatments, gear, food, and coping with vertigo, which he'd suffered from in the past. I learned a hell of a lot from him in that half-hour. It seemed that up until now I'd been doing a lot of things wrong despite my lengthy preparations. Clive had also walked all the way from Minehead – that day! 30 miles in that heat – over that terrain – how? I was astounded and impressed. It took me two and a half days to complete! He was doing Minehead to Padstow in one week. He was extremely experienced and had a positive attitude, whereas I wasn't and did not! A teacher by trade, he helped me enormously for which I'm eternally grateful. It was almost pitch black before he set off to camp further on. He seemed quite unruffled by the thought of walking the cliff ledges in the darkness. I struggled to cook the rest of my sausages in the blackness but they did go down well with the other half of the loaf and some brown sauce. I fumbled around in the gloom trying to put the stove, the used pots and utensils outside before crawling into the sleeping bag. I was asleep by 9.30 p.m. for the first time.

Day 3: Wednesday 16 April

I'd slept much better and was up early, packed away, and walking by 7 a.m. in order to avoid the heatwave predicted to last all week. I had trouble packing the cooking gear away as it was all covered in congealed sausage lard. Great name for my new band: "Congealed Sausage Lard". Must make a note of that. The tent itself had become an untidy pork-sty overnight too. This spelled the end of the cooking. I couldn't put up with the mess any longer. There was a lot of climbing again – now graded "severe" – the worst grading of all. It was sheer coastline and high cliffs with hazardous narrow walking ledges, dazzling sea, and dynamic views across the Bristol Channel to South Wales on the far side. As it was still early the sea breeze made conditions pleasant for a while but it was definitely a terrible day for vertigo. As I turned inland to cross the Heddon valley, I looked way down below me, hundreds of feet to the River Heddon itself, spying a miniscule dot that was Clive's tent beside the silver ribbon of water. Feeling extremely Heddon-istic now, it took me all of forty-five minutes to descend and cross the river to reach the beautiful spot where he'd pitched in the dark the previous evening. He knew the region inside out and had picked the best camping spot on the entire coast: a lush tree-lined valley with a flat bottom through which gurgled the fantastic River Heddon. It was 20 feet wide, shallow, and fast-flowing at this point where it neared the end of its journey.

Clive was relaxing by his tent, worse for wear, when I spotted a huge wine bottle lying beside him, which he must've polished off the previous night. I couldn't believe he'd carried that extra weight and bulk, especially after lecturing me the previous evening about cutting out all non-essential items. His eyes had come out on stoppers. He'd paled, almost unable to speak when I'd proudly shown him my collapsible yellow plastic bucket that weighed a mere 8 ounces! Needless to say I posted it home at the earliest opportunity after witnessing his adverse reaction to it. Hence I couldn't figure this wine bottle business out, though later reasoned that if he happened to be an alcoholic, the bottle of wine could be classified as an "essential" item. He didn't show any characteristics or mannerisms of an alcoholic and I didn't think it appropriate to ask. As a result I was kept in suspense, wondering if the bottle was an "essential", thus justifying the immense weight. Or was it an undisciplined, heavy waste of space? *Or*, in other words, a "non-essential"! The trouble was that Clive had placed this notion of "essentials" and "non-essentials" so firmly in my teeny brain that I'd become obsessed with it to the exclusion of all else. I kept in touch with Clive afterwards and can now divulge to the readers that he is *not* an alcoholic but, like me, he likes to reward himself with a bevy or two at the end of a tough day. It was a bloody huge bottle though, but after walking 30 miles in a day I reckon he deserved it, even if it had turned out to be a "non-essential".

We had another chat before I wandered off to look at the point where the river flowed into the Bristol Channel some 400 yards north at Heddon's Mouth. I had it in mind to bathe but it was windy and cold when I got there, so I observed the ancient lime kiln before returning, finding Clive slowly packing away.

I set off to climb the west side of the valley, another long zigzag grind in the ever increasing heat, in total contrast to the cool shaded valley below. An hour later Clive caught me up. We stopped for a final chat high on a narrow cliff top ledge with a sheer rock face to our left and a big drop to the water below to our right. One of the things that he stressed to me was that "mental attitude" was far more important than physical fitness. This would come automatically in a couple of weeks if I was able to get that far. Mental strength and determination was the most important. Part of this, for me, was the fact that I had to overcome or at least cope with vertigo. Standing on that precarious cliff ledge chatting was something I would've never believed I could've done, but I *was* doing it. This gave me confidence and confidence tends to breed yet more confidence. The pain in my shoulders and feet was the other major problem to deal with, but I kept walking through it no matter what. I took a photo of Clive before we wished each other luck and shook hands. He went on ahead of me. I walked slowly until the heat finally became too much. At 11 a.m. I plonked myself down under a tiny solitary tree on the side of a steep valley and had a slug of my precious water, which was fast becoming my favourite drink for the first time in my life.

Whilst resting I read a newspaper I'd found on the café table in Lynmouth – essential or non-essential item? It was full of all the latest celeb gossip and rubbish, but strangely there was no mention of the Iraq war, which started a month before. Strange. After half an hour I left my miniscule oasis and set off again in the shimmering heat. I soon came across a total prat who looked like Burlington Bertie, about thirty-five going on sixty-five. He was immaculately dressed in full 1930s garb: plus 4s, straw boater, striped shirt, cravat (essential or non-essential item?), and ludicrous pince-nez spectacles. He was walking briskly along wielding two poles in a stupid-looking circular motion. He looked like he was riding a penny farthing. I stared at him in amazement.

When he addressed me in an toffish, snooty, full-of-the-joys-of-spring-type manner, with, "Wonderful morning, by Jiminy, hey what?" I replied, "Not really," in a dry "Len-*nonic*" or even "Len-*nacious*" manner – i.e. in the style of John Lennon. He didn't speak again. I was glad.

I was getting worryingly low on water again as I had had to keep drinking to avoid dehydration in the high temperatures. It's amazing how much the body craves and needs when thirsty. The path turned inland again. I came across a beautiful spot under a patch of trees in a small valley by a stream with a wooden footbridge bridge (essential or non-essential item?). It was lunchtime. I decided to stop until the sun was past its zenith. I stripped naked before immersing myself in a rock pool and soaping myself down. The sea was 100 yards below me and nobody was around. I also washed all my dirty clothes and hung them on the little bridge to dry. Being desperate, I decided to risk drinking the stream water – upstream from my bathing spot, obviously. The situation demanded drastic action. No habitation or animals were apparent as far as I could see above me. I popped a purification tablet into my bottle, filled it up from the stream, and left it to dissolve for ten minutes, laying the bottle in the water to keep it cool. It tasted fantastic and I felt fine. After half an hour I drank another gallon or two! I had a snooze, covered up by a small, strategically placed towel (essential or non-essential item?). Extremely essential, as it happened, for a young Aussie couple suddenly appeared from nowhere. She was really gorgeous and pleasant, while he was a huge thick lummox who could barely string a sentence together. It's not fair. How did he get a woman like that? You can probably tell I haven't got one. As we chatted, a frail-looking old chap crossed the bridge, carrying nothing but an empty coke can, which he filled from the stream and drank straight down. No namby-pamby purification tablets for him. He refilled the can and set off up the side of the steep valley in the blazing sun, wearing no hat. The couple went. I stayed. The old boy returned an hour later, not dead from typhoid or cholera. He filled his can again and returned to wherever he'd come from.

My laundry was dry in under an hour but I stayed in that shady spot until about 4 p.m., feeling reluctant to swap the safety and tranquility of my own private oasis for grim sweltering pastures unknown. When I finally did leave, it was still baking hot. I climbed forever upwards towards the Great Hangman before taking a signed cliff ledge path to Blackstone Point with the worst drop to date to my immediate right and a sheer cliff face again to my left. After quarter of a mile of terror, during which I dislodged numerous stones that tumbled terrifyingly over the precipice, I reached a complete dead end where an ancient disintegrating sign stated bluntly: "Danger – No Further Access." It looked like there'd been a rock fall or something equally disastrous decades earlier. As I stood there staring I realised I must've gone horribly wrong somewhere, for the ledge had a disused, overgrown look about it, as had the shabby sign. The path appeared lethal, abandoned years ago, but why the hell had it only occurred to me now when it had should've been bloody obvious all along? My heart jumped into my mouth at this realisation. I knew I'd no option but to turn back and retrace my steps along the crumbling ledge. The light was fading fast, making it even more frightening, as I was disorientated. My stick, which I always carried in my right hand, could no longer push me away from the cliff edge. I had to swap it to my left hand. This felt all wrong so I swapped it back again, even though it was rendered useless in my right hand. I froze on the spot numerous times, thinking I may go over the edge. Being alone I knew nobody could help me. I'd have to make it back somehow or die!

I moved at a snail's pace, fumbling my way along, trying not to look down or panic, praying I'd make it. The relief when I finally stepped back onto *terra firma* was incredible. I flopped down in the first field I came to. For a second I was close to tears with the sheer terror of the situation I'd inadvertently found myself in. Stupid really, but vertigo is a terrifying thing, as fellow sufferers will know. I had to make my way inland now and somehow get round the back of the Great Hangman as I couldn't face searching for the front of it! The guidebook was useless. I was lost again and it'd be pitch-black in less than forty-five minutes. My right heel blister was so painful I could barely walk. I was limping along akin to Long John Saliva but with *five* wooden legs and *nine* parrots hampering him (essential or non-essential items?). I soldiered on regardless whilst whimpering and desperately looking for somewhere to camp. This was my first real low point of the trip, what with being lost, the heat, the pain, the fright I'd had, the worry about camping, plus the sheer exhaustion of it all. It led to anxiety and distress. All I wanted to do was to get into my sleeping bag, close my eyes, and forget about everything. I thought about trying to faint – Basil Fawlty-style – to get out of my awful predicament, and would've done, but couldn't induce a fainting fit no matter how hard I tried.

I stumbled on for another mile across open farmland where there was no chance of pitching whatsoever, before coming to Knapp Lane; a straight 5-foot-wide grassy path bordered on both sides by claustrophobic thick hedges, blocking out potentially visible landmarks. I started along it, thinking I'd soon find a gateway into a field where I could camp, but there weren't any. After a draining mile of Knapp Lane I was all in, weak and shaky. I must've been nearing Combe Martin when I finally found a gate on the left, but it was locked and topped with barbed wire. There was, however, a fresh green meadow beyond it. With great care I scrambled over the gate, dropping exhausted into the long grass, unable to move, never mind pitching the tent.

After five minutes I laid out the ground sheet, praying I wasn't trespassing, when suddenly I froze, hearing strains of human voices coming from the other way up Knapp Lane. As they got louder I discerned children's voices, along with a man's. Seemingly they'd come to feed a horse in the opposite field. As I sat in silence, hardly daring to breathe, they stood in the lane talking, not more than 6 feet away on the other side of the hedge. I heard every word clearly. I also heard the unmistakable sound of keys unlocking a metal gate. Please, God, don't let it be *my* gate! I didn't have the strength left to pack up and move on should I be evicted now, at twilight. I planned to act like I was gravely ill if my cover was blown by "blubbing" whilst also writhing on the ground clutching my belly. This was bound to invoke sympathy and wouldn't be far from the truth anyway. Surely they'd pity me and let me stay after that? I breathed a sigh of relief, realising they'd unlocked the gate on the opposite side of Knapp Lane. Maybe I'd get away with it after all. They stayed for about ten minutes and a great weight was lifted when their voices faded as they left in the direction from which they'd arrived.

I pitched the tent quickly as it'd become freezing – radiation – a bitter night after a scorching day. I felt too tired to change the dressing on my foot, so I lay in the dark, shaking and shivering. I felt peculiar. I don't know what it was. Possibly mild hypothermia, caused by going from being boiling hot to bitterly cold within fifteen minutes. I couldn't sleep in this state, so I ate a Pepperami sausage, which tasted fantastic. I think it was the salt. I ate another and eventually stopped shaking. This had been the toughest day so far. I didn't think I could take many more like that. I felt disheartened as I drifted off to sleep. After an okay start today had been far more difficult than the awful climb out of Culbone two days earlier. How much worse could things get?

Day 4: Thursday 17 April

I awoke at 7.30 a.m. feeling almost human again. No sign of the DTs from the night before either, or any other ill effects for that matter. My first priority was to change the plaster on my right heel, which had become red raw and huge. I hadn't really got the hang of those Compede things yet. Surely I must've been doing something wrong, as the plasters kept falling off before I could get my sock back on! Wow, all this fascinating foot saga stuff must make enthralling reading.

It was a relief vacating the area at 9 a.m. after not being evicted. I continued down in the sunshine to the end of Knapp Lane, which was only a couple of hundred yards further ahead. I'd almost made it to the end last night without knowing it. I joined a main road, following it for over a mile down the narrow valley, into Combe Martin, which is apparently the second longest village in England – don't ask the bleeding obvious because I don't know! Today was another scorcher. I was feeling thirsty, not to mention peckish, so I visited The Harbour Café and ordered the sumptuous-sounding "Farmhouse Breakfast" – a full English with all the trimmings, bread and butter and a pot of tea. I really needed to get my strength back up again. Suitably nourished, I looked out of the window towards the picturesque village for a while before chatting to the even more picturesque waitress, who replenished my water bottle for me before I waddled out into the main street, filled to the brim with lard. I ambled to the harbour where I emptied my entire rucksack and placed the contents in a neat line on top of the harbour wall so I could decide what to keep and what to post home or discard. Clive's words were now indelibly etched into my brain for life: "Get rid of all non-essential items." I was totally ruthless but it was good fun too. I managed to lose about 7 lbs., including some thermal clothing and loads more already redundant stuff, like my poor doomed folding bucket, which had never harmed anyone or been used in anger yet.

I cadged a cardboard box from the post office sweets counter, only to deal with a fat ugly woman on the parcel counter, who deliberately set out to *not* be helpful. Maybe she was married to the miserable Ken Dodd-esque git from the Lynton Tourist Information. She got flustered and irritated when I asked how much my parcel weighed in pounds instead of in kilograms.

She rudely stated, "We only have kilograms in here."

Why are people like that? There's no need for it.

It didn't ease the situation when I provocatively said, "In that case, I'll take 10 pounds of kilograms please … and could you wrap them individually for me too?"

Some people in the queue smiled but "fat and ugly" didn't see the funny side of it. She continued scowling at me, though it was hard to tell!

She made herself look stupid in front of everyone with her petulance and bad attitude. The chap beside her proved more than helpful, perhaps compensating for her rudeness. After it was sorted out I returned to my spot on the harbour wall where I sat and ate a whole large Original Creamy Müller Yoghurt in one go. Banana *was* my favourite but they don't make it any more – *pigs*! I followed this with a can of good old British Sprite – or is it bloody American?

Combe Martin looked lovely bathed in sunlight with its dinky harbour and long single street. A local chap really upset me by telling me that it was not the second longest village in England after all. Apparently it was all lies! He said that the myth probably came about because of four reasons. First, Combe Martin holds the Guinness World Record for the world's longest street party. This could easily be confused with longest village street! Secondly, many people measure Combe Martin from one "You are entering Combe Martin" sign to the other, but one of those signs is placed in an unusually long way from the village – approximately 1 and a half miles – which can lead to confusion. How stupid! Thirdly, human error: on a hot summer day when you walk uphill from one end of the village to the other it feels like you've walked further than expected, so to save their pride, people exaggerate the distance walked – arrogant *fools*! Fourthly, Combe Martin has always had several lively pubs, and there's a saying in the village that, "At The George and Dragon they talk about my sprained thumb and at The Dolphin they talk about my broken leg," meaning that in the pubs of Combe Martin many stories really do get exaggerated. Maybe such is the case here. What kind of village was this anyway, where nobody's sure about anything? He went on to tell me more about the village that in bygone days it used to produce silver. The mines were located on the eastern ridge. Evidence of tunnels can still be seen, as well as the remains of a wheelhouse used to lift ore from the mines. Apparently there are items in the Crown Jewels made from Combe Martin silver. Or was he "exaggerating" about that too?

One of the village's most unusual buildings is The Pack o' Cards pub built around 1700, by George Ley, reputed to have been funded by his gambling successes. It originally had fifty-two windows, thirteen rooms, and four floors, matching all numbers from a pack of cards. An annual procession down the main street known as "The Hunting of the Earl of Rone" features "The Rare Hobby Horse of England" and a fictitious character called the "Earl of Rone", as well as a "fool", some grenadiers, drummers, music, a donkey, and hundreds of dancers in festive dress. The custom was banned in 1837 owing to "licentiousness and drunken behaviour", as well as the death of a drunken parishioner who fell off of a wall during the wild festivities. It was resurrected through public demand in 1970. Also nearby is Combe Martin Wildlife and Dinosaur Park which is similar to a normal wildlife park except this one boasts live dinosaurs too!

I found the gents' in the car park for my daily ablutions before speaking to a nice old boy of eighty-four in his neat garden alongside the harbour. He was scraping the remains of his breakfast off his plate into his herbaceous borders. He was obviously a bachelor. I half expected him to chuck his blue and white willow pattern plate into his dustbin afterwards. He'd lived in the village all his life but even he wasn't sure about anything either!

All tasks completed, I set off for Ilfracombe at 11 a.m. For a change the terrain was not too severe, enabling me to enjoy it a bit more for the first time, despite my painful feet and shoulders. After a few miles I passed through a low-level open campsite where I applied the customary Ibuleve gel to all my aching parts, before watering my whole head under an outside tap. I filled my water bottles followed by the Tilley hat, which I donned before leaving.

I'd already got a problem with my digital camera and couldn't take any pictures for some reason. I needed to get it checked as soon as convenient. It was a pity, as the views were great again, and would've made lovely photographs. I pressed on and stopped for lunch in the petite Hele Bay at an outdoor café overlooking the beach. I had half a chicken, chips, and a pot of slop to try rebuilding my strength. I chatted to "Cockney Geoff", a delivery driver, who said he'd done some amateur boxing but decided to pack it in, as it hadn't gone well lately. The final straw came when his cruel "fans" nicknamed him "Rembrandt" because he spent so much time on the canvas! You can't beat the old ones. He mentioned going to Hertfordshire for the Bank Holiday to see his young daughter, as the heatwave was predicted to last another week. I sat there nodding my head as my mind wandered off towards more pressing matters.

After a long break I set off towards the principal seaside resort in North Devon, the hilly town of Ilfracombe. I arrived at 5 p.m. after getting lost in its suburbs, which later inspired me to create, rather surprisingly, an upbeat song called 'Up, Down, and Round the Houses', complete with catchy hook that was to recur in my head constantly throughout the walk, along with many more sombre and downbeat melodies unfortunately. Once in town I sought out a photographic shop. It was a small one and they were unable to examine my camera, so I bought a disposable for a fiver to keep me going until the next big town – Barnstaple – still a couple of days away.

I went to the harbour for a massive toffee ice cream, bought from a lady in a kiosk, who resembled a 150-year-old version of Brigitte Bardot. Maybe it *was* her cos she hasn't worn that well, has she? This could be a case of the pot calling the kettle black though, for I'm not exactly a spring-oil painting myself. I still rate the young BB as the sexiest woman of all time. I sat on the wall eating my tasty treat a fantastic evening, with Ilfracombe looking beautiful bathed in the deep golden glow of the late afternoon sun.

I loitered with intent (to sleep) around the town for a while, catching a few shops that were late closing. I looked at shoulder bags in a fishing tackle shop. I don't know why, as I'd already got one and couldn't possibly carry another. I rang Mum and Dad from a call box in the harbour and was delighted to hear everything was fine back home, BB included. I left the harbour in the deepening glow at 6.15 p.m. and climbed up to the top of Capstone Point, a landmark in the town but was totally Point-less – ha, ha! – as I arrived back exactly 100 yards from where I'd started an hour earlier! The view from the top wasn't worth it either, as I had to climb up through the western suburbs, out of town, and in doing so would get the same views again only far better from much higher up. Capstone pork-belly *pigs*! The breeze felt cooler as usual when the sun was setting. I searched for a place to pitch. I was a couple of miles out of Ilfracombe, high up on the cliffs when, I found a flattish area of short grass that was also sheltered. A few people were still out walking their dogs as I put up the tent. They'd all gone by dusk when I prepared to sleep. It was about 9 p.m. and, thankfully, I felt much better than on the night before. I hadn't died yet and was feeling pleased with myself until realising I'd only done about 42 miles, meaning there were still 588 more to go. I figured I'd better stop larking about and get a move on tomorrow!

Day 5: Good Friday 18 April

I woke at 7 a.m. feeling well rested and unzipped the flysheet to reveal yet another lovely morning. Looking back over a sunny Ilfracombe, it seemed puzzling again as to why the locals nicknamed their town "Ilfra-gloom". But who was I to argue with them? I packed away before leaving at 8 a.m., having realised it always took exactly *one* hour to perform this task, unless something went drastically wrong, which forced me to begin again.

I strolled casually along the cliff tops, which made a pleasant change from strolling desperately, before descending slightly inland into the beautiful village of Lee Bay at 9.30 a.m. This was where Mark Wallington of the *500 Mile Walkies* fame had stayed at the amazing Duff Farm during bad weather, after walking the path twenty-two years ago. Today the weather was perfect. I sauntered down the long lane with its colourful spring flowers, birds twittering, and old cottage gardens. This was my favourite place so far. The setting for the picturesque village was a deep combe, heavily wooded in places, with a variety of interesting buildings scattered on either side of the single lane. I felt concerned about being too late to get any breakfast, when a lady jogger approached me.

When I asked if there was a café or shop in the village, she said, "Yes, you could try the Fuchsia Tea Garden, but you're a bit early."

A bit *early*! It was that kind of place, lazy and sleepy like me. The pleasant looking Fuchsia hadn't even opened when I arrived, but a woman soon appeared at the side door. A passing delivery man asked her if I could have something to eat! She made me a two big bacon sandwiches and a pot of tea, setting me up nicely for the next stage. While she was topping up my water bottles I asked her about Duff Farm. She said it was now a private house and had been modernised, which saddened me, and was back up the lane, thus I wouldn't be seeing it this time after all. It was great sitting in the tea garden, relaxing. Why couldn't this rare and peaceful moment last forever?

Before leaving I bought more plasters for my blister, which was worsening by the minute. The unfathomable Compede had been disastrous so far. Therefore, I opted for some conventional plasters, this time simpler and much cheaper. I spoke to a well-to-do old lady, watering plants in her garden. She said Lee had an extremely mild climate owing to its sheltered position, and was locally referred to as "Fuchsia Valley" during the flowering season, as many hedgerows are ablaze with the scarlet flowers. This explained the "Fuchsia Tea Garden" bit too. The hub of the village is centred round St Matthew's Church, built in 1835, and the nearby village hall and Pixie Meadow; the venue for many a village fete in bygone years and present times too. She wished me luck.

I continued on the narrow path running alongside the old Grampus Inn – where Mark had spent the evening – and over a small bridge. My path crossed a meadow where I stumbled upon a little stone-built gents' all on its own in a perfect setting amid the greenery. With nobody around this was too good an opportunity to turn down. I shaved and washed my hair and clothes. I hung them on a nearby fence to dry. It only took fifteen minutes. That's how hot it was. I spent half an hour there and did the lot. I heard workmen doing something outside for a few minutes then they were gone. Nobody else disturbed me. I retrieved the freshly laundered clothes, which were bone dry – too dry, in fact. So much so that I doused my hat and top again before putting them on to try staying cool for as long as possible.

I set off for the coast and was soon at the bay itself. The first thing I noticed was the imposing Lee Bay Hotel, which seemed overlarge for such a small bay, and would've looked more at home in Brighton or Bournemouth. Once again, who was I to find fault or tell the people of Devon how big to build their hotels? There must've been a market for a hotel of that grandeur in the dinky little Lee Bay once! The small rocky cove, with its impressive coastline on either side is regarded by some as the jewel in the crown of Lee Bay, and by *me*, for what it's worth. It was also refreshing to see that the place had remained untouched by the hand of time, with its many little rock pools and small sandy beach. Even on that sweltering day it was still a tranquil spot indeed with none of the usual bucket-and-spade hoards.

It was 11.30 by the time I sadly left Lee Bay behind, bound for my next port of call at Woolacombe. I passed the glistening rocks at Bull Point with its lighthouse, but became diverted inland for some reason. As I walked along a small twisty-turny lane, I found a lighter, a dog clip, a penny, a comb, and a 5 pence piece, all within ten yards. It must be my lucky day, I thought, especially as there was no chance of finding a police station to hand them all in! I missed most of the scenery during the next half-mile or so, as my peepers were glued to the tarmac in case of a more spectacular windfall, which never materialised.

I soon found myself in the middle of Mortehoe another pretty village clustered round the square-towered church of St Mary. Quite a few present day tourists were here, relaxing with drinks outside the pub in the sun. I bought my first Cornish pasty of the trip from the village shop, plus tomatoes, a coke, and a raspberry yoghurt, and sat on the church steps to eat them. Not fully satisfied, I returned to the shop for a Magnum – the ice cream, not the champagne. It was almost 2 p.m. by the time I got back on the road, but things sort of went downhill from here.

After descending and rounding a bend in the lane, I was confronted by Bank Holiday mayhem! The beautiful yet hardly visible sands of Woolacombe beach were crammed to the hilt with thousands of sun-seekers, bathers, lummoxes, bronzers, lady-boys, and surfers. At least half the population of Europe was present by the look of it. I'd previously seen the place out of season and deserted, so this chaotic scene came as a shock. I had to make a choice whether to take the road that curved round and through the town, skirting the beach, or aim in a straight line for the distant Baggy Point some 3 miles away, which entailed ploughing through the middle of the crowded beach. I decided to grit my teeth and do the latter route, as if I went like hell it'd only take about an hour to cross.

After chatting to some friendly Italian surfers I stepped onto the blazing beach and attacked it with gusto. Unlike anybody else I was fully clothed, carrying a gigantic rucksack, and I got some strange looks from the seven-eighths naked, lobster-red sun-worshippers as I marched round and over the top of them. The sand was soft yet tough walking. I sank 3 or 4 inches into it with each frustrating step, rapidly sapping my strength. Kids were shouting, crying, and screaming. Frisbees, beach balls, and various other scary objects were flying about. I pressed on with grim determination. After an hour the density of bodies decreased. Getting to within 400 yards of the end, I plonked down on a big driftwood log for a well-earned rest. Suddenly, as I looked down, there was blood everywhere – my blood! My nose had started bleeding profusely the first time in at least thirty years, probably owing to my superhuman efforts during the last hour, combined with the heat and my lack of fitness. I pinched the middle of my nose for two minutes. All was well again. This was thankfully a one-off occurrence. I was fine afterwards. Luckily the blood missed my clothing, so no harm was done.

After a fifteen-minute break I resumed the short walk to the base of the large, beautifully-named promontory, Baggy Point, with no further problems. I found a welcome water tap outside the gents' where I saturated everything and guzzled down as much water as humanly possible before starting the tough climb up the cliff. As I walked along its flattish top, I spotted a couple near the edge, waving and making strange arm movements to a small orange boat far below the cliff and quite close in.

Being nosey, I asked the girl – who was German – if they were waving to friends in the boat. She said the orange craft was a lifeboat and three surfers were stranded out at sea. The boat couldn't spot them, being level with the water. The girl and the chap could see them from on top of the cliff, hence they were signalling directions to the lifeboat, which had managed to pick up two of the three. The third had drifted out of view and they could no longer see him. I handed my monocular to the chap. He spotted the unfortunate surfer straight away, pointed out the angle to the lifeboat, and the surfer was soon rescued. I watched the whole episode and felt relieved when it was over. After a brief chat with the couple I carried on.

I saw a man running towards me with a mobile phone clamped to his ear. I heard him anxiously say, "Where was he last seen?" Instantly grasping the thread of the conversation I thought it was time to intervene. I stopped the guy, who was a coastguard, and explained that the rescue had been successful. He thanked me before we went our separate ways.

As I ambled off I felt sort of like a micro-hero for doing my bit. Lucky I'd bought that monocular. I congratulated myself. It occurred to me a few minutes later, when I'd come back down to earth, what if *another* surfer was missing and I'd told the coastguard not to bother? Oh my God! It'd all be *my* fault if a body was washed up in a week's time. Some bloody hero then! Well, it was too late now. I tried thinking about something more pleasant instead. I spotted an older hippy hiker who I'd seen near Mortehoe earlier. Next I spoke to a fantastic flame-haired girl, who was with her horrible boyfriend. He wasn't horrible really. I was envious. I also met a friendly holidaying couple sitting in a small sheltered ornamental garden with a pond, off the path, like an unexpected oasis and a tranquil spot. We chatted before taking some photographs of each other before going in opposite directions. Several people were walking the picturesque path round the end of Baggy Point, but I enjoyed the relative peace after the chaos of Woolacombe Beach.

Eventually I arrived at Croyde Bay, with its incredible rock formations, prior to arriving at the sandy beach. These rocks are so spectacular that it's hard to imagine how it all happened. The steeply angled thin layers and sheets look like they've plummeted to earth and embedded themselves in the ground at a million mph to produce this stunning effect. This would take some beating from a geological point of view, but obviously not from a horticultural one. A profusion of sea birds of all varieties were diving and fishing on the rocks. I got an Oasis drink – Summer Fruits flavour – which was to become my favourite soft drink of the trip, along with their Lemon/Citrus ones. I sat at a table on the edge of Croyde beach with my drink. Afterwards I watered everything at a tap before crossing the smaller, less crowded sands.

I climbed up to the old dilapidated coastguards hut that leaned and teetered at a terrifying angle near the top of the cliff in the late afternoon. Goodness knows what was holding it up. It looked like it was about to disintegrate and crash down the cliff, though hopefully not while I was immediately below it. I met the busy main road at the top where I'd no alternative but to turn right and walk along it as there was no pavement. The guidebook warned walkers to be cautious. I don't really see how though. You either risk it or you don't and I did. After a mile or so of well-dodgy road walking I came to the imposing Saunton Sands Hotel. On my right this huge oblong structure looked out over sands and the Taw estuary 3 miles away. It didn't occur to me at the time that I'd be looking back at this hotel from across the other side of the estuary for the next week or so. This landmark could be seen from virtually everywhere to its south.

I sat on the wall for a five-minute breather before weaving down to the beach to purchase my second Cornish pasty, which turned out to be awful, being one of those curry-style failures. I still ate it though. Waste not, want not. I purchased a cold lime drink for a change and it was good, almost making up for the pasty. I walked south along Saunton Sands beach for half a mile or so until I was too tired to go further. It was getting late and the cool evening breeze had sprung up. I headed into the huge maze of sand dunes that stretched for miles to try and camp. With nobody around it seemed like a good place to pitch – but it wasn't! No sooner had I struggled to erect the tent in the wind and sandstorm, twenty teenagers appeared from nowhere with carriers full of booze intent on partying not 20 yards from me. At first it wasn't too bad, but as the drink took effect the racket started. Shouting, laughing, screaming, squealing, and swearing, while I was trapped in my tent as it was dark now.

I got quite worried when I heard them shouting, "Look at that f****** tent! Who's in that then?" I kept quiet, grasping my walking pole. It got really spooky when someone yelled: "Who's got the ******* matches? I wanna start a ******* fire."

I had visions of being burned alive. All went quiet at about 11 p.m. as they appeared to have drifted off. I remained edgy all the same. At 12.30 a.m. another load of kids arrived and it all kicked off again. This lot stayed an hour. Luckily it was now blowing a bitter gale and it became too cold for them.

All twenty or so passed within 2 feet of me as they left, with one drunken smart alec chipping in with, "This is your early morning wake-up call, mate! Huh, huh!"

I wanted to curse at him but bit my lip instead, not wanting to risk a confrontation in which I'd be drastically outnumbered. I also kept telling myself that they were only kids having fun. After all, I must have been one once, mustn't I? (not sure?) This would never have been my idea of fun even then. I failed to sleep for more than an hour all night, partly owing to the strong winds that blew the tent sideways, and partly from the fear that the kids may return with more sinister intentions. It was a bad night; my worst so far. I resolved to take greater care over where I camped in future. I decided to camp only in remote areas or on authorised campsites. Easier said than done though, especially when that sun starts setting and you're somewhere grim.

Day 6: Easter Saturday 19 April

I gave up trying to sleep by 7 a.m. and started wearily packing away, amid cold winds and flying sand that infiltrated everything. I left the desolate dunes at 8.10 a.m., miraculously finding my way back to the windswept beach. I'd love to be able to say, "I sauntered sartorially along Saunton Sands" that morning, but I certainly did not. More like, "I staggered shell-shocked and stupefied." I made straight for the water's edge as the tide in the sand was harder there, thus easier to walk upon. The tips of the waves lapped at my old boots as I route-marched due south for an hour in a straight line, towards Braunton Burrows and the River Taw estuary. It started spitting with rain. The wind was so cold that I put on my Berghaus Gore-Tex jacket to stop it cutting right through me. In contrast to the last few sweltering days it was a dull morning. It was a sandy wilderness and there wasn't another soul in sight. I thought to myself, Only a fool would be out in this – *me*.

After entering the nature reserve of the Burrows, I sat in a sheltered spot by an empty car park to eat a brown pear that, after being battered around in my rucksack, had seen better days. I also pondered on my current plight. Apart from the problem with my camera, my debit card had got cracked somehow, and therefore may not work in a cash machine. I had only got about £50 left, causing some concern with the Bank Holiday underway and with no sizeable towns until Bude, which was about a week away. I had to sort something out today, which entailed going into the middle of Barnstaple and looking for a Nationwide and a Jessops.

I carried on through the boring old Burrows. This was normally a wildlife sanctuary but not today. No self-respecting wildlife would venture out of its hole in these wintry conditions. I soon picked up the old railway embankment, climbing up the side of it, onto the precarious path. Of course, once on the top, the gale felt more icy and ferocious, continually blasting me in the face as I slowly progressed. The surrounding land was flat, with the embankment raised up 15 feet above it, giving the winds free reign to batter me at 70 mph. It felt like I'd gone from the Sahara Desert to the Antarctic in twenty-four hours. This was miserable walking to say the least. 3 miles of this would've been enough to even finish off the intrepid explorer Sir Ranulph Fiennes. To think I'd been looking forward to this rare flat stretch for days. At one point, being unable to climb down the embankment, owing to the barbed wire and large rocks on either side of it, I forced open the door of an old shed on the side of the slope, and fell in out of the wind. It was stacked full with old planks of wood and jagged, rusted sheets of corrugated iron, all at a 45-degree angle, making it impossible to sit or lie anywhere. I leaned uncomfortably on it, realising I was covered in wet, rotting, brown and green, foul-smelling seaweed or something possibly even more vile. Whatever it was, it was all over my clothes. I had to get out of this nite-time nightmare immediately. I flung back the door, nearly flinging it off its rusted hinges, and pulled myself out, back into the relentless gale. This was my idea of hell. After another mile I was nearing the town of Braunton. I was finally able to climb down from the embankment where I found a mini roundabout in the road. I staggered round it several times. Totally unable to decide which way Braunton actually was, such was my battered and numb mental state, I took a wild guess and somehow found my way into the town.

Whilst staggering through a small park, overcome with exhaustion, I considered lying down to sleep on a metal bench in the freezing gale. Finally though, I walked into the town wondering how I was going to get through the day. This fatigue was unbearable, preventing me from thinking straight. My instincts were barely working. It was too early to find a B & B to sleep, so I found a chemists and bought some double-strength Ibuleve gel and a roll of medical tape to hold on the Compede, as I considered giving it one more try. They didn't sell speed or cocaine or I may have bought some of that too!

I headed for Squire's, Devon's most famous fish and chip shop, where I'd eaten three years previously whilst holidaying in Ilfracombe. Photos of a smiling John Major adorned the window, along with pictures of other "celebs" tucking into their tasty Squire's fish and chips. It was pretty packed but I was given a table to myself by the lovely manageress who took my order of mixed white fish with prawns in a sauce, plus chips, of course. The warmth of the room was making me nod off at the table as the room started to fill up, but fifteen minutes later there was still no sign of my meal. The family next to me had meals delivered first, despite them ordering a good ten minutes after me. They were sent back, however, when the young waitress knocked over and broke a glass into their meals. I felt sorry for her. She was embarrassed and probably hadn't worked there long. Finally I got my meal, but felt guilty eating it, as by now there was a queue halfway down the street, staring sullenly at us through the windows, willing us diners to eat up and vacate the tables as quickly as possible. This was hardly conducive to the enjoyment of one's meal.

So, after rushing my dinner without being able to savour it, I left my rucksack and went to the toilets to have a quicky and to try reviving myself. I was in a state of semi-undress and semi-consciousness, with shaving cream all over my fizogg, when an old battle-axe of a waitress rushed into the gents' to force me out! First I got a telling off for monopolising the gents', then another one for blocking the aisles with my rucksack, which was apparently too heavy for anyone else in the entire establishment to move, hence causing complete mayhem and gridlock in the café. Cut off in my prime, I hastily dressed in mid-ablution, with one side of my mush still all stubbly, somewhat put out by the arrival of "Matron Grimly" in the supposed sanctuary of the gents' room. People ogled at me as I made my way back to the table, with half a beard on show, and the remnants of shaving cream all down my front. I could feel their eyes boring into me: "So *that's* the man who caused mayhem and held everyone up!"

I paid my bill, feeling deflated, embarrassed, and unable to think of anything nice to say to the lovely manageress, lest I should get a telling off from her too. I drifted away feeling cheated. I stood over the road at the bus stop opposite, in full view of the fifty diners, who were still staring at me from the café windows.

"Yes, that's him over there! Isn't he horrible? Should be damn-well ashamed of himself!"

I asked a woman about buses. I was in luck, thank goodness. I needed to get away from Braunton in a hurry. A bus arrived two minutes later and I left the jeering crowd behind. I bought a ticket for Barnstaple, a 3-mile journey, which took about thirty seconds! I did say I wanted to get away in a hurry, didn't I?

Whilst struggling with my pack, the driver said, "Come on, come on, ain't got all day!" He added he was very late, revving up the engine, before proceeding to drive like Stirling Moss at breakneck speed, trying to make up for lost time, taking corners on two wheels, ignoring red lights, blasting his horn at OAPs to shift them, missing them by inches.

I thought to myself, I've survived all those frightening cliff ledges, nosebleeds, searing heat and freezing gales, only to be killed in a horrific road accident, on the edge of Barnstaple. It wouldn't look good in the local paper back home either. Better to fall off a cliff whilst trying to rescue a child's dog or be lost at sea after saving a drowning surfer's life. Oh no, don't remind me! We did finally get to the town centre and I thanked the driver for not crashing, asking if he'd ever considered Formula 1.

Barnstaple, the capital of North Devon, is an ancient town, being granted its original charter in AD 930 by King Aethelstan, grandson of Alfred the Great. Surely that must be the same Alfred mentioned in Ilfragloom. It was a busy Saturday afternoon in the town. The place was bustling with shoppers as I walked towards the main area. I spotted the traditional indoor Pannier Market with its varied stalls and glass roof, which I'd visited on previous occasions, it being one of my favourite markets. Many other fine buildings and attractive alleyways were dotted around and beside the Pannier market, running along its 100-yard length, stands the quaint old Butchers Row, built in 1855. This consists of about ten shops with pilasters of Bath Stone and wrought iron supports to an overhanging roof. Only two of the shops remain as butchers, though the new shops sell local agricultural goods. Today there's the Norman mound and remnants of the original castle wall, the ornate Queen Anne's Walk and the thirteenth-century Long Bridge, to which I'd be heading once business was sorted. At 2.05 p.m. I started asking people if there was a Nationwide Building Society.

Turned out it was one minute away. Approaching it I saw a Jessops on the opposite corner from the Nationwide. Perfect! *No*, not really! First, the Nationwide was closed. A door sign stated: "Saturdays 9 a.m. to 2.00 p.m." I'd missed it by ten minutes. Barnstofools! How can they open till 3 p.m. in Hereford but close here an hour earlier? Was it a different time zone or something? I'd no alternative than to risk putting the damaged card into the hole in the wall. Luckily it worked. I drew £300 so I could manage for a long time without having to risk the cracked card again.

I strode boldly into Jessops and handed over my camera. The first thing they did was test the CF card and, to my dismay, told me it was full. I'd only taken thirty pictures. How could it be full? When they brought the images up on their computer screen it seemed like I'd failed to transfer all 200 pictures and video clips taken since Christmas. I thought I'd transferred them to my PC before I'd left home but evidently hadn't. Oh, why *me*! I asked if they'd download the images onto a CD for me to post home, enabling me to re-use the card from scratch. Of course! Their computer wasn't working properly, thus it couldn't be done. As I didn't have time to traipse all over Barnstaple looking for a place that *may* do it, I was forced into purchasing another CF card. I felt like a total mug, as it cost me £140 for a 512 Mb. Card. As I winced at the price, the manager commented it should've been £280, but I was in luck, as it'd been reduced to half price in the sale. Half bloody price! I should cocoa Jessopigs! I was extremely miffed, but what alternative did I have? It all seemed so simple with hindsight, but at least I could use my camera again.

I found *Milletts* where I bought a few protein bars before leaving the crowded town by crossing the old river bridge and aiming for Westward Ho! I would've loved going round the old Pannier Market but it was too late, plus I couldn't carry any bargains that I may have been lucky enough to find there anyway. I'd also spent 140 horrid quid and needed to economise on everything else. I left it for my next visit. I stopped at the beginning of the tarmac cycle path to Instow, sat on a bench, treated my blisters, and rubbed Ibuleve gel into my shoulders and calves. I saw signposts for the famous Tarka Trail (otters) everywhere upon setting off up the broad track towards Instow. For a change the walking was flat. The wind, though still strong, was coming from behind now, pushing me along instead of holding me back. The *Berghaus* jacket (only 12 ounces) was brilliant. I was glad to have this.

I met several families on hired bikes, struggling towards me in the wind. They asked me how far it was to Barnstaple. I was able to comfort them by saying, "Only ten minutes and you're there." I came across a lonely little "old" railway station – Fremington Halt – which served as a little tea room/museum. It'd been reconstructed and was identical to the original, which had long since crumbled away through years of neglect. Inside was cosy and old-fashioned, with about half a dozen people relaxing. I ordered a pot of tea and started feeling slightly better. The crippling fatigue had worn off. I'd got my second wind. I looked at all the old photos of the station, adorning every wall, taken in bygone days. They were most interesting, unless you can't stick trains.

Later I went outside to put my rucksack on and spoke to some Italian cyclists, before hearing a girl's voice say, "Overend! What the hell are you doing here?"

I turned to see the lovely Diane from Jonathan Preece Estate Agents back in Ross-on-Wye! We'd met in the street in Ross a few weeks before and had both mentioned we were going down that way, but this was a ridiculous coincidence, especially in a remote little place like Fremington Halt. It transpired she was on holiday with her boyfriend and had been driving around seeing the sights all day. After a chat I took a picture of her, put my rucksack on, and left in a much happier mood than I'd been in all day. It's amazing how a little event like meeting someone you know can re-energise and invigorate you, changing the mood of the day. I should really have had more tea with them, but needed to press on.

It was 3.30 when I continued along the flat cycle track that, according to the book, went all the way to Instow. This suited me fine as it was easy walking. Once there, I'd be at the confluence of the rivers Torridge and Taw, where they collide at the large estuary. At one point, I felt a sudden sharp stabbing pain under the toes on my right foot, like a knife. I thought, What the hell was that? I didn't know at the time, but it turned out to be the start of the most painful blister I've ever had. Lucky I didn't realise exactly how painful, or I may have packed up and gone home on the spot!

The weather improved as I neared Instow. The conditions became pleasant, with less wind. Even the sun popped out. I came to some picturesque cottages and, to the north, sweeping views across to the other side of the estuary from where I'd walked that morning. The gigantic Saunton Sands Hotel dominated the skyline. I walked with difficulty, limping into Instow at 6 p.m. in search of the ferry to Appledore, but as I should've known, there weren't any at this time of year. I spoke to two young local girls on bikes about alternative routes, but it seemed I'd have to, other than swim the mile or so across the estuary, walk inland to Bideford, cross the road bridge, and then head back up to Appledore along the other side. I didn't relish the thought of all that unnecessary walking. It was getting late, my foot felt grim, and I couldn't see any potential camping spots ahead. It looked mostly like main road walking to Bideford, which didn't bode well either. For some reason I still felt quite cheerful though as the day had improved as it progressed. I gave Mum and Dad a quick ring from a call box to say Happy Easter before going into John's Supermarket for some grub. A great atmosphere existed inside the little store, with local people milling round and chatting. I chatted too and bought a huge pasty, tomatoes, and a big bottle of cider.

I set off up the road eating my tasty pasty, heading towards Bideford. After 200 yards, however, I suddenly realised I'd left my indispensable Leki walking pole behind. Oh no! I couldn't manage without that. I hurried back, hoping the store hadn't closed with my precious pole locked inside. I knew that when moving on from somewhere I must ensure I was carrying three items: 1) Rucksack. 2) Shoulder bag. 3) Walking pole. As long as I could remember these items everything would be fine. This time I had got the three items but, unfortunately they were: 1) Rucksack. 2) Shoulder bag. 3) Cornish pasty! The poor old pole was forgotten. Nearing the store I spied four people waving to me, holding my pole. It was the lovely family I'd chatted to inside the shop who'd also something to do with the management. I said thanks, took my pole, and was about to leave when they offered me a lift to a campsite near Appledore. No way would I get that far on foot after the horrendous inland detour. I took them up on their offer. This definitely wasn't cheating, as the inland detour wouldn't have been necessary if the ferry had been running, which it should've been.

They squeezed up in the car to make room for my gear. I also spilt flaky Cornish pastry on their seats, but they didn't seem to mind. They were really nice and chatted about my walk on the fifteen-minute journey through Bideford, on to Knapp House camp site. They assured me I wasn't cheating. It was 7 p.m. when they dropped me off and waved goodbye. I was in a rural setting again. The campsite looked most welcoming. I went up to the big old house to try finding someone to pay, but there wasn't a soul about.

I returned to the field, where a Londoner, standing by his caravan, said, "Camp wherever you like and pay in the morning."

So I did.

Suddenly the evening became freezing. I got the tent up quickly, near the bottom edge of the field by some trees, and clambered straight into the bag without further ado. I was worried by this drop in temperature, as I'd posted home all my thermal clothing, apart from one fleece, during last week's heatwave. Oh Gawd! Had I been a bit premature? "One swallow ..." etc. I wrote up this journal, drank the whole bottle of cider, making me feel much warmer and more cheerful, and managed a good night's sleep. About time, too.

Day 7: Easter Sunday 20 April

I woke at 8 a.m. after my much needed kip. I was exactly one week into the walk. It'd been tough and traumatic so far. A good night's rest proved essential and most welcome too. I packed away before going to the house to pay. Once again I couldn't find anyone. I had a shower and brush-up in the outbuildings and prepared to leave without paying. Before I got to the gate a car pulled up beside me. It was the owner. I could go to prison for this. I explained I'd tried to pay twice, but couldn't find anybody. He smiled, saying it was normally £7, but he'd let me off this time. A most kind cove, I must say. I felt elated as I wandered up the road in the general direction of

Appledore. I'd saved myself seven valuable notes too, pretty damn good. It was grey and blowy again, but at least it wasn't raining. I met an ancient countryman, in his nineties perhaps, who tried his best to give me directions. A lovely old gent, Billy Hill was his name, but even though he'd lived there all his life, he couldn't get the words out coherently and got all mixed up. He seemed so excited at being asked for directions that it'd completely thrown him! I didn't care though. It was great to listen to his beautiful Devon accent. I couldn't go far wrong this time as it was only a mile to the town along a main road. As I bade him a Happy Easter I thought about all the changes he must've seen throughout his days. He appeared cheerful enough despite of them though! I sat on a bench at the top of the hill opposite some houses, taking a quick drink of water and rested.

As I walked down the final hill into Appledore nobody was about but the cheery Easter bells were ringing out. Lilac and cherry blossom were on the trees. Life was great. I felt unreasonably cheerful and optimistic, the best I'd felt since the start. The sun almost came out to welcome me too, but decided against it at the last minute. Down by the harbour I watched an old seadog preparing his boat for a fishing trip and peered across the estuary to Instow where I'd stood peering towards Appledore the previous evening. I took a few pictures before amazingly discovering a quayside café that was *open*! Inside was warm and cosy. Three old ladies were behind the counter but I was the only customer. I ordered a "Farmhouse Fry-Up" to replenish my strength. I read a Sunday paper that was lying on a chair and enjoyed a big pot of tea. The breakfast was huge. I could hardly stand afterwards. After letting it go down for an hour I waddled up to a small supermarket to buy some chocolate bars for later. I usually got Mars, Twix, or my favourite Snickers, normally the giant-sized ones!

It was drizzling by 10.30 a.m. as I weaved my way through the quaint passages of Appledore. I soon discovered the amazing Irsha Street, a narrow cobbled street, full of ancient, terraced, brightly-painted, former sea captains cottages, all picturesque, with some dating back as far as the Elizabethan era. I met a lady resident who was sorting out her window box. She pointed out a cottage that was up for sale. It was expected to sell for around £80,000. What a bargain! Its owner, who'd gone into a home, had lived there for many years, during which time the house had never been modernised. Many original features still survived. I took photos and vowed to return soon to snap it up and move to Appledore. I didn't, of course.

Not appearing to be making much progress, I became irritated with myself, stopping every ten seconds for some reason or another. I finally struck out passed an ancient pub and the lifeboat slipway bound for Westward Ho! I walked miles to the coast around a totally exposed golf course in the wind and drizzle. In the distance I could discern the familiar scary silhouette of "The Haunted House", the last building on the skyline on the far side of Westward Ho! I'd once been frightened to death outside it by the sudden unexpected appearance of a "toothless old hag", who'd emerged from the derelict building into the puzzlingly well-kept garden, causing me to run like the clappers! Bet she was a beautiful duchess in reality. I didn't have my specs on at the time, but a "hag" makes the story much scarier. This had happened several years previously when I'd visited the town, but the ghostly memory had always stuck with me and now I had to walk past it again! With the rain beating down, my *Berghaus* jacket came into its own again, proving to be indispensable in these wet, miserable conditions.

Several Easter walkers were about, despite the bad weather. I managed to chat to some of them en route. When I reached Westward Ho! an hour later I stopped in the first beach shelter I encountered to re-Ibuleve my shoulders. Westward Ho! as a town isn't nearly as wonderful as its name suggests. In fact, it's a bit of a let-down. I don't think Charles Kingsley would've been too impressed with the town that stole its name from the title of his book either. It's a faceless, straggling, run-down resort with no apparent redeeming features and no real centre. Several chip shops and tacky gaming and gift emporiums were apparent, but little else. From where I stood it didn't deserve its exclamation mark! Strangely though, the drabness and drizzle sort of suited the place. I couldn't imagine it looking any other way, or why anyone should want to holiday here, especially when there're so many more beautiful places in Devon.

After gelling myself up, I set off along the windy prom without dawdling, and into the public toilets adjacent to the Haunted House. Here I completed my Ibuleve-ing, treating my calves and re-doing my foot plasters while the going was good whilst keeping an eye out for the old hag. After one last look back at the spooky building, which appeared to be hanging off the cliff edge, I stepped off the road, onto the grass, before climbing steeply once more. Both feet were extremely painful now, especially the right one, which had two huge blisters on it. I came to some lovely high woodland areas with bright yellow daffodils and millions of bluebells carpeting the ground under the trees. This kind of scenery made a real change. I really enjoyed it. My water was getting low as I was drinking a lot, particularly on the tougher climbs.

With evening approaching I found myself catching up with a couple who were walking ahead of me towards Bucks Mills. We got chatting. Del and June were about my age. They lived inland nearby and did B & B. They gave me a card for "Wretcher Fewforence" (a future reference or possibly a name for a punk guitarist). We entered the swish village of Bucks Mills at 7-swish, when it immediately struck me that this place was the antithesis of Westward Ho! June kindly knocked on the door of a large terraced cottage called The Anchorage in order to procure water for me. I was afraid to do it myself for fear of scaring the occupants. Apparently a young girl answered the door, so it was lucky June had knocked, as she looked far more respectable than I. Anyway, the girl took my water bladder and kindly refilled it.

The three of us walked inland up the village street with its stream, which followed the bottom of the valley, talking until we reached a small wooded car park, cut into the hillside at the top. I thought about asking them about B & B for the night but, judging by the stylish card they'd given me, it would've probably been way beyond my meagre means. We shook hands before they got into their car and drove off. I thought, That's it. I'm not walking another step tonight. I pitched my tent on a small patch of grass on the verge of this leafy tree-lined and empty car park. St Anne's church was close by. The nearest cottage was about 50 yards from me so I wasn't too worried about being disturbed. Bucks Mills didn't look like a particularly noisy or violent place. It was a pleasant evening, but there were a few spots of rain as I ate my instant-ish noodles on the picnic table, with three squirrels watching enviously. I kept telling them that the noodles tasted like cardboard but they didn't believe me.

For some reason I'd put the tent up badly this time. I hadn't quite got the hang of it but felt too tired to start again. Also I was in a sheltered spot so it shouldn't blow away. I listened to Radio 2's "Easter Hymns" on my tiny radio earphones. They'd never sounded so good. All was peaceful and lovely for the first time. I grew weary before drifting off to the strains of the beautiful 'Finlandia' by Sid Bailey-ous. It must have been around 9 p.m.

Day 8: Bank Holiday Monday 21 April

I woke in the car park at 7 a.m. and lay there for half an hour. It'd rained during the night but had since stopped. I packed up and left by 8.30 a.m., but felt puffy-eyed, rough, and with a sore throat too. I hoped I wasn't coming down with something ghastly. The old plates were causing problems from the offset again. I retraced my painful steps the half-mile back along the stream and down into Bucks Mills to pick up the coast path again. This stream, which divides the village, once used to power the old corn mill, marking the boundary between Parkham and Woolfardisworthy Parishes. Before the consecration of St Anne's church, the coffins of those who died here had to be taken to Parkham, or if the deceased lived on the other side of the village, they were carried along the "Coffin Road" (now a public footpath). I definitely wouldn't have slept in that car park if I'd read the guidebook the night before!

I didn't descend to the small harbour, as I was anxious to get going again, but stood above it, looking out to sea before departing. I'd hoped to find a village shop somewhere in the vicinity but fell out of luck this time. I expect the less-brainy Braunds blew it up a couple of hundred years ago. For centuries "Braund" – a surname rooted in the West Country and North Devon – has close associations with the village of Bucks Mills. At one time most residents were related to the infamous Braunds. Known for being rogues, their past ferocity in scaring away newcomers contributed to the formation of a tight-knit family community. As I made my way up the coast path between the cottages, I saw two lovely black kittens, rolling and gambolling on the cobbles before me. I couldn't resist playing with them for a minute or two before climbing up through yet more cottages and west out of Buck's Mills. I was heading for Clovelly, or "Old Clovvo" as I like to call it, which was about four hours away. My feet were killing me and I'd no way of relieving the agony. I limped on, stopping every few minutes for a short sit down. The pain was now beginning to take much of the pleasure out of the walking, making it difficult to appreciate the glorious views, the wild flowers, the woods, and birds, whilst feeling nauseous. I hoped the blisters would've eased by now, but they worsened every day. I became depressed, wondering if the agony would ever stop, or would I have to pack it in? I was concerned that I may end up in hospital with septic feet if I wasn't careful. I was pushing my luck by forging onwards. Something would give eventually.

The sun appeared as I came to the densely-wooded cobbled Victorian walkway that runs high above Clovelly. It's named "The Hobby." I renamed it "The Hobble" before hobbling along it, doing my best to chuckle and lighten-up a bit. Mental attitude, that's what it was all about, according to Clive. I caught glimpses of the picturesque harbour way below through the occasional gaps in the trees, and then followed the path down through more dense woodland, arriving at the harbour in Clovelly at noon. A quick walk onto the harbour and a joke with the retired fishermen, who, having been forced to give up their fishing, were now trying to commandeer tourists for pleasure trips on their small boats instead. The sea was calm and flat as a mill pond, but I responded to their sardonic offers of, "Boat trip around the bay, sir?" by quipping, "I'm not going out there in those conditions; far too dangerous." I don't know if they realised I was serious!

Clovelly, overlooking the Bristol Channel to its north, is a huge tourist attraction and has been for many years, famous for its history and quaint beauty. It's remained virtually unchanged in appearance over the last 200 years, consisting of one steep, car-free, cobbled main street with its cluster of ancient wattle and daub cottages and a few shops on both the sides of the rocky cleft. Donkeys and sledges that originally carried baskets of fish now carry children, goods, and produce up and down the slope, as it's too steep for wheeled vehicles. Its steepness is what's really saved Clovelly from modernisation and ruin. Thick woods shelter the village, rendering the climate so mild that even tender plants are able to flourish. Although its population is around 1,500, not surprisingly it always seems to be packed with visitors who have no option but to leave their vehicles in a car park above the town and *pay* to enter the village via its large visitors centre. This doesn't put anybody off though, nor does the steep descent, followed by the crippling ascent back, all on foot. I saved myself a few bob this time, getting in *free* by entering from the east via the coastal path, avoiding the visitors' centre.

Fishing was the main occupation for at least 1,000 years with herring being the prize catch. In 1814 more than 3.6 million herring were landed here. The locals could buy five fish for a penny! There are only two herring men left now, namely brothers Stephen and Tommy Perham. Once they retire, that'll probably spell the end of the trade that's kept the village alive for centuries. My solution to the problem is to never allow the Perham brothers to retire.

I frequented the only pub in Clovvo to attempt cheering myself and my feet up. In the Red Lion, beside, the quay, I had a quality "steak and pudney kidding", a pint, and finished off with "sticky poofy todding" to build up my strength. This *did* cheer me and my feet up. Full to the brim, I had to climb up to the top of the steep cobbled village street, which nearly cheered me back down again, stopping on the way to buy yet more plasters, a Mars, Snickers ... I had to bear right before the shop/museum, in case they got me, and leave sunny safe Clovelly behind for more exposed pastures unknown.

After a lovely grassy walk out towards the cliffs I came to a large carved wooden gazebo with benches underneath its flat square roof. Four pensioners were sitting there, who took some pictures of me with my camera. After a cheery chat I was off again. All too soon the path, which had entered some steep woods, became difficult with overhanging brambles and thick undergrowth making progress hard. Something seemed amiss and unnatural. After smashing back the dense vegetation with my pole I came to a once beautiful, but now overgrown and dilapidated, little folly, bearing upon it a shabby plaque. It appeared to have been built in 1932, dedicated to a Dame Diana Hamlyn. I later discovered she was a member of the influential Hamlyn family, who used her share of her father's fortune to improve the estate. Sadly, according to the plaque, the folly itself had fallen into ruin and been restored twice already, but it was obvious that a third restoration was long overdue. But up here in this overgrown wilderness, what would be the point? I took a picture before making a steep descent through more undergrowth. I was concerned now, as surely no part of the well-trodden SW Coast Path could be this inaccessible? This was more akin to a jungle, rather than a much-walked National Trail. Finally I emerged from the wilderness onto a better path where, through the trees, I could discern the sea. Nothing unusual in that, but this time it was on my *left* when it should've been on my right. I continued, hoping I was on some kind of hairpin bend and that the trail would resolve itself and become normal again.

Suddenly the same pensioners I'd left behind an hour ago were approaching me! They were clearly amused to see me, taking great delight in saying I was going the wrong way and would soon be back in Clovelly. I was gutted. I'd wasted an hour and all that energy. To make matters worse I couldn't comprehend where I'd actually gone wrong. They told me to follow them, so I walked with them for ten minutes in to a small valley that I didn't remember seeing before. I checked the guidebook. This was double-

Dutch to me by now. I hadn't a clue where I was and set off in desperation across a stream by means of stepping stones, to the strains of much yelling and whooping from the two old ladies, interspersed with shouts of, "Mind you don't fall in the water," followed by raucous belly laughter. They were *vicious* eighty-year-old hoodlums! I was on the right path this time, thank goodness, with feet not hurting as much. I made for Hartland Point with its unusual radar tower. The globular shape was visible from several miles away. A feeling of anticipation and excitement came over me upon realising I was now completely alone and approaching one of the wildest and most remote parts of the whole of England. I traversed many grassy fields high on the edge of the cliffs. It was mainly flat now, but the wind was powerful up there. It felt isolated and spooky in the ominous greyness of the afternoon, but a new kind of tranquillity washed over me. Suddenly I became aware of it, and my senses were immediately heightened like a wild animal that's in control, but at the same time on its guard, sensing every sight, sound, and smell in its proximity. I knew I'd never forget exactly how I felt at that moment and still haven't forgotten. I can feel it as I write. My heart is pounding again, as it had on that grey windy afternoon.

I was getting into a definite rhythm with my walking and feeling much fitter, but in certain gloomy conditions I was also starting to hear music in my head, humming it aloud in the most remote areas and on the steep ascents. This music was in time with my stride patterns and was dark and melancholic, either in a minor key, or sometimes comprising the notes of the pentatonic scale, with strong Celtic-sounding melodies, accompanied by the rhythm of my footsteps, the cries of the seabirds, and of the wind. I wasn't sure if I was regurgitating music I'd heard before, or whether I was subconsciously "composing" it as I walked. I couldn't tell which. Once the music started it invaded my brain, overpowered any other thoughts and it wouldn't stop. It kept on repeating, evolving, forming endless loops in my head that I couldn't erase, almost driving me crazy sometimes. The same themes could also recur every day, usually until the weather or landscape, or both, changed completely. Sometimes I'd attempt singing something cheerful out loud in order to oust the depressing music, but once I stopped singing it'd usually resume within minutes, returning me to square one. The only "cure" seemed to be to change my circumstances, like chatting to people or descending to a town or village for a break. Sometimes, on sunnier days my head would be invaded with pleasanter music, or even a song that I knew and liked. I've read about other walkers who have had similar "music-loop" experiences, and I put it down to the rhythm of the stride pattern, dull ominous weather, plus the remote loneliness. It was something I had to learn to live with throughout the walk. I became used to it, but it was always a relief when it finally stopped. I christened it my Nasty Note-Mares.

The solemn atmosphere of the afternoon was further added to when, striding out purposefully, I spotted a little plaque placed on the edge of the cliff. On closer inspection I saw it was a tribute to each crew member of a Wellington bomber from the second Squadron, 480th Anti-Submarine Group, RAF St Eval, near Newquay, which had been under the command of Captain George O. Brousard. On 22 January 1943, while approaching the coast in bad weather, the radio operator had asked the 19 Group controller to home the aircraft into St Eval. Unfortunately the request was made on the wrong radio frequency. The controller attempted to respond but it was too late. The aircraft slammed into cliffs, killing everyone on board on impact. I shuddered at the thought of it as I stood in that desolate windswept spot thinking, What a lonely place to die.

At 6 p.m. it was getting colder by the minute, though a watery evening sun was now appearing. I came across a flink of twenty or so lovely black and white calves lying down under a hedge, sheltering from the harsh wind. They weren't stupid, having found the best spot in the field. Meadow after meadow, stile after stile, I pressed on walking as quickly as possible, like a man possessed. I needed to reach Hartland Point and get round it tonight, out of this wind, in which I couldn't possibly pitch my tent. I could tell that the sunset was going to be fantastic, as the sky ahead was a rich red-golden colour. With about an hour to go to Hartland Point I saw a tiny dot moving on the distant horizon. Soon after I could discern it was a human being approaching. Within ten minutes we came face to face. This chap was called John, a serious walker with a big rucksack. He looked like Jesus, was probably fifty, but appeared thirty and extremely fit. He was walking from St Ives to Minehead. He'd done this every spring for the last ten years and travelled this far in ten days. We only chatted briefly as the shadows were lengthening and we were both anxious to press on. He said he'd had a bacon sandwich in the café at Hartland Point half an hour ago, which surprised me, as he looked like a veggie. They'd told him they were going to stay open to catch the sunset. He needed to camp (best of luck son) and I needed a bacon sandwich. We shook hands and went quickly on our separate ways. I raced the 2 miles at breakneck speed, using up all my reserves of strength only to find the café closed. What a downer. I continued disgruntled, passed the huge Ministry of Defence radar dome, on to the daunting Hartland Point itself, another 400 yards ahead.

Before the point itself, I came to another plaque set into a freestanding rock, overlooking the Atlantic. This one paid tribute to the "Glenart Castle", a lone hospital ship which had been torpedoed and sunk by a German U-boat in 1918, 18 miles off the coast from Hartland Point. Hospital ships were unarmed, traditionally painted white with highly visible red crosses. At night they carried full navigation lights, with a green band around the ship, and with the red crosses illuminated even in the darkest military blackout. They could be seen to be hospital ships and therefore not a legitimate target. Some U-boats became desperate and started ignoring the rules, attacking any shipping they could find. In this case, killing 155 unprotected doctors, medics, nurses, crew and patients. Only 31 survived, but that's the

Nazis for you! The Germans are great now, apart from the Müller Yogurt Gestapo who stopped producing banana flavour on purpose cos it was my bloody favourite.

Upon arriving at Hartland Point things were quite scary, with all the elements – well, not fire – going berserk all around me. The wild Atlantic was lashing the rocks 300 feet below. A hurricane blew ferociously. What an amazing sight to behold in the brilliant red and gold sunset, with the distant island of Lundy visible to the north-north west. I held on to a wire fence for fear of being blown away, as I peered over the cliff to the old lighthouse. This one was built by James Douglass in 1874, and its powerful lamp is 120 feet above sea level. It's still going strong although it's now automated, like most of the others, with its own helipad. Down below on the rocks, less than 400 yards from the lighthouse, lay the decaying hulk of the "MS Johanna", a Dutch-owned cargo ship, driven aground by gales in 1982. The crew was rescued by lifeboat and helicopter. I couldn't hang around in that wind, as I had to find a place to camp, which didn't look too hopeful as I turned the corner, face-on into the gale, and struggled south.

The terrain became rocky and ludicrously steep. I wondered if I should've taken a leaf out of those calves' book and camped behind a hedge 5 miles back, but I'd no option but to keep going. I was panicking as the light was fading fast. I was freezing in the wind. Ten minutes later I came to a tiny rock-strewn river valley way down below me where I could distinguish a patch of grass that would take the tent. This was 50 yards inland from the Atlantic. On the downside, a noisy waterfall was crashing down beside me. I'd no time to worry about trivialities like that though. I scrambled down quickly and set up in the wind. It was great to crawl inside my sleeping bag and zip up the tent for some respite. I ate a Cornish pasty and drank some water. It was too windy to try brewing up inside the tent! I slept from about 9 p.m., but was disturbed periodically by torrential rain on the tent walls, by gales, and that damn waterfall that provided an incessant din, making me wish I'd packed some earplugs. However, I was cosy inside. The sleeping bag came into its own that night. Good old Snugpak.

Day 9: Tuesday 22 April

I awoke at 7 a.m. with the sound of the thundering waterfall, which had swelled to the size of Niagara, ringing in my ears. It was still gusty but also a fine morning. I felt okay and packed away slowly, feeling lucky that I hadn't been swept away during the night by the raging torrent several feet away. I left the dynamic setting at 9 a.m. for even more dynamic settings, which were on show as soon as I climbed up the northern face and down the southern face of the first of about fifteen steep-sided river valleys. The full horror of what was ahead came home as I stood on the top, from where I could see headland after headland, stretching way into the distance to the south. It was daunting to think I'd have to climb and descend all of them.

The landscape was noticeably different after rounding Hartland Point, extremely high with rugged metallic silver-grey cliffs, with jagged and precipitous rock formations and the angry Atlantic Ocean below. Today was calmer than the previous evening, but still ominous-looking as it pounded the cliffs with amazing force. The first piece of land a traveller would arrive at to the west is America. Nothing existed in between.

My right foot had gone again. This was really a problem now. I staggered into Hartland Quay at 10.30 a.m. The only buildings in sight on this sunny morning appeared to be part of the Hartland Quay Hotel. These buildings incorporated a gift and sweet shop, a shipwreck museum, a pub, and a restaurant. Apart from hotel accommodation, all the traveller needed was here, only the shop and shipwreck museum were shut. The shop was due to open soon, though I would liked to have taken a gander at some giant shipwrecks in the museum. In the meantime I found a cloakroom beside the hotel reception desk. With nobody around, I nipped in and did the lot. It was pure luxury to shave and wash my hair in hot water for a change. Later I emerged looking neat and tidy. Nobody told me off either.

I proceeded to the roomy Wrecker's Retreat for a huge meal consisting of rack of lamb with red wine and rosemary, sticky poofy-todding to build my strength up, and a cool pint of bitter. I had a table to myself but another half dozen people were eating too. It was far too hot in the bar as the sun shone directly in through the large windows, forcing me to order another pint to keep my body temperature below its customary 118.6 degrees. The cost for the meal and drinks was £10. I was full and tipsy for a mere "Edward Jenner."

I stuck my head into a few rooms to see what the old hotel was like. I loved the residents' lounge, which looked very 1920s, with old huge old-fashioned sofas for guests to sprawl upon. It cost £25 for a single room. I swore to return one day and book in. I haven't yet, of course, and it's probably gone up to £150 a night now. I wrote up my journal in the bar before stocking up with "eats" at the shop, plus as much water as I could carry for the foreboding "severe" terrain ahead, as the book described it. I rang Mum and Dad from the hotel payphone to tell them they may never see me again, but they were out.

I managed to get my mate DR at work. He told me he was fed up with his office job, to which I replied, "You ought to be out here walking these cliffs, son. You'd soon wish you were back at your desk then!" I told him he'd probably be reading about me in the newspapers soon when they found my body at the bottom of a cliff.

It was after 1 p.m. when I climbed out of Hartland Quay. The weather, with a cooling breeze, couldn't have been better. I took some pictures on the top, feeling staggered by the sea views yet again. This was definitely the only method to see the coastline properly. I was surprised at having to walk 2 miles over fairly easy grassy uplands, before hitting the tough river valleys again. Eventually I came to the spectacular Speke's Mill waterfall and took some video footage for posterity. I did about six valleys that afternoon, pausing often to rest, drink water, and take in the superb scenery. I met various people, including Andy; a strange curly-haired walker, who was lobster red, with a big pack, but no stick. The fool! My motto has always been, "A Man is not a Man until he's got a Stick", even before I became a walker. Ask my two nephews, Ben and James. I drummed it into them from the age of two onwards and it hasn't done them any harm. The guy said he was walking to John o'Groats but seemed aimless. He'd got a few months to kill and nothing in particular to do – more money than sense, the lucky sod.

I came to a beautiful stone hut built on the cliff edge, constructed in the 1960s for the writer, poet, pacifist, and playboy Ronald Duncan (1914-1982), although it looked more ancient. (Sorry, it should have been "playwright", but I thought I'd make him sound more rakish.) He was best known for preparing the libretto for Benjamin Britten's opera, The Rape of Lucretia, though he wrote loads of other stuff including the script for the 1960s film, Mole on a Girtercycle, starring the gorgeous Marianne Skinfull – in black leather – along with some moody garlic-munching French git who practically ruined the film single-handedly.

I entered, discovering a table, chairs, and a frame on the wall containing details of Ronald's life and works. I slumped into a chair to rest from the blazing heat, gazing out of the window at the magnificent sea views. Two empty Perrier bottles sat on the table – probably left by that French git – which I checked unsuccessfully for droplets of moisture. I spotted a large bowl on the floor containing about an inch of water, obviously left for parched cliff-walking dogs by some considerate animal lover. I was tempted to get down on all fours and slurp up the thirst quenching nectar, as my own supply was getting low. I even convinced myself that no sensible dog would be out walking today. The water would probably evaporate and be wasted if someone didn't drink it, so it might as well be me. At the last moment my conscience kicked in: what if some lost little woofer were to stagger in all alone with an injured paw, having limped for miles in search of this hut, knowing in his little heart that if he made it, a bowl of life-saving water would be waiting for him? This being his only hope of survival unless I'd already drunk it! The thought of it was too much to bear. I left the bowl and water alone, bowed out gracefully, and went on my thirsty way.

High on the top of the cliffs I met a German chap in his shirt sleeves – no actual shirt, just the sleeves. Aged about thirty and carrying only a large 35 mm. camera, his name was Bernt. He spoke a little English and we got chatting about various things. He'd lost his mate, whose description exactly fitted that of Andy the walker I'd met half an hour earlier. I'd already told Bernt I'd seen his mate, when I suddenly realised I hadn't. Our conversation became confusing, until I realised his mate was not English but German. Andy the walker – an Englishman – wasn't his mate after all!

I tried explaining in pigeon German: *"Nein, nein,* you no go-looky for him! He *nichts* your *freund Verstehen.* See?"

He stared at me blankly before stating, *"Ja,* I search him now. Where goes he travel?"

It was awful but I eventually got through to him somehow, after almost having to physically restrain him from chasing after Andy, who must've reached Birmingham by now. He said he and his missing mate were on the cliffs looking for a famous house where Deep Purple had rehearsed their 1971 album, *Fireball.* This was news to me. I was unable to help him. He said he'd seen Ritchie Blackmore's Rainbow at the Hammersmith Odeon in 1976 and asked if I'd ever seen them.

"No, but I've seen Ritchie Hammermore's Blacksmith at the Rainbow Odeon in 1977."

He looked bemused. So did I! Strange how references to Purple/Blackmore kept cropping up on the walk. *Lorna Doone,* etc. When I became aware of his passion for most early 1970s rock I blurted out that I'd been a founder member of Mott The Hoople. I wouldn't normally bother mentioning this, but it seemed relevant under these exceptional circumstances. I thought it may be a slight consolation to him if he failed to find the Deep Purple house. He looked at me in disbelief. At first I thought he was going to have a heart attack. He went all kind of shaky and silent before looking like he was about to burst into tears. I couldn't tell if he was happy or suicidal at the news.

Finally, he looked at me suspiciously; his Teutonic logic telling him, "Zis *swinehundt* must be an impostor vy vood a veal vock musician out here be?"

Anyway, he still turned round and walked back south with me. We carried on chatting, mostly with him firing non-stop musical questions at me whilst trying – unsuccessfully – to catch me out.

"I forgotten so, tell me please, vot vas zat *gruppen* again? Zie vons vich sang, 'Allus zie Jung Deudes'. Vot vas its name? I demand zie truth now. *Schnell!*"

We descended steeply after ten minutes to another river valley, discovering his long-lost mate sitting by their car in the sun. To my amazement, he looked like a more handsome Aryan version of the aforementioned poor old Andy. Bernt covertly told his friend Marcus, in German, what I'd told him, aware that I couldn't understand what they were saying. I got the gist, though. They both eyed me with suspicion. After a ten-minute rest it was time for me to go. We all shook hands vigorously, and although doubtful of my credentials, they were good guys really. I wished them luck with their search for "*Fireball* House."

Another thing becoming apparent was that I was *not* a "morning person" when it came to walking. Without fail, I felt grim and knackered every morning, struggling until about 4 p.m., barely covering 5 miles, till suddenly I'd get into my stride, covering twice that distance during the late afternoon and evening. By this stage I couldn't do 20 miles a day because of the severe terrain and my poor old plates. Later on I'd start to motor. The weather was fantastic. I needed to press on, aware that it couldn't last much longer. I'd only had one rotten morning thus far, around the Saunton and Braunton dunes.

I gave up at 7.30 p.m. before Morwenstow, my target for the day, and a place I was intrigued by. I pitched the tent in a lovely spot in another small valley by a stream without a beastly waterfall this time. I lay inside, looking at the sea below. I spotted a massive white object, completely stationary in an otherwise empty sky. It resembled the shape of the hull of a huge ship which appeared to be sailing through the sky from right to left and coming towards me! I shivered at the sight of it because of the tragic maritime history of the region. It seemed too perfect a shape to be a cloud as it had clearly defined edges. What the hell was it?

Many shipwrecks occurred along this section of coast. One of the most famous was the *Caledonia*, which sank here with all hands but one in 1842. I read about it a couple of weeks ago and thought this cloud-like hulk could be the ghost of the *Caledonia* and a harbinger of doom – oh no! I scared myself stupid. Morwenstow at that time had been the parish of the eccentric gaudy dresser, Reverend Robert Stephen Hawker (1803-1875), who – apart from writing many stories, poems and hymns – is credited with reviving the custom of Harvest Festival. He was known as a practical joker in his younger days. He owned a pet pig that he took for walks and banned his pet cats from church for killing mice!

Lying alone, miles from civilisation, gazing at this abnormal sight in the sky, I don't mind admitting feeling uneasy. The "ship" stayed intact for more than an hour, but in the two minutes it took to boil my kettle it'd vanished, putting the wind up me even more. I assumed whatever it was had rapidly diffused or evaporated, but still can't explain its presence. It was enough to give this grown man the collywobbles! When I got home I found three silly-looking photographs of my orange guy ropes, a smidgen of heather and gorse, and a huge empty area of sky. I presumed the camera had gone off by mistake until I realised these were the shots of the ghost ship, but it was nowhere to be seen. A shiver ran through me whilst staring at the almost bare PC screen.

As dusk approached I zipped myself in and listened to Classic FM on my headphones. I listened to the Five Variants of 'Dives and Lazarus' by Ralph Vaughan Williams, my favourite composer, and it sounded better than ever before. I felt calmer after that. I woke several times during the night, aware that the temperature outside had dropped considerably, but I was as snug as a bug in a rug. Thankfully I never saw or heard one single ghost.

Day 10: Wednesday 23 April

I woke properly at 7.30 a.m. to another lovely but breezier morning.

After leaving by 9 a.m. I climbed an extremely tough cliff – not a good thing to do that early in the morning – before heading inland for Morwenstow with my right foot worse than ever. A normal person would've jacked it in by now, but I'm not at all normal. I saw the church half a mile away but owing to the pain it still took twenty minutes to get there. It was sunny and pleasant as I strolled, in total agony, round the beautiful churchyard, which was alive with spring flowers. Sunrays shot through the gaps in the foliage above, giving the serene effect of a dappled pattern of light and shade. I soon found myself standing in awe at the authentic white-painted figurehead of the *Caledonia*, which had been salvaged from the wreckage, including the bones of its captain and crew in the earth 6 feet beneath. I shivered again at the thought of it. Pleasantly I was the only visitor, giving me chance to absorb the atmosphere and solitude for a while. The church is dedicated to the Saints John the Baptist and Morwenna, featuring Norman architecture. The nearby vicarage was built for Hawker, boasting chimneys in the form of the towers of various churches associated with him. I took some pictures and looked round the lovely church before my thoughts turned to practical matters, like food. The nearby Rectory was now a tearoom. I headed there and entered the ancient low-beamed room. Although someone was moving upstairs, I couldn't attract their attention. At a loss as to what to do, I sat on a garden bench, not prepared to give up yet.

A girl appeared; a paying guest, who offered to make me a pot of tea, along with some cake and biscuits, all for free. I don't know what the owners would have made of all this, but it was excellent from my point of view. She came from New Zealand, explaining why she was so lovely, as people from New Zealand always are, unless they're murderers, of course. Her name was Joella. We chatted a while. She made no attempt whatsoever to murder me.

I wrote up my journal till 10.30 a.m. By then it was time to go, as I intended to reach Bude today, by hook or by crook, but most probably by foot. By that I do mean *foot*, not *feet*. My right one felt like it was about to fall off. I limped back to the coast, arriving at Vicarage Cliff, where I met an older couple with a lovely English bull terrier named Meg. She was well trained, remaining quiet as we conversed.

They pointed out where Hawker's Hut was. Although it was a dodgy climb of 30 feet down over the edge of the cliff to a narrow ledge, I felt I had to visit it whilst there. It was worthwhile too. The driftwood hut was built into the rock with a rugged door and a sturdy bench seat inside. I thought about Hawker sitting there 150 years ago with the storms raging outside, telescope clamped to his eye, opium pipe in hand, pen and paper at the ready, forever scanning the horizon for potential shipwrecks. Hawker is also said to have entertained such notable guests as Alfred Lord Tennyson and Charles Kingsley in his hut. It's good to know that the tiny hut is now owned and preserved for posterity by the National Trust as their smallest building. Afterwards I wished I'd spent the previous night in the hut, as it would've been exciting, but I hadn't known if this would've been possible until now.

I took a picture before scrambling back to the top of the cliff to resume my trek. Two weeks ago I could never have made that death-defying descent. Maybe I was gradually becoming more comfortable regarding my vertigo. I was getting accustomed to being high on the cliffs with the sea far below, whereas near the start it fazed me. I crossed at least five more river valleys that day. The sun, counterbalanced by the cool breeze, made ideal walking conditions. Only my feet made the going tough. I needed to reach Bude to find a chemists before closing time at 5.30 p.m. I passed many gigantic coastal radar satellite dishes and masts before stopping at a National Trust beach café in Sandy Mouth where I ate heartily. You can always trust the National Trust! For starters I had some big prawn sandwiches, Porn-ish casties, a pot of slop, a can of Sprite, followed by a giant strawberry ice cream cone. I chatted to the waitresses for a while, got my water bottles refilled, and struck out for Bude.

It was 3.45 p.m. and several tourists were out on the cliffs enjoying the fine weather. After a few conversations I found myself "rushing gingerly" as much as I was able, as I needed to find a chemists before closing time, otherwise I'd be forced to saw off my right foot with my pocket knife. Over an hour had passed by the time I limped badly into Bude town centre, but I made it in time for the shops. The blister under the middle toes of my right foot was hell by now. I was worried about not being able to continue my walk, as it'd cost too much to stay in a hotel for a week until my feet recovered. I made straight for the chemists. They gave me some pads to place under my toes and sold me some more Compede, Ibuleve, foot care ointments, and antiseptics, and telephoned another chemists down the road to find out if they'd got this special blister spray. They told them not to close until I arrived to collect it. I hobbled quickly and bought the magic spray. I'd spent around £40 on foot treatments and other creams, gels, and medicines at only two weeks into the journey!

I bought a blackcurrant and clotted-cream ice-cream before walking down the hill, only to scurry back up two minutes later to retrieve my pole. I'd left it behind again in favour of my ice cream. Three items to carry: rucksack, shoulder bag, and ice cream instead of pole this time. I went down into the town centre to phone Mum and Dad and sister "J". All was well back home. After exiting the phone box and looking round a bustling Bude, I realised that the last time I'd been here it'd been horrible. Admittedly, it was an hour-long visit, but it'd been deserted, boring, and looked like a different town to the lovely one now before me. The only other thing I remembered from my previous visit was the big punch-up in a gift shop involving half a dozen people. This ended up spilling into the main street.

While escaping unscathed, I'd said to my girlfriend, "Nice town, Bude. Remind me never to return!"

Yet here I was, four years later, and everything was wonderful with no evidence of any fisticuffs anywhere. Bude lies near the mouth of the River Neet. The modern name is a shortened form of Bude Haven; a corruption of the name Bede Haven, meaning "Harbour of the holy men", intimating that Bude may have been a landing place for early Christians. Its earlier importance was as a harbour and then a source of sea sand useful for improving the local moor-land soil. The Victorians favoured it as a watering place and it became a popular seaside destination in the nineteenth century. Present-day Bude is predominantly a centre for tourism and also surfing with two sandy beaches and close proximity to several others.

After a quick lie down in a park, I was offered a *free* bus ride, back up town to the top of the hill again, from an off-duty driver named Dave. I finally raided Somerfield's to stock up with orange juice, quiche, Cadbury's cream, a Müller yoghurt, tomatoes, a banana, and a bottle of Wyre Piddle beer. I wanted to live in style for a change! I posted the Morwenstow postcard back to my parents and left sunny Bude by way of the old harbour and canal.

Heading south on the coastal path I trudged on in great pain for two hours. I couldn't find a place to camp and always got worried around 7 p.m. if I wasn't in a suitable area or couldn't see one in the distance. I met a couple of mature backpackers, Tim and Anne, who seemed clued-up. They were doing John's End to Land o'Groats with massive backpacks. They'd taken ten days so far. I didn't envy them, especially when I later discovered only one in twelve walkers who undertake LEJOG actually make it, with many giving up after one or two days. Technically, my walk was tougher than theirs, but nowhere near as long. During the conversation they were pumping me with questions about gear, camping, weather, tips and the like as if I were some kind of expert. Not wishing to disillusion them, I answered knowingly and confidently. Amazingly, they were hanging on my every word, taking in all my "expert" advice. After parting company I realised I'd actually learned a hell of lot about backpacking during the last fortnight. I felt chuffed, realising that when it came to backpacking, I was no longer green behind the ears!

I continued searching for anywhere to pitch, as the light was fading fast. Just before Widemouth Bay at St Philip's Point, I found a sad apology for a valley that was no more than a slight indentation in a grassy meadow, with a measly stream about a foot wide. I put the tent up as quickly as possible, with much cursing in the annoying breeze and the fading sunrays. Whilst unrolling the sleeping bag I spotted a small sign on a post 30 yards away. I thought it best to check it out. I immediately regretted it upon reading the words in the twilight: BEWARE! ADDERS BREEDING AREA. Bloody hell! No way was I packing up and moving on now. If I got killed by irate or randy snakes it was tough luck. Climbing into the tent I realised that, in the panic, I'd managed to erect it *over* the tiny stream. The long grass kept it hidden. I could feel the trickling water under the plastic as I lay in the dark, praying my bathtub groundsheet wouldn't leak that night.

Luckily it didn't. I kept sliding down the tent whilst drinking my beer though. I was on a slope – not one of my better choices for a camping spot. But Cheggers can't be boozers! I heard rain for much of the night. It was cold too. The forecast stated that a change was coming. I didn't want a change but knew it'd have to come all the same, as Bob Dylan predicted in his 1964 song.

Day 11: Thursday 24 April

I awoke at 7 a.m. As I far as I could tell I was still alive. I hadn't been bitten to death by sexually frustrated adders or drowned in the stream, which had swelled to a worrying 3 feet in width under the tent, owing to the heavy rain during the night. I felt "just" alive, having slept dreadfully again. I treated my feet with the freshly acquired products, packed away with the river flowing beneath me, and left by 9 a.m. I'd long since dispensed with the idea of breakfast or a cup of tea in the tent, it being too awkward and time consuming. I now started the day with a couple of swigs of juice or water, and maybe a pasty, a sandwich, or a Mars Bar, and get on the road as soon as possible.

I hadn't walked far when I collapsed in pain. My right foot had reached the point of no return. This was the closest I'd come to abandoning the walk and was seething with rage.

I yelled out: "I am not packing it in! Not now I've come this far!"

It was a damp morning as I hopped into the shantytown that was Widemouth Bay. Even through the pain I saw what a disappointment this place was. It was made even grimier by the dismal weather, not that I was at all concerned about stuff like that, being solely preoccupied with my right foot. Nothing was open, nobody was around. I sat on a bench outside a closed beach café in the drizzle and removed my boot. The raw blister appeared more horrific than ever. I took out the special gauze pad that I'd placed there ten minutes earlier and replaced it with yet another Compede plaster. I'd been using them incorrectly by only peeling off *one* side of the backing strips. No wonder they kept falling off. Why couldn't they make the instructions simpler, or alternatively make *me* more intelligent? I'd spent 15 bleeding quid on them before learning how to use the buggers properly!

After setting off five minutes later the pain wasn't as bad. Crossing the beach, I met a lady walking her dog, Bonny, who was enthusiastically fetching and then smashing up plastic coke bottles. The lady saw me limping. She offered to run me to the A & E department at Boscastle Hospital; a twenty-minute drive away. I couldn't accept a lift as it'd be cheating (dimwit). I felt ridiculous saying this but felt I must continue alone, unless it became impossible. Turning inland, onto a road and up a steep hill in the wind and rain, I wondered if I was taking the whole thing too seriously. It'd be idiotic to jeopardise my health for some stupid ideal. If I kept walking and my foot went septic, I really would be in trouble. Blood poisoning or gangrene could even set in. The thought frightened me so much that I tried not thinking about it. It occurred to me that the twenty-minute drive to Boscastle would take me the whole day to walk, assuming I could make it. I felt depressed again. The climb seemed endless. All morning I regularly stopped to don or remove my waterproof jacket, for if it wasn't raining heavily I couldn't bear wearing it, being so hot and sweaty from all the climbing. I think my body temperature must be 20 per cent higher than everybody else's. I would constantly meet oncoming walkers throughout the trip, all wearing thermal hooded jackets, zipped up, with scarves, gloves, heavy trousers, and gaiters. Unless it was pouring down, I could wear nothing more than a short sleeved wicking top, with lightweight trousers or shorts, and was still swelteringly hot. What's wrong with me? I'm too scared to find out.

The doctor would say something like, "Most interesting, Mr Watts. According to the test results, you're technically dead. No human can survive with a body temperature of 118.6 degrees Fahrenheit. It's curtains for you, my old beauty, sometime within the next ten minutes, I'd say."

I only cooled down if I stopped walking for a while, even in the coldest of conditions. I must find courage one day to discover why I'm like that. Perhaps I've got two hearts, plus huge arteries, but only half a brain. No, I'm definitely too scared to find out. I'll continue sweltering in silence.

On the cliff tops the weather improved, perking my spirits. The sun came out but the wind increased, blowing me sideways if I didn't watch my every step. Some fabulous sea views were apparent, plus some lovely wooded valleys, full of spring flowers and stunted trees bent over at the same angle. A couple approached after not meeting a soul for hours. The woman had run the London Marathon. We chatted for five minutes before going our separate ways. Today's walking proved exceptionally difficult with frightening climbs and descents being the worst so far. The most worrying thing was that I'd been led to believe that the Hartland Point to Bude section was the toughest on the entire walk. I was now finding this part far tougher, so what was coming next?

At about 4 p.m. I sighted the small scattering of houses way below that was Crackington Haven. I'd imagined, while looking at my road atlas from the comfort of my armchair, that it'd be a cracking little "haven". You can't win 'em all. Using my pole, I picked my way tentatively down to the beach where I immediately spotted the ugly and incongruous Coombe Barton Inn. I was rather taken aback, having imagined it to be an ancient seventeenth-century, half-timbered, character inn. Mark Wallington wrote about an evening here during his 1981 walk. I didn't like the look of the place, which was posh in a 1970s run-down kind of way. Several people were sitting outside drinking beer on the terrace. I entered to buy a pint, only to be ejected by a horrified manageress, who didn't like the look of me one bit.

"Sorry, we're closed!" she said brusquely, and when I asked if I could buy a beer to drink on the terrace, the expected reply was, "No."

Nobody else was present, so they may have closed. I didn't argue with her and instead ambled down to the beach café, which appeared more inviting, but wasn't licensed for alcohol. It was a bustling friendly area, thus into the café I went. After asking what kind of sandwiches they did, the young waitress – Holly – quoted the usual list: cheese, ham, cheese and ham, ham and tomato, cheese, tomato, and ham, etc.

She said proudly, "We also have avocado with prawns."

I baffled her with my stupid comment, "Oh great, I'll 'ave a cardo, then. No, on second thoughts, make that two cardos!"

She sensibly ignored me, making a mental note to herself: "Imbecile."

I started with an avocado and prawn sandwich, which was fabbo, followed by a beetroot, garlic, and mayonnaise salad, a pasty, several cakes, orange juice, and a pot of tea. I rounded it all off with a gargantuan butterscotch ice cream. It may seem like excessive amount of food to the layman, especially considering I'd eaten a quiche and a yossive great maggot earlier, but I did need to keep my strength up. I was burning billions of calories with my over-the-top exertions. One great thing about this walking lark is you can virtually eat *anything* and still lose weight. By now I looked trimmer than I had for years, while gorging myself on chocolate bars, cakes, full breakfasts, roasts, fish and chips, and the like. I pondered that if I stopped walking for a day or two, my weight might suddenly balloon out of control; a case of *The Picture of Dorian Watts*. I'd look in a mirror and see myself at 40 stone, instead of the fit-looking gent I'd become over the last two weeks. I felt good though, apart from my demented plates of meat. I promised I'd be nice to them if they agreed to get me through the rest of this ordeal. The strange thing is that from this point onwards my feet sort of went numb, becoming less problematic, so the reader won't hear as much about them from henceforth. Hurray, do I hear you exclaim?

I ended up talking to Holly's granny, who was having an afternoon cuppa. She swore by "wellies" for walking. I doubted she'd done 630.4 miles in them though. Before leaving, the lady owner gave me the recipe for the tasty beetroot, mayonnaise, and garlic salad, which appeared to contain nothing more than those three ingredients. Perhaps there was a secret one that she wouldn't give away, like salt or pepper. I thanked everyone for their kindness and set off across the small beach after taking a photo of the café.

By 4.45 p.m. I couldn't tell what the weather intended doing, which was most perturbing, as I'd checked the guidebook over tea, discovering something therein that made my blood run cold. One mile south of Crackington Haven is the highest cliff in Cornwall; the imaginatively named "High Cliff", rising to 735 appalling feet with a terrifying sheer drop to the rocky foreshore below. I had to climb it next whilst attempting not to die, as it was also classified as southern Britain's highest sheer-drop cliff! The Great Hangman back in Devon, where I'd taken a diversion by mistake, has a cliff face of 820 feet. The long ascent was unpleasant, but the weather held. I stared at the ground, not at the sheer drop. Once on top I donned my oxygen mask, my crampons, grabbed my ice axe, and carried on (only kidding). I came down but was soon climbing yet again. This was taking its toll.

By 7 p.m., with nowhere to camp, desperation set in. These cliffs were exposed with few natural havens in which to pitch a tent. This was always a worry, especially if the weather turned. Eventually I came to a sheltered river valley, a few miles out of Crackington Haven. I pitched up. Once inside the tent I felt relieved. I put on my headphones and listened to Classic FM. I heard my all-time favourite piece of music, 'Fantasia on a Theme by Thomas Tallis', by Ralph Vaughan Williams. Wow, this gets better every time I hear it, always moving me to tears without fail. Soon after I heard another dynamic yet ominous piece, 'Mars, the Bringer of War', from Gustav Holtz's *Planets Suite*, which is the most frightening piece of music I've ever heard. Its building relentless warlike rhythm and its swirling, swooping, angry, crescendos invoke the terror, anguish, and desolation of war. I had to put Radio 2 on afterwards, hoping to end the evening on a lighter note. After 'High Hopes' by the old Pinks (Floyd), they played 'Black Books', a great track by Nils Lofgren, followed by the brilliant 'Can't Stand The Light', by my favourite all-time band The Contrast, from Peterborough. Next came 'Kayleigh', by "Old Marrow" (Marillion), during which I started to nod off. A line from that song was voted one of the worst lyrics of all time: 'I was walking in the park, dreaming of a spark'. I must admit it's certainly a worthy contender for the No. 1 slot.

By 10 p.m. the rain and gales began and continued all night. In these noisy conditions it's virtually impossible to sleep, along with the worry that the tent might take off or flood. With no respite I barely slept.

Day 12: Friday 25 April

I couldn't pack away in the morning as the conditions were no better. I laid there, shattered, waiting for a break in the weather. At 1 p.m. it grew calmer, so I started to pack up. After half an hour the storm resumed, forcing me to stop again. The boredom was stupefying. I could only lie there twisting and turning, thinking about how bloody miserable I was. So that's what I did until 3 p.m. when the wind dropped. Time to get out of there fast. There was a lot of swearing as the groundsheet flew 30 feet up the side of the cliff with me in hot pursuit. I was wrestling with it for about ten minutes before taming the wild beast in it. The air was blue with my cursing. Suddenly, amid the mayhem, a bloke strolled past without looking up. He was unperturbed, like a ghost. I reckon he was one from the *Caledonia* shipwreck.

I hurried on towards Boscastle, realising I wasn't going to cover much ground with it being late. The weather held and once more there were some incredible cliff top sea views, though I wasn't fond of the narrow ledges around this region. The Nasty Note-mares started again. This time, predictably, it was Mars (no the music, not the chocolate bar, you idiots!). Although a fantastic piece, it was ugly and unnerving once it became lodged in my brain. The same passages played over and over with their menacing raucous, and sometimes discordant phrases, along with the unyielding insistent rhythm. I tried ignoring it but it wouldn't stop.

I realised that since Widemouth Bay I'd only seen three other humans, two being me in a mirror in the gents'. I felt exhausted and downhearted until Boscastle came into view about 3 miles away. The grassy path was a more even now, but the lack of sleep affected me, along with the nagging Note-mares. I felt myself drifting into a weary trance – not a good thing to do when cliff walking. I looked down from the top Boscastle harbour, which appeared like a tiny model in its calm, sheltered, olive-green waters. It looked fantastic and the orchestra in my head stopped playing Mars. The deafening silence was wonderful. Although small, this is the only natural harbour for 20 miles along the coast. Whilst walking above the harbour into the village I decided it was time for a proper night's sleep to recover from the previous two weeks. I was going to stay in my first B & B of the trip.

I found myself in the Harbour Restaurant drinking lots of tea. The pretty waitress – Odette – proved friendly and helpful. She offered to look after my rucksack, allowing me to travel light and search for a B & B. I tried a couple that were fully booked before being sent to a bare building appearing more like a conference centre than a guest house. Yet when the lady answered the door with a welcoming smile and a friendly hello, I knew this was the place for me. The price for a single room was £27. Being a cheapskate this made me wince, but I hadn't time or energy to look further or to try haggling the price down. The lady – Anne – was lovely. The place looked clean so I checked in. It was called Lower Meadows. I collected my rucksack, which I never felt comfortable about leaving anywhere where I couldn't see it. My whole world was in there, but it was still safe and sound with the trustworthy Odette.

I ordered steak and kidney pie with chips, which was gigantic but boring. I wished I'd had lobster afterwards, after all you're only young once (55 actually). Odette helped me with my directions for the next day and spoke of this mystical place I should visit in Rocky Valley, near Tintagel. She drew a rough map, advising me to "Look for the ribbons in the trees".

At 7 p.m. I left for Lower Meadows, pausing at the phone box by the stream to call Mum and Dad and my mate Rick, whom I'd hopefully be meeting in a few days' time. Walking up the peaceful High Street in the golden evening sunlight, I passed several closed craft and gift shops, the Museum of Witchcraft, past a former water mill, a tea garden, a couple of restaurants, a bakers, a greengrocers, plus a couple of old character inns. I noticed that many of the old houses had stone and slate porches, with large flagstones leading up their garden paths. Back at Lower Meadows my en suite double room was plush and comfortable. It felt strange to be in a luxurious setting after two weeks of roughing it. I could get used to this, but mustn't. I put the TV on, which seemed peculiar. To my amazement the Iraq war was over and we'd won! I felt relieved and surprised. I'm glad I didn't know then what I know now. I spent the evening pottering and sorting out the contents of my rucksack.

I wrote up my journal before reading up on Boscastle, which only a hundred years ago was a thriving port. The coming of the railways ended the isolation of North Cornwall. A mile or so up the River Valency is St Juliot's church, which was worked on by Thomas Hardy when he was an architect. Much of his novel *A Pair of Blue Eyes* is based around this area.

It was wonderful to have a shower after having cold water washes in streams or public conveniences. I treated my feet with various ointments and antiseptics. I turned in at 11 p.m. and slept soundly in the comfortable bed.

Day 13: Saturday 26 April

I was brought back to life at 7.55 a.m. by my fab Timex alarm watch. I showered before heading to the sunny conservatory for a big breakfast. Anne introduced me to the couple on the table beside mine. They were from Essex and in their sixties. The lady was friendly but the bloke was a "pale show-van-ist mig fighter". He was big and aggressive with a skinhead, covered in tattoos. He ignored me completely, preferring to bury his head in his crossword puzzle. His wife and I chatted about my walk, their grandchildren in Canada, his ferrets, and her Women's Institute. Occasionally the man looked up, making some derogatory jibe at her, usually about the size of her breakfast, and how she was fat enough already (which she wasn't), trying to humiliate her in front of me and a younger couple sitting at the third table. For her it was like water off a duck's back. By ignoring him she made him look even more ridiculous.

When he failed to finish the crossword, he took an unhealthy interest in me, staring directly at me, asking menacingly, "Well now, my friend. What do *you* do, then?"

Now bored with his wife's indifference towards him, he felt like trying to intimidate someone else. Being nearest, it had to be *me*! I imagine it was like being interrogated by Reggie and Ronnie Kray. I managed to remain polite but non-committal. It was difficult as I didn't want to get into a punch-up in such a lovely guest house. I left the table once I'd eaten.

Anne had washed and dried all my laundry for no extra charge, neatly folding it to boot. The £27 cost was good value for money. After packing up, I thanked Anne and Adrian and walked out of the door at 11 a.m., heading back along the Valency into Boscastle. I felt sorry for them having to put up with and wait on that nasty git, but I was sure that 99.9 per cent of their guests were much nicer – sort of like me.

Within a minute it started raining. Although it wasn't heavy, it was worrying as the sky had turned from blue to dark grey. I had to pass by the Visitors' Centre, so decided to go in for a while and learn a bit about the area. After fifteen minutes I crossed the road and went into the Harbour Restaurant. Sadly it wasn't Odetta's shift. With the rain looking grimmer I wrote up the journal, dallying for a while, trying to blend into the background to avoid getting slung out into the rain. I wrote, "I want to walk" as I was bored, not because I liked walking. The rain eased off so I decided to bolt for it. I slid on my Gore-Tex jacket, which felt uncomfortable, owing to the exertion and because my body temperature was 20 per cent higher than everyone else's!

As I climbed up out of Boscastle, heading south, the rain suddenly belted down, like I knew it would when I'd got nowhere to shelter. Sod's Law again. I passed an elderly lady walker, sitting on a bench, wearing soaking waterproofs. As I drew level with her she wanted to chat! All I wanted to do was get out of the wind and rain. After apologising I hurried up the cliff. Huge, frightening, waves crashed against the lone grey island at the harbour entrance. This was my first real experience of the awesome power of the Atlantic. So far the sea had mostly been blue and calm, apart from Hartland Point, but even that paled into insignificance compared to this. I wouldn't have wanted to be on a ship, not for all the tea on a tea clipper in China. Somewhere above the harbour entrance I must've walked past the famous "Boscastle Blowhole", which is audible after low water under certain sea conditions, as the water surges in. I'd neither seen nor heard anything in my haste. To be honest, I couldn't have cared less. What did interest me was the small turreted folly on the cliff top that I was aiming for. I hoped to shelter by it, or preferably *in* it. When I reached there it was blowing a hurricane. I pressed my back against the outer wall, working my way round to the less windswept side. Through a small window above I discerned man and a woman – both coastguards (or murderers) – peering out to sea with binoculars.

I beckoned to them, hoping they'd open the door and say, "You can't stay out there in this weather. Come in and have a hot cuppa and some pasties and wait till it clears up. There's a bed in the corner if you fancy a kip."

Unfortunately they politely ignored my frantic arm gestures and continued looking nonchalantly out to sea, binoculars glued firmly to their eye sockets, thus making it easier to avoid my panic-stricken gaze. It struck me that they must be accustomed to this kind of thing and knew how to keep their castle to themselves. "An Englishman's/Cornishman's home is his ... blah, blah!" I found it ironic that whilst being prepared to save any number of sailors in peril out at sea, they weren't going to let any simpering landlubber in distress beside them disturb their tranquility. Failing to make any impression upon them, I soldiered on along the cliff tops towards

Tintagel.

At length the weather improved. The sun came out, but to make up for that I got horribly lost for the nine-hundredth time. I became angry at being forced inland, unable to figure out where the path had gone. This route couldn't possibly be right. I was going to miss the amazing place that Odetta described yesterday. I ended up, inexplicably and furiously, on a main road, left with no option but to follow it south. I came to a solitary craft shop by an area of woodland, where the friendly Welsh lady owner, holding her lovely newborn baby, gave me directions to Tintagel. She sent me through some woods, back towards the coast, which seemed strange at first, until I found a beautiful valley with a rock-trewn gurgling stream and the odd ancient building. This place seemed magical, almost like fairyland, and I ambled through it, taking in the ambience. I came to some ancient, crumbling buildings, and then lo and behold, saw all the ribbons in the trees I'd stumbled across in Rocky Valley by accident! I was ecstatic after thinking I'd missed it. Odetta was right about it being a spiritual place. Many myths and stories of witchcraft are associated with this place, yet it felt tranquil. I put my hands on the wall like Odetta explained, wondering if she was a white witch.

After a few minutes of reflection I continued through the pleasant valley, alongside the stream in the sunshine, hardly believing I'd gone through hell an hour earlier. This sheltered valley was the first real respite from the full-on winds since Bude a few days ago. I met the odd person walking their dog and customary greetings were exchanged. After a mile or so the path started to climb, leaving the stream below to my right. I met a friendly blonde lady named Gay. We chatted for ten minutes. She offered me a coffee and a lift in her motor-home. I declined, having this big thing about not cheating on this walk, meaning I couldn't accept lifts.

Gay featured heavily in TV documentaries eighteen months later, after Boscastle suffered terrible floods. Her motorhome and possessions had been swept out to sea. She helped the villagers get back on their feet by cleaning, painting, and decorating for them, for nothing. In return, they surprised her by clubbing together to buy her a brand new campervan. It was a lovely ending and it couldn't happen to a nicer person. Good luck to you, Gay!

From the coastal end of Rocky Valley the views down to the sea were fantastic with the foaming stream pouring into the blue-green sea. Sadly, it was time to leave. I turned south, hitting the cliffs again. The sky turned grey and I had to negotiate a nasty sheer ledge before reaching Tintagel. I was learning to cope with the vertigo. Although I still felt uneasy, I had no option but to grit my teeth and walk through everything that was thrown at me. I tried not to look down or think about the drop as I rounded the side of the cliff. As I neared "Aluminiumtagel" – a place I invented right next to Tintagel; it's as believable as King Arthur and his cronies – it started to drizzle. I walked on to its neighbour, the more famous Tintagel, found a café by the car park, and hurried inside to shelter. It was actually called the Beach Café, despite having no beach. I ordered a large mug of coffee; the worst of the entire trip, possibly of my entire life, plus an even horrider piece of dried-up chocolate cake. The coffee remained almost "jet-brown" no matter how much milk I added. I asked at the counter if they'd made a mistake and given me Bovril in error, which they weren't too happy about, but then they didn't have to drink it. I bought a Cornish pasty, which turned out to be surprisingly good. Quite a few other people were sheltering too. I spotted the little old lady I'd passed a few hours previously on that bench in the rain. I couldn't imagine how she'd arrived before me. She certainly hadn't overtaken me. Thinking I may have appeared short with her earlier, I asked to sit at her table for a chat. She was an interesting lady. Her name was Elizabeth. She was sixty-five but had a childlike innocence about her. She was also eccentric and chuckled a lot. Elizabeth lived in Hanwell, West London, where I'd previously lived for many years. Her husband never joined her on walking holidays. She'd written several novels, with some degree of success, until she'd run out of ideas. She said that her books were in the style of *The Thornbirds*. I'm more of a biographies man. I never touch novels. I like *real* life, such as *Star Trek*, *Star Wars*, *Lord of The Rings*, *Thunderbirds*, and *Dr Who* – I'm having you on. I hate them all. Anyway, we had a nice chat for half an hour. Elizabeth had bypassed Rocky Valley and taken a more direct route, which explained how she reached old "Tin-Tackle" before me.

I left the café at 4.45 p.m. bound for Port Isaac. Nothing was open on this gloomy Saturday afternoon. I wasn't going to bother walking inland to see the village of Tintagel. I reckoned the chances of seeing King Arthur or Sir Lancelot were slim on a lousy day like this. Their armour would get rusty. The climb out of "old Tinto" was a steep one, but for once the weather fooled me by improving again. Blue sky appeared everywhere. Puffing my way up to the top, high above me and straight ahead, I saw a colossal square building perched on the top facing the sea. It was a couple of hundred yards inland and looked like an extremely upmarket prison. I gawped at the turreted structure in disbelief, wondering what the hell it was, when I saw a sign inside the barbed wire that read: "Camelot Castle Hotel". Wow, it certainly was in a stunning location, but I'd a feeling the cost of staying would be much more stunning, even if it did resemble a prison.

I climbed again after passing Tintagel Head, before turning to look back over the famous Island where, through the ages, fact and fiction had mingled to create the tales of King Arthur's court at Camelot. Mostly it was fiction with more fiction mingled in, methinks. However, we English do love our romantic tales of chivalrous knights, magic, love, and intrigue and would rather believe it all to be true. Anyway, these tales are all inextricably linked with the enigmatic ruins of Tintagel Castle, perched on a remote promontory of land.

After half an hour I encountered a windswept Youth Hostel on top of

Glebe Cliff near Dunderhole Point. I felt overjoyed, having never stayed in a Youth Hostel. This one looked great but also looked shut. It was. I wasn't sure whether to hang around until it opened or walk on with it being only 5.30 p.m. A strange Swedish hippie girl was sitting on the ground outside, chanting. She was obviously a witch. After a quick chant with her, "witch" confirmed my suspicions, I departed whilst looking back to ensure she wasn't following me on her broomstick. After another 2-3 miles I came to the ultra-posh settlement of Trebarwith Strand. It was about 7.30 p.m. and I thought about B & B-ing it as the weather was looking well-dodgy. On entering an un-ultra-posh cheap-and-nasty-looking pub called The Fort William, I asked the barmaid – who was "scaring a mini-wirt" and "a toe-cut lop" – how much a single room would cost me. I couldn't help thinking, even though she was "Latin dressed as mum", she was very attractive all the same.

She returned after consulting the landlord, announcing it would cost £65, to which I replied, "I want a room for one night, not the whole week!"

When I rose from the floor I said I wouldn't pay more than 20 quid … I left despondently. I'd politely written, "No thank you" in my journal. As I climbed the path high up above The Fort William, I looked down on its roof, full of massive holes and needed replacing. I thought to myself, 65 quid for that! I'd need ten buckets in my room to catch the rain. After a mile or so I came to a deep little valley with a stream that would suit my purposes for the night. I camped before dusk. For a change I fell asleep before 9 p.m., but was awoken by loud banging noises and flashes in the sky. My first thought was that there was a ship in distress. I poked my head out of the tent, gazing seawards, not finding anything out there. I craned my neck to look inland towards the village of Delabole, spying a huge firework display in mid-flow! It was 11 p.m. in April. What the hell were they celebrating in the middle of nowhere? I couldn't get back to sleep for hours after that, so had yet another bad night after such a promising start. Delabole pork rapscallions!

Day 14: Sunday 27 April

I awoke still fuming at 7.45 a.m. I packed horribly and as a result it was 9.15 a.m. before getting away. I forever climbed the cliffs. They were higher and steeper than ever before. This was beyond belief and by far the most difficult walking to date. I became depressed, having been led to believe that things would get easier after reaching Bude. The weather was dull again with severe gales blowing in my face. These horrible conditions were conducive for those Nasty Note-mares to invade my brain. Once again the gradual building, persistent rhythm, and intimidating mood of Holtz's 'Mars' drove me crazy as I struggled upwards, face contorted in pain, trying to get to grips with the almost impossible terrain.

I arrived on the edge of Port Isaac via the adjoining hamlet of Port Gaverne at 1 p.m., physically and mentally exhausted from my ordeal.

Following a quick sit down on the nearest wall I practically fell into an open art gallery to ask for directions and food. Here I met local artist Katie Childs with her lovely original paintings of the area and her fabulous wild hair. I wasn't about buying a picture and stuffing it in my rucksack, but think she understood and recommended The Watershed for lunch. I found it quickly and had the best meal of the trip so far: Sunday Roast with all the trimmings, followed by home-made apple crumble and a couple of pints of real ale. I chatted to the waitress, the lady owner, and her boyfriend, who happened to be the superb chef too. They'd only opened two weeks previously but the meal was *brilliant*. They were interested in my walk. The owner asked if I was going to be passing through Polzeath. When I told her I was, she asked whether I'd mind going into TJ's surfing shop and asking her brother to give her a ring as she'd lost his mobile number! I left feeling horribly bloated and even more tired. I ambled down the hill into Port Isaac. If I'd been wealthy I would've sought out a little B & B and gone straight to sleep after a hot shower, but I wasn't wealthy, I was poor, so kept walking.

Another sizeable traditional fishing village, this one has fared better than most over the years, remaining largely original and unspoiled, possibly because, like Clovelly, it's difficult to access, being off the beaten track and away from the major routes through Cornwall. The fishing nowadays is mostly confined to "crobs and labsters" as the silver darlings (herrings) have long gone. Despite its isolation, the village has unfortunately had several visits from the famous. The ugly devils flock here, especially the TV companies who seem to run amuck in the locality at every opportunity. The 1980s BBC drama serial *The Nightmare Man* was filmed here, and it was a location for the 1997 film, *Oscar and Lucinda*. The poor old village hall has even been decorated by the team of TVs "DIY SOS". God help us! The ITV series *Doc Martin* has also been filmed here, though the village has a fictional name of "Portwenn". *Saving Grace*, a successful comedy, was filmed in and around the Port Isaac. In recent years the village has become home for part of the year to a growing number of celebrities, including the designer Laurence Llewelyn-Bowen. I've liked him and his wife very much since seeing them on *Celebrity Who Wants to be a Millionaire?* Things go downhill fast as you've got that irritating forever-beaming-benignly, actress/presenter/sexy (not!) guru ***** ******** (you've got to guess who), and someone from a TV car boot programme who'll remain nameless, as I'm not that keen on them either. I had thought about moving to Port Isaac, but not now. They've put me off. The village is also home to the famous sea shanty singers, The Fishermans Friends, whose name suggests they may be somewhat brinzely. However, they do still perform on The Platt in the old harbour, and all over the world too. Since my journey they've become an international force and released several top selling CDs and are definitely not very brinzely at all.

I checked out the scenic old harbour before discovering "Squeezy Belly Alley", where I bumped into an artist named Dave, as he was squeezing his ample belly out of his cottage. He'd moved here from Cheltenham a few years ago and loved the place. I couldn't help thinking afterwards that Dave seemed a bit of a funny name for an artist. Dave Van Gogh? Dave Rembrandt? Dave-enardo De Vinci? Dave Angelo? It didn't seem right somehow. Then again, there is David Hockney, if you like that kind of art. Back in a harbour-side sweet shop I met an elderly mother and her middle-aged daughter. They came from Broadwater Green, Worthing in Sussex, near where I had lived in the 1950s. We chatted like long lost friends even though we'd nothing else in common. Next I saw the best-looking woman so far, in a gift shop, buying fudge and chocolates. An American, I think. I didn't dare speak to her with me being too scruffy. I bought a giant-sized bar of emergency fudge before setting off again in light rain for Polzeath. Again it proved difficult with never-ending ups and downs, easily as bad as, if not worse, than the notorious Hartland Point to Bude stretch. Feeling half dead, I came to Port Quin, a sad deserted ex-fishing village. There wasn't a soul around and although all the buildings appeared to be intact they also looked empty and disused; a veritable ghost town.

Port Quin was abandoned on two occasions, once when the pilchards failed, and then again, when sometime in the nineteenth century, all the men were drowned during a terrible storm whilst fishing one night. Because of this it's still sometimes referred to as "the village that died". The women of the village, unable to continue without their men folk, left Port Quin when their hardship became intolerable. The fishermen's cottages fell into disrepair, ruin, and the sea. The fish cellars are still there but the port and harbour are mainly tourist attractions now, with just a scattering of National Trust-owned properties and a couple of private houses left. It's rumoured that Viking longboats came ashore here and the remains of one is buried somewhere nearby, but nobody seems to know where! Port Quin is also one of the places that inspired Marcia Willet during the writing of her book, *The Golden Cup*. Sir John Betjemen also had a special affection for this neck of the woods too. His last resting place can be found at St Enodoc's Church in the dunes of Daymer, just south of his beloved Trebetherick. The church at St Endellion is dedicated to St Endelienta and has many legends about the saint who gave her name to this church and parish. One tale suggests that she was the daughter of the Welsh King Broccan, another that she was the god-daughter of King Arthur (naturally), who helped her when a local lord killed her cow! The high ground upon which the church stands renders its tower visible from some considerable distance and was a landmark from the sea. I sat on a wall and rested in the grey, gloomy silence, pondering awhile on Port Quin's mega-gloomy past. Some jolly tourists from the Midlands arrived by car, lifting my spirits somewhat, and we chatted about the sorry state of poor old Port Quin, trying to make light of all the disasters.

After I'd walked round the sizeable, empty harbour, I began another climb, which naturally caused the rain to come down again, but I was getting used to it by now. I quickly stopped to don the waterproofs, only to have to take them off ten minutes later. The headland on the south side of Port Quin is known as Doyden Point, and upon its summit stands the dinky Doyden Castle; a tiny, turreted, stone folly. It was built in 1830 as a retreat for some local businessman, where it's reputed that the partying and gambling were particularly excessive! Now it's a National Trust holiday property, as is nearby Doyden House. It looked so cosy and inviting, with a plume of smoke coming from its, chimney as I passed by some 200 yards inland of it. I looked longingly, wishing I could just knock on the door, go in, and sleep for a whole month. I carried on in gales that seemed to be strengthening the further south I went. The coastline was beautiful and more rugged than ever, but it was impossible to enjoy it, feeling exhausted whilst the weather was threatening too. With the Nasty Note-mares bugging me again I began looking for somewhere to pitch the tent at about 7 p.m. Before I could find a suitable patch of greenery, the heavens opened and it bucketed down. No way could I pitch in that. The waterproofs were back on and I made an all-out dash for Polzeath. I was soaked, weary, and unable to find that bloody town, despite being within spitting distance of it. I could see the twinkling lights but there were so many valleys, coves, and inlets to circumnavigate that it took forever to get there. It was dark by the time I reached the edge of Polzeath. As I walked towards the lights of the town, I spotted a stupid idiot flying a kite in the gales on the beach for *fun*! He'd no idea of the torment I'd been subjected to for the last three hours and wouldn't have cared either. Here he was *enjoying himself*! The barefaced cheek of it!

I felt like grabbing him by the throat and screaming into his face, "It's all right for *******s like you swanning round here, having the time of your life, while I've been out there in *hell* for three hours!"

Instead I passed by, cursing the foolish dolt under my breath. I stumbled into a phone box with the guidebook open on the B & B page. I rang a Mrs Pauline White at Seaways. In a panic-stricken shaky voice I asked if there was any hope. *Yes*, she had got a room. Thank God! Now to find the place – another saga. She tried giving me directions, but as I had no clue where I was, this wouldn't be easy. It transpired that I was in old Polzeath but had to cross the wide beach to get to New Polzeath. It was now dark, which didn't help as I traipsed across the wet sand. Once in New Polzeath I began climbing a hill by way of a main road, unaware if it was the right way or not, when I saw three pensioners talking 50 yards away at the top. When I approached them to get directions I gathered they were having an almighty row. One old lady, who had a gob the size of a parish oven, was shouting and yelling. The other one was in tears. Meanwhile an old bloke stood looking on. So did I. After a minute, not wishing to get involved, I turned round and walked back down the hill, muttering to myself in sheer frustration, "Why me? Why bloody me?"

I flagged down a car in desperation. The driver got out, leaving his wife inside, and his engine running in the middle of the road, directing me back to where I'd come from and up a different hill. Oh misery me! I popped into a small supermarket and bought some beer from a cool-looking black dude who was the only person in there. I finally staggered up the last hill at 8.30 p.m. and knocked on the door of the large detached Seaways in the pitch dark, over an hour since phoning them. I was soaked and knackered. It was heaven to get inside, despite being told off for knocking on the wrong front door of the house – they all looked the same to me. I changed into some dry gear and came down to the TV lounge. I was soon drinking a pot tea and watching the box with Ken, Pauline's hubby. We chatted about sea shanties, folk music, and suchlike.

I staggered up to my room at 10.30 p.m. It was only a Bengal Sid (single bed), but it was comfortable. I managed a bit of laundry before turning in and hung up all the wet gear in the shower. The effort required to do any tasks was immense, but I knew I'd regret it in the morning if I didn't get it done. I fell asleep at 11.30 p.m.

Day 15: Monday 28 April

The next morning I showered, treated my feet, and had a good breakfast. I chatted to Ken and Pauline as I was the only guest. Afterwards I rang Mum and Dad from the payphone, informing them I hadn't been found dead in the sea at Redruth. Some poor devil had. Dad was bound to think it was me. Back in my room I wrote up the journal prior to sorting out my rucksack. Ken showed me his vegetable patch for a full half-hour. Not being a gardener, I didn't find this overly-fascinating, sorry to say.

I made my excuses and set off for Padstow. It was dry and sunny as I headed for good old Paddywack (Padstow). On the way through New Polzo I called in at TJ's surfing shop to say hi on behalf of the lady to the Watershed's brother and asked him to ring her as she'd lost his number. He was delighted to get the message after wondering why he hadn't heard from his sister for ages. My good deed for the day done, I proceeded to walk the flat wide path alongside the beach, on to the shore at Rock. During the 3-mile walk to the Padstow ferry I noticed my feet were not so painful today, only aching a bit. I waited with a few other people at Rock for the little yellow "Black Tor Ferry." It cost £1 to Padstow. This was okay, but I complained when I wasn't given a nice ticket for my memorabilia collection – you only get a ticket if you're doing a return journey. Everyone else got one and to make matters worse they laughed at me for asking. Padstow bacon pigs, the lot of 'em! This was to be my first estuary crossing. Despite feeling worried, it all went off okay without incident. It took about ten minutes to get across to Padstow where I alighted, still in one piece, and strolled around the bustling harbour in the sunshine. All was lively and scenic with the ever-present gulls eyeing any sandwich or ice cream within their peripheral vision. I'd heard a lot about the place but had never been here before, so it was a pleasant surprise to find it even lovelier than I'd imagined. Padstow lies near the mouth the River Camel and in its partly sheltered estuary, a couple of miles in from the wild Atlantic coast. After looking in several shop windows I sought out St Petroc's Hotel. I looked at the menu on the door to see if I could afford to lash out. It wasn't dirt cheap.

Whilst trying to make up my mind, two female staff members trapped me by saying, "While you're deciding, we'll take your rucksack inside and look after it for you." With that they dragged it across the pavement, into the restaurant, without me having any say in the matter. I remained unsure when I entered apprehensively, but they said, "Here's your table. What would you like to drink?"

No turning back now. I didn't live to regret it though. Fifteen minutes later I ate the best sea bass I've ever tasted; sort of grilled/barbecued, with its crackly caramely-brown skin facing upwards, with loads of great veg, a lovely selection of breads and a pint to round it off. Quantity and quality, "the worst of both belds!" I decided against a dessert, as they were 6 quid each. I nicked half a toilet roll before departing. Hundreds were piled up in the gents'. I did this periodically so I always had tissues on me for general use, including my hay fever, which I expected to strike me down any day.

I wandered down to the harbour and bought a toffee ice cream for dessert. As I was adjusting my pack, holding the ice cream cone, I somehow fell accidentally into a ladies' shoe shop and ended up staying for ten minutes, talking to the lovely owner, Eve. She related how she loved life in Padstow and how she walked 3 miles into town every day from her coastguard's cottage. It was lovely to talk to someone who loved their life the way it was. A nice interlude but I couldn't dally for long. I posted more excess baggage back to Mum and Dad's house in a jiffy envelope before leaving Padstow, making for the coast at Stepper Point. I was feeling exhausted after my big meal, but bravely carried on.

Some distance off the path I spotted Eve's quaint terraced cottage, which was a fabulous spot to live, before turning south along the wild Atlantic coast. I came to a coastguards' hut, and then a tall stone-built "thingy" that I learned was a "Day Mark" tower. These were built to serve as navigation beacons for seafarers during the daylight hours. This one is referred to locally as "the Daymark", but I would've named it "the Darkhouse", as it seemed to be the exact opposite of a lighthouse. The cliffs were lower here but it was still not easy walking, especially as I hadn't yet recovered from my large lunch. I walked all afternoon, exhausted, wishing it was 7.30 p.m. so I could sleep. The weather was pleasant, apart from the gales that I was trying to ignore. I came to a couple of bays where I couldn't even get a pot of slop to keep me going. I gingerly circumnavigated the dangerous Round Hole collapsed cave. Someone died the previous year after tumbling into it. It was horrid peering into its wild foaming depths. I shuddered before running down the slope to safety.

In the village of Trevone I was furious when a waitress clearing up said indifferently, "Sorry, we're closed."

It was obvious that one minute earlier they must've been open. Despite assuring her I'd sit outside to drink, I got nowhere at all. I trudged on thirstily to the *massive* Harlyn Bay caravan site. I was still thinking about how great my seafood meal had been when suddenly my whole belly heaved in agony, which only meant one thing: I needed to find a gents' right away! There was no chance on the cliff tops with this monstrous caravan site stretching for miles. Nothing remained but to crouch in a fast-flowing rocky stream off the path, which tumbled over the edge of the cliff, into the sea. Hardly ideal, but these were desperate times. I got back onto the path in the nick of time, as a happy holidaying family appeared a few yards away. Unfortunately though, as I'd opened my shoulder bag a few minutes earlier, a strong gust of wind had caught the entire wad of toilet paper, whipped it up into the air where, in the blink of an eye, it had unrolled itself to at least 30 feet in length and then flown up into a tree above the stream. I now had to point out to sea in order to divert the family's attention away from the long reams of luminous pink tissue flapping wildly from the branches several yards above and behind us! I felt weaker now, but followed the path past all the caravans, around Cataclews Point, out towards Trevose Head. By 7 p.m. it was getting windier. I decided to camp before hitting the large exposed promontory itself. I needed to find a sheltered spot but it was going to be difficult. I was already being blown upside down, inside out, and sideways. I found some broad sheltered grass verges, but some swish detached houses beside them prevented me from pitching. I carried on. I was getting too near to the exposed Trevose Head, so was forced to camp right *on* the grassy path itself. I was in the bag at 8.15 p.m. A gale blew outside and it rained heavily. I'd made the correct decision this time, as I was snug and warm. I slept well and long that night.

Day 16: Tuesday 29 April

I was awoken by a woman calling out a bright, "Good morning!" as she passed by with her dog on the other side of the nylon, a foot from my sleeping bonce. It was only 7.30 p.m., but that was it. I couldn't risk going back to sleep whilst blocking the path with the tent. Luckily it wasn't raining, so I started packing away, which again proved difficult in the strong wind. A bloke frightened me to death by coming over a nearby stile from nowhere. I only spotted him when he was right beside me.

I exclaimed angrily, "What did you want to go and do that for!" but managed a wry smile.

I left at 9.40 a.m. and soon came to Trevose Head with its fine white lighthouse standing guard over the dangerous reefs below. I walked south all day in wind and intermittent rain past Booby's Bay and Constantine Bay. The views were more boring now, nowhere near as dynamic as before. One highlight, however, came whilst viewing the famous Red Arrows practising their aerobatics overhead. I got talking to a gruff ex-Teddy boy in his late sixties, sitting on a bench watching them. The sad thinning remnants of a once-mighty quiff just managed to cling to the front of his shining cranium. He started reminiscing about the 1950s and the good old days when he used to bike down to Cornwall from his native London with his ton-up mates. They'd meet at the legendary Ace café on the North Circular Road, pick a destination at random, and then go for it. Fifty years later, with his wife dead and his mates dispersed hither and thither, here he was, sitting alone on a bench with his memories on a grey drab afternoon after catching a train down from London on impulse. It must've been an anti-climax for him. I could tell he was hurting inside, wondering what the hell he was doing here, longing for those good old days. He wasn't looking for sympathy but I felt sorry for him all the same. We had a decent chat during which I attempted a few jokes and funny stories in hope of cheering him, and myself, up.

After 20 minutes I walked on. Not long after I got caught in a violent hail storm on top of a cliff with nowhere to shelter. This lasted fifteen minutes. Although I wore my waterproofs, I wasn't quick enough this time, and got drenched through. When the hail stopped the sun emerged again, but I was soaked to the skin and furious about it. Almost immediately I saw four people, who looked like Germans, dressed in lederhosen Hawaiian shirts and summery gear, appearing dry and unruffled. Where the hell had they been during the deluge? This sort of thing happened fairly regularly. It infuriated me. I'd never see a soul when the heavens opened, but as soon as it stopped people would pop up everywhere, looking like they'd been lying on a beach all day. I hated them.

I was longing for a cup of tea when I arrived at the National Trust café at The Bedruthan Steps. An elderly local couple I'd met on a beach earlier had recommended it as a good watering hole. It was more than good, it was great. I had a large prawn salad with a baked potato, followed by two large shortbreads and a pot of tea for £8. I had a good laugh with the staff, the manageress in particular, who was a friendly lady with glasses, aged about thirty-five. When I emerged, well rested and full of prawns, I spoke to the friendly and informative National Trust warden – John Case – who was on duty at the hut outside. We chatted about the legend of the Steps and about the area in general.

I wandered over to the cliffs and took a photo of the famous volcanic stacks that make up the Bedruthan Steps. A Cornish giant was supposed to have used them as stepping stones in order to cross the bay. After the big build-up they weren't much to write home about. I chatted with two women out looking for skylarks. As John had pointed out, they could often be seen flying and hovering overhead in the area. Bloody pests, polluting the sky like that! Must get myself an air rifle next time. (For the benefit of the RSPB, I'm only kidding.) As we talked, a bloke wearing a vest and a pair of trendy Speedos jogged up to us, joining our conversation. He bored us all stupid by explaining about his "basal metabolic rate", which is the amount of energy expended while at rest in a neutrally temperate environment in the post-absorptive state. No doubt you knew that already.

I left at 4 p.m., aiming for Newquay, trudging through the showers and gales for the umpteenth time. Somewhere high above Watergate Bay, way in the distance, I saw a figure coming towards me, behaving suspiciously on the cliffs. Getting closer, it transpired to be an "anorak", with a gleaming bald dome, reminiscent of St Paul's on a wet night. He'd spotted me at the same time. As a result he'd rushed to a sheltered spot that he was familiar with, ready to camp quickly in case I'd beaten him to it! What a loser! He actually admitted this when we met, the miserable wretch that he was. Pathetic, especially as it was mid-afternoon. I never camped before 7.30 p.m. Who in their right mind would camp wild, five hours before dusk? I imagined the cooty-headed chump lying there in his tent, bored and twiddling his thumbs until late at night, all through his own stupid fault!

Newquay finally came into view with an ominous black cloud hovering above it. There was nowhere to pitch. As I approached the edge of town the huge black cloud burst open, tipping it down. Even with the waterproofs I was getting soaked. I dived into a bus shelter in a built up area. Knowing I was near to Porth Beach, I sat down with the guidebook to search for lodgings. The reasonably priced "Porth Beach Hotel" appeared to be 50 yards down the road, so I risked the rain to get to it. It was a big yellow building, though not beautiful. Would they take the likes of me in the state I was in? I crawled into the foyer, sopping wet like a drowned rat, feeling like a scruffy old trimp (a thin tramp), and rang the bell for service.

I fully expecting to be slung out or at least told, "I'm extremely sorry, sir. We're full up at present. There's a nice skip at the end of the road, sir. Why don't you try that?"

Instead though, a quiet middle-aged chap appeared, announcing he could give me a double room for £20. I could've hugged him. It was Carl, the owner. He said afterwards that he'd felt sorry for me, being caught in that awful storm, and hadn't been put off by unkempt, soggy appearance. The room was warm and comfortable, en suite with two beds, TV, kettle, etc. Everything a man or an old trimp could want. I was to return the following year for a week-long break, £120 all in, including food, double room overlooking the sea, wine, late night bar – no questions asked.

It was great to be indoors and safe again. I showered and watched *Emmerdale Farm*. I did some laundry and placed it on the radiators to dry overnight before nipping down to the hotel bar for a few bevvies. This Hotel Bar was pure luxury. Only two blokes were there, including barman James – Carl's son and heir to the business – and an old fisherman. Another friend of theirs arrived and we all chatted. I drank bitter. James made me a large gammon sandwich, which I ate, along with a packet of cockles in vinegar. Amazingly 'All the Young Dudes' came on the jukebox. I laughed and said, "This is *my* band!" I don't think they believed me and I didn't elaborate. We chatted about fishing, music, and other stuff. James's lovely girlfriend

Hannah turned up. She complained that she'd spent £80 on a hair-straightening gadget before realising she could've got a better one for free. Her hair wasn't curly though. Presumably it must've worked to some degree, so at least she hadn't completely wasted the money. At some point a chap of about ninety-eight came in, all doubled up, leaning on a stick.

James asked him, "You know about music, Freddie. Ever heard of Mott The Hoople?"

The old timer immediately said, "Of course I have. They were my contemporaries, for Gawd's sake! How's Ian Hunter these days?"

I told him Ian was fine and asked how he knew about the band. He'd seen us playing somewhere in the early 1970s. He was a great bloke but I had to chuckle to myself as I thought, How time flies! Most of our old ex-fans would probably be over sixty by now, no longer the young dudes, like us! After four pints – a lot for me – I turned in, feeling Natalie Tokered again. For some reason I didn't sleep well though.

Day 17: Wednesday 30 April

I got up at 7.30, showered, and was down at 9 a.m. for an excellent full English breakfast, with masses of extra toast. I sat with a very Spuck-ish (odd) bald bloke from Chester, who was on a failed surfing holiday having injured his chest at sea. He was returning home later, all washed up. I was dreading him trying to show me the repulsive injury over breakfast, so kept leading the conversation away from the subject. I phoned my mate Rick Battersby and his lovely wife Tatts (Sarah). They were on holiday from Dorset. We intended meeting up for a day or two. Rick mentioned they were in Padstow, up the road. He arranged to pick me up from the Porth Beach Hotel at 1 p.m.

I left my rucksack in my room and walked into Newquay at 11 a.m. It felt strange and fantastic to be walking without all the crippling weight I'd been carrying for two weeks. Without that pack I would've been able to sail round the coast path with ease. What a drag that I was going to be stuck with it for another 400 miles or so yet. I bounced along like a man twice my age ... or do I mean double?

Once in the town centre I bought a new monocular for 19 bloody quid at a chemists. I'd lost my original one in the dark, in the phone box, on the edge of Polzeath a few days earlier. I also purchased a whistle (£3), as I'd somehow lost the old one without even blowing it once, which wasn't fair. I bought more plasters, despite not suffering foot blisters now. Most of the feeling in my feet had gone, apart from a dull ache, which was present most of the time. I went into a fishing tackle shop to look around. I got chatting to the fishermen who looked bemused when I spoke about carp, as they were more used to talking about and catching sea fish for eating, not for releasing again like I did with carp. I got an Oasis drink Summer Fruits, which was now my firm favourite, after trying all flavours over the past two and a half weeks. At nearly a quid a throw I couldn't afford to like it too much though. The weather was okay, but looked like it might rain later, as it did on most days.

I rang Mum and Dad, leaving a message. At least they'd know I was okay in Newquay. I nipped into a Kodak shop and bought a smaller pouch for my little Nisis camera. Back in the street, I realised that a fantastic-looking woman was walking alongside me with her not-so-fantastic-looking friend. They didn't notice me, which was as well, as I might have got reported for ogling with my mouth agape and tongue hanging out. I asked a copper about buses back to Porth Beach before chatting with a chap who owned a blue Mercedes like my lovely old cream one, which I'd tragically sold for £46.75 in a rip-off car auction before leaving home. Some pig got a real bargain. I hope it breaks down on him. Some great-looking vehicles were around. I soon spotted an amazing old VW camper that had been customised and was low to the ground. I took a picture of it. I enjoyed pottering round Newquay. This made a pleasant change, especially as I wasn't weighed down with over half a hundredweight of gear, plus I was always in a hurry to get on and walk. Not today though. This was my first real rest day of the trip.

After a leisurely stroll I caught a bus back to Porth Beach and somehow got dropped behind the hotel, from where I couldn't find my way to the front. This was all very dodgy. Finally I found the correct back door and banged on it before Carl arrived, laughing at my misfortune. He let me in via the busy kitchens. Rick and Tatts had arrived, looking great, and reckoned I'd lost loads of weight. We decided to go eat at the same National Trust café at the Bedruthan Steps where I'd visited yesterday.

When we went inside the busy café, the lady manageress, hardly believing I was back again, shouted aloud for all to hear: "Oh no, not *you* again!" We all burst out laughing at the same time.

"I like it so much here I'll be coming in every day from now on for the foreseeable future."

I had an even bigger and better prawn salad and jacket potato this time, sticking to the same meal with it being so good first time round. Afterwards we all had a cream tea – splendid. Outside we watched the Red Arrows rehearsing again. I took some wobbly video of the event, largely based on guesswork. I also took some of Rick and Tatts, who were much easier subjects to film, as they didn't move about quite as fast. After a quick potter on the cliffs we cruised back up north, into Padstow. What luxury, travelling in a *motor car* again, yet it also seemed alien to me. We do take things for granted in our normal daily lives, don't we? We strolled round the harbour and took some smiling photographs of each other before sticking my head round the door at CJ's to say hello to Eve again, but unfortunately she wasn't there. I posted my old pouch, tripod, and several other unused bits back to Mum and Dad's house, lightening my pack by another pound or two. Rick and Tatts treated themselves to a wooden cooking spoon, causing much merriment for some reason, and a few other bits for camping.

The weather was sunny now. We returned to their campsite a few miles south of "Paddywack" at 5.30 p.m. It was called Atlantic View, and the old farmer said I could camp for £1.50 – that's what I call a bargain! I pitched a few yards from Rick's big tent. Luckily no other campers were nearby. The campsite was near the coast, but I didn't remember passing it, probably because a thick hedge separated it from the path. Rick made a big pot of tea and we all chatted, having lots of laughs. At 7.30 p.m. I took them for a meal to say thanks for ferrying me about. We settled on The Farmers Arms, a couple of miles up the road in a village, after asking a few locals if they knew anywhere good to eat. They couldn't have liked us much, as the food there was extremely average. Tatts had cold spaghetti bolognese, containing *no* Bolognese whatsoever. It was essentially boiled mince in water, with no sign of tomatoes, onions, herbs, or any kind of sauce! It had virtually no flavour. We semi-complained, but didn't want to get too nasty, being on holiday. My chicken was okay-ish, as was Rick's gammon, so we sort of joked about it to the lovely waitress rather than going berserk as I normally would in these situations. The "couple pie and astard" was good anyway. She gave us extra "pig-bortions" as if to compensate for Tatts' lack of bolognese. A pleasant evening.

We returned to the campsite at 10.15 p.m. as Tatts, being heavily pregnant, felt exhausted. I was asleep by 11 p.m. but got up to wizzle three times. Rain was beating on the tent and the Thermarest air mat was ineffective as the valve had been leaking for a week. Each night I'd blow it up, only to wake to find it deflated with my hips aching as they pressed into the hard ground beneath the thin groundsheet. £65 and it lasted a week. Useless, but I wasn't prepared to fork out for another one. I'd have to put up with this for the whole trip. How bloody annoying! I was later given a free replacement, but that didn't help during this time.

Day 18: Thursday 1 May

I gave up trying to sleep at 7 a.m. I lay there with a bad bellyache. I was going off that pub now. Rick came over at 8 a.m., all bright and breezy. I managed a faint smile when he said the kettle was on. I diligently wrote up my journal before Rick reappeared, beaming and carrying an even huger teapot than before. We drank eleven and a half cups each, chattering away by my tent, trying not to wake Tatts, who continued sleeping soundly about 20 feet away. Rick and I drove to the shower block. It was pretty Spartan inside, but what can you expect for fin-pound wafty (£1.50)? The showers were somewhat primitive, accepting numerous 20 pence pieces, which seemed to run out every few seconds. As a result it cost me £1.00 for my shower, taking me over the £2.50 mark for my stay. While I showered, the old farmer came in. According to Rick, he started tidying up before wiping down the porcelain sinks with my used hay-fever-nose-tissues that he'd found lying on the floor, having fallen out of my pockets when I got undressed. Very hygienic, I must say! Rick didn't have the heart to tell him. I was in the shower wondering why he was chuckling like an imbecile as he continued trying in vain to hold a normal conversation with the baffled farmer throughout the unseemly episode.

Rick and I drove the 6 miles back to Padstow to see the aforementioned "'Obby 'Oss" festival, which began the previous night. Apparently, at the stroke of midnight, the townspeople start singing the 'Morning Song', after which the merriment and revelry begins. We left Tatts sleeping at the campsite. She needed lots of rest and didn't fancy having to walk far or stand around for hours. The weather was warm and sunny when we managed to find a parking space. Not easy in the packed town. Thousands of people were descending on Padstow for this ancient fertility festival. Padstowians from all corners of the globe often return home for this four-day bash. We walked among the crowds, down to the harbour area that'd been dressed with greenery, with flowers placed around a maypole, where it was bustling and heaving with all manner of folk, locals and tourists alike. The atmosphere was electric with an air of expectancy, although we couldn't actually see much action. Lots of girls and boys, mostly around the ages of ten-fourteen, were in traditional dress. We were packed in the crowd, unable to move much, but could see up some of the narrow streets.

Suddenly the crowd ahead of us roared, "Ooooooohhhh!" as an 'Obby 'Oss jumped out of a nearby building, terrifying everyone in its proximity. The two main 'Osses are apparently named the "Old", and the "Blue Ribbon." We caught a glimpse of an 'Oss that was a tall man (on stilts?), swathed in a hoop-framed, voluminous, "horsy" costume, complete with head, chasing all the nearby children, while being goaded on by acolytes known as "Teasers". If a young maiden is caught and pulled under the costume, the child would then be destined to have many children of her own one day. Before too long I expect the PC brigade will insist that the festival be toned down, or even banned, despite its long tradition. I was recognised by several people who remembered meeting me while walking up on the cliffs over the last few days. This amazed me. I didn't remember any of them. I said hi to Eve in CJ's. She remembered my name and asked how my trek was going. I introduced her to Rick and we chatted for several minutes as people weren't actually trying on many shoes while the 'Osses were about. We stayed in Paddywack for a couple of hours, soaking up the party atmosphere, before leaving for the campsite. We were told that the festival itself ends at midnight – May Day – when the crowd sing, to the accompaniment of dozens of accordions and drums, of the poor old 'Obby 'Oss's death, until its resurrection the following May Eve. Therefore it "lives" for one day a year. The partying continues for days until everyone's had a skinfull. I ate half a cheese pasty and half a large lardy cake, in order to build my strength up.

I packed my gear neatly with nothing hanging off the outside of the rucksack and felt I was getting the hang of it now. Tatts was up, feeling rested, so we set off for Newquay at 1 p.m. I found the Tourist Information Office to ask about the Gannel ferry. Oh deary me (or words to that effect), there wasn't one! I'd have to find a tiny grim wooden footbridge in order to cross the river Gannel estuary, providing it wasn't high tide, in which case the bridge would be submerged and inaccessible. This meant having to miss walking the length of Fistral Beach if I were to make it across the Gannel at low tide.

We did some hurried shopping. I bought a load of sandwiches and drinks, having no idea where I was going to end up that night. An attractive female customer chatted to me in Superdrug, mainly about the nutritional merits of the various sandwiches on offer in the fridge. I told her I usually went for the *biggest* ones available for the *lowest* possible price, regardless of what's in them or how nutritious they were.

The three of us left Newquay town centre and drove off in search of the River Gannel. After fifteen minutes and forty U-turns we weren't any closer to finding anything even resembling a river. Horribly lost and despondent, we ended up in the middle of a nondescript modern housing estate, which seemed all wrong, yet according to the guidebook was correct. Baffled and frustrated, we got out of the car and walked in opposite directions in search of the elusive River Gannel. I headed down a well-mown suburban slope that miraculously took me to the north bank of the estuary, exactly where I needed to be. I called to Rick and Tatts. The tide was out, exposing the wide, muddy sand flats. As I looked to my right I saw, downstream and in the middle of the mud, a horrid ancient 18-inch-high "plank" that about spanned the 8-foot-wide trickle that was the river Gannel. The slimy blackened wood looked like it was rotting from the constant tides. We stood looking at this excuse-for-a-footbridge and then at each other.

Rick said in astonishment, "Surely after all the fuss, *that* can't be it?"

It was. In less than half an hour the tide would come in and that Gannel trickle would have widened to 50 yards, submerging the gruff miniscule "bridge" to a depth of several feet until it went out again. I didn't want to leave my friends, especially for the gloomy wilderness ahead, and wondered if I should go back to the campsite with them for one more night. We were knackered. I'd never felt less like walking in my life, especially after being softened up by that easy two-day break, but there was no option. I had to go. A tear was in my eye as I left because it'd been such a lovely couple of days with my very special friends, despite Tatts' spaghetti-un-bolognese! They were going to return to their tent to listen to their new radio before sleeping for the rest of the day. No such luck for me as I walked the slippery mossy plank to misery. They told me later that they'd watched me walk half a mile or so and saw me talk to someone briefly before disappearing.

I climbed the cliffs, passed the severe drops around Pentire Point West, and Kelsey Head, and on to Holywell. The rain that'd been threatening since Newquay finally started pelting down. The path was winding about all over the place, owing to the numerous inlets and small headlands, making me feel like I wasn't getting anywhere. To add to this it was a dismal afternoon. Apart from the rain and gales, the scenery was becoming increasingly eerie. It was certainly the least enjoyable walking of the trip. I found myself constantly looking over my shoulder to see if I was being followed, even though there wasn't another living soul about.

On the way to Penhale Point the path skirted round before entering a large redundant MOD. training ground – Penhale Camp – that was particularly grim with the path weaving through and all around it. I couldn't seem to leave the place behind. It was miserable, derelict and creepy, with barbed wire everywhere, plus warning signs: "Beware! Unexploded Shells." It was hateful and I desperately wanted to get out of there. With relief, I eventually saw the long sandy Perranporth Beach stretched out below me. Not wishing to attempt the extensive soggy undulating dunes ahead of me in the downpour, I descended and walked the beach itself where the sand was firmer. The beach stretched about 3 miles ahead, so I set off in earnest to tackle it. As I got towards the halfway mark I encountered a river flowing across the beach in front of me, into the sea. Unable to walk a single step further, I was left with two choices, both being equally loathsome. The first was to turn and retrace my steps north for 2 miles, climb up the cliff, and then walk the same distance south again, only this time in the unfeasible dunes that I'd already avoided. The other option was to climb up the sheer 150-foot dunes to my left, which would bring me out on the cliff top, where I could turn right and get to Perranporth easily and stay the night. I opted for this despite realising it'd be horrific. Unfortunately I'd underestimated the horrific-ness. It was the worst thirty minutes of my life, including having to endure the diabolical Manchester band, Electric Mud; the worst band I've ever seen live onstage at Mr Smith's in 1970!

By the time I'd managed to climb about 20 feet I was up to my thighs in sopping-wet sand, which eventually gave way. I slid back down to the bottom again. It'd taken five minutes to climb all that way, only to end up back at square one! After several more energy-sapping attempts I wasn't making any headway and started wondering if I should give up and go back, even though it'd take over two hours to get to the spot I was now looking at. This was a 50-yard climb above me on the top of the dunes. I tried climbing again, from a spot 30 feet further along the beach. I persevered, putting every ounce of my strength into that climb, stopping to rest every few feet. I kept sinking and slipping backwards, but was inching towards the top. After twenty minutes I was three-quarters of the way up when I stopped for the fiftieth time to rest. Looking up, sweating and swearing, I saw three people sitting comfortably on a bench at the top, watching me struggling in the sand below them. I hated their guts! I couldn't believe they could sit there looking without helping me. This meant I couldn't fail now at all costs. I had to get to the top or be a laughing stock. Ten minutes later I pulled myself up and collapsed with exhaustion. The three people had vanished, saving me the bother of killing them. Even though it was still raining, sweat was pouring off me as I lay there, trying to get my breath back. I remember thinking, Why am I doing this putting myself through this nightmare? *I hate walking*! It took ten minutes before I was able to pick myself up and carry on south towards Perranporth.

I decided to B & B it, as the weather looked even more ominous, despite the rain stopping momentarily. I saw Perranporth below from the cliffs but it was still 2 miles away and the sky was turning blacker. I made an instant decision to pitch where I was, at an unsheltered spot on the bare cliff top. This transpired to be one of my worst decisions of the trip. With it being only 7 p.m. I could've carried on. I may have got a soaking, but could've dried everything off in a B & B later. It was hard to pitch in the strengthening wind but I managed it before the deluge came. This continued throughout the night with the gales howling and pressing the tent walls flat against my face. Unable to hear my radio through the din, I lay awake, bored yet terrified in case my shelter was destroyed. At 1 a.m. I used both hands to grasp the tent pole through its nylon sleeve above, fearing the tent and myself would be blown over the edge of the cliffs. It was a frightening and depressing night as I drifted in and out of consciousness. I learned another valuable lesson that night: never camp in an exposed spot, no matter what!

Day 19: Friday 2 May

I'd barely slept and felt delirious with tiredness. By daylight my rucksack, plus the all the gear on my groundsheet, was soaked through, amidst puddles of water. It was like Hades but far worse. It was still raining and the gales were even stronger, making it impossible for me to pack away. I was trapped in my tiny tent indefinitely. I'd taken to holding onto the tent fabric itself, fearing it would tear away from the pole with the ferocity of the wind. At one point I took the plunge of emptying my full wizzle bottle, as I needed to go again. I pulled back the tent flap in the gale, removed the bottle lid, and flicked the contents away as hard as possible. The whole lot blew back in my face at twice the velocity – all two pints of it. Thank you very much indeed, God! (Or words to that effect.) My one consolation was that I wouldn't starve if I had to stay there, as I had enough food to last a week if I rationed it out. Surely the weather would change before then, though it was hard to imagine it improving at that moment. I felt like I was being paid back for the beautiful weather I'd experienced during the first ten days of the trip. It was also going to affect my daily average mileage that had, until now, improved, along with my time schedule. What a waste of valuable walking time this was, especially as I'd done so well until now. Somehow I managed to scrawl a few miserable notes in my journal before dozing off through exhaustion at 5 p.m.

It looked like I was going to be stuck for another night, however, I came round at 6 p.m. feeling pleasant and warm. The sun was out, plus it'd stopped raining. I frantically packed away, despite the ongoing gale, realising this may be my only brief window in the weather. Taking the tent down in this exposed spot proved to be a nightmare. Removing the pole and packing it into its small stow bag was impossible. I shouted and swore. Well, who was going to hear me on those cliffs in that deafening gale? A happy family of four, that's who! As I looked up in mid-curse, this family was leaning into the gale 3 yards away. What the hell were they doing out in this? I stopped swearing in disbelief, but carried on when they'd walked another few yards. They'd already heard me. What difference would it make now?

I ran away at full pelt, twenty-five hours after arriving. I raced 2 miles down the hill, across the dunes, and down into Perranporth. Incredibly, a few hardy surfers were round the beach area. It felt good being back in the real world after my vile stint away from it. I found a phone box and managed to book a room at the cleverly named "Perranova" Guest House (£18), run by a Mrs Honey. She gave me directions across the town and up another hill. I popped into a small but busy supermarket to obtain large mounds of chocolate (comfort food) and two cans of cider. Whilst paying at the counter, the nozzle came off my water hose, causing the contents to jet out in all directions, over me and on the floor. I apologised to the lady on the till, feeling like a complete prat, as everyone else in the queue was looking on, smiling. I would've tried joking my way out of it, but felt too knackered. After leaving quietly and embarrassed, I called at a fish and chip shop.

As I stood wearily in the queue waiting for my order, some stupid git looked at me and said, "Got back from Iraq then, have we, mate?"

I was so tired that it didn't occur to me what he was on about. When I realised he was referring to my camouflage rucksack, I smiled limply and said sardonically, "Very funny, mate. You're a proper wag, aren't you? I don't think!"

Everyone in the queue laughed at him, which made me feel good, if somewhat smug. At 8.45 p.m. I arrived at Perranova, a strange-looking "tall bungalow". Mrs Honey was a pleasant, elderly Cockney lady who made me feel welcome. I was her only guest. She gave me a downstairs room with two beds, a telly, and a kettle. I ate my fish and chips supper with numerous cups of tea before doing my ablutions before getting too comfortable. Although not en suite, the bathroom was next door, featuring a *bath* – heaven on earth, after my hell on earth earlier. This was my first bath of the trip; a great chance to soak my old plates of meat, which I'd been unable to do since leaving home. I watched TV all evening after polishing off half a dozen chocolate bars with loads more tea. Madonna was being interviewed by Jonathan Ross. What a bore that woman is. I'm not over-fond of him either. I can't stick all that showbiz bullshit full stop. Still, they sent me to sleep, so I should be grateful for that. Unsurprisingly, I slept soundly this time.

Day 20: Saturday 3 May

I was awoken by the good old reliable Timex alarm at 7.30 a.m. and had another luxurious bath. You can't look a gift bath in the plughole, can you? I had a lonely but tasty breakfast in the conservatory, overlooking a grey Perranporth. I could see the spot a few miles back across the bay where I'd been trapped on those exposed cliffs. Urrrggghhh!

Mrs Honey came in with more toast and tea. I took a picture of her on the balcony. There didn't seem to be a Mr Honey but I couldn't really ask in case he'd kicked the bucket or done something equally inconsiderate. She reminded me of Vera, my old Cockney neighbour in Acton, who was like everyone's second mum. I liked Perranova and Mrs Honey.

I packed away and left at 10 a.m. The second I stepped outside it started raining, as it always did when I left the B & Bs. I put the waterproofs on and reluctantly set off up the cliff in the same gale I'd been stuck in for two days, wondering if I should return to Perranova and stay another night. My first visit to Perranporth hadn't exactly filled me with joy. It'd been one that I'd prefer to forget altogether, so I decided to press on and put some mileage between myself and it. I felt rough for about an hour before settling into a better walking rhythm. I've found out since that it's not a good idea to have a large cooked breakfast before walking, as a lot of energy is needed to digest the food energy that could be used for the walking. I don't expect I'll change my habits, unless I win the lottery. The point being that by eating a massive breakfast there are two distinct advantages. First, if the B & B costs £20 and you can eat breakfast for £8 and drink tea and coffee in your room for £2, you'd only be paying £10 for your bed, bath, heating, and laundry facilities. Secondly, by eating a gigantic breakfast you wouldn't need another cooked meal that day and could get by on sandwiches or snacks, thus saving a lot of invaluable time and money. I will, no doubt, continue to gorge myself to the eyeballs at breakfast, even if I have to waddle until late afternoon.

It was drizzly but quite fascinating walking as I'd finally come to the first of many mining sites that I was to pass through. Apart from fishing, mining was the main industry in Cornwall. I was close to Cligga Head where copper and tin mining were prevalent for many years. The sites have long since fallen into ruin. There were many ghostly overgrown, tumbledown, stone buildings, pit shafts, and hunks of rusted metal and ancient, contorted, abandoned machinery. Strange mesh grills covered many open shafts, preventing people, animals, and debris from falling down them. It was spooky to think that this had once been a thriving industrial site over a hundred years ago. When the mining became unprofitable, the area was left abandoned to the elements. Nothing ever replaced the mine workings, so they were gradually being reclaimed by nature. Hundreds, if not thousands, of men had laboured here over the centuries. Now there was me alone.

After an hour of this fascinating backdrop I came down to the tiny Trevaunance Cove. It was time for a break so I went into The Driftwood Spars pub and ordered half a pint of shandy and a pot of tea. I chatted to the attractive young barmaid and a pleasant, but not particularly attractive, old chap. I felt happy there and could've stayed all day, but conscience got the better of me after forty-five minutes. After a quick brush up in the upstairs gents' I said my farewells and stepped outside into the drizzle at 12.30 p.m. I turned to take a photograph. Looking back at the welcoming pub I felt a pang of loneliness before turning towards the cliffs again without looking back.

I came to St Agnes Head. As I rounded it, the gale suddenly hit me full on, lifting me bodily off my feet, almost taking me over the edge, such was its terrifying force. The rucksack's weight assisted the gale as I stumbled, trying to regain my footing. I got quite worried for a few minutes, not really in control of my own movements, but luckily the path soon veered inland and then ran parallel to the dangerous drop instead of being on top of it. At least if I fell it wouldn't be fatal. I kept going, bracing myself against the conditions, while at the same time learning how to position myself for maximum stability. A few hundred yards ahead I recognised the old engine house of the famous Wheal Coates tin and copper mine, complete with chimney, which was below me on the cliff and had been beautifully preserved. The weather was too rough to go down and look at it closely, but I wandered round some other buildings on and around the path. I read potted history boards and plaques as I sheltered from the elements for a while.

A couple with a toddler was looking round. The chap had the child on his shoulders as they wandered silently in and out of the ruins. He and his wife hardly spoke. He strolled off with the child to view some other ruins. The woman – a vision of great beauty – stayed and chatted to me about various bits of history. I liked her very much. She was knowledgeable, warm, witty, and blonde, with a kind of melancholy vibe about her. She was wearing no make-up, aged in her early thirties.

After a lovely five-minute conversation she suddenly turned towards me, grasped my jacket collar with both hands and, adjusting it, said affectionately, "You'll catch your death if the rain gets in there."

It was a special moment. Our eyes met for a split second and we kind of connected. Suddenly her husband's voice echoed from somewhere, breaking the spell.

"Come over here and look at this big ugly thing."

Whilst gazing at me, giggling quietly, she called back to him with: "I'm already looking at one!"

We both cracked up laughing before shaking hands and saying goodbye. I left knowing I'd never see her again. I didn't even know her name – ships that pass in the night, and all that. I felt sad for a while. It was like *Brief Encounter*, only briefer.

The next landmark was the nondescript village of Porthtowan, which looked pretty dead on this grey day, apart from a nice old engine house perched on the hillside opposite. Not bothering to stop, I walked straight through and out the other side, part of the way with a weird couple who I couldn't shake off. I'd made the mistake of asking them for directions, not realising they both made two short planks look awfully thin. Apart from not knowing the area, despite being locals, they bored me rigid. They had an air of "serial killers" about them, so felt glad to ditch them when the climb proved too much for them. I saw a great dog with its owner on the cliffs, sort of medium-sized with a heavily-lined, crinkly face, shrivelled-up ears, and a miserable look. It was as if she was saying, "I'm not as old as I look. I'm only two. Honestly." I took some video and a picture, though she was rather nervous when I tried stroking her. The chap said it was either my hat or my rucksack. At least it wasn't *me*. I met another local chap with a small dog who was going my way, so we walked together for a mile. Conversation was difficult, owing to the continuous din of the gale. He did, however, point out a few interesting landmarks to me before turning back to his car, parked in a cove. I carried on towards Portreath. Even though the walking was strenuous and the winds were carrying light rain, I stuck it out all afternoon without flinching – crying yes, but flinching? Not me!

The path left the coast at around 4.30 p.m. and headed inland. I ended up walking down a small road from which I saw the houses of Portreath below in the deep valley to my left. Feeling weary, struggling under the weight of the pack, I had a seminal moment that stuck in my mind forevermore. I came to a large house named Gull Rock on my left, with a shallow gateway off the road which led to a pair of white gates. In a sloping field beyond was a turreted, octagonal, Victorian-looking structure with modern windows – a kind of folly. Being exhausted, I reeled, virtually falling into the gateway sanctuary for a breather. Whilst standing there, leaning on my pole, I studied the small structure and reckoned it to be something to do with an old railway or a waterworks maybe. It was a smoke outlet above a tunnel which ran under the cliff I was standing on. Whatever it was, it'd been refurbished and converted into a kind of summerhouse, as I could make out some stacked chairs inside it. In a stupor of weariness, I gazed at the lovely house with its views over the coast, harbour, and Portreath itself.

In a trancelike state I began praying and day-dreaming that someone would open the door and say, "You can't stand out there in that wind, you poor fellow. Why don't you come inside? I've cooked a massive shepherd's pie and there's a spare room if you want it. Or I'll open the folly and you can sleep in there if you like."

Needless to say nobody opened any door and a couple of minutes later I was forced out of my dreamlike state by the icy wind and into action again, shivering from standing still for two minutes. I always remembered that bizarre moment of passive frustration and hardship. I can remember those feelings now as I type and am reminded of how tough it was. I'll never forget that Gull Rock gateway.

Whilst descending the hill to Portreath I decided that, despite the money, I was going to try for a B & B once I got there. I was in danger of overdoing things. Half an hour later I was there, without even seeing the harbour, but wasn't sure if I found the actual village centre. Portreath is spread along a stream valley away from the beach, with the village clinging to both slopes. The main centre, a small parade of shops, was about 300 yards inland from the seafront and harbour. It's a centre for surfers and holidaymakers.

I found a phone box where I spent forty-five minutes trying to track down a B & B for the night. I booked a room at Benson's up the road. It did seem a bit early to stop, but what the hell? I phoned Mum and Dad for ten minutes, which cheered me up as always, then found a small supermarket where I bought two cans of cider, sausage and egg sandwiches, Pepperami, yoghurts, and loads more chocolate bars and cakes, all for tonight's supper. I never ceased to be amazed at how I could stuff my face with as much junk as I liked and still lose weight. Shame it wasn't like that at home.

I followed their directions *uphill* – where else? It seemed like miles, until I could cut across and get to Benson's, which I found at the very top. It was a classy chalet bungalow overlooking the harbour, albeit from a mile away. Once there, a row broke out over the cost of a room that stated £20 in the guidebook, but when the manageress demanded £25, what could I do? I reluctantly agreed to pay. It was great value, but I'd have to eat an extra fiver's-worth of breakfast, meaning I'd have to eat fifteen quids-worth of grub altogether so that the bed would only rush me a tenner. My luxurious double room featured a balcony and sea views, with loads of Kit-Kats and chocky bars thrown in – two quids-worth at least. Now I only needed to eat thirteen quids-worth of brekky. I was terrified of ruining the white lacy bed linen and white carpets with my muddy boots and wet gear. I put all that stuff in the shower before lazing around in the plush room, feeling guilty that I hadn't done a couple more hours of foot slogging. It would've been impossible to camp in those gales anyway. Besides, it had been an interesting day's walking if not a full one.

After some laundry and writing up my journal I watched TV all evening, eating everything I could find and drinking my cider, interspersed with cups of tea and coffee. Oh no! *I'm a Celebrity, Get Me out of Here* – total drivel, but I had to watch something. Thankfully I fell asleep during it.

Day 21: Sunday 4 May

I was up at 7.15 a.m. with the alarm, showered, and down to the conservatory for the *biggest* breakfast so far. It was a help yourself-style buffet, which suited me down to the ground. I ate about ten individual portions of various cereals and yoghurts before emptying the hostess's trolley. It contained sausages, bacon, scrambled and fried eggs, hash browns, tomatoes, mushrooms, fried bread, beans, and the rest. The only other guests were a middle-aged couple who'd already had breakfast. After a couple of pints of fruit juice, ten cups of tea, eleven rounds of toast and marmalade, I was ready to go back to bed. Before I got up to leave I chatted to the couple who were walking the coast path using two cars and doing a bit at a time in weekly stretches three times a year. This would take them two years to complete.

I smiled politely but felt like saying, "I don't know how you can be bothered with all that kafuffle and hassle. Why not walk the whole lot in one go, like me? It's the only way, yer cowardly milk sops!"

I crawled back to my room to pack, bloated to the eyeballs, feeling like going back to sleep. I took a photo of the nice manageress, who'd forgiven me for bickering over the extra £5, and of the equally nice waitress before leaving at 10.20 a.m. I didn't fancy walking back down to Portreath and then back up the coast path again, especially as I was on the southern side of town and already pretty high up. I "improvised" the route instead. This was not a total success, as about half an hour after crossing a deserted rare breeds farm there was still no sign of the sea. I'd come horribly unstuck and taken a wrong turn somewhere. I found a main road and got lost on that too. In the end, with no compass or proper map, I decided to guess and jumped over a gate into a private field, following my instincts, which had already let me down on several occasions. I kept going across some more private land climbing high fences and praying I wouldn't get shot by an angry farmer. After a worrying forty minutes I saw the Atlantic ahead of me and an SW Coast Path acorn marker before me. It felt good to be "legal" again, even though the walking wasn't good and the weather was turning grim again. I was already feeling low when I noticed that even the coast was horrid today, with big tarmac car parks alongside the path, with the sea and rocks right below.

I stopped in a miserable empty roadside café at the pleasant sounding Hell's Mouth for a pot of tea. The only redeeming features were the two fantastic looking waitresses, who unfortunately only appeared from the kitchen occasionally. I got lumbered chatting to the boring café owner – a scruffy middle-aged bloke – for ages about irrelevant routes, etc. I walked on after forty-five minutes, feeling miserable. The weather was getting me down. I didn't like it round here. Maybe it'd seem different on a lovely day, but it was not a lovely day, it was an abominable one. I continued out to the grassy Navax Point and round the promontory to Godrevy Point where the rain really belted down. The setting for Virginia Woolf's *To the Lighthouse* was supposedly the lighthouse on the rocky Godrevy Island.

As I approached the long beach leading to Hayle, the rain was so heavy that I was forced to shelter in the less than salubrious gents'. After ten minutes I gave up standing inside the doorway in case any blokes thought I might be brinzely. I donned the dreaded waterproofs and climbed down to the exposed 4-mile-long beach to walk the official path across its huge expanse. The next ninety minutes was like nothing I've ever experienced before or since. All I can say is that no human beings should have to endure horrors of that nature, *ever!* To begin with, the beach was not as it first seemed. Within ten minutes I came to a deep fast-flowing river, racing across the sand. No way could I wade that channel, so I tried going inland to cross it. I scrambled across, falling in between some huge slippery rocks, soaking my feet and legs. I was forced to follow the river inland for half a mile before discovering a footbridge to cross over and then all the way back out to the beach again. I now had the long, hard slog through the soft sand to Hayle. The problem was that the tide appeared to be coming in 50 yards to my right, while 50 yards left were high un-scalable cliffs. This meant I'd be cut off by the tide and drowned unless I moved at high speed to the far end of the beach 3 miles away. This was easier said than done as the gales and rain were blowing me backwards. I was sweating in my waterproofs, sinking into the sand under the enormous weight of my pack. I had to go flat out, so the feeling of abject *terror* was added to the list of awful minuses that increased whenever I looked right and saw the sea getting closer. Few people were in sight and those that were visible were at the far end near Hayle. I couldn't rely on anyone to save my life. I raced on panicking, screaming, swearing, sobbing, and praying alternately. I would stop for five seconds or so, exhausted, only to force myself forward the instant I'd got a fraction of my breath back. It seemed like an eternity but eventually I made it to Hayle, by which time the waves were lapping a mere 2 yards from my feet.

When I knew I was safe my behaviour was reminiscent of a soldier in an old war film who was lost in the desert without water. I staggered forward, spun round a few times, finally collapsing on the ground in a crumpled heap. I lay motionless in the wet sand, breathless, sweating, and totally done in. I wondered if anyone had been watching me. Probably not, otherwise I would've undoubtedly heard an ambulance siren by now, which someone would've called after seeing me topple. I lay shaking for ten minutes until feeling able to walk on. The terrifying night in the tent above Perranporth had paled into insignificance compared to this episode. The memory of it seemed like a kiddies' tea party with jellies and ice cream now. I pottered through a derelict industrial site with a dozen dodgy-looking yobs tearing round on beaten up motocross bikes. I kept my head down, stalking on. Even this was like paradise compared to Hayle Beach.

After crossing the estuary I came to the big old viaduct at Hayle and attempted to negotiate its complex traffic system. I carried on, determined to get out of hateful Hayle and make for the beautiful St Ives, a place I knew already. I asked an elderly woman, who looked uncannily like my old guitarist mate Dave Tedstone, for directions. She walked the 400 yards with me to a big road junction.

I couldn't help at staring her, desperate to blurt out, "You *are* Dave Tedstone, aren't you? Come on now, own up. You can tell me straight. Nobody frowns upon gender realignment in this day and age." I managed to restrain myself though, which pleased me afterwards, as I may have ended up with a black eye whether it was him or not.

It seemed like an awful town, grubby and ugly, nothing like what I'd come to expect from lovely Cornwall. I went into a small supermarket and bought an ice cream and an Oasis drink. After spending twenty minutes in a phone box trying to book a room in St Ives. I got one at Rosenfred, Porthellen Row, run by a Mr and Mrs Archer (£24). With under 6 miles to go I took it easy, chatting to some teenagers whilst enjoying my ice cream. They'd already given me directions in the supermarket and were strangely curious about what I was doing and where I'd come from. It fazed me somewhat, as I didn't think teenagers would be interested in anything like backpacking or conversing with an old bloke. Of course, they'd never heard of Minehead or the SW Coast Path, so I told them I'd sort of walked from Bristol.

Two fourteen-year-old girls shouted to some younger boys on bikes: "Hey! Come here! This bloke's walked all the way from Bristol!"

They pedalled over out of curiosity and disbelief. One lad aged about ten was wise beyond his years. He asked if I *had* indeed walked all that way, and when I nodded he looked at me and said with astonishment "But *why*?"

I couldn't give him a straight answer, so mumbled something nonsensical like "You'll understand when you're older, sonny!"

They kept peppering me for another ten minutes with the kind of questions that almost convinced me what I was doing was pointless; that I should pack it all in and return home. They were good kids though and made me laugh. They didn't even try mugging me or try to cadge anything off me. After saying cheerio to my new "fan club" and shaking hands with each and every one of them, I walked under the vile viaduct twice more to get on the right road. I located the main one to Carbis Bay and St Ives and set off. This entailed walking a mile south-west and another mile north-east, in a huge circle round the Hayle estuary to Lelant. I hated this kind of thing as it was so longwinded. After an hour I ended up less than half mile, as the fly crows, from the centre of Hayle across the bay, where I'd come from. My feet, although no longer blistered, were hurting quite badly, having been through a great ordeal today and the last two and a half weeks.

I stopped to wizzle by a blue telegraph pole on a tarmac path in the middle of a grassy area, parallel to the road, before resting several minutes. Afterwards I came to a petrol station with a weird cash machine inside. I withdrew £200. I dislike having less than £50 on me in case of emergency. I got to the edge of St Ives at 6.30 p.m. I'd done at least 20 miles in grimmer than grim conditions. It's amazing what the human body can cope with when pushed. According to the chap on the phone, Porthellen Row was on this side of St Ives, up a small hill for a change. I stopped to ask the way in a grand roadside hotel. The desk clerk directed me to the pleasant-looking Victorian terrace, which I found with ease.

Rosenfred looked delightful from the outside. Inside, however, it was a different story. It was outdated and tatty, not having seen a lick of paint since at least 1967. My room was rundown but as long as it had a clean bed I didn't really care. It actually had two single beds, both clean. The TV was at ceiling-height and lacked a remote control, so I left it permanently on ITV. There was no en suite, but that never bothered me. Gerry Archer, the forty-something owner, thought he was a comedian, constantly coming out with one-liners, double entendres, and the like, but he wasn't amused when I asked for a plastic bowl to soak my feet in. In fact he was horrified. This baffled me, as it didn't seem like such an unreasonable request. He must've had walkers staying before. Yet he seemed perplexed and insulted. He muttered something about not having "that kind of thing round here", so my poor feet would have to survive without a soak. I watched *Emmerdale Farm* before nipping into St Ives for a scan round and for some tucker. It was now a sunny evening with lovely light. It's obvious why artists flock here to paint the views.

The town was busy on this lovely Sunday evening. I had plaice and chips in The Balancing Eel café off the harbour (£6). The food was fine but I felt uncomfortable as the waitress obviously couldn't wait to get rid of me, close up, and go home. She wasn't rude, but kept wiping down tables all round me and turning off lights, and turning the sign on the door to "Closed", and glancing at her watch every twenty seconds. Most off-putting, but I wasn't going anywhere till I'd finished. Funnily enough, as I left ten minutes before closing time, a couple came in, requesting a pot of tea. She had to oblige.

I wandered round town in the fading light, looking into the heaving pubs and restaurants, all full of fun and laughter. For the first time on the trip I felt lonely. Everywhere people were having a good time and I wasn't part of it. I wasn't miserable; more melancholy, and although I consider myself to be a bit of an outsider, I wished I could've joined in somewhere for a while. I phoned Mum and Dad from a call box by a big church. This cheered me up. All was fine with them and old BB too, who'd been doing a hell of a lot of rolling and gambolling. I really missed my old bulstrode. I tried my mate DR and J my sister but they were all out. Thanks a bundle! I'll remember that when they try calling me one day! I didn't feel like going into a crowded bar alone so I bought a Ross blackcurrant cheesecake for

99p. from a small Spar supermarket before returning up the hill to Rosenfred. I gorged most of the cheesecake with a couple of cups of slop, but only managed an hour of TV, as I was so tired I didn't even notice what was on. I was spark-out by ten, after the hardest of hard days.

Day 22: Monday Bank Holiday 5 May

I was up early with the lark, which proved to be a real nuisance, as I had to fight with it over the bathroom. I finally showered and went down to the old-fashioned breakfast room, feeling well-rested and perky for once. The room was full of guests. I got chatting to a friendly couple on the next table – a chap with long hair and his girlfriend – and also with the Archers themselves. Mrs Archer was chatty and surprisingly glamorous (for him). She told me they were off to New Zealand on holiday later and were worried in case I may want to stay another night. No chance! I packed briskly and left Porthellen Row at 10 a.m., out into the warm sunshine. This was the first really hot day since Hartland Quay over two weeks ago. It was amazing how different I felt in this lovely weather. It changed the perspective of the walk.

Not knowing where I may end up that night, I stopped at a baker's shop and bought some cheese, ham, and pineapple sandwiches and cakes, plus another pile of chocolate bars to keep my strength up. The path today was graded as "severe" again, so I was quite worried. The weather was on my side and I was now super fit. I ambled along the harbour, encountering a mini-car boot sale, where I met a lovely old couple. He was an ex-commando and resembled a ninety-nine-year-old clone of Jasper Carrot. I visited the harbour side gents' for a last minute wizzle before heading through the winding streets and past the lovely Tate St Ives Art Gallery. I'd no time to go in, as I'd some severe terrain to negotiate. The last time I'd visited the gallery I'd spent most of the time in fits of laughter in front of the works of art (?) which had been on display, one of them being the contents of a vacuum cleaner bag that had been placed meticulously halfway up a winding staircase. The resulting "work of art" was given some ludicrous title like *Green Jazz Moon on a Winter's Day: File Z-17*, and in the fortnight it'd been on display it'd been re-hoovered up every single day by the cleaning lady! As a result, every day the gallery staff had no option but to empty her Dyson back onto the stairs and attempt to reassemble *Green Jazz Moon on a Winter's Day: File Z-17* as accurately as possible, praying "the artist" didn't turn up to see what had become of his masterpiece! One of the friendly staff in the café related this story when I'd complained about "that mess on the stairs", which I'd inadvertently trodden in on the way up.

As I climbed the cliffs going west it was sunny and wonderful, with a cool breeze making walking conditions perfect. The colour of the sea was a sparkling blue-green with multiple white horses floating across top of the water. It's so obvious why artists love it here. I must have visited the place three or four times and it's never been a disappointment. Despite the guidebook's "severe" warning, I'd been looking forward to the coast path today for various reasons, like the scenic walk to Zennor and the legendary pub, The Tinner's Arms. Before long I realised why the route was graded "severe", as though not quite as steep as the Tintagel area, it was extremely difficult and ponderous as the "path" was stony and dangerous, with massive boulders to negotiate regularly, with lots of dodgy scrambling to be done. It'd be easy to break an ankle, get stuck in the rocks, or topple over the cliff edge in places. Concentration was essential and much caution needed to be exercised. If there was a break between the stones the ground would be wet and boggy until the rocky outcrops resumed, allowing no respite.

A surprising number of people were out walking, taking advantage of the fabulous weather and views. The colours of the sea were breathtaking. I couldn't help stopping to gaze at it every few minutes. I ensured I always stopped walking before gazing out to sea. The one disappointment was not sighting any dolphins, basking sharks, or seals. I hadn't seen one sea creature in the whole three weeks yet. After about 6 miles of this irregular, strenuous environment I felt knackered, but was suddenly re-energised by an outcrop of beautiful blondes! Two girls from Bath were doing a circular walk. I'd written in my journal, "One was yours", directed at nobody in particular, but meaning she was grim the other was gorgeous, tanned, about twenty, friendly, and definitely *mine*.

After an animated ten-minute conversation, during which much flirting and giggling was going on, she asked, "Are you going to the pub at Zennor?" After saying I definitely would go if she did, she added, with a sexy smile, "I'll see you there later, then."

I left with a renewed spring in my step, thinking confidently, I reckon I'll be okay there. Haven't lost the old touch. Yep, I'm still a contender! I was dismissing the fact that she was about twenty and I was nearly 56! Within five minutes I encountered two beautiful blonde Germans, sunning themselves at the side of the path. A similar conversation ensued for ten minutes before they said that they too would see me in the pub at Zennor later. I left with a spring in my other step, this time thinking, Yep, it's a good idea to have a couple of reserves, just in case. I hurtled along, wondering how I was going to cope with all these fantastic blondes at the pub, and which one should I go for when push came to shove? It wasn't going to be an easy choice. I'd have to reject most of them, causing much upset and jealousy among them. I was thinking I'd have to be tactful when I stumbled across four more! This was getting ridiculous. To cut a long story short, after another friendly chat, they also said they'd see me later in the pub at Zennor. Hee, hee, hee! What a predicament. How could I choose between all these beauties without offending the majority by turning them down.

I left the path at Zennor Head and walked half a mile inland to the legendary Tinner's Arms. Not only was this the famous pub that people had been telling me about since Minehead, but it was also the village to which my father had come on holiday in the mid-1920s when he was only six. Dad was a Geordie lad from a Gateshead family. Times were tough up there before the depression, but his best pal had somehow obtained an extra rail ticket for Dad to visit Cornwall with his family one summer. Although seventy-five years had passed, Dad had vivid memories of that holiday, and specifically of The Tinner's Arms, where the local fishermen and miners lifted him up onto the huge pub table, encouraging him to dance and sing songs from the north-east, including 'The Blaydon Races'. He went down a storm and there was much laughter as the little lad with the funny dialect performed all his party pieces. He never had another holiday, so didn't returned to Zennor, which I thought was a terrible shame. Anyway, it was for this reason more than any other that I wanted to see the Tinner's Arms for myself and take some photos to show Dad. I arrived there at 2.30 p.m., as it started drizzling.

The unassuming stone building contained no frills or gimmicks, being an old-fashioned pub brimming with character. I doubted it'd changed much since Dad was here years ago. Only half a dozen people were inside when I ordered my pint of Sharp's local beer and a meal. As I chose a table in a window I noticed a large scruffy man of sixty.

Full of the joys of spring at having made it this far I gave him a cheery, "Good afternoon! Lovely day, isn't it?"

He didn't reply but his face contorted slowly. One eye fixed me rigidly with an icy kind of stare, while the other mockingly roved around my person in disbelief, as if to say, "How dare you speak to me, you hippy tosser! What the **** has it got to do with you anyway?" He never uttered one word. He didn't need to! He banged down an empty ash tray in disgust and stormed off.

It came to me in a flash: Yes! This was the notorious rude landlord that I'd been warned about in virtually every establishment since Minehead. He hates *everyone*! The entire population of Somerset, Devon, Dorset, and Cornwall knows of him and his loathing for the public in general and particularly for his own customers. There he was in front of me proving that point. I realised then that I hadn't been singled out from the crowd for this treatment but that this was actually the norm. Rather than feeling offended I felt honoured at being insulted by him. It would've been a real let down to have caught him in a rare good mood and been treated the same way as you should be treated in any old pub. I giggled to myself as he disappeared angrily up the stairs, slamming the door behind him, never to return.

When I approached the bar, the pleasant bespectacled barmaid whispered, "You've really done it now." I told her I'd only mentioned it was a lovely day, to which she replied, "Ooooh, that's the worst thing you could've done! He hates people that talk about the weather ... or anything else, really." I asked if there was any chance of him reappearing. She shook her head, saying, "No, he's usually had enough by 3 and has to go to bed, but because of you it's earlier today." I changed the subject, telling her about Dad dancing on the pub table in the 1920s. She immediately pointed across the room and said, "It'll be that table over by the fireplace." She explained that the big refectory table had been in the pub for a couple of hundred years. I almost fell over before taking a picture for Dad.

I had a good fish pie and another pint of Sharp's bitter. I was to become a bit of an expert on beer during this trip, before which I'd never noticed any difference between all the various brews. A pleasant young couple came in and sat on the table beside me. They were from Leamington Spa. She had an internet-based retro-clothing business and was doing well. It set me thinking about all the junk – sorry, antiques – that I'd have to get rid of when I returned home. Another couple from Northampton came in and sat at my table. The lady, sitting next to me, was hilarious.

When I told her about the full horror of my walk she said, "You should write a book called, *The Man Who Hated Walking*." I loved it! I told her I'd probably never do it, but she said she'd look out for it and definitely buy it.

So here it is at last!

I wished I'd got her name so I could thank her for the title and the inspiration. She was probably the first person to suggest that I write a book.

Anyway, *thank you, madam*, whoever and wherever you are.

Two friendly brinzers came in and sat nearby, joining the conversation. After five minutes I made some excuse and sloped off to get another half-pint of Sharp's, neatly avoiding getting a round in. By the time I returned to the table I'd drunk it, so nobody but I was any wiser. There was still no sign of any blondes. I figured they'd probably done a detour, got a bit lost, but would be here any minute. The beer was kicking in and I came over all unnecessary. I felt like camping next door to the pub in the field next to the youth hostel, but as it was only about 3.30 p.m. I thought I should probably carry on walking for another few hours yet. Of course, if the blondes turned up and wanted to party all night I'd have to forget about the walking and camp here after all, though I'd probably end up spending the night in one of their luxury hotel rooms. After another half-hour I seriously wondered what'd happened to those blondes. How could all eight of them have got lost? I went outside for a quick look for them, but as it was drizzling I went straight back indoors for another half of Sharp's. I'd been in the pub for two and a half hours and there was still no sign of even one blonde. It was looking like I'd been stood up by all of them! It would've interfered with my walking schedule anyway, so it was probably for the best I thought, crying into my beer.

I finally set off for the coast, drunk out of my head, at 4.30 p.m. Within five minutes the sky turned black. It rained heavily again so the waterproofs were donned. Aarrgghh! So uncomfortable. I climbed past Gurnard's Head, which I renamed "Gurnard's Horrible Old Head", owing to the severe muddy, wet terrain. Soon after leaving it behind I saw a cottage on the cliff top and, still being drunk, took a picture of a roof rack on a van parked outside! As I descended a steep cliff into yet another narrow valley, a huge mountain of a cliff blocked my way ahead. I gazed with fright at its Everest-like proportions. Its high ridge seemed to stretch from the coast itself for several miles inland. It was named Bosigran. I didn't like it one bit. The guidebook urged me to "head for the highest point in front of you", but when attempting this I could find no path through the thick gorse and tall scrub blocking my way. I'd no option but to follow the valley bottom inland, climb a grassier slope up the side of Bosigran, and walk along the top back to the sea. I managed to climb the slope but things started going horribly wrong. The top of the cliff was fenced-off, inaccessible farmland, forcing me to partially descend and walk along the side of the steep slope. I was sinking down a foot or so into thick mud and water with every step. Running water seemed to be everywhere. The effects of the booze didn't help either. It baffled me how a bog could exist on such a steep slope. Gravity didn't make any sense up on Bosigran. That Isaac Newton bloke should've come to Bosigran and done his sums again. I kept trying to regain the crest of the ridge but every time it was fenced off with barbed wire. I spotted a farmhouse but couldn't reach it, otherwise I would've knocked on the door and given them a piece of my mind before begging for assistance and a bed for the night. After an hour and much cursing I finally came down to sea level and the coast again, totally lost.

I walked in any direction, hoping for the best. Needless to say I got the worst. The weather had improved but I found myself on a large flat coastal plain, consisting of many small medieval-looking fields, all separated by ancient high walls, resembling a huge maze. I walked as "south" as I could, but kept having to make detours to do this. There was no sign of any habitation whatsoever and it was 7 p.m. I was panicking about where to spend the night. I hated the thought of camping because I was lost. After climbing a dozen high walls and dropping to the ground on the other side I still hadn't got anywhere. I found a grassy spot along the edge of one stone wall but it was hardly ideal. I scanned the horizon with my monocular. The only visible feature was an old engine house chimney about a mile away further south and inland. As the ground was flat, I decided to head for it. With many diversions it took an hour to reach the overgrown remains, which seemed spooky as I passed close by them in the diminishing sunlight. A shiver ran through me. The area was definitely haunted, probably by the ghosts of dead miners who'd met their ends in some terrible pit tragedy. No way was I camping near those buildings.

After several more yards I approached a minor road and immediately felt relieved. I set off at a brisk pace hoping to beat the veil of darkness that would soon descend. Within a few minutes I heard a car engine approaching from behind. This sounded comforting, as I hadn't seen any sign of human life since the Tinner's Arms. I'd even be glad to see the horrid landlord now – gladder still to see those blondes who'd let me down. A Land Rover passed by, but pulled up 30 yards ahead and reversed back towards me. I was slightly concerned by this development out there in the middle of nowhere. Was I about to be butchered *Texas Chainsaw Massacre-*

style by a local madman? No, it turned out to be a friendly young couple, Diane and Johansen, who'd recently moved to Cornwall from London. They offered me a lift. Without worrying one iota about cheating I jumped into the back, grateful to be going anywhere.

I asked them to look out for any B & B signs. After a mile and an unsuccessful stop at a deserted holiday complex, we came to a stone farmhouse with a handwritten B & B sign stuck in the hedge beside it. This was Higher Pendeen Farm. It looked good, but was anybody home? Diane and Johansen agreed to wait while I checked the place out. I walked through the cottage garden, up the path to the front door, where another hand written sign read, "Knock on the window to your right." Before reaching the window, I hesitated. I had visions of terrifying the inhabitants with my dishevelled, gruesome appearance at the window whilst they sat on the sofa engrossed in the telly. I was also worried about what I may see through the aforesaid window, like a man throttling his wife, for example. Staying put, I reached over to the window and knocked. I returned to the front door to wait.

A lovely lady opened the door. When I asked if she'd got a single room for the night she invited me in after agreeing a price of £20. I dashed back to the Land Rover to thank Diane and Johansen. I also took a quick photo by the vehicle. They'll never know how grateful I was for their help. Once inside the beautiful farmhouse the lady – Alice – made me a big pot tea. We chatted in the kitchen for about half an hour and it appeared I was the only guest that night, so I'd have the large lounge to myself. Alice said everyone gets lost on the awful Bosigran. I went up to my heavily-beamed and cosy room and unpacked before doing some laundry. No telly was apparent, but who cares? It was clean and comfortable. As it was only 8.30 p.m., I decided to try staying awake until at least 10 p.m., so came down to the chintzy, cottage-style TV lounge with my sandwiches. World Championship Snooker was on, featuring Mark Williams versus Ken Doherty; my favourite player, along with good old Ronnie, of course. I watched until 9.15 p.m., but soon found myself nodding off. It'd been another long, tiring day, so I'm afraid I left poor old Ken in the lurch by turning in before the end. I went out like a light. I never did find out who won so if you're reading this, Ken, drop me an email and let me know. There's a good chap.

Day 23: Tuesday 6 May

I awoke to the strains of the Timex alarm at 7.30 a.m., feeling refreshed. When I flung back the curtains it was a lovely sunny day. Land's End, here I come! Ablutions completed, I went down to the kitchen for a tasty brekky. Alice and I chatted cheerfully as she cooked my big full English. She related how she and husband Gray had decided to let the prettiest part of the house for B & B, while they lived in the less salubrious half, affectionately nicknamed "The Hovel"! At one stage, with two kids at college to support, they'd considered downsizing to provide extra funds. Alice obviously loved the place far too much to leave. I didn't blame her. It was wonderful.

After breakfast I packed away my gear and took a photo of Alice in the doorway. She told me she was going to an auction in Penzance later to buy some dining chairs. When I asked how far it was she said it was a ten-minute drive. I was amazed, as it'd take me three days to walk to Penzance following the coast path. I burst out laughing when she offered me a lift, saying, "Get thee behind me, Satan!"

I left in brilliant sunshine after getting directions for Pendeen lighthouse, which was on my route and wasn't far away "as the fly crows". It was a perfect day, for which I was most grateful, as I was due to hit Land's End later if all went to plan. On the lane back to the coast I bumped into a couple walking two dogs. During our chat they asked me to tell their relatives – who were walking someway behind them – that Bengy the Alsatian was walking with them, so there was no need to worry about his whereabouts. I conveyed this message minutes later and was thanked profusely for it. After a friendly "doggy chat" I was off again. Where the path split I saw the Pendeen lighthouse half a mile to my right, but I turned left towards the famous Geevor tin mine. The coastal scenery was fantastic, the sun was shining, the sea was translucent blue, and there was virtually no wind.

I walked through the spooky mine workings and saw some huge conveyor belts working noisily 100 yards away. Maybe tin mining is carrying on in secret. I became aware of a walker half a mile or so behind, catching me up, slowly but surely. I guessed by his demeanour he was another "proper" hiker. I sat on a low stone wall to rest and wait for him, partly out of curiosity, partly because I didn't want the embarrassment of being overtaken by another backpacker. Only one had done it so far, namely Clive Parkinson, and I'd excused him cos he was such a good bloke. As he approached I thought it *was* Clive. This guy had the same short hair and navy shorts and shirt. As he got closer I saw that it was a much bigger chap, also very fit-looking. He laughed and said something like, "I thought I was the only mug out walking today."

His name was Peter Sykes. He'd walked all the way from St Ives that morning! The first thing I asked was, "You must know Clive Parkinson cos you're like him only bigger."

The name didn't ring any bells. Obviously they weren't brothers. He'd left St Ives at 6 a.m. and had got this far in seven hours without stopping. He said he'd got lost on Bosigran for the sixth time in his life. I didn't feel so bad about it now. He was an ex-army man, possibly SAS, aged about forty-five, with a colourful character. We chatted about walking for twenty minutes. He was heading for a pub in Sennen Cove where he'd sink a few pints before walking round Land's End on to Porthcurno, where he intended camping for the night. He'd walk around 40 miles in *one* day by the time he got there! I can't foresee myself managing that, but he was ten years younger than me, so I wasn't doing too badly. He wasn't doing the whole path, only a section of it, so he was able to make it in a dash, rather than a plod, like I had to. He was a funny laid-back guy. He was also a smoker and a drinker, which amazed me, as he was walking 30-40 miles a day. Had I been bionic I may have walked some of the way with him. Anyway, we said cheerio and off he went ahead of me.

Amid the Lelant mine workings I met a middle-aged German couple. He thought he was a funny guy. I didn't. Neither did his wife. His sense of humour was stereotypically German. I wished I'd had a tape recorder with me to capture the way he guffawed at his own un-funny jokes, while his poor wife stood glumly looking at the ground in embarrassment. After leaving the mine workings behind, the scenery became fabulous again, featuring hundreds of old engine houses, with their chimneys crumbling, dotted about all over the landscape. Some were perched on narrow ledges above the Atlantic in various states of decay, set against a backdrop of the sea, the rocky cliffs, and grassy slopes. On a cliff top viewpoint I caught up with Peter, sitting on some rocks. He pointed out the distant Isles of Scilly on the western horizon. We could also see the small promontory that was Cape Cornwall a couple of miles ahead. Below us it looked spectacular with its chimney glistening in the sun. We parted company again and he said he'd be in the pub at Sennen Cove if I fancied a pint later. I let him go on before following slowly, enjoying the land and seascapes, not to mention the terrific sunny weather.

I found a narrow tree-lined valley through which a bubbling brook flowed towards the ocean. I followed its leafy shade for a while, talking to a friendly farmer out walking three dogs. The brown dog had only three legs but was as agile as his pals as they romped around, having tremendous fun. I continued alone, drenching my dependable Tilley hat in the stream, filling it with the cool water, and plonking it back on my head ecstasy. Water had become my favourite commodity in the world, both for drinking and for cooling me down. After leaving the stream I came to the small headland at Cape Cornwall with its own engine house and chimney. The views out to sea were spiffing, especially the unusual rock formation known as The Brisons, consisting of the two islets a mile out to sea. These are said to resemble former French president De Gaulle lying on his back in the bath – and they *do*!

Sadly there was no café, but there was a snack van. I got myself a tuna-mayonnaise bap and a cup of tea before sitting down to gaze at General De Gaulle and the surrounding scenery. I set off up the sun-drenched cliffs again at 3 p.m., chatting to several visitors on the way up, including a lady basking in the sun beside the path. Her husband, who'd been playing golf on the cliff top course, joined us for a ten-minute chat. As we passed the time of day, the farmer with the three-legged dog appeared and joined in too. It was all friendly and pleasant with no stabbings or shootings whatsoever. The path to Sennen was extremely up and down, not to mention twisty and turny, besides being horribly rocky again. Although I could see Land's End far away in the distance, it didn't seem to be getting any closer. I took it easy in the sun, so it was a two and a half hours before I reached Sennen Cove.

I said hello to some surfers before checking in at the gents' in the car park. Next stop was the pub. I stuck my head round the door, asking for Peter Sykes. The barman looked at me blankly so I left. Peter must have passed through earlier and was probably nearing Porthcurno by now, drunk out of his brains, but still doing 10 mph. After buying twenty Land's End postcards, stamps, and an ice cream, I headed out of Sennen, bound for the western tip of England. High on the cliffs I was forced to make an inland diversion, owing to a recent shipwreck, but not before peering over the edge to see big cranes unloading the cargo. I was fascinated by the sight of it.

Afterwards I came to Dr. Syntax's Head, one of my favourite names of the trip. It's a nineteenth-century name for a rock formation resembling a human head. It's probably named after a fictional character, perhaps created from satire of Dr Johnson, who has his own rock formation beyond Land's End, below the hotel, named "Doctor Johnson's Head." Because of the diversion, the final section was a flat, much-walked and cycled path, proving much easier than the real coast path. This came as a relief after another hard day. 400 yards from Land's End I met a middle-aged Essex couple who'd moved to the area and had finished a training session with their dogs in a nearby field. We walked towards Land's End together, chatting merrily, while deep inside I was getting excited about finishing Stage 1 of my journey. I can't explain the feeling I got on arriving at Land's End, but it was wonderful. I grabbed their hands and shook them frantically, hardly believing, yet overjoyed, that I'd got this far. They responded by getting into the spirit of things by patting me on the back, laughing, and congratulating me. It was all emotional even though we'd only met ten minutes earlier. The chap took their dogs to the car park while his wife accompanied me round the buildings to the famous Land's End mileage marker post. She took two photographs of me with my camera for posterity. Unfortunately I look as ugly as sin on both of them and about 159 years old to boot. But as Buck's Fizz once said, 'The Camera Never Lies'. I wished it had this once. We were allowed to take photographs free of charge, as it was 7 p.m. Peter – the photographer – was packing up to go home, saving me £8. I felt proud for completing the first major hurdle of the long walk. Even if I failed to do the rest, at least I could now go home without feeling any shame, knowing I'd achieved something that few others have. I felt quietly confident, aware that the toughest part was behind me. I'd covered about 260 miles, meaning I had around 370 to go. I felt optimistic but totally knackered. I needed to find somewhere to sleep. Before that I had to find a phone box and tell Mum and Dad the good news. I found one nearby in the now deserted De Savary theme park complex, which was quite eerie with not a soul around.

They were delighted for me, laughing when I said, "Told you I wouldn't give up, didn't I?"

I phoned my mate DR, who congratulated me before giving me some more good news: our cottage was about to be let again after a five-month gap. At last! Thank goodness! (The deal later fell through. Pork Sausage-y dolts!)

Before leaving, I bumped into an interesting Irish yachtsman who told me about a campsite inland back towards Sennen! As everything was closed, I left Land's End shortly afterwards, walking inland and uphill – forever uphill – for forty-five hateful minutes until arriving there. It was imaginatively called "Seaview" and looked okay, not too crowded. I put up the tent – which was still soaked from the night of horror above Perranporth – in a quiet corner of the large field. I hadn't camped since that dreadful night and it'd been packed away for almost a week. Luckily it hadn't gone too mouldy and dried out within fifteen minutes of being pitched. I was quite close to the main gate and shower block, which would make things easier in the morning.

It was gone 8 p.m. when I headed uphill again to find "The First and Last Pub in England", the only place to eat round here. The evening sun was lovely but the pub was grim. The interior had been semi-modernised, appearing characterless, despite being old. The barman was a thirtyish, tattooed, earring-ed, arrogant git. He gave the same reply to *every* question I asked.

Q: "Could I have a pint of bitter, please?" A: "No problem." Q: "Do you do bar meals?" A: "No problem." Q: "I'll be sitting over there." A: "No problem."

The curt way in which he spoke sounded insolent. I ordered Hawaiian chicken with chips and vegetables, which was quite palatable.

Halfway through my meal a bloke rushed out of the kitchen dressed in full chef's garb, meat cleaver in hand, only to ask me politely in a strong eastern European accent, "Mille okay, sir?"

Somewhat taken aback, I replied, "Yes, very nice, thank you."

What else was I going to say while he was brandishing a lethal weapon inches from my head? He was delighted by my reply and spoke humbly.

"Oh, sank you so vare, vare mush, sir! I sank you so mush! You are mose kind! You are a good, sir!"

He backed away, bowing and smiling, into the kitchen. It seemed like a peculiar thing to do in an ordinary pub with an ordinary bar menu. This was no gourmet restaurant. Maybe nobody had ever liked his cooking until now and he was desperately seeking approval with a meat cleaver. His politeness *almost* counterbalanced the belligerence of the two-word barman.

Back to the bar for another pint. "No problem" was the predictable reply. I glanced at the coins he'd given me, feeling sure I'd been short changed.

"I'm sorry, but I seem to be a pound short."

He looked blank, said nothing, walked over to the barmaid and whispered something to her before disappearing into a back room.

She came over and said, "Sorry, sir, but you were given the correct change."

How the hell did she know? I didn't kick up a fuss, not wanting to end an otherwise lovely day by getting into a punch-up over a quid. I sat down disgruntled, hating the barman more than ever. I'd thought of two words I'd like to say to him! To make matters worse, when I returned to my table, two blokes were sitting at the adjacent one. I couldn't help but overhear the one-sided "conversation", which really depressed me. One was a smartly-dressed Dutch businessman; the other was a scruffy loud-mouth Cockney prat. One of those who's white but thinks he's a West Indian. An extreme cross between DJs Brandon Block and Tim Westwood, but far more mouthy and much worse than either. They were sort of in the music biz. The prat was excitedly "bigging himself up", attempting to impress the Dutchman by telling him how *he* had got the UK dance music scene sewn up single-handedly. He was bragging about how brilliant he was at DJ'ing, and mixing "tunes".

"Listen, man, at the end of the day, I can belch into a f****** mike, *yeah*? Mash it up with delays and beats, bro, innit; mix in some cool f****** effects, believe it, *yeah*? Sorted, *yeah*? It's another f****** No. 1, *yeah*? There's f*** all to it, bro, innit. I do it 24/7 for real, bro. I got No. 1s comin' out my f****** ****hole, innit, *yeah*?"

I could hardly believe my ears. It was like listening to Ali G except this guy was neither funny nor clever. What an absolute charmer. What would poor old Vaughan Williams, or even good old Ozzy Osbourne, think of this approach to making "music"? I also had a feeling that this idiot wouldn't know a No. 1 if it smashed him in the chops, like I wanted to. I didn't recall hearing many No. 1s that matched his lurid description, either. I wondered if I should ask the chef if I could borrow his meat cleaver for a couple of minutes. I could deal with the barman and this nincompoop in one fell swoop. Well, two fell swoops actually, unless they happened to be sitting with their heads together. I felt sorry for the Dutch chap, who looked unimpressed, nodding without speaking. I put up with the constant stream of egotistical rubbish for about the five minutes it took to drink my pint. I was squeezed past their table to get out.

As the fool looked up, I couldn't control myself any longer and blurted out angrily yet controlled, "It's because of no-marks like you that there's so much rubbish out there. You're a disgrace and should be banned from recording anything *ever*, *yeah*?" He didn't say a word, but his mouth gaped open at my audacity. I turned to the Dutchman and said, "He's full of crap, not talent, but you must've realised that already."

They stared at me, but neither uttered a word. I left the pub, wondering what the hell such an odd-matched pair were doing at Land's End and walked down the hill in the twilight to the campsite in a sombre mood. The day had been amazing except for the last hour. What an anti-climax! I was in the bag by 9.30 p.m. but didn't sleep well, waking several times in the darkness following distressing nightmares, involving throbbing dance music, with the repeated words, "No problem, bro," and "I've got your pound, *yeah!*" with burping sounds all over the top! Whilst tossing and turning I became aware of heavy rain on the tent. My feet were badly aching and I'd nasty twinges in my lower back. I'd felt a good sense of achievement by getting this far but the shine had been quickly taken off. I wondered whether my aching body could hold out to Poole Harbour, 370 miles away. I felt like I was getting a cold or, worse still, hay fever that could stop me dead in my tracks.

I drifted off into an uneasy slumber, muttering, "I must go on. No problem, no problem, sank you vare mush, sir, no problem, bro. I must go on, innit, *yeah?*"

PART TWO
Land's End to South Haven Point

Day 24: Wednesday 7 May

I woke at 8.20 a.m. to a grey morning after a troubled night. I felt like I was coming down with something too. It took forever to get organised. I packed at the speed of a senile snail, getting everything wrong and having to begin again several times. With the rain threatening I became grumpy at my inability to get the hell out of there. I finally made it to the shower block and got everything done, apart from shaving – I couldn't be bothered – before departing at 11.40 a.m. It'd taken three hours since waking to leave – useless. I didn't mean to go without paying but halfway down the hill to Land's End it struck me that I hadn't done so. All the elation from arriving the previous evening had evaporated as the reality of my new situation took hold. I was still in a stupor of exhaustion mixed with the misery of not being halfway yet, of my bad back, a cold, the impending bad weather, and the disappointment of that pub last night. No way was I going back up that hill to pay, so I resolved to pay twice next time I stayed there, which I haven't quite done yet. I didn't hang around at Land's End, owing to the time pressure. A pot of tea would've been nice, but I'd wasted half the day already – buffoon.

It was drizzling as I set off from Land's End sometime after noon. Despite easier walking today, it soon struck me that the hateful strong wind, which had dogged me all down the north coast, was still right in my face, even though the guidebook promised it wouldn't be there after rounding the corner. I wasn't happy about this and would complain to the Cornish Tourist Board if it continued. Greeb Animal Farm is a charming smallholding perched on the cliff top a mile beyond Land's End, featuring ducks, goats, and other species, plus small craft workshops. Several visitors were milling around. It cheered me up. I would've stayed longer if I weren't so late. The views back to the Longships lighthouse and rocks were spectacular with the grey sky and a rough sea. I took several photos before moving on. The drizzle ceased and I started feeling cheerful again until getting badly lost – very badly lost! As the coast path was fairly flat here I could see the sweep of the cliffs and the sands of Nanjizal – or Mill Bay – a mile ahead, plus a broad path rising from the beach going east in my line of travel. In reaching the beach without any proper mapping, I became slightly confused. The yellow National Trail arrow-with-white-acorn distinctly pointed straight ahead uphill along this splendid easterly path. This seemed like the obvious route, but I noticed a scruffy apology for a path slinking off to the right through low vegetation, up a steep cliff, seemingly onto a headland. This measly winding path must surely be for birdwatchers or boring geology students. The bold straight one with the markers must be mine so I took it. I presumed I'd be cutting off a boring corner and return to the coast ten minutes later.

All seemed well for a mile or so until I became aware that this path was turning left (north-east) inland, away from the coast. Undaunted, I figured it'd presently swing in a southerly direction and I'd see the English Channel bang in front of me again, so I kept going. Unfortunately, not having bothered bringing a compass, I'd lost track of which direction I was walking. I would've never made it as Boy Scout. I was becoming agitated, knowing by now I'd definitely gone wrong back at Nanjizal and was up the creek from hell, in a barbed wire canoe with an egg-whisk for a paddle, heading for Niagara Falls! When you're on Shank's Pony and you've got Hobson's choice, there's no worse feeling than being lost in a remote area. I'd passed several people earlier on the coast path but inland there was nobody at all. There are hundreds when you don't need them, none when you do – typical! I found a stately-looking house and decided to knock on the door until fierce dogs barking through wrought iron gates made me think again. By now I was on lanes. The terrain had flattened out. I considered retracing my steps, but that meant walking downhill for half an hour to Nanjizal, and taking that horrid little path up again. No thanks! I kept walking. Along the way I muttered to myself, mainly about being an imbecile, inadequate signs, etc., with loads of choice swear words thrown in for good measure. I resented being lost – not because it seemed stupid on a "simple" coast path – but because of the time wasted and energy expended trying to get back on track. I'd have to walk until dusk today to compensate for all the self-induced delays.

I eventually came to a village sign: Trethewey. Never heard of it. Wasn't much there either, apart from a few cottages and a phone box. I was thinking about dialling 999 and screaming for help when I spotted a signpost to Porthcurno on the side of the lane. What a relief, even though it was nearly 2 miles away. Now knowing which way to go I rang my mate Rick, as a phone box is not a common occurrence on coastal paths and cliff tops. It happened to be his birthday too. Of course there was no reply. So much for my altruistic intentions. I bet he wouldn't believe I'd rung to wish him Happy Birthday. I turned onto another lane and headed for Porthcurno. The lane followed the steep-sided valley down through the village towards the sea. I spotted the large imposing building on the side of the hill. The famous Telegraph Museum proudly displayed on an outside board: "Home of the Victorian Internet"! Old Marconi and his mates did loads of trial broadcasting round these parts. Porthcurno is also famous for its old beach hut from where communication cables were laid to carry signals to everywhere in the world in bygone days. It was all pretty quiet but the sun had come out and things were looking up.

I came to a pub called The Cableworks. Inside it was impersonal huge and empty with tired 1980s décor. There was a large TV, pool table, games machines, and plastic kids' toys strewn hither and thither. I can't say it was pleasant, but feeling peckish I decided to eat anyway, as I may not find anywhere later. I'd learned not to look a gift horse in the mouth, to my cost. I ordered a BLT baguette, a pot of tea, and a pint of shandy for a change. I wrote out some postcards whilst the incessant jabbering of the *Loose Women* bugged me on lunchtime telly. The food was okay but felt glad to get out of there into the warm sunshine and head downhill towards the coast.

I found a path to the famous Minack Theatre, which is a must for all visitors to this area. A Roman-style amphitheatre chiselled out of the solid rock during the 1920s overlooks the sea, supposedly by Rowena Cade, a lady of great vision and determination, and her gardener. I think they had a lot of outside help, as much dynamiting must have taken place. I'm not inclined to believe that Rowena and her gardener would be allowed to blast away willy-nilly with high explosives without some *very* expert supervision. That said, the result is beautiful. This amazing cliff top structure has provided an incredible setting for plays, concerts, and other spectacles every summer for decades.

When I arrived I paid a reasonable £2.50 entrance fee, entitling me to walk around the small museum that explained – with old photographs – how it all came to be. The café was open too. This really annoyed me, as I wished I'd hung on to eat here with the great sea views. So I had another pot of tea and a bit to eat anyway before pottering about, taking pictures. Several rod-and-line anglers were perched precariously way below on the rocks, probably after the elusive bass. What a spot to fish from, though rather them than me. I'll stick to carp fishing. It's far less dangerous, unless you happen to die, of course. I browsed the gift shop for a souvenir, finally plumping for a green cotton baseball cap emblazoned with the words, "Minack Theatre". I bought it in a fit of glee, though at £7.50 it was pricey. It was also light and practical. I could've easily sat there in the sun all day and stayed for an evening show, as the weather looked perfect. The waitress said that the actors had paused mid-performance a few nights earlier for the whole ensemble to watch a "mound" of dolphins swim by. It can't be a "school" of dolphins, surely. That's whales, isn't it? Whatever they're labelled, Shakespeare's Bottom was cut off in his prime for ten minutes that evening.

It was mid-afternoon before I headed towards the vertical, terrifying descent to Porthcurno beach to resume the coast path on the other side of it. The golden sands and brilliant blue sea bathed in rich sunlight were such a sight to behold that I forgot about my vertigo. I was getting used to heights now. This feeling was reinforced when I met a couple climbing towards me. The woman was struggling with the thought of the drop below us.

Like an old pro I said in a "hilarious" manner (I don't mean "comical", but rather in the style of mountaineer Sir Edmund Hilary), "This is a doddle, madam. You'll be fine. Don't look down. Keep your head upright like this" (gesturing). "Keep going up and suddenly Bob'll be yer uncle and you're at the top. And don't do anything I wouldn't do! Ha, ha!"

I ended up sounding more like Tony Hancock than Sir Edmund. I think they really believed I was an expert rock climber or better still a real mountaineer … or did they? I wound my way down the sheer cliff, pleased with the way the day was turning out after a miserable start. The walking was tougher again but I was fit enough to cope with it. The scenery was becoming gentler with more vegetation – including some trees – than on the north coast. The wind, having dogged me for over 200 miles, had turned into a pleasant breeze, proving most welcome on this boiling afternoon. I picked some wild flowers to press in my journal. Don't ask what they were, as I'm not exactly Percy Thrower. Suffice to say they were yellow, ruling out Sea Pinks, and sort of round and flat as I'm now looking at them squashed between the pages. No longer worried about my schedule, I chatted to several friendly walkers coming the other way. After descending again I came round a corner and found myself in a lovely little cove where a few small fishing boats had been dragged onto the sand. Half a dozen fishermen were tending to their pots nearby. It was an idyllic scene, reminiscent of bygone days. Unlike other tiny coves I'd passed through, this one had an old substantial cottage plonked in the centre, almost on the beach itself, facing the sea. I got chatting to five ladies who were pottering around, enjoying the afternoon sun. Four were in their eighties, revisiting the haunts of their youth. The younger fifth one was looking after them. They informed me that this was Penberth Cove. They were all cheery and our cameras worked overtime as we posed, mostly with the cottage forming the backdrop. These turned out to be some of my favourite photographs of the trip.

I left for the next set of cliffs feeling invigorated. I mused on how the day had begun as one of the worst of the trip but was somehow turning into one of the loveliest. The way things can change unexpectedly, particularly when it's for the better, is the beauty of this kind of travelling. Six hours earlier I'd felt as miserable as sin, yet now with gorgeous weather and no sign of a cold or a dodgy back, memories of the dismal pub vanquished to the metaphorical recycling bin. I felt like I could walk all night. Despite the terrain being once more "strenuous", I had a spring in my step by evening. Near St Loy's Cove the path wound down to a beach through some beautiful green woodland. This really surprised me. I hadn't experienced anything like this on the north coast. In this soft shaded area some huge white flowers were growing in abundance among the overhanging trees. I hadn't a clue what they were but with their large trumpet heads they appeared to be part of the orchid family. I am, of course, "leaking as a speyman". I was later informed by folk less horticulturally challenged than I that they were wild lilies.

I ambled on, taking it all in, at one with the world. On a small stony beach I encountered a young chap sitting on a rock. He was from Chicago, named Mark, and was walking the opposite way to me. He'd broken his main rucksack belt buckle and was trying to improvise some kind of repair. I was always worried about this kind of disaster happening to me, so much so that I carried a spare buckle. My buckle, unfortunately, wasn't compatible with other rucksacks but he didn't seem too bothered. Mark seemed a practical kind of guy. I left him in a jovial mood to climb up again, this time into the deep-red evening.

Being early May the evenings were still drawing in by about 7.45 p.m., so I started looking for a pleasant sheltered site to pitch for the night. As mentioned earlier, it always gets difficult in the evenings. As usual a gentle panic began to set in. Nothing drastic this time though, as I was very chilled. Turning round a bend, I became aware of a fleeting glaring light, falling sporadically across the path ahead – most eerie. In approaching the spot, the blinding light was appearing every few seconds, seemingly coming from the seaward direction. When I got there I found myself looking down a flight of dead-straight stone steps to the sea. Lo and behold, 40 yards away at the bottom was the answer to the riddle: a lighthouse! This was the beautifully named Tater-Du beacon. Having no mapping I was taken by surprise. It's Cornwall's newest lighthouse, built of local stone in 1965 after a ship was lost nearby two years previously. It originally featured a powerful foghorn system, comprising no fewer than seventy-two tannoy loudspeakers housed in a stone-built honeycomb grid, visible from its seaward side. This system has been replaced by a state-of-the-art fog-warning gadget, no doubt bloody "digital" like everything else nowadays. For the anoraks who may be reading this, the new-fangled gadget is a Pharos Marine Omnidirectional Electric Omitter. It sounds two one-second blasts every thirty seconds during fog.

Being a lover of lighthouses my first reaction was to camp near to the base of it. Luckily my brain took over from my heart and I deduced that pitching anywhere in the vicinity of that powerful beam, not to mention the foghorn, would be a nightmare. Instead I walked on and soon found myself, without warning, on the edge of the beautiful Lamorna Cove. It was dusk. Nobody was about, nothing was happening. I contemplated trying a harbour-side cottage for B & B, but being a lovely night I decided against being a wimp for once. After retracing my steps for 100 yards I pitched on a narrow strip of grass, tight under the stone cliffs, within spitting distance of the sea. I fell asleep after a short time. I was aware of rain in the night but felt warm and cosy, soon drifting off again into a deep slumber.

Day 25: Thursday 8 May

Awaking at 8 a.m., I first thought it was a dull day, as I couldn't feel the sun on the tent. However, after looking out of the flap, I realised with me camping underneath the cliffs my tent was in the shade. The sun *was* out and the harbour was bathed in its golden early-morning rays, looking wonderful.

Lamorna Cove is at the end of a lush valley watered by a stream running down to the sea where there're a few cottages and an old inn bordering the narrow lane. Apart from the natural beauty of this cove with its tiny quay, built from local granite that's quarried nearby, and its old fishing boats, Lamorna is perhaps best known for the Post-Impressionist artists who stayed here in the early twentieth century. One of them – Lamorna Birch – was so impressed that he took his name from the place. Born Samuel John Birch, he moved here shortly after the turn of the century. Before long he was followed by other artists, many of whom were associated with the famous Newlyn School. Laura Knight is probably the best known of the group, which continued to grow over the years. Others included Harold Knight, Alfred Munnings, Dod and Ernest Proctor, Charles and Ella Naper, and Robert and Eleanor Hughes. Augustus John was also a visitor to the picturesque hamlet. The colony was somewhat fragmented by the onset of the First World War, but Lamorna Birch himself remained for many more years. Today it's still a popular location with painters, potters, craftsmen, and writers continually flocking there, including John le Carré and Derek Tangye.

I took my time packing, while airing my bag properly in the sun for half an hour before leaving at 9-ish. My first port of call was to be the Lamorna Cove café, which I'd noticed the night before, but was thwarted when the lady inside refused to open for me, despite my pleas and tragic sobbing when I attracted her attention. In fairness she said if I could hang on half an hour she'd open then. I couldn't hang on though. If you gotta go you gotta go. I wanted to get going early, so, contenting myself with a single cereal bar, I headed for the sun-drenched hills. This was another beautiful yet tough stretch. By mid-morning I encountered some scattered bungalows and cottages with subtropical palms growing in their gardens; a welcome indication of the mildness of the climate to come. Fabulous sea views were apparent over the roofs, though one scene was marred by an objectionable long line of laundry flapping in the breeze, blotting out my first view of the stunning St Michael's Mount across the bay. This shouldn't be allowed. Minor pork pigs! I thought about reporting it to Penzance Town Council, but thought better of it. I was feeling charitable today – live and let live. I'd see St Michael's Mount from at least 42,000,000 different angles in the next few days anyway. It was time for eleven whole elevenses as I sauntered into the picturesque fishing village of Mousehole – pronounced

"Mouzle" (like "cows") or the closest you can get to that. Mousehole is probably best known for its Christmas illuminations, created each year to raise money for charity, and also for Tom Bawcock's Eve, a unique celebration held every 23 December. This festival is the origin of the local dish "Star Gazey Pie", named in honour of the legendary Mousehole fisherman Tom Bawcock, who braved the fierce elements sometime in the sixteenth century, to go out fishing alone when it seemed certain that the locals were destined for famine. The tasty but gruesome-looking pie is served in the village pub, comprising a mixture of fish, eggs, and potatoes, with grotesque baked fish heads protruding through the pastry top with their dead eyes staring skywards. Not everyone's cup of pie!

After visiting the village shop for supplies, I ate sitting on the harbour wall in the company of a persistent gull. I stupidly gave him bits of my superb pasty – big mistake – and he grabbed at my banana skin as I binned it. At least that kept him quiet for the few minutes it took to polish off my ice cream, biscuits, and cranberry juice. It was breezy, but pleasantly on this hot morning.

Heading towards Newlyn, I followed the path skirting the curve of the bay at a lower level, offering glorious views to St Michael's Mount and beyond Cudden Point to The Lizard peninsula. I came to a small plaque on the seaward side of the path next to the redundant lifeboat house. I was expecting this as it's the poignant memorial to the crew members of the ill-fated *Solomon Browne*, the Penlee lifeboat, which was lost with all hands on 19 December 1981 in hurricane conditions, while attempting to save the eight-strong crew from the stricken cargo ship *Union Star*, which suffered engine failure in atrocious weather conditions. The sea was so rough that the *Royal Navy Sea King* helicopter was unable to lift any of the crew from the *Union Star*. Lifeboat coxswain Trevelyan Richards made several attempts to get alongside, managing to rescue four people who jumped from the *Union Star's* wheelhouse onto the *Solomon Browne*. The lifeboat made another attempt to rescue the remaining four when radio contact was lost. Her last message was "We've got four off at the moment; going back for the others." Ten minutes later her lights disappeared. The lifeboat was completely wrecked with the loss of her crew of eight. Nobody survived the *Union Star* either. In total there were sixteen casualties. A local journalist witnessed the catastrophic event from a cliff top, unable to do anything other than watch the unfolding tragedy. He saw *Solomon Browne* lifted out of the water by the ferocity of the waves, only to be smashed down moments later at right angles across the central deck of the *Union Star*, lifted up and swept off again by another huge wave. The lifeboat should never have been launched in those conditions. If that brave crew had time to think they must've realised the odds were against them, but they still went, such was their dedication to saving lives. These men of the RNLI are the real heroes, not bloody celebrities, pop stars or pampered footballers. I sat for a few minutes by the plaque. The lifeboat house has never been used since. Inside hasn't been touched since that fateful day. The equipment all remains as it was left before the *Solomon Browne* was launched. A sad epitaph trapped in time in this quiet spot. Despite the beautiful sunshine, as I reflected on the tragic events, I felt my eyes filling with tears. It was time to move on.

The colourful fishing boats and quaint back streets of Newlyn soon appeared, jolting me happily back to the present. There was much hustling and bustling around the harbour, not surprising for the largest fishing port in Cornwall. I stuck my head inside a large quayside warehouse. It was a hive of industry with tons of fish, crates, and ice. Men were packing the seafood in ice, working rapidly to keep it fresh, shouting to one another, oblivious to my nosey presence. One bloke did pause for a moment to stare at me as if to say "Who the **** are you?"

Further down the road were signs for several art galleries, which came as no surprise, as Newlyn's history is firmly tied to the art world. It was made famous in the 1880s and 1890s by its "Newlyn School" artists' colony, which included the painters Thomas Cooper Gotch, Albert Chevallier Tayler, and Henry Scott Tuke. The largest current collection of work by the Newlyn School is held by Penlee House Gallery and Museum in nearby Penzance. Newlyn was second only to St Ives for its celebrated painters. Artists realised that the natural light in this corner of Cornwall, both north and south coasts, had unusual properties that were conducive to painting. I hadn't time to visit any galleries on this trip. Besides, I'd more important fish to fry whilst in Newlyn. My first port of call was the small post office where I bought a large ice cream and a cold bottle of Oasis. I cadged a cardboard box and sat outside the post office in the warm sunshine, emptied the contents of my rucksack onto the floor, and went through them with a fine toothcomb again. I was determined to get rid of any unnecessary weight by posting stuff back to Mum and Dad, as the pack was still killing me most days. I managed to lose about 2 lbs. this time, plus roughly 8 ozs. of accumulated rubbish. I'd posted almost 12 lbs. of gear home since three weeks ago. It was getting easier to lighten-up now as the weather was becoming more summery, allowing me to keep the minimum of clothing. I retained only my camo army fleece in case of cold weather. If I'd known what I know now, I would've sent home much more clothing. Nowadays – 2008 – apart from lightweight waterproofs I carry one pair of trousers, one pair of shorts, two short-sleeved wicking tops, an 8-oz. fleece, and a 14-oz. Primaloft jacket for emergencies. Everything is lightweight polyester and gets washed several times a day in hot weather, rung out, and put back on whilst still wet! It sounds strange but it's very refreshing and it dries quickly. In 2003 I carried more than double the amount.

By the time I'd taped up the box and posted it, my rucksack felt considerably lighter. 2 and a half lbs. is 2 and a half lbs.! Presumably the pack now weighed 43-45 lbs. Some passers-by saw me packing. They asked about my trip. People seemed to be interested whenever I said I was doing "the lot" in one go. I always got comments like, "Oooohh, what's it like? I've always wanted to do what you're doing." Or, "Which is your favourite bit?" "Where do you sleep?" "What about going to the toilet?" The most common question must be, "How do you get the time off work?" I felt quite flattered by this as it suggests that I must look young enough to still be working. My answer was usually, "I didn't get time off, I packed it in," which was true. Occasionally people asked if I was doing it for charity, to which I'd reply defensively, "No, because I don't yet know if I'm capable of doing the whole walk and don't want to acquire money under false pretences and fail." This was quite true.

In my thirties I may have done it for charity "for the crack" with a few mates but I was too busy earning a living back then and was also very unfit. On through Newlyn in the sun next and along the "prom" into Penzance where I promptly got lost. Amazing how I'd lasted this long, it being 2 p.m. I'd got lost here last time in exactly the same place. I passed the large shack with its souvenir shop where I'd bought many tacky presents for my staff whilst on holiday in happy bygone days. On the main road across the small bridge I spotted several large fish in the salt water below. I reckoned they were grey mullet but could be wrong, not being a mullet expert. I don't think they were red mullet though because they were grey! Penzance gets its name from the location of the chapel of St Anthony that stood on the headland to the west of what became Penzance Harbour over a thousand years ago. Model Jean Shrimpton and cricketer Jack Richards each have a guest house here. Penzance was the birthplace of the famous chemist Sir Humphry Davy, who didn't have a guest house here, but worked on many scientific important discoveries. He's possibly best known as the inventor of the Miner's Safety Lamp, or Davy Lamp, and there's a statue of Davy at the top of Market Jew Street, near the house where he was born – which wasn't a guest house!

Heading past Penzance railway station situated right on the front, I found myself walking inside a kind of stone-curved sea wall. I came to a dead end and was lost for the second time today, ten minutes after the first time. Forced to retrace my steps, I managed not to get into a rage for once. I didn't really want to arrive back at the station shouting and screaming. Someone might report me. The men in white coats would come, preventing me from finishing the walk. For the umpteenth time, I did really hate walking again for that twenty minutes, and wouldn't have minded being arrested. At least I wouldn't be lost if that happened.

Finally back on track, I followed the sea wall by the railway line round the edge of the bay. Next destination Marazion, pronounced however you like! I walked on top of the wall to avoid the road and railway lines, but couldn't get down as it'd got higher without me noticing – pork council pigs, building it up like that without telling anybody! I had to jump from a great height, risking everything, but luckily all went well. The next section was great. A 4-mile gravely track, about 8 feet wide and, for a change, completely *flat*. This was the only level bit I could remember since Saunton

Sands in that awful gale. Quite a few holidaymakers were walking this stretch but I found myself motoring effortlessly, overtaking everyone in front of me on this wonderful flat path. I realised how fit I must've become. I felt turbocharged with no back pain. I enjoyed the next hour greatly. Approaching Marazion, some old derelict railway buildings and ancient carriages were 20 yards off to the left of the path, before the railway lines. I loved the way they looked but it seemed odd that they were allowed to exist at all. They were certainly not a beautiful site as far as most people would be concerned, but perhaps they belonged to the railway company who no longer had any use for them, but couldn't afford to modernise or convert them, or be bothered to knock them down. I hope they're given listed building status and left there indefinitely as they look great as they are to me and, no doubt, to many railway enthusiasts too. By the time I entered Marazion I was route-marching, doing at least 5 mph. I felt so good that I found it almost impossible to stop. Yet when spying an inviting sign off the path ahead, displaying "Cream Teas £2.99", I managed to force myself. This was the first cream tea of the whole walk, which seemed strange, as I'd walked through Somerset, North Devon, and three-quartes of Cornwall without finding so much as a single measly scone till now. This was remedied at last as I tucked into the large tasty treat whilst sitting at a table overlooking the splendid "St Mickey's Mount"!

A crew-cutted American adorned with large cameras asked me earlier, "Hey *you*, buddy! Where's that Saint Mick's Mountain or whatever it's called?"

What made it even better was that we were looking across the causeway, straight at it, bang in front of us, but he hadn't noticed it. I *loved* it!

I said, "See that massive black thing blocking out the light? Well that's it. But you've got the name slightly wrong." I added cheekily, "It's not called Saint Mick's Mountain, it's called Saint Mickey's Mouse!"

He gave me a quizzical look but I'm sure he believed me. I never got a photo of him, which is a pity, as I wanted one for the cover of this book. St Michael's Mount – its actual name – is a tidal island 400 yards off the Mount's Bay. I hung around taking in the view for a good hour before having to pull on the pack again, which felt much heavier after my long rest, despite my earlier efforts to lighten it. Up through the pretty but touristy village of Marazion with its pubs, galleries, and shops, I inevitably got lost again for a few minutes before finding the right path. More cliff walking now. Why couldn't it have stayed flat for a few more miles? I met several other holiday walkers and stopped to chat, as I tended to do as often as possible on the difficult ascents. I climbed gently again through woodland to a broad path. It began to level out above Prussia Cove when I came upon an unusual building, or rather buildings, as the property appeared to be bisected by the woodland path. It looked very "Arts & Crafts", simple and unfussy, but I wanted to find out what it was doing here in the woods and what was its history?

Ambling between the two "halves", I noticed a large wooden door partly open, allowing me to look into the building on my right to the seaward side. I pushed it slowly, half expecting an echoing creaking noise, à la Castle Dracula. No such sound emanated. Someone had kept this door well oiled. Inside was indeed totally Arts & Crafts and very beautiful, featuring a large room with a sizeable banqueting table. Stylish yet plain benches, coffers, carved cupboards and chairs, paintings or fabrics adorned the walls. Wow, what a pad (man)! I saw a man at the far end writing at a smaller table. He spotted me at the same time, making me feel like an intruder. Had I stumbled into somebody's home? I humbly apologised, explaining I'd seen the open door and was curious to know about this unusual place. He smiled, saying that many people felt the same and, much to my delight, he invited me in. We got chatting. Roger was about forty and another New Zealander. He explained that the house was called Porth-en-Alls, built in the early 1900s in the romantic Arts & Crafts style reminiscent of Lutyens (told yer). The house was listed and designed by a Philip Tilden in 1911 but never completed, owing to the Great War. In order to optimise the glorious sea views the design had resulted in an unusual arrangement whereby the main entrance is via the top floor, passed the bedrooms, descending to the living rooms on the middle floor and further rooms below. While obviously Neo-Elizabethan in design, the architect had managed to chuck in some of the latest structural developments of the day. The house is one of the earliest to use ferro-concrete beams. I spotted that immediately of course but didn't want to brag about it to Roger in case I made him feel inferior. The fixtures used were top quality and much of the original furniture remains to this day. Porth-en-Alls has a large garden and a private beach called King's Cove, about 20 yards below for the exclusive use of house residents. It's possible to swim and dive at all tides and to keep small boats or inflatables safely. Roger and several friends had rented the entire property for a couple of weeks every year for the past five years. They came for one holiday and liked it so much they returned every summer. I told Roger I liked everything about New Zealand, mentioning that one of my favourite rock bands were from Auckland.

When I said they were called the Mutton Birds, he replied, "That's incredible! Don McGlashon is a really good friend of mine."

McGlashon being their brilliant singer/songwriter. I almost fell to the flagstones in disbelief. I'd met Don too and chatted to him at a Mutton Birds gig in Bristol. Roger went on to tell me he'd been the president of a record company he'd formed in the 1980s called Flying Nun Records. I almost fell off the cliff at hearing this. Having had several record shops myself, I was quite familiar with Flying Nun. They were a good label who'd signed several of the top New Zealand bands. It was a real pleasure to meet and chat to this interesting guy. We discussed Crowded House (of course), Martin Phillips and the Chills, and many other NZ bands. As we chatted I sort of forgot that it was getting towards evening. Upon realising this I panicked, declaring I must rush off. He said I may be able to stay somewhere there if the others agreed – they were currently out sightseeing. I couldn't hang around though in case there wasn't any room for me, so we exchanged email addresses and numbers before I hurried off, down through the woods. I felt quite exhilarated at this chance encounter and thought how it is a small world. We must be the only two people within a 100-mile radius who know the wonderful Mutton Birds. Everyone should know them really cos they're brill, as are my really favourite band The Contrast, from Peterborough.

The terrain became much gentler, enabling me to make good time around the bay and over Kenneggy Sands. This region was the base for the notorious Carter family, big-time smugglers. They used all the tiny coves like Piskies Cove and Bessy's Cove to stash their booty until it was distributed. It was fascinating seeing these little remote beaches. After Hoe Point I was back on familiar territory. I was nearing Praa Sands where I'd stayed on a fab "Sun" holiday back in the 1990s – nineteen quid for the whole week, no questions asked, guv! I remembered that the chalet had been slightly run down. My "bedroom", situated behind the main door, was a cubby-hole in the wall, about the size of a sideways-on bathtub with a tiny mattress. After one night of agony in that I slept on the sofa for the rest of the week. It was better than a tent though. The pink evening glow over land and sea was so beautiful as I walked through an upmarket housing estate. When I came to the beach, Praa Sands itself, it occurred to me to pitch *on* it. Surprisingly there were no signs prohibiting anyone from doing anything whatsoever, so I pitched on some short grass in the open area about 40 yards from the sea. Soft sand existed beneath the grass, so the pegs weren't too stable. As the weather looked like staying fine I risked it anyway.

Apart from chatting with two surfers who were packing away, I saw nobody else. Lounging in the tent with a soothing cuppa, looking out over the harmless waves, I heard their gentle lapping on the shore. I was getting drowsy at 8 p.m. and nodded off to the tranquil sound of the sea.

Day 26: Friday 9 May

The night was not as good as the day had been. I slept badly as the sea was too loud! Must write to the council to complain about it when I get home. I woke sporadically amid dreadful nightmares. Each time I was either too hot or too cold. It had seemed an ideal place to camp the previous night but had turned out to be a bad choice. When I finally awoke around 9 a.m. I lay motionless for half an hour, incapable of getting out of the bag. I felt horribly weary and gruff. Eventually I needed to make a start and crawled out into the dull morning. It'd rained overnight, making the tent wet when I packed it away. This made me even more mardy than I was to start with as the pack would be even heavier now. As I pulled on my three-week-old boots, which by now looked about 100 years old, I noticed that the left one was falling apart. *Great!* Three weeks of agony and now, instead of moulding itself comfortably to my foot, it was going to give up the ghost instead. Thank you very bloody much! I ranted before groaning in despair. I haven't mentioned my feet for a few days because they're not there anymore! By "not there" I mean I can't feel them. Complete numbness from the ankles down is infinitely better than the agony experienced during the first three weeks. As I knelt, struggling with the rucksack zips, I became aware of a diminutive figure, passing from right to left across my line of vision 10 yards away, silhouetted against the sea and sky. In my zombie-like state I could barely distinguish the shape yet alone the gender. I did notice the head shape, the close cropped hair, and the gigantic rucksack, which looked equally as large as the figure carrying it. A tiny hand waved in my direction. I spluttered a croaky, disgruntled, "Morning!" The figure moved on, leaving me no wiser. It took an hour and a half before being ready to walk. After a lone cereal bar for breakfast I frustratingly trudged off at 10.30 a.m. shouting, "Useless boot! Useless git!"

It was a windier morning but the sun was trying to force its way out from behind the grey matter. I passed a crumbling engine house on the cliffs. Later I overtook the diminutive figure resting some way off the path. The weather started improving along with my mood. It never ceases to amaze me how I can feel like death on wheels, not to mention suicidal, yet when the sun appears an hour later everything looks rosy again and I feel fine. It's not always the case but generally I seem to end up feeling okay on most days. A mile or two before Porthleven I almost fell over a Scotsman, sitting on a big rock on the path, eating bread and cheese. A slight, balding figure, he was wearing full Scottish garb. He was a lovely old boy, well over seventy, and was walking Land's End to John o'Groats. He had a large hand-written sign on his pack to prove it too. He was hiking 30 miles a day! He only weighed about 7 stone but these wiry walkers have less weight to carry on their frames and are capable of monstrous physical feats of endurance. Bigger individuals, like yours truly, tend to struggle more. He'd been a lifelong backpacker and was unfazed by the immensity of his forthcoming trek. He was laidback and hilarious. Named Iain MacDonald, he was reminiscent of some character from an early 1950s film comedy, like the gentle Scottish tale, *The Bridal Path*, featuring Bill Travers. It seemed like Iain MacDonald had been plucked from that very film. I took to him immediately. He discussed his food rations at great length, explaining that he ate lots of bread and cheese. Another favourite "dish" of his was dry muesli with cheese, porridge (what a surprise), with guess what? Yep, right first time: cheese. I wondered how he could eat that all the time cos I couldn't. After a few minutes I walked on but he soon came running along behind me calling, "Hey, Overend Watts! Let's walk together for a while!" So we did.

He was a real upper, but all too soon we had to part company when

Porthleven came into sight. He was going to leave the coast and circumnavigate the town in order to press on. I, not possessing any muesli or cheese, wanted to eat and look round the town. I visited the gents' but failed to shave as there was no hot water. This was a bit worrying, having not shaved for five days, since The Farm B & B at Pendeen. I was trampy-looking now and I like to stay relatively tidy on the trail. Well you never know who you might bump into. Kylie or Danni Minogue, Michael Parkinson, a "cavity" of herons, the England cricket team, the Queen; you've got to be prepared at all times! I did wash, however, and rinsed some clothes out. I left feeling smarter and headed for the town centre. I bought a pasty and cakes at the bakers, some supplies and ice cream at a sizeable supermarket, where a nice-looking girl kept smiling at me in the queue. I reckoned I was all right here with no hurry to leave Porthleven. I could have a few days' rest. Suddenly I realised that a tall handsome chap less than half my age was behind me in the queue so that was that! Downcast, I took my grub onto the harbour and put it on a bench with my pack and went into a pub to get a beer. Two guys were perched on barstools but there was no sign of the barman. After five minutes I ran out to check on my gear outside, worried that the nice-looking girl and handsome young chap might conspire to nick my stuff to add insult to injury. Back inside the pub a very offish barman appeared and served me silently with a pint of lager-shandy. The blokes on stools sat there embarrassed at the icy silence. Unsurprisingly it was the most expensive pint (for 2003) of the entire trip, weighing in at a massive £2.70.

When I queried the price he shrugged, mumbling, "You should've had straight lager. It's the same price."

Thanks a bundle for telling me afterwards, mate. Not enjoying the tension, I left the ice-cold pub, taking my ice-cold shandy outside where the wind was now ice-cold too. I felt like going back to exchange the drink for a hot coffee but was too scared of the barman. I ate my pasty miserably, crouched uncomfortably behind the harbour wall, avoiding the wind. I'd also have to contend with the bloody ice cream I'd bought earlier when the weather was warm. I couldn't waste it so forced it down, wincing at the pain of every frozen mouthful. It made my teeth, throat, and neck hurt. I blamed that nice-looking girl for starting the downward slide twenty minutes earlier.

Porthleven is the most southerly port in the country, originally developed as a harbour of refuge, back in the days of sail. I left here much grimmer than when I'd arrived an hour before. I climbed up through the small streets veering east, studying the guidebook intently. It wasn't long before the inevitable happened: I was lost before getting out of Porthleven. A bloke appeared, walking in the opposite direction. As he was obviously a local, I accosted him before he could escape. They often tried running when they saw me looking at them, so the element of surprise was crucial in these kinds of situations. Trap them before they have time to think. In this case I wish I hadn't bothered. The conversation went something like this, but much longer:

Me: "Could you tell me if I'm on the correct lane for the coast path to Gunwalloe?"

Git: "I suppose you could go on a bit further if you want, but if I were you I'd, erm ... now let me think ... I know a shortcut, erm ... now let me think, erm, go back down the hill into Porthleven, take the second on the left – or is it, erm, straight on?"

Me: "Please, I want the coast path going eastwards."

Git: (ignoring me) "If you do a right – no, I tell a lie. I mean left, I think it is. Head inland for a mile or two, follow a stream – no, a pond, for erm, 2 miles-ish, passed a farm – or is it a church? Anyway, it's really nice there. There're herons too. You can get to Helston easily from there. You can't miss it. You like walking, don't you?"

Me: "No, I don't like walking. I loathe it. I don't want any shortcuts, streams, churches, farms, or ponds, no matter how 'really nice' they are. I hate them all. I can't stick herons either. I've seen billions of them since Minehead. They just stand there like boring statues. If you've seen one you've seen 'em all! Oh, and Helston is in the wrong direction. I want the coast path *eastwards*! It's that funny narrow, winding thing next to the sea. Do you know where it is or not?"

Git: "Well, erm, if you go back down the hill into Porthleven and, erm, turn left to this shortcu –"

Me: "– Get this straight, mate. I'm *not* going down any hill into any town. I've just climbed up from there! It's the *wrong way*! I don't want any shortcut." Shouting in his face: "I *want the bloody coastal path!* Surely you must know it?"

Git: "There's no coast path round here. I've lived here all my life, but if you go back down the h –"

Me: (wanting to punch him up the bracket) "– Aaarrrggghhh! *No!* Forget it! I'll find the ****** path myself!"

Git: (in a huff) "Well if you won't listen to me it'll be your own fault when you get lost. I won't be able to help you then."

Me: "You're *not* helping me! I'm already lost, you pillock! That's why I asked you and you're wasting my valuable time. You're hopeless! You're pointing in the opposite direction. I've had enough! I'm off! Thanks for **** all, mate!"

As I walked away he called benignly after me: "You could try turning right instead."

I ignored the imbecile. I skulked off eastwards, shell-shocked, shell-suited, in my shell, and, in a nutshell, in a rage. I only wanted a simple answer to a simple question. Surely this wasn't too much to ask? Obviously it was too much to ask. Was it *my* fault for not explaining my case clearly enough? No, it was *him*. It all boiled down to the fact that I hate people and they hate me.

50 yards up the road was a large sign for the coast path. I'd endured the most frustrating ten minutes of my whole life all for nothing. The tone was now set for the rest of the afternoon. I'd used up all my reserves of energy trying to communicate with that oaf. Now I felt physically and mentally weakened. I felt like packing it all in. This wasn't a common occurrence with me, but at that moment it'd have been so easy. Compounding my glumness now was the stricken boot. It was getting worse by the hour. The next sizeable town where I might be able to get new boots appeared to be Falmouth, maybe three days away. The toe of the boot was developing "crocodile's mouth syndrome". My sock even started poking out like a comedy black tongue. I soldiered on but the walking was boring and repetitive, up down, up down, through lots a small coves. That bloke was still bothering me too. How can you meet a lovely old chap like old Iain MacDonald one minute and a total tosser the next? I reasoned that it's all down to being on the same wavelength as someone, and also plain common sense with the ability to *listen*. Some people haven't got *any*. That bloke may well have been from another universe. There was no point of contact or any common ground between us. Maybe I should have just punched him up the bracket after all.

After heading up a winding road, passing by a grand peach-coloured nursing home on the top overlooking the sea, I chatted with two local lady walkers. No problems there and no need to thump either of them. By teatime the sky had taken on an ominous thundery quality, but the golden evening sun was also in evidence, behind the clouds, giving a fantastic translucent effect. My mood started changing to one of wonderment at the incredible light. It was still like this when I arrived at Mullion Cove, another lovely ancient harbour with two sea walls jutting out into the bay. Here I found the village shop/café, which was of course closed. The owner was doing jobs around the place. He sold me some supplies and made me a cuppa. He told me about the history of Mullion and we talked in the spooky "sunny blackness" before I set off on the steep climb out of the cove. I'd always wondered what the Lizard coastline was like, having never seen it previously. I wasn't disappointed.

Although the sky was blacker still, the sun was shining on the nearby black roofs, giving off their own spectacular reflections. JMW Turner could've captured it beautifully on canvas but the silly sod wasn't there. I was concerned in case of a sudden downpour but once on the top I walked on in a trance-like state through a kind of mystical landscape. I'd never experienced any conditions quite like these. It made for terrific walking even though I hate walking most of the time. Now well and truly on the Lizard Peninsula proper, the terrain was very rugged. High jagged cliffs and dark-green sea crashed below to my right. To my left a level grassy plain seemed to stretch inland for miles. By the time I reached Predannack Head there were no more buildings or signs of habitation – wonderful. Part of the large plain was a disused airfield. I could see overgrown concrete runways and discerned some rusted hulks in the distance. These were redundant aircraft that had been abandoned many years ago when their shelf life ran out. This all added to the ghostly experience, giving me an uncanny feeling of a sense of isolation and loneliness as I walked, but also of peace, tranquillity, and warmth. It's difficult to explain but everything became surreal. I was swallowed up by, but also at one with my desolate surroundings. All my senses were heightened. I came alive for the first time that day. I was the only soul for miles and it felt magical to be there at that particular moment. I was filled with a feeling of anticipation and excitement. It was undoubtedly one of the loneliest and best evenings of the whole journey.

I made good time for two and a half hours beyond Mullion, but felt spots of rain on my face at 8 p.m. and decided to camp in the wild before it bucketed down. I'd passed Vellan Head some miles back and could see more steep ascents and descents ahead. As I began one of these descents I spotted a funny green plateau about 20 feet square, 30 feet below me. It was near the cliff edge above Sandy Cove, appearing ideal if slightly precarious. I'd be okay as long as I didn't sleepwalk. I clambered down to it and pitched the tent with some wild sheep looking on. Wild? They were bloody furious! The rain was still spotting but the anticipated mighty downpour never came, which always annoys me when I've taken the trouble to pitch early. However, it'd been a long day with emotional highs and lows too – that b*****d bloke! – so I was ready to camp anyway. I certainly wouldn't find a lovelier or more remote spot than this, so I wasn't too annoyed on this occasion. After pitching, however, I was rather put out by the arrival of half a dozen long-horned cattle that began grazing around my tent, too close for comfort. The sheep had vacated the area. Too late to move now. I'd have to risk being trampled to death or dragged violently over the precipice by these large spiked herbivores. I tried to forget about them. The view out to sea was awesome (except I hate that word).

Now famished, I lay in the tent looking at it whilst first downing a chicken and veg cuppa soup, a "pornish casty", a "pike paw", a ham and coleslaw roll, along with an Oasis drink. For pudding, a giant-sized Snickers bar. This brought me back to that old Viz chestnut: is a giant-sized Snickers bar a normal-sized Snickers bar to a giant? Or indeed, is it a fun-sized Snickers bar to a massive giant? By the same token is a normal-sized Snickers bar a giant-sized Snickers bar to a dwarf? Or is a normal-sized Snickers bar only a fun-sized Snickers bar to an exceptionally tall dwarf? This riddle could be applied to *every* size of Snickers bar compared to *every* size of human being that exists! If you were miraculously able to decipher it, you'd have to start all over again with every other type of chocolate bar in the world compared to every size of human being in the world and possibly every variety of animal in the world too, including dinosaurs, whales, and fleas. I wish I could give you readers the answer here but I'm afraid it's quite beyond my capabilities. It needs Professor Stephen Hawking to do the mathematics. I'll mention it to him after he's worked out the how the world began, the meaning of life, and whether God exists or not. After pondering on the subject for half an hour and getting no closer to the answer (Snickers bars, not God), I gave up and wrote up my journal and some postcards purchased in Mousehole. I was in the bag by dusk and asleep pretty soon. Slept well too and luckily didn't sleepwalk either. I did dream about tall dwarfs and short giants for a time.

Day 27: Saturday 10 May

It was 7 a.m. when I awoke to the sound of gentle rain on the flysheet – oh no! Happily it soon stopped. Shortly after I felt the warming rays of the sun on my face through the nylon skin – yippee! I love that sensation as it usually bodes well for the day ahead. I'm not at my best in the morning but I felt good for once. The long-horn threat had come to nothing and when I opened the flap there wasn't a single animal of any variety in sight. The sea was a glorious shade of Mediterranean blue. My superb view of it was bordered on both edges by the sides of the green valley. As I took a photo, a large ocean-going liner appeared in the frame, a mile out at sea. I took some video footage too. Definitely one of my better camping spots. I love those photos. I packed away cheerfully and whistled some of 'The Lark Ascending', by Vaughan Williams, but screwed up the solo violin bit; my whistle going all squiggly when it went up high. I gave up and did a fine rendition of 'Strawberry Fields Forever' (by Vaughan Williams) instead.

I left in beautiful weather, still whistling gaily. The terrain was strenuous again but I was enjoying myself. After several steep rocky ups and downs I met a chap called Torsten on a cliff top. Despite his name he was a very nice guy. He and his wife Julie were strolling round, waiting for the café at Kynance Cove to open at 10.30 a.m. I'd heard about this café and was looking forward to breakfasting there. It was only about 9.45 a.m. so I slowed down a bit. It was nice ambling for a change instead of pacing it out, especially in this area in this gorgeous weather. I saw the huge rocks off Kynance Cove ahead with the brilliant sunlight bouncing off them. You can't get much better than that, I thought.

Before the final descent to Kynance I looked way down and saw the small white café. I recognised the diminutive, close-cropped figure from Praa Sands coming out of the front door. Another walker had told me he'd met a tiny Canadian lady who was doing the SW Coast Path alone like me. I deduced this *must* be her. I watched her struggle to put on her enormous pack, thinking she had some guts. I began climbing down, thinking I might introduce myself and maybe have a cuppa with her, but she'd disappeared long before I got halfway down. It struck me, as she'd come out of the café door, it may have opened early. According to my watch there was forty minutes to go before 11 a.m. When I arrived the curly-haired manager saw me and invited me in, even though they weren't officially open yet. When he led me into the luxurious kitchen to fill my water bottles I could hardly believe my eyes. It was bigger than the café itself for starters. All was stainless steel and spotless. Very reassuring if you're going to eat. He was a baker who prepared and cooked all the food on the premises. I was well impressed. He explained that the Kynance Café first opened in 1929 and had, until recently, relied on spring water and a generator for power. When the café became the property of the National Trust in 1999, mains water and electricity were installed and the place was completely renovated.

Having the café all to myself I picked the choice table, right in the window, overlooking the cove itself. Wow! Kynance boasts several small islands of spectacular multi-coloured "serpentine" granite rock, with stacks and arches hidden amongst the towering cliffs. The rocks are called serpentine because they resemble the mottled-green skin of the serpent – or "Lizard", hence the name – having been polished by the sea over thousands of years. These predominantly green and red rocks are distinctive to Kynance Cove and the Lizard Peninsula. I saw nothing else like them anywhere else. Stone-turning shops in the nearby village of the Lizard turn the serpentine into interesting ornamental shapes and objects. Another outstanding feature of the cove itself is that at high tide a sandy beach facing the water on two sides and a small island – that becomes a tidal island – are cut off. The cove became popular in the early Victorian-era, with many distinguished visitors, including Alfred Lord Tennyson, appreciating its beauty. That guy certainly got around, didn't he? It's amazing he had any time left to write poetry.

A huge brown Labrador suddenly appeared at my table, momentarily scaring me by barking loudly, bringing the owner running out from the kitchen. The dog calmed down immediately. No further noises emanated from him afterwards. His name was Charlie and he sat staring balefully at me until my food arrived. He occasionally lifted his paw, hoping it'd lead to him getting something to eat. I'd ordered two bacon and tomato baguettes and a pot of tea, out of which I got four mugs. The food was really tasty. Charlie thought so too. So tasty in fact that I ordered some home-made shortbread and another pot of tea from which I got four and a half mugs this time.

Between courses I wrote the rest of my postcards, with Charlie looking on, just in case. He finally gave up and next time I saw him he was sitting outside with his paw up to some tourists having a snack at a table on the small lawn. No wonder he was so huge. I got a lovely photo. I stayed at that café for ninety minutes. It was too great to leave. It was noon and quite a few people were milling around now, so in the end I made the effort and scrambled over some low rocks that were being washed over as the tide was coming in. I climbed up the rocks, out of the cove. I decided this was my favourite since Penberth. I chatted to some elderly walkers sitting on a bench through the large car park at the top. This must've been where I'd parked on previous holidays but had never been down to the sea before. I could soon see the lighthouse and buildings on the end of the Lizard a mile away, with the obsolete lifeboat station at the base of the low cliffs. There were several brief encounters with the tourists on this fine day. Whilst photographing the old lifeboat house a young honeymooning couple came along. We struck up a conversation, laughing for ten minutes before going our separate ways. Their names were Ian and Suzanne from London. I wished them a long and happy marriage. Walking off, I thought "ships that pass in the night", feeling sad that we'd never meet again. I often got this feeling with particularly lovely people.

Much as I was tempted, I didn't stop for more tea in the Lizard café, even though it was an old haunt of mine from bygone days. I didn't want to get bogged down by stopping too often. It was lively there and I enjoyed the atmosphere as I passed through on the path. There were many hellos and suchlike from the numerous visitors enjoying themselves in the sunshine. Looking out to sea, I was standing on the southernmost tip of Great Britain, after standing on the westernmost tip a few days ago. It was from here that the first sighting of the Spanish Armada took place on the 29 July 1588. Also, the biggest rescue in the RNLI's history occurred here on 17 March 1907, when the 12,000-ton liner *SS Suevic* hit the Maenheere Reef near Lizard Point. In strong gales and dense fog, RNLI lifeboat volunteers rescued 456 passengers, including seventy babies. Crews from The Lizard, Cadgwith, Coverack and Porthleven rowed out repeatedly for sixteen hours to rescue all on board. Six silver RNLI medals were later awarded, two to Suevic crew members.

I passed the impressive Youth Hostel; the most luxurious in the country, formerly a hotel. Not that I'd be staying in it. I passed by the massive scary, sea-facing foghorns on my left – none of that wimpy digital "Pharos Marine Omnidirectional Electric Omitter" rubbish here. I prayed they wouldn't go off as I hurried by them. I would've probably got blasted off the cliffs into the sea if they had. I got by safely, leaving the crowds behind, deciding it'd be a good idea to wear my shorts for the first time. Why I hadn't done so before in all that hot weather beats me. I stopped on a quiet section of the path and took the shorts out of my pack, realising why I hadn't worn them before. They were tight luminous green and black Bermuda shorts. It hurt my eyes to look at them. I'd bought them because they were on sale for a quid (twenty years ago) and thought they might do for in the garden. They'd even proved too gruesome for that purpose when I was alone. For some reason I'd deemed that they'd be suitable for this trek and stuffed them into my pack before leaving. It was too late for vanity. I struggled to get my trousers off and pulled the shorts on before anyone appeared on the path and screamed. My legs were hideously white, a condition that was accentuated more by the bright sun, giving them an almost translucent green quality, not quite matching the shorts. I'd feel like a total fool until they browned.

As people came towards me I tried to avert their gaze by pointing out to sea, saying stuff like, "Look at that yacht! Magnificent, isn't it?" Or if there was nothing out there to comment on: "Look at that horizon! Glorious, isn't it? Wow! You missed that dolphin." It seemed to work.

The masses of wild spring flowers were incredible around this part of the Lizard. Some even grew down the vertical cliff faces towards the water. I almost went over while leaning to take pictures. Whatever happened to my vertigo? That's two phobias gone now: vertigo and spiders. I've been fine with arachnids ever since I managed to hold that huge tarantula, named Diana Ross, at Tropiquaria, in north Devon a few years back. I came to the Devil's Frying Pan, a large collapsed cave on the right of the path, with a thin rock arch above it. On its seaward side there was no lard or giant sausages sizzling in it though. Round the corner was the tiny but fabulous olde-worlde village of Cadgewith with it small beach, fishing boats, quaint pubs, and white-washed thatched cottages scattered about. This place had got the lot, appearing to be about as perfect a Cornish fishing village as you could want. It was bustling with sightseers, but I couldn't complain, being a kind of sightseer myself, albeit one of a superior nature! Fishermen were pushing their boats down the beach to go fishing. I spotted a freshwater stream winding down from the valley, trickling over the sand and shingle beach, into the sea. Despite its idyllic look, I got the impression that Cadgwith was still a real working village with these fishing boats still going out every day, as they must have done for hundreds of years, not for long-gone pilchards anymore, but for crab, lobster, mackerel, shark, and mullet. All round the cove were reminders of the past. Pilchard cellars, winches, the old lifeboat house, apparently used until 1963, memorials to much-loved fishermen who'd lost their lives at sea, are all carefully preserved, yet somehow still form part of everyday life. I stopped by a small table outside a café, glancing at the handwritten blackboard. It read, "Crab sandwiches, prawn baguettes," etc.

As I was taking it all in, a well-built blonde of about thirty-five came out to clear the table and said curtly, in a strong Cornish voice, "You want something?"

I asked politely, "Have you got any crab sandwiches, please?"

Rolling her eyes with boredom, she said, "What's it say on that board?"

I tried to say, "I thought you might have run out of crabs," but it fell on stony ground.

She said, "Do you want one, then?"

I stuck to an uncomplicated, "Yes, please."

The crab sandwich was incredible. The sign outside said "Sarah's" and when I asked if she was Sarah she didn't roll her eyes. Although she was gruff, there was a kind of warmth about her too. We had a brief chat during which she gave me directions out of the village. I liked her a lot. I've since seen her on Rick Stein's TV programme, talking about Cadgewith crabs, on which she wasn't quite so gruff. After the sandwich I quite fancied an ice cream, so went into a bar-cum-café sort of place. Whilst ordering a

Roskilly's choc and strawberry combination cone, I became aware of raucous laughter coming from a nearby table. Half a dozen couples in their early thirties were sitting round a big table drinking and were all looking at *me!* When they saw me looking back the laughter stopped abruptly and they looked away. As I took my ice cream and paid for it I became aware of muted sniggering from the same table. I looked round again. The sniggering ceased and they looked away again. I thought, What the bloody hell? Suddenly it hit me: they were laughing at my luminous green shorts and my luminous white legs – b*****s! I wanted to crawl into a hole and die, but did the next best thing by silently skulking, like a scolded dog, out of the place in total embarrassment with my ice cream between my legs. I didn't look great in my shorts but this really brought home that I must look totally ridiculous – not a nice feeling. Should I change back into my army strides, I pondered? No! Sod the lot of 'em! What a bunch of ignorant pigs they were. If they'd been fifteen-year-olds I could've understood the giggling, but they weren't. They hadn't even the common decency to curb it until I'd left. I'm going to carry on regardless, stiff upper lip and all that. Surely my legs would be tanned in a couple of days in this weather. The cotton shorts might fade a bit in direct sunlight, especially with a couple of hot water washes to aid the process. I became angry, wanting to go back in and have a go at them, but that would've been acknowledging that they'd got to me, so better to walk away.

After finishing my ice cream on a bench I'd calmed down. After heading into the small shop for some supplies, and then north through whitewashed cottages back to the coastal path, I passed several tourists, none of whom laughed at me or appeared to notice my shorts or legs. That was the only unpleasant experience I had regarding the latter for the rest of the walk. I really got the momentum going that afternoon, eating up the miles rapidly in the summery conditions. On a lofty cliff top above Black Head I bumped into three great characters who reminded me of *Three Men in a Boat*, by Jerome K. Jerome. The first thing that struck me was that they got on like a house on fire, having a wonderful time hiking together. The second thing was that they were all loony! They were talkative and there was much humorous verbal sparring between the four of us. One was a journalist, one a lawyer, and the other a doctor. I loved their exhilarating presence. I mentioned earlier about the importance of wavelengths, well we were definitely all on the same one. I mentioned it was going to be my fifty-sixth birthday in a few days.

The lawyer said, "Wow! You're in great nick for your age." When I pulled a miserable face, he asked, "What's wrong with that?"

"I'll tell you what's wrong with it. *You* said it!" Pointing to the doctor: "I'd be a lot happier if *he* had said it!"

We all laughed. They were fascinated by my long trek and asked numerous *sensible* questions about it. I enjoyed answering them as they were so enthusiastic. They wished they had time to do the whole lot too.

After fifteen minutes we shook hands vigorously and said our cheerios. As a parting shot they asked how long it'd take to get to Cadgewith where they'd booked lodgings for the night. When I said it was about two and a half hours away they were horrified, believing they were much closer. After they recovered from the shock they started laughing again.

The journalist said, "Come on, you wimps! Last one to Cadgewith pays for dinner!"

As I looked back at them they were chattering and chortling as they walked south. "I told you it was 8 miles, you dolt!"

"Don't you 'you dolt' me, you large-bodied nincompoop!"

"Oh, leave him alone, you bald-headed coot!" the doctor chipped in.

Seeing their close companionship made me feel lonely for a split second but I walked on enriched by our jovial exchange.

I passed Chynhalls Point and soon covered the short distance to Coverack. Although it was only early evening, it was like a ghost town as I followed the road around the bay, through the village. The sun was setting, bathing all around me with its deepening-red glow. I met a mother and daughter out having an evening stroll. They said a café was a bit further on. I perceived there was a distinct lack of anywhere open. Rather disconcerting, as I'd eaten most of the Cadgewith grub. When I spotted the café it was shut too. I noticed a chap messing about by the side door. When I accosted him he offered to flog me a couple of pasties to keep me going. That would keep the wolf from the tent flap tonight.

Coverack appeared to be a larger fishing village. The guidebook stated it was noted for its water sports, including windsurfing, sailing, and diving. Not far inland was Goonhilly Downs, where stands the famous BT satellite earth station. Somewhere nearby was a Youth Hostel, but I was wary of them. Not wishing to share a room with strangers, I didn't bother looking for it. I sauntered out of Coverack, intent on finding a camping patch within the next half-hour, as the red light was turning grey before fading. At the end of the village I caught up with an attractive woman of about forty, named Christine. She was walking her white Scotty dog. We chatted as we walked. She lived in Pembridge, not far from me, and was on holiday with her semi-invalid husband who, unable to walk, was back at their rented cottage. No! Nothing happened if that's what you filthy beasts are thinking! We're not all like *you*! We got on well and chatted away without realising that the little doggy had vanished.

Christine shouted in alarm: "Angus! Angus! Come here, Angus!"

After a couple of minutes we decided to separate to search for him, when suddenly he came bursting through the undergrowth with something vile in his mouth. We couldn't get it off him, and didn't want to really, but he soon dropped whatever it was in the long grass and scurried ahead again, sniffing the ground as he went looking for something even viler. We continued to chat and laugh again until we realised, in horror, that he'd done another runner. Christine called out again and again. After he failed to materialise after a few minutes she really started to panic.

"What am I going to do? This is terrible! I know he's gone forever!"

As if on cue, he came belting out the trees, carrying one of them! Christine was relieved, as was I. He was a loveable little fellow, despite his antics. This same pattern was to continue for a further twenty minutes with his absences becoming longer and our panics getting worse each time. When it eventually became too unbearable we said our goodbyes and she turned back for Coverack. I hurried on, realising I'd virtually blown it now – regarding somewhere decent to camp, that is. Only ten minutes of daylight remained, so, as "Cheggers can't be boozers" again, I pitched on the first bit of flat grass I discovered. It was a small field, about 50 yards long, 10 yards wide, adjacent to the beach. I looked on the ground for signs of animals but could see none. I also noted that the only way in or out was via two stone stiles, one at either end. It looked ideal, apart from the sound of the waves. Once inside the tent I "cooked" a cream of vegetable cuppa-soup, which I devoured with my two pasties. It was rounded off with a pile of milk chocolate. Well, why not? I'll walk off the calories tomorrow. This was one great advantage of the strenuous nature of this long walk. As previously mentioned, I could eat *anything* I fancied, yet still lose weight.

As I prepared to baton down the hatches for the night I was aware of water being everywhere. What the hell? It took a minute before I found the culprit. My platypus water bladder had sprung a leak somehow. I may have caught it in a rucksack zip when squeezing in all my supplies at Cadgewith. I mopped up the spillage with my wonder towels and all was soon okay again. Luckily I'd a spare with me and no harm had been done. I managed not to flip my lid for once. I was too tired anyway. It had been another good day.

Day 28: Sunday 11 May

I was awoken by a deafening bellowing noise about an inch from my head! In a terrified zombie-like state I pulled back the flap to reveal a bloody great black bovine bonce. Its large pointy horns were inches from my face and huge eyes stared at me. The monster raised his head and bellowed again, obviously not happy about my presence. The feeling was mutual. The morning air was filled with bellowing from every direction. I peered round the massive black obstacle to see at least twenty more cattle homing in on me. It looked like curtains this time. How the hell had they got into the field? Surely they weren't brainy enough to climb the stone stiles? I closed the flap and hid inside. I heard the stomping, panting, and bullish excitement outside as they surrounded my shelter. I've never been afraid of cattle when hiking amongst them, but this was different. A mate of mine had almost been killed when his tent had been trampled whilst carp fishing on a lake. His frying pan had been crushed like a piece of silver foil by hooves. Now eighty hooves were about to do the same thing to me. If I'd been religious I would've prayed. In fact I did anyway just in case there's a God after all. As I hurriedly packed I noticed all had gone quiet. Gingerly opening the flap, no sign of the beasts were apparent. They'd vanished like Angus the night before. I got out, observing that they'd gone, but how and where? This puzzled me, as I could see a fair distance in every direction. Maybe Scotty (or Angus) had beamed them up or was it all a horrible nightmare. As I packed away feeling lousy, I reasoned that a local farmer must have spotted my little tent parked in his private field, which had got his dander up, so he decided to punish me by letting in his biggest, wildest bull and a load of cows, allowing events to take their course. He must've removed them by a secret gate after he'd seen me scared out of my wits. I wouldn't be camping there again, would I? So job done! I left feeling very billy goat gruff.

Easy flat walking began proceedings, with a gentle climb through the massive grey quarry on Lowland Point, with loads of sheds – I like sheds. I've got three at home – dormant cranes, and large machinery strewn around. Warning signs about blasting and not straying from the path were apparent. Being Sunday it was silent. Any other day would be a deafening hive of industry. It was an okay morning weather-wise, if somewhat grey. The coast was not so steep here and I was looking forward to reaching Port Hallow later. That would be the exact halfway point of the trip. Before that I'd be passing The Manacles, the notoriously dangerous rocks a mile off the coast where numerous ships had foundered over the centuries.

A mile beyond the quarry a SWC Path marker pointed inland, away from the coast, which seemed unnatural to me. I came to a halt, examining the options. The obvious thing to do was to ignore the sign and climb down the low cliff, cross the sandy beach for half a mile, and climb up to the coast path like I'd done on many occasions. Scanning the beach I saw that it became very rocky a few hundred yards in. Maybe there'd be no way through these rocks. I spotted a man with a dog below walking across the sand from the rocky area. There must be a way through if he's done it, I mused. I climbed down the narrow path, onto the beach. The man and dog had disappeared but I could see a row of fresh footprints in the damp sand. I followed the tracks in the opposite direction knowing they'd lead to a route through the rocks. The low cliffs 30 yards to my left were approximately 30 feet high. The sea was about 30 yards to my right.

After a five-minute walk I came to the start of the rocks, but instead of seeing footprints heading into them, they turned right, heading towards the water. I followed them to the water's edge. They turned right again and back in the direction I'd come from. It hit me that man and dog had been on a large circular stroll and hadn't gone through the rocks at all! My language at this point was not pleasant. I kicked out at an innocent piece of driftwood, which did no good at all, also doing nothing to improve that state of my left boot. Not wanting to walk back to where I'd started, I decided to climb over the rocks. At first they weren't too large but within a few minutes they became massive. After a twenty-minute struggle, during which time I'd only travelled about 300 yards, I saw only higher, larger rocks ahead. I was fighting a losing battle and turned back in fury. Climbing back over the same rocks, I noticed they were being washed over by waves. The tide was coming in rapidly. It'd take at least twenty-five minutes to get back to the end of the beach from here. It occurred to me, in horror, that I may not make it! I looked at the low cliffs, now on my right, and scrambled over the rocks to get to them. Once there I attempted to climb my way out of trouble, but the unsympathetic vertical rock face with a 45-lb. pack proved too much. I gave up after five minutes, aware I'd have to beat the incoming tide if I were to get out of this alive. Trying not to panic, I scrambled back as quickly as possible on the now slippery rocks. One false move and I could fall into a crevice. I finally made it to the beach. With only an 8-foot-wide strip of sand left I ran that last 400 yards and stepped with great relief on to the narrow path that led to the cliff top. My heart was pounding. It'd been a close shave. Exhausted, and in a bad mood, I rested at the top, feeling foolish for having taken such a risk. You should never underestimate the sea. I didn't ever again. I also cursed that man and his dog for misleading me. It was all their fault. I took the path inland as directed. I understood now why it did this.

The village of Porthoustock was deserted as I entered it. I spotted a little stone-built gents'. I decided to do my ablutions seeing as it was a Sunday morning. Having not shaved for almost a week this was to be a priority. Shaving and washing hair were always the trickiest acts to perform in public toilets. The former because there was rarely a hot water tap or mirror, the latter for the same reasons, plus the added difficulty of stooping awkwardly over a tiny sink, usually with no plug, and unavoidably splashing water everywhere. It could also be embarrassing if anyone came in while I was in mid-rinse with no shirt on. Tongues could wag. With nobody about I lit my tiny gas stove to boil enough water to shave and also for a cuppa while I was about it. While this was happening I washed my hair and had an all-over scrub. Halfway through, the door opened, almost knocking me over. Two blokes in wetsuits came in for a wizzle. I quickly pulled on my top and apologised for my gear being spread out all over the tiny room. Within minutes about a dozen more blokes in wetsuits arrived and the place was heaving. A laugh was had by all and they told me they'd been diving on wrecks off the Manacles. I asked about treasure, "skellingtons", Davy Jones's Locker, etc., and got some interesting replies. Once they'd left I noticed my gas cylinder had run out, forcing me to shave and make my cuppa from lukewarm water. Although peckish, I didn't bother to eat any cereal bars, as I'd been told there was a superb café in Porthallow.

I felt a bit better as I progressed, until it suddenly struck me that while I'd been panicking to stay alive earlier, I'd missed seeing The Manacles. I was gutted. No way was I going back now though. I passed another classy-looking hotel that boasted teas, coffees, and lunchtime meals. It looked inviting yet expensive so I walked on. I was starving by the time I arrived in Porthallow. I saw the café and immediately realised that it no longer existed! The sign was still there but piles of old furniture was strewn about inside the redundant building. There wasn't much choice of a pub and if they didn't serve food I'd be knackered. After opening the door of The Five Pilchards – a respectable-looking old pub – I was aware of manly laughter. This ceased abruptly the second I became visible to the half-dozen or so guys at the bar. Apart from them the place was empty. These locals continued to glare at me as if I was from another planet. I shuffled towards the bar where they sat.

The landlord, who'd been chatting with them, said coldly, "Can I help you?"

I felt like leaving but was in a dilemma with the café being gone. I asked if they did food. When he said they did I ordered a pint, grabbed a menu, and retired to a table round the corner, as far away as possible from this ice-cold atmosphere. As I sat down there was a burst of deafening laughter from the bar, obviously at my expense. It reminded me of the film *Straw Dogs*. It was upsetting, as I'd done nothing to antagonise them. I didn't look particularly offensive either, as my lurid shorts were in the pack, it being a cooler day. I never understand why people have to behave like that. Okay, they may not like tourists, but surely there's no need to intimidate them. They were bullies, but I wasn't scared, just saddened. Tourists or Grockles, as we're called, bring much needed money to Cornwall, but some don't care about that. Besides, a harmless backpacker like me is only passing through, appreciating the beauty of their land, not buying up loads of property or starting a business that could wipe them out. I was an older guy and presented no kind of threat to them. In my experience the majority of Cornish people are wonderful and have been very kind to me, but these isolated pockets do exist and are very unpleasant. Surveying the menu my heart sank at the prices. Once again I really had no choice but to eat here. I kicked myself for not checking out the classy hotel. It couldn't have been worse than this. I plumped for chicken and chips but didn't want to go to the bar to order it. Fortunately the landlord appeared with my pint, and now, out of sight and earshot of his compatriots, was more genial. I got the feeling he felt embarrassed by their behaviour, but was in a tricky position, caught between a rock and a hard place, like me earlier on that grim beach. When the meal came it was average, just about conforming with the trades description act in that it was indeed chicken and chips. Sadly though, that's all it was; a mound of chips with a piece of chicken on top, with no peas, vegetables, roll, salad, or even a measly sprig of parsley. I ate it with no seasoning as I couldn't face another visit to the bar to get it. I ate my banoffie pie glumly too. Even my favourite pudding couldn't cheer me up. Instead of being chuffed at being halfway I sank into a depressed state, not knowing if I had the will to continue. It'd been a tough day of downs and further downs right from the second when that huge black shape woke me up. I caught the landlord as he passed and paid the bill. It was £14.00, about a fiver more than it was worth.

I left by the side door and looking back at the hanging sign, said to myself, "That's the first and last time I'll ever go in there."

Back on the path again the grey-blue clouds were threatening rain, but there was some sun too, so I wasn't unduly worried. There were a couple of light showers on the way to Nare Point but nothing drastic. I felt slightly more optimistic by the time I got there. I was greeted by the sight of some wild ponies grazing in the low shrubbery. I spotted a tiny one barely a few days old sticking close to its mother. It was no bigger than a collie dog. I managed to get some video of the beautiful little creature without disturbing it. Sights like this always cheer me up. The view from the tip of this low peninsular was stupendous. Straight ahead I could see Rosemullion Head across the Helford estuary a couple of miles away. It'd take 10 miles of walking to get there. I'd first have to zigzag west to east four times, along the south bank of Gillan Creek, back east again to Dennis Head, back west again, up the wide expanse of the Helford river itself, take a ferry from Helford village to the other side in order to walk east to Rosemullion Head. A very tricky and frustrating bit of coast to negotiate; beautiful yet daunting, seeing it spread out all around me. Some people might cheat here, but not me, even though I wanted to. I'm *British*, for God's sake! Before setting off west inland, I took in the view to the north-east, where I'd be travelling over the next week or so. I could see the Roseland Peninsula with the dark bulk of the Dodman beyond.

As I turned inland to get around Gillan Creek, it began raining, heavier this time. Out came the waterproofs. It was short-lived, so the uncomfortable items were quickly removed. I soon ran out of path though, owing to the tide being in, and was forced to climb an extra 2 miles, steeply up a field of long wet grass, going back south again. I grew angry at getting lost through no fault of my own. It took a huge amount of energy to climb in what I knew was the wrong direction. The chest-high wet grass made it almost impossible. Luckily nobody was around to hear the screaming. On the top of a ridge I came to a lane where I turned right to correct myself. I came to a sign that read, "Manaccan 1 Mile". I could easily get across to Helford from here but I'd be missing out Dennis Head, which I couldn't bring myself to do, knowing I'd regret any cheating later. I ignored it and took the lane back east to Dennis Head. I passed several cars parked on the edge of the lane and saw a sign saying "Garden open teas". I was tempted to go in but, still feeling grim, didn't think I could be sociable with the locals. On the way to St Anthony I found a Citizen wristwatch on the path near a puddle, not an expensive one but it was working. I could hardly leave it there, not having seen one person since Porthallow. It was doubtful that I'd find the owner on the path. It'd hardly be worth handing it in at Falmouth – the next town – as it was so far away, so it looked like I'd gained a watch. Ten minutes later I realised I'd lost my spectacles – the ones I'd had since the start and really loved. That's karma for you! It began raining. The dreaded waterproofs had to be donned again. I'd *really* hated walking today and it was only 5 p.m. The showers were over by the time I got to the small beach café at St Anthony. I was the sole customer. I bought a white chocolate Magnum – my least favourite but that's all they had – and a coke for a change. I spent five minutes wrapping duct tape round the toe section of my left boot. The wet had caused it to "crocodile" even more. It'd only be a temporary measure but unless a proper repair could be done soon I'd be walking barefoot. The lady there was friendly and helped me with directions before I set off for Helford. I felt worn out, owing to the emotional and physical hardships of the day.

The woodland walking along the south bank of the river was beautiful, and the rain was gone, cheering me up slightly. After 2 miles I turned south again to get round the little creek before Helford. It was all overhanging trees and tiny secret creeks, all beautiful and very Daphne Du Maurier-ish. I began thinking about stopping soon. I'd really had enough and the weather was still unpredictable. On the edge of the village I found a phone box – it must be fate. As I couldn't go any further or face camping, I went inside and pulled out my guidebook. Under B & Bs I found a Mrs J. Davies at Pengwedhen. Twenty-two notes sounded good to me. Mrs J. Davies answered my call in person. When I asked about vacancies she seemed uncertain. After a short conversation, during which I said I was desperate and would sleep anywhere, she said she'd find a space for me. She sounded like a lovely woman. I thanked her and, after I got rough directions, said I'd be there in twenty minutes. The first thing that struck me about Helford village was that it was posh; very posh. In fact it was far too posh for the likes of me! Nobody was about as I sauntered through taking it all in. It was hard to believe that this sleepy place was once an important port with trading ships unloading large quantities of French rum, tobacco, and lace on its quays. The Ship Ahoy looked inviting. I tried the door but it was locked. At 6.30 p.m. it was too early for a swift half. As I walked away a chap came from around the side. I asked if he knew where the B & B was. He told me it was 400 yards away and said it was a bit tricky to find, pointing in its general direction.

Within one minute of setting off towards the harbour I was lost. I kept trying different lanes and footpaths, all of which were wrong. I retraced my tired steps each time. It's bad enough getting lost under normal circumstances but when you're dead on your feet and grumpy to boot, it really is terrible, like one of those nightmares where you're running but standing still, unable to get anywhere. I was getting frustrated when I saw a lovely detached house on the lane like a fairy tale cottage with little arched windows, surrounded by trees. I knocked on the door to ask for directions, struggling to keep my cool. When it opened I was amazed to see the lovely lady who'd served me in the café at St Anthony two hours earlier. I felt better immediately. We had a laugh about having to get directions from her again even if it meant tracking her down and knocking on her door. I asked if she knew where Pengwedhen was. She said it was next door and I'd love it there. 30 yards down the lane I found the gate from which a path led up through a lovely garden. The house was hidden away at the top. Arriving there I saw a beautiful 1930s "bungalow" ringed by trees. Half a dozen good-looking people were laughing and drinking cocktails whilst sitting on a large decking area, overlooking the Helford estuary and harbour way below. It was a spectacular view down over woodland. Mrs J. Davies got up and came over. I introduced myself complete with trail dust.

She said, "Call me Judy," and made me feel very welcome. She took me to my room, which was genuine art deco and cosy. "Why don't you leave your stuff here and come join us for a drink on the patio?"

Even though I was knackered I couldn't resist an invitation like that. Ten minutes later, after a quick wash and brush up – thank goodness I'd shaved that morning – I was sitting down hobnobbing with the party, admiring that view. Judy had made a pot of tea especially for me. I drank it, punctuated with sips of brandy. The atmosphere was convivial. I was introduced all round and became the focus of attention for a while as they plied me with questions about my trip, not to mention more brandy. It turned out they were all sailing friends of Judy and her husband Nigel. Only one couple was staying apart from me and they were still out. As I sat relaxing in comfort in this splendid place with this friendly crowd it all suddenly seemed a far cry from the rest of my day. It was surreal again. Until now I'd probably had the second or third most miserable time since I'd started. I couldn't begin to convey to everyone how awful it'd been, and didn't want to either, as it may have put a damper on the fun. I made jokes about my misfortunes, saying I really hated walking, but don't think they took me seriously.

At one point someone said, "You see that huge yacht down there? It belongs to Roger Taylor, Queen's drummer."

Someone added, "He often visits Helford. He's supposedly a decent guy."

I couldn't resist saying, "Yes, he is a great guy."

They all looked at me in astonishment and said, "You know him?"

"Oh yeah," I replied cockily. "Queen used to be our support group."

Their eyes came out on stoppers and someone said, "Well who the hell are *you*, then?"

Too deep in to extricate myself now I started laughing and said, "Don't get too excited! You've probably never even heard of my band."

When I told them the name was Mott The Hoople, most of them *had* heard of us. Nigel seemed quite impressed, which led to me getting yet another drink! One of the ladies had been an early member of Pan's People. Our paths had never crossed until now but we'd met some of the same music biz crowd in the old days. Nigel said that Hugh Cornwell, the ex-Stranglers' front man, had stayed in my room for a few days the previous year. I said that was far more preferable than someone like Joe Dolce of "Shut Up-a-Your Face" fame staying in it, in which case I would've demanded another room! After an hour or two the guests left. I chatted to Nigel and Judy for a while. Their amazing home was owned by the National Trust, of which Nigel had been a long-serving officer. It'd been built from scratch in 1926 by an old colonel, who, having retired from the army in India, and seeing the potential, bought up an old sloping potato field with a great view on which he planted trees and built the house. He was there for many years. The building had remained virtually unchanged and was now listed. The light switches worked in reverse as they would've in the 1930s. Nigel and Judy were serious sailors too. They were planning a long adventure in their small yacht for 2004, off to Jamaica, the West Indies, and all round the Caribbean. Now that's what I call a real adventure. We came inside when it rained. By the time I went up it was almost 10 p.m. but I still had a good soak for half an hour before watching the end of Ray Mears' *Survival*.

I said aloud to the telly, "Yes, Ray, that was me today. You'd have been proud of me, my old son."

I don't think he would though, especially not the screaming and screeching bits. Bet he never does that, unless he's trying to mimic some wild creature so he can eat it. Anyway, I had the best night's sleep for two weeks. What a great find Pengwedhen had been. I do get things spot on occasionally.

Day 29: Monday 12 May

Up with the Timex lark, feeling refreshed – never thought I'd say that. Another soak in the big bath – you've got to when you get the chance. Downstairs for breakfast and blow me down with a bargepole! Guess who was there already? Only Ian and Suzanne – the lovely honeymooning couple from the Lizard – that's who! Unbecredible! (my own newly-coined adjective. D'yer like it? No? Nor do I.) They say it's a small world and on this occasion they're damn right. Needless to say there was much handshaking, nattering, and giggling. Of all the places to stay we'd both chosen this little B & B tucked away from all the bustle of tourism. They were returning to London after breakfast and were somewhat downcast about it but said they'd return, as did I. After a fine breakfast they left and I went out onto the decking and sat talking to Judy and Nigel in the sun. It was a beautiful day and I could feel my fortunes changing. I won't allow any misery today. When they asked how I'd slept I said fine, apart from that bloody Hugh Cornwell who kept hogging the duvet all night. I was freezing! I learned that Judy hadn't intended letting anyone else stay the previous evening as my room wasn't made up. She'd got friends round, but said I sounded so glum and desperate on the phone that she changed her mind. This explained the original conversation when she'd sounded lukewarm. If you ever read this, Judy, I want to thank you from the bottom of my heart for that decision. My stay at Pengwedhen was one of the most enjoyable of my entire journey. I'll never forget it and will return one day if you'll have me, providing Hugh Cornwell isn't hiding in or under my bed. Judy left for an appointment, something to do with their daughter being the British surfing champion. Wow, that's really something! Nigel and I continued chatting whilst supping tea. He was a really laidback guy. The conversation was interesting and easy. I didn't want to leave. Finally I fetched the rucksack and shook hands carefully with Nigel as he'd got a massive bandage on one arm from some kind of horrific DIY accident. I didn't delve too deeply in case it was too gruesome.

It was noon before I reached the small quay and stood on a ferry platform to await the boat to take me the short distance across to Helford Passage. I was joined by a party of four friendly holidaymakers. We chatted amicably and I pointed out Pengwedhen to them, which stood out alone among the thick woods on side of the hill above us. The tiny red and white ferry appeared and we got on for £1.75 per head. Can't complain at that, though I did just the same. I constantly looked back at Pengwedden as we crossed the river until it disappeared behind the hill. Once on the other side I found a quiet leafy glade among the trees and changed into my shorts, determined to get brown legs while the hot sun shone. With no sign of rain and fine views along the north bank of the Helford River, what could be better? Bluebells, that's what; millions of them in the cool shady woods. I was walking through by the water's edge. I got into my stride, walked well and quickly, but without missing a trick. My senses were on high alert. I was aware of every sound and smell apart from the visual delights of my surroundings.

There were many small coves as I made my way back to the coast. I'd come naturally to that state of mind and body that I was always striving for, but is impossible to achieve, apart from occasionally, like now. I stood on Rosemullion Head and looked back to Nare Point. Much had happened since I was there twenty-four hours earlier. I wondered if that little pony was enjoying the sun too. I didn't pause for long, as I was thinking ahead to Falmouth and the ferry from there to St Mawes. Not having used these ferries before I wanted to get to them as early as possible to check the times. At 3 p.m. I grabbed a quick BLT baguette at the Swan Pool Cove beach café. There was a cool breeze as I sat outside, chatting with two couples. Everyone seemed so interested in my jaunt. I liked relaying interesting bits of it to them. In the gents' I changed back into my trousers before hitting the town. I didn't want to inflict my legs upon the hordes of people there. I soon reached the outskirts of Falmouth and road-walked past the guest houses and residential streets, up the tree-lined road, around the whole of Pendennis Point without an inch of cheating.

Pendennis Castle is one of two similar compact fortified castles built here by Henry the Eighth in the 1500s to protect the entrance to the wide estuary known as the Carrick Roads. The other is a mile across the water on the point at St Mawes. Between them they could cover and fire on any enemy shipping that dared try infiltrating Falmouth harbour or the many surrounding waterways. I had a list of vital stuff to do in Falmouth, as it was the first major town I'd passed through since Penzance. Before the town itself I passed several massive cranes, dockyards, and quays that held many cargo ships, luxury cruise liners, tankers, and all manner of shipping. Some tankers were over 400 yards long. Falmouth is most famous for its harbour, which together with Carrick Roads forms the third deepest natural harbour in the world.

The first thing to take care of on the list was to replace the lost spectacles. Walking into a bright Falmouth, I immediately came to Trago Mills; a large wooden warehouse-style department store on the quayside that sold good quality products. Inside I found a nice pair of folding specs in a case for an "Uncle Ivor" (a fiver). Next I'd been told at Pengwedden that there was a great Brummie cobbler in Falmouth who could perform miracles on your footwear. After a few inquiries I found his small shop in the main street not far from the ferry point. I nervously asked him if there was any hope for my left boot.

"Let's have a look, kidder," he said, in a thick midlands accent. I knew he was a great bloke immediately. There was an intake of breath as he studied my left boot in depth. "It ain't beautiful but I'll do summat with it any road," he said, with a reassuring grin.

If you can't trust a Brummie, who can you trust? After all, I'm one myself. He worked on it while I went and bought a pasty, sandwiches, and a drink from a nearby bakers. Wearing one boot I got a few funny looks! Five minutes later I collected the other boot. It looked amazing. He'd performed a miracle.

Despite my protestations he refused pointblank to take any money from me, saying, "Nah, forget it, kidder, it's only a rough job. The boot's knackered really and might not last. See how it goes."

I left a quid on the counter saying, "At least get yerself half a pint on me, kidder," lapsing into the vernacular myself, much to his amusement

"If yer gonna do the dialect at least do it proper like me!" he laughed.

I only had about fifteen minutes before the last ferry to St Mawes, so I bolted straight into the nearby Millets to buy another lightweight wicking top. I liked the one I'd already got but needed a spare, having sent most of my heavier un-wicking tops home after realising they were useless. For the benefit of the uninitiated, a wicking garment is one that draws moisture or perspiration away from the body through its fabric, where it simply evaporates on the outside. The best fabrics for wicking are quick drying polyesters or polyamides. The worst is cotton, which should *never* be worn for any physical activities. Lecture over. Two minutes later and fourteen quid poorer, I rushed out again, making for the ferry terminal on a quaint jetty. On the way I noticed a nice pair of Berghaus fabric walking boots in a

"25 per cent off" in an outdoor shop window. I'd bear them in mind. It was about 5.30 p.m. when the last ferry of the day left Falmouth for the twenty-minute crossing to St Mawes. It was named "Queen of Falmouth" but, despite this being a bigger boat, I remained apprehensive about stepping onto it after a nasty experience in 1971 on the Calais to Dover ferry. The sea had been as rough as Cape Horn that day. I'd sworn never to sail again after that. Yet after checking several times with the captain whether the ship was likely to sink or not, I plucked up courage and took the bull by the china shop and went on board, where I stood up the "sharp" end. I believe in nautical terms it's called the bow. It was quite choppy in Carrick Roads but my fear subsided as I became enthralled by the fabulous views in every direction. These were enhanced by the light as the sky was bright blue with large, fluffy, white, grey, and black clouds. There was a strong breeze. I took out my little Nisis dv2 and filmed bits of the crossing along with some cheery but idiotic commentary: "I'm on a ship, that's land over there," etc., stating the bleedin' obvious.

The only other passengers were an older couple on holiday. We chatted about the visible landmarks. After fifteen minutes we neared St Mawes Castle. On our port side, on the end of a premonitory, was the second of Henry's protective forts. Starboard was the impressive green landmass of St Anthony's Head, complete with lighthouse. We sailed right up between the two of them into the wide beautiful Percuil River, and presently the quaint cottages and harbour of St Mawes itself came into view to our port. Please note: I'm sounding like a seadog already. From the water St Mawes looks like a Mediterranean fishing village with its ancient buildings and old stone harbour wall. As we landed I realised this place was very upmarket. There was also an air of quiet nonchalance among the people strolling about, almost as if they were unconcerned about the rest of the world, and they didn't look like tourists.

This village is special, partly because it is so far off the beaten track and difficult to access by road, being right on the southern tip of the Roseland Peninsula, thus not en route to anywhere else. The majority of tourists tend to omit St Mawes from their list of holiday "must dos", so it's managed to remain unspoiled without any touristy gimmicks. I felt good here. It was around 6.30 p.m. by the time I'd had a quick look round the centre and all had gone quiet. The village store was open but the twenty-odd other shops had closed. I thought it was time to move on. I would've liked to have been there earlier to imbibe the atmosphere properly but this wasn't to be. When I returned to the tiny harbour, however, to my dismay I was told that the last ferry to Place – my next destination – had left half an hour ago. Oh dear. I thought they ran until dusk but had got it wrong. Wondering what to do, I wandered back towards the buildings. The sky darkened and it began to rain. I thought about getting cheap accommodation. The Ship & Castle and The Idle Rocks hotels didn't look cheap though. I went into the bar of St Mawes Hotel. It was noisy and full but fell silent as I made my way to the bar. Oh no, not again! It must be something to do with rucksacks. The barmaid leaned across. When I asked about rooms she said they were full. I thought she would, but she said I may find something on the lane along the sea towards St Mawes Castle. Not wishing to outstay my welcome – or should I say "non-welcome" – I got out of there pronto and headed up the lane.

The rain had stopped for now, but I wasn't convinced. I tapped on two or three doors of cottages which displayed B & B signs, but was told they were fully booked. They were all civil and I'd no reason to doubt them. They said "Keep trying." Unfortunately, as I approached St Mawes Castle, I'd run out of buildings and options. With nowhere to stay it appeared I'd have to walk the 12-mile detour round the Roseland peninsular to get to Place, the only alternative to the ferry that I'd missed, and camp somewhere along the way. 12 miles for no good reason – I was not happy. A moment later I was even less happy when the heavens opened and I got soaked to the skin within seconds. I ran towards St Mawes castle to shelter. Inside, not wishing to spend four notes merely to shelter – the price of the castle museum – I felt obliged to at least buy an ice cream in order to lurk about without guilt.

With the place being empty, I got talking to the curator who, understanding my predicament, produced a business card from under the counter saying, "You could try this place, it's not far away."

It said "Newton Farm B & B." He gave me directions and I set off into the countryside and away from St Mawes. At least the rain had eased off. After ten minutes I'd seen nothing and started worrying that I'd have to camp somewhere in the wet grass. The name "Newton Farm" may paint a pleasant picture in most people's minds, maybe of some kind of idyllic rural scene, but not to me. It's also the name of a formerly notorious council estate in Hereford which, back in the early 1960s, was anything but idyllic, unless you happened to love trouble and punch-ups galore. Not having returned there since "the good old days" I can't vouch for it in 2003. It was with mixed feelings that I spotted a sign on the edge of a small estate off the lane, stating "Newton Barn." Another read, "Newton Cottages", "Newton House", or similar. It all looked modern and "Newton-y" too. I asked two guys working on a car about Newton Farm. They pointed at a small close and said that was it over there. It looked good. I nervously tapped on the door, knowing this was shit or bust. A huge figure opened the door in the semi-darkness. I shot back a few feet. In the fading half-light the outline looked like a cross between Frankenstein and Frankie Howard!

When it didn't speak, I stuttered, "H-H-Have you got a s-s-single room p-p-please?" sort of hoping that it hadn't.

After a pause a man's voice whispered, "You'd better come in. It'll be £24."

Although still apprehensive, I felt relieved at the same time. No camping in the rain tonight. Mr Hancock was a quiet but lovely Cornishman. In proper lighting he didn't look like either of the aforementioned questionable characters whatsoever. He was in fact a handsome gentleman and well-preserved, despite being eighty years old. The room was comfortable if a bit "girly" for me, with a white lacy bedspread, etc. It was immaculate though, with everything I needed. He left me without reeling off a list of house rules, which was good. I unpacked, lay down, whipped out my pies and sandwiches from Falmouth, and gorged down the lot. I spent a relaxing evening watching the box, including seeing ex-cricketer Phil Tufnell win *I'm a Celebrity, Get Me out of Here!* High drama, I must say. I wrote up my journal and suddenly realised it was my birthday tomorrow. It had completely slipped my mind. I was going to be fifty-six and shuddered at the thought. It seemed like only yesterday since I didn't celebrate my fortieth. On that occasion I still had my doomed antique shop in Chiswick. I remembered clearly that I'd sat in the shop all day without taking so much as a penny piece. I hadn't seen or spoken to a soul, so closed up at 6 p.m., drove to Acton High Street, got a takeaway curry for one, drove back, ate it alone in silence, and was in bed by 7.30 p.m. I remember thinking, as I'd climbed into my single bed, It's all over! Amazing how sixteen years later it's *not!* Back to the present and surely my fifty-sixth would be better than that? It'd all depend on where I ended up tomorrow night. I drifted off into a deep sleep. It'd been a lovely day.

Day 30: Tuesday 13 May

The Timex alarm going off was not at all nice, but with last orders for breakfast at 8.30 a.m., I didn't have much choice. I dragged myself to the plush 1970s-style bathroom in a weary state before remembering it was my birthday. Down to the small breakfast room where three couples sat in embarrassed silence at their individual tables. When I said a polite good morning I was met with more silence. I sat a few feet away at my own table, remaining silent myself. You could hear the sound of crunching toast and slurping tea. The full English itself was fine but the company left a lot to be desired. This kind of thing only happens occasionally, as someone usually breaks the ice. Nobody was going to do so this morning. At least we weren't all stuck on one communal table together. That would've been even worse. I felt like jumping up and shouting out loud, "It's my birthday! What's wrong with you ******s!"

It must've seemed quiet even for poor Mr Hancock, who was a quiet man himself. You could hear a pin drop as he weaved his way between the tables silently handing out the breakfasts, teas, and coffees. After what seemed like an eternity, all three couples left without uttering a word. One woman did nod shyly towards me though. I felt relieved and spread myself out a bit. Mr & Mrs Hancock soon came in to clear the tables.

When they asked if the food was okay, I replied, "Yes, very good, thanks. It's my birthday, you know!"

We got chatting about various things for over an hour. They were a lovely, interesting couple. She was younger than him and had been an Essex girl! They'd met in the 1950s while she was on holiday in Cornwall. He was born at Newton Farm in the 1920s when it *was* a farm, and he'd lived there all his life, apart from his army years. He'd seen many changes too. All of the farm outbuildings he'd played in as a lad were now converted into houses, along with some newer ones that now make up the estate surrounding his original farmhouse. He offered me a lift down to St Mawes harbour so I could get the ferry. It felt strange being in a moving vehicle again. The last time must've been at Pendeen a couple of weeks ago when I got a short ride in that Land Rover. It was a beautiful morning now. It took two minutes to negotiate the network of tiny lanes that led steeply down to the hub of the village. I hadn't seen these the previous evening.

The harbour was a bit busier than yesterday with lots of little boats and the odd bigger one coming and going. I called Mum and Dad from the phone box to tell them I was fifty-six, in case they'd forgotten, and to sing "Happy Birthday to *me!*" They even joined in for a line or two! Everything is fine back home, including old BB my bulstrode, which is always nice to know. After the call I'd a quick look round the classy shops and galleries, followed by a visit to the post office for some birthday chocolate and postcards. There was an extremely camp local, ranting about how he hated all tourists. I had to smile. It was no use me trying not to look like one with my massive rucksack giving the game away. I couldn't believe he was complaining about living in such a beautiful place with tourists or not. There weren't many of them anyway. I felt like saying, "Why don't you move to St Kilda, cos you don't get so many of them out there?"

At 11 a.m. the tiny ferry for Place arrived. I boarded via the stone steps without so much as "eyeing a bat-lid" as it was only a river crossing rather than the open sea this time. I was the sole passenger for the ten-minute crossing to St Anthony-in-Roseland. £1.50 is a bargain, I suppose. It was breezy and bracing but fine as the little boat took me and the captain over the picturesque Percuil River towards the wooded shore and hillside of the St Anthony-in-Roseland peninsular. En route I spied a large isolated house to my right, almost on the beach of another small headland. This was a magnificent location with glorious views. The captain said that, owing to its seclusion, The Rolling Stones had stayed there in the 1960s to "get it together." I'd love to get something – anything – "together" there myself. Shortly afterwards the honey-coloured and stately Place House came into view. *Wow!* I forgot about the Stones' house immediately. I'd move into Place House instead! It'd been the former home of the Spry family and it struck me that there must be big money in lard! I stepped onto the tiny rough slipway a few minutes later, thanked the captain, and turned right, finding the now narrow and grassy SW Coast Path. I met a Brummie couple with an English Bull Terrier and a Border collie. Around the next corner I was greeted by a full-frontal of Place House with its towers and beautiful aspect, sheltered from the bad weather like a true country mansion. The little church tower and wooded hillside behind made for the perfect backdrop. This was gentle scenery, making a real change from what I'd got used to during the last four weeks. The house was not open to the public, so I walked round its boundary, into a lovely wooded setting where the little church of St Anthony-in-Roseland nestled. There was a real sense of total peace and tranquillity here among the wild flowers growing in abundance and the ancient gravestones in the little glade. I spied a medieval stone coffin in the sunshine. The church was no longer in use but was kept in good condition. I opened the door and entered. I was the only one here and spent a few minutes looking around.

Out into the bright sun again and, not really wishing to leave the glade, but realising I had to, set off up the hill towards St Anthony's Head. I wished I could've caught the ferry last night and camped near the church. It would've been ideal. Gaining height again I felt the strength of the wind blowing in my face. By the time I was out of the trees and on the top it was almost gale force and quite cold. The views from on the top were breathtaking. I couldn't be bothered about putting on my fleece. As I rounded the grassy tip of Carricknath Point, the sea was a vivid sapphire with numerous white horses. St Mawes Castle and Carrick Roads were to my right, with Pendennis Point and its castle, along with Falmouth, straight ahead across the mouth of the estuary. I turned due south and made for St Anthony's Head. Along the side of the cliffs the trees petered out as I headed back to the coast proper. It became windier and cooler too. I found a pleasant toilet block (if toilet blocks can be "pleasant") after passing the lighthouse and old gun batteries on the tip, where I refilled my water bottle and sheltered briefly out of the wind. Bracing myself, I set off around Zone Point, determined to get down to some serious action. I walked very well, feeling much better knowing I was, at last, travelling in the right direction again, north-east or east. I got used to the wind and greatly enjoyed passing through this unspoiled area. Apart from a few people near Towan beach I saw nobody for 5 miles or so.

Suddenly I came round a corner and bang! Without any warning I was in Portscatho! The village hadn't been visible from the path but was certainly a pleasant surprise. Sheltered from the vicious south-westerly winds it'd had a pilchard fishing fleet in days gone by. Some fishing continues today on a small scale. After passing some white cottages I came to the post office. I fancied an ice cream so went in and was served by the lovely post mistress, named Penny. I reckoned she was in her late twenties. I was the sole customer and asked about directions out of Portscatho and what obstacles may lay ahead. She smiled, grabbed an ordnance survey map off a shelf, and beckoned me outside, into the sunshine. Penny explained about the area and coastline ahead. She was quite an outdoor enthusiast herself. She'd led Girl Guides on walks and knew what she was talking about. She pointed out Nare Head, beyond Gerrans Bay, and the dreaded Dodman beyond that. We got on well, chatting for about fifteen minutes, ·

during which time I mentioned today was my birthday. She said it was a pity I was passing through, as there was a good restaurant in Veryan, a few miles inland. I wasn't sure what she meant by this, but felt the urge to ask her to come out with me that night for a birthday meal. She was very attractive and would certainly be great company. It'd make my birthday quite special if she agreed. Unfortunately, me being me, I began seeing the negatives. Even if she agreed – which I doubted, as I was old enough to be her father – where would I stay afterwards? At midnight, probably slightly worse for wear, I couldn't really ask to kip on her sofa. Neither could I wander miles back to the coast or camp in the dark either. She may even be married. I couldn't ask without it looking bloody obvious. There was also the humiliation of almost certainly being rejected. "There's no fool like an old fool" sprang to mind. If that happened it'd ruin my birthday, as I'd dwell on it glumly for the rest of the day. Also, she hadn't hinted that strongly so I could've read it all wrong. So as usual, I did nothing. I took a couple of pictures of her in the sun, said thanks, and gave her an "uncle-ish" peck on the cheek.

I wandered up to the small supermarket to stock up, feeling depressed at my own downright cowardice. I used to be good at "chatting up the birds" when I was young but not anymore. I bought some pasties, cranberry juice, Sopperami pessages (Pepperami sausages), and a pile of chocolate bars to keep my strength and morale up. It was a friendly atmosphere in there with some gentle banter.

I felt like asking the couple serving, "Could you go down to the post office and ask the post mistress if she'd like to come out tonight, please?" but didn't.

With my luck they would've probably changed shifts in the meantime and I'd find myself on a date with a gruesome ninety-year-old post mistress instead! I noticed some great-looking scallops in the fridge going so cheap that I asked what was wrong with them. Had they gone off? Thankfully they laughed instead of throwing me out. They explained that they were caught locally and there'd been a surfeit recently. I couldn't buy any though as they may go off in my pack. I wouldn't be able to cook them till camping about six hours later. I left Portscatho still kicking myself for being a spineless jellyfish. At one point I turned back, determined to take the bull by the gate in a china shop before it was too late. After a few steps I realised that the bull had now turned into a tyrannosaurus rex whilst I'd turned into a gutless wonder, so I headed for the cliffs instead – pillock! At Nare Head I looked back round the coast to Portscatho and thought about what might have been – pillock! (twice more!). After that I saw a horrid bloke walking his dog and gave them a wide berth.

There were lots of twiddly bits of coast that afternoon before I came to Portloe; another unspoilt fishing village, squeezed into a steep valley at the western end of Veryan Bay. Upon a small shingle beach rested a few fishing boats, mainly used for catching lobster and crab potting. Hence I'm giving you a potted history of the village! These are all that's left now, though there was once a small drift fleet and a seine fishery. Up the hill and the Portloe Lugger Hotel, a seventeenth-century inn, is reputed to have been the haunt of many smugglers. One of the landlords – Black Dunstan – was hanged for smuggling in the 1890s. The liqueur licence was withdrawn and the inn ceased trading. After a variety of uses, including a boat-building shed, the structure was renovated. It reopened in 1950 with six bedrooms. It's now a swanky hotel.

I walked on after a quick call home from the village phone box. All remained good. It always cheers me up speaking to Mum and Dad. Being anxious, however, I didn't hang around but carried on through coastal woodland paths. I was looking to camp but couldn't find any clearings among the trees. Strangely, I did see a B & B off the path, but couldn't get any answer when I knocked. I bumped into an upper-class old colonial type who, when I expressed my anxiety about camping, told me not to worry, as there were some ideal flat bits about twenty minutes further on towards Portholland. Relieved, I practically ran to try beating the failing light. I ran for forty minutes before realising the old colonel hadn't got a clue. I could've killed him! Eventually I found a miniscule flat area big enough for the tent but right on the cliff edge. I'd no choice so attempted to pitch. It was a nightmare in the bitter wind, taking me twenty minutes. It was almost dark and some small holes were appearing in the tent pole sleeve, making it harder to pitch each time. The language was not nice but nobody heard me, being the only person fool enough to be out in this wind. Once inside I got straight into the bag to try and warm myself up. I ate my cold pasty, washed it down with cold water, and wished I was in that warm restaurant at Veryan with Penny the lovely post mistress – pillock! (three times over!). Overall it'd been marginally better than my fortieth but, given the turn of events, still pretty pathetic. I was determined that my fifty-seventh would be fantastic to make up for it. I dozed off at 9-ish but woke feeling chilly several times during the night.

Day 31: Wednesday 14 May

The sun's rays on the tent woke me at 8 a.m. Fabulous! It didn't last long though. The rays stopped dead halfway between the sun and the earth. I felt a black presence above me and looked out to see a gigantic raincloud filling most of the sky. I packed slowly, expecting a downpour, which was extra worrying with me being on the cliff edge. Could I be washed over it, Back-stack and Laurel (and Hardy)? By the time I was ready to leave the cloud had gone and all was well again. I'd live to fight another day. My first stop, after a mile or so, was another little stone-built gents' in Portholland for my daily ablutions. Portholland is divided into East and West halves. Both are tiny clusters of houses. They're joined by a peculiar concrete reinforced beach, exposed only at low tide. I crossed over and climbed up to the path again. On the way up I found a lovely summerhouse for rent, all by itself on the right of the path. It was on a patch of flat grass featuring brilliant views looking out to sea. I peered inside: very bijou but cosy, all for the princely sum of twenty notes per night. I wrote down the phone number for future reference. On the top the wind had dropped to a light breeze. This was splendid hiking weather now. The path was fairly even, making things much better.

In the middle of nowhere I was suddenly overtaken by a Jack Russell terrier. The little fellow slowed down and walked a couple of yards ahead of me, sniffing the grass and flowers as we passed them. I wondered if he was lost as no owner was in evidence. He seemed quite content to potter along with me, never making a sound. Once or twice I tried patting him but he wasn't having any of it, veering away elusively each time. A mile on I saw a man approaching. I asked him if my little friend belonged to him. He said no but he'd seen him alone on the coast path before. We agreed that he was simply out enjoying himself, not lost. This man was a well-built old Cornishman, probably in his seventies. Born and bred in this area, he had a broad, rich dialect. It was wonderful listening to him speak. *He* didn't seem to resent this tourist being in his native Cornwall either. No chip on either of his broad shoulders. I mentioned to him that, despite the beautiful weather, I could hear distant thunder, seemingly coming from a seaward direction. He laughed, assuring me it wasn't thunder but warships on manoeuvres, firing shells way out at sea. We weren't too far from Plymouth, so that's obviously what it was. As we talked, the little dog sat down a few yards away. He was waiting for me! I set off eastwards again with the Dodman Point looming large now. I must say it was great having the little terrier for company. He seemed so at ease and appeared to know every inch of the path too. I was still slightly concerned, however, in case he was wandering too far from home and may not be able to find his way back alone.

Suddenly I remembered a notice I'd seen by a pub on the north Cornish coast two weeks earlier. It'd mentioned that a Jack Russell had gone missing and had been posted by the distraught owners. It also mentioned that they were concerned about him falling down one of the many redundant open mine shafts. I'd felt quite upset when reading it. Surely this couldn't be the same Jack Russell? That was two weeks ago. All the same I whipped out my "dog-eared" map (pardon the pun) to check. To my horror, I realised St Agnes – roughly where I'd seen the notice – although 200 miles away by coastal path, was less than 20 miles away across the middle of Cornwall as the fly crows! I considered this could be the same little woofer that was missing after all. He could've wandered that distance quite easily if inclined. He was still pottering along ahead of me quite unconcerned. I could see he'd got a brass disc on his collar. Despite trying to tempt him with some chocky, I still couldn't catch him. He wriggled out of my hands each time. He liked me but not enough to let me pick him up. I stopped by a gate leading to a lane, took the pack off, and sat on the ground. The doggie came to me for a bit of pepperami. I managed to grab him. He wasn't too happy about it, but before escaping I managed to read the name "Mac" and memorise the accompanying phone number. As this was a potential emergency I took out my mobile phone and dialled the number. Another broad-spoken Cornishman answered. I told him about the notice, that I'd got "Mac", and where I was.

He laughed and said, "Not again! He's always wandering off and loves walking the coast path. He's got a girlfriend down there too. I'll be down in five minutes to get him if you can hang on."

I could hang on but Mac obviously couldn't. He'd wandered off while I was speaking to his master! Mac was definitely not the dog from north Cornwall then. Presently, a beaten-up old pickup truck arrived with a beaming farmer on board.

"Where is the little so-and-so, then?" Embarrassed, I explained that he'd vanished again. The farmer said, "He'll come home when he gets hungry; he always does."

Thankfully he didn't seem too bothered. We had a long chat in the midday sun. This good Cornishman gave me permission to cross any of his coastal fields if I felt like a change from the actual coast path. It was most kind of him. I did that and it was delightful. It felt lonely without little Mac trotting ahead of me though, having got used to him in the last few miles. At the delightful Porthluney Cove I found a nice café where I ordered breakfast, consisting of two bacon and sausage sandwiches, ice cream, and a pot of tea for the tillerman. All went down very well. I sat outside in the sheltered warmth and chatted to two couples who were visiting the floral gardens, famous mainly for their magnolias, at the nearby Gothic-styled Caerhays Castle. The castle was completed in 1807, designed and built by John Nash of Brighton Pavilion fame. We could see it a few hundred yards inland.

As I took a picture I became aware of a commotion and, looking up, caught sight of old Mac, chasing two huge German Shepherds across the field between us and the castle! The sight of them running for their lives with the tiny Jack Russell barking and hot on their heels cracked us all up. After he'd seen them off he strutted over to us as if to say, "Job done. Now where's my treat?" Needless to say he was given all kinds of titbits but still wouldn't let anyone touch him. This great character made my day. He soon disappeared after his treats. I left too, making my way ever closer to the mighty Dodman.

The climb up was tough but I made it to the tip where there was a cross with an inscription, informing me about the second coming of Christ! Very useful information if you're that way inclined. It fell on stony ground as far as I was concerned, but I did like seeing all these inscriptions and unusual yet often pointless monuments. The Dodman headland is also one of the most prominent in Cornwall and served as a lookout point during the

Napoleonic wars. A watch house from the period still stands there. The remains of a defensive earthwork from the Iron Age are still visible, the ditches and banks of which are over 15 feet high in places. With the rounding of the Dodman I felt relieved that yet another major hurdle was now behind me. I'd been looking at its bulk for four or five days. It'd be visible behind me for a few days before fading for good.

I soon descended into another charming port, called Gorran Haven. It was tea time and there before me in the village centre was a bakers shop, named Cakebread's, which looked irresistible. I sat at a table outside after ordering a cream tea from the friendly staff. Life was good again as I relaxed in the sunshine. I felt ultra-fit today and, looking at my legs, realised they'd become very *brown*! I checked my left boot, which wasn't looking good, but seemed to be holding out for now. A lady walker joined me at my table. She'd tried to order a cream tea, but the proprietor told her that I'd got the last one. She had to make do with an ordinary tea. Feeling guilty, and being a perfect gentleman, I offered her half of mine, but to my great delight she rejected the offer, saying that her ordinary tea would suffice. I didn't pursue the matter any further fearing she may change her mind – it's a woman's prerogative, you know. Anyway, my cream tea was huge and amazing. I was also given a pot of tea for six without even ordering it. The lady was on holiday with her husband who was off playing a round of golf nearby. Meanwhile she'd walked the coast path from Charlestown near St Austell, a fair old distance by any standards. This girl was no slouch! Her husband arrived to collect her, frustrated with his round like so many golfers. I don't know why they do it. I don't know why I walk either. It's horrific most of the time, as you'll realise after reading this, or if you've walked any distance yourselves. I expect you'll all pack it in for good soon. You know it makes sense. We said our goodbyes and went our separate ways.

I stocked up in the wonderful Cakebread's with the usual stuff, but this time the goods were of a far higher quality than normal, all baked on the premises too. On the little sandy beach I met a local couple who gave me the low down on Gorran Haven. It was another traditional fishing village that'd hardly changed over the years. It also boasts a fifteenth-century Tudor-style church, which I couldn't be bothered to walk to, and also a nearby ancient inn that I *could* be bothered to walk to for a pint of real ale. I'd worked up quite a thirst from lazily chatting on the beach. This inn has a dubious history, but haven't they all around these coasts? The ale was strong and I left feeling slightly woosy, hoping there wouldn't be any narrow ledges to negotiate this afternoon.

My next destination was Mevagissey, or as I've renamed it, "Mega-vissey." I headed by the picturesque Chapel Point, onto the road at Portmellon, which leads uphill and downhill into "Mega" itself. The views over the twin harbours were almost tropical-looking as I descended steeply, still on the road. Several large spiky palms were growing about the place.

The village, which I'd visited once before, seemed much bigger than I remembered. It was a veritable teeming metropolis now. It was a larger fishing port but picturesque all the same. Its streets were crowded with tourists, especially round the lovely twin harbours, which were crammed with all manner of seagoing craft. Many of the ancient fish cellars have been converted to a variety of uses, but their thick stone walls and the unchanged look of the tiny streets retain the quaintness of "old Mevagissey". Fishing is still important too, as is the hiring of boats to visitors for angling, normally fishing for shark or mackerel. There's a ruined village nearby – Portgiskey – where all of the cottages, cellars, and boatyards were abandoned in the late 1800s. Horticulture-wise, the Lost Gardens of Heligan are very close and the Eden Project is about 7 miles away. Unfortunately I wouldn't be going that way this time, but have been when it was in its infancy. A famous visitor was George Bernard Shaw who wrote his play, *The Doctor's Dilemma*, while staying in Mevagissey in 1906. He also became a surfing champion and won a large silver cup for coming second for his performance in the Pontin's karaoke competition the same year.

Nearing the centre I glanced in some shop windows. In an antique shop the first item I spotted was a pack of Iraqi playing cards sporting a smiling Saddam Hussein on each one. They were on sale for an Edward Jenner. I loved them, but couldn't carry them. This was my kind of shop. Upon further inspection I realised that the window was full of the most amazing artifacts, featuring all kinds of rare items, ranging from authentic Titanic memorabilia, Marilyn Monroe and JFK, to Lord Nelson. No boring "brown wood" or any of the usual "antique" dross. This was no run-of-the-mill antique shop. What exactly had I stumbled across in this little town? It was like an incredible yet much smaller version of my own shop, which I'd packed in after twelve years. Whoever's shop this was they'd got it dead right. The sign above read "Cloud Cuckoo Land" – perfect. Mesmerized, I stumbled towards the central door, to the side of which was a collage of photographs. On closer inspection I noticed they were snaps of famous rock stars, all standing next to, or shaking hands with, the same guy, whom I didn't recognise. I took him to be the owner. I spotted pictures of a beaming Robert Plant and Jarvis Cocker among others. There was nothing else for it; I had to investigate. I pushed the door open and saw a man, a girl, and a dog sitting at the rear of the shop. I struggled inside with my massive pack getting dangerously close to an early 1980s grotesque, but no doubt priceless, figure of Lady Diana. Suddenly, a vicious-looking dog leapt up at me, barking deafeningly. The man quickly restrained it and dispatched it to the back room with the girl. I was left alone with the owner who looked familiar, though not from the pictures by the door. We got chatting about the shop and he told me his name was Paul. He was about forty and looked like a "muso". He wouldn't be drawn into mentioning which bands he may have been in. It turned out that he'd had a unit in Alfie's Market, off the Marylebone Road in London. I'd been there several times, as it was London's premier retro indoor market; a fantastic place that'd take days to check out completely. He'd been in there for twenty years, had made many contacts during that time, hence the stock. He'd now decided to move back to his native Cornwall, particularly Mevagissey. Maybe he wasn't a muso after all, but looked familiar anyway.

He said I did too, blurting out, "Come on, which band was it? Don't keep me guessing!"

We had a laugh and I told him it was Mott The Hoople. Without further ado he reached straight down behind his counter and pulled out an ancient Mott The Hoople LP as if on cue.

I said, "How the **** did you do that?"

We laughed again and he said, "You should reform the band."

"What? And end up owing a fortune again? Not likely!"

I stayed for half an hour. We chatted mainly about his wonderful stock and his own personal collection of Nelson rarities. He also possessed an authentic letter and an "autograph" by Bonnie Prince Charlie! All too soon it was time to go. I said I'd be back one day to have a proper look, shook hands with him, and left. A fascinating half-hour. Straight into a bakery next. I do buy fruit occasionally but not today. The blonde girl that served me was the tiniest person of the trip. She was eighteen, well under 5 feet, and pretty. As we chatted, the subject of her size came up somehow. I got all tangled up with my words, aware that I could be treading on eggshells.

"You know what they say. The smallest presents arrive in the loveliest parcels." I tried correcting myself by adding, "What I mean is the shortest people arrive in the tallest – *no*! – nicest packaging!"

She smiled throughout as my words petered out pathetically in sheer embarrassment. I guess she was used to stuff like that. She still served me with a smile, so not too much damage done, but it could've gone either way. Finally all "pied-up", I'd a quick look round the picturesque harbour with its old watch-house, followed by setting off up the steep path through the cottages, out of "Mega", back onto the coast path. The climb up around Penare Point was horrid and strenuous. As I puffed and heaved my way up I wondered how the hell do you get Bonnie Prince Charlie's autograph?

Maybe some soldier shouted, "Hey, Charlie! Stop fighting for a minute and let me hold your sword, there's a good chap. There're some fans here that want your autograph. It won't take a minute. Ooherr, look out! There's a Pontin's Redcoat behind you!"

Is that how it was done, or did they bring a pile of publicity photos for him to sign while he was eating his porridge in a cave? Pondering on issues such as this often took my mind off the severity of the actual walking, which was nice – idiotic, but nice. From the top I saw the full sweep of Pentewan Sands way below, stretching north for a mile, and the large camping and caravan site running parallel to it. The sky was still a lovely shade of cobalt blue but the forecast for tomorrow was for heavy rain. It was 7.30 p.m. so as I walked down I decided to knock it on the head for this evening. I'd had a decent day so far, so let's quit while I'm ahead for once. At the campsite gatehouse, despite my protestations, I was forced to fill in a myriad of complex forms. Goodness knows why. I'm simply a solo backpacker staying one night. Why do they have my name, address – don't forget your postcode "sir" – phone, mobile phone, email address, vehicle registration number – they still asked for it even though I was on foot– vehicle registration document, motor vehicle insurance, National Insurance Number, reason for visit, how did you hear about us? Why did you hear about us? Bank details (I made that one up), but it did go on and on ad infinitum. I found it all pointless, mind-boggling, and left most boxes blank as I simply couldn't fill them in.

After ten minutes they finally said, "That will be £5, sir."

I paid up and asked for a printed receipt, plus a handwritten receipt, a VAT receipt, all free maps of the site, a book of all campsite rules, a copy of every single tourist brochure they'd got, *their* vehicle registration number and bank sort code, just in case I wanted to block-book for a party of 100 people in advance one day. It was after 7.30 p.m. before I found a convenient spot to pitch. I wanted to be fairly close to a shower block in case of bad weather. Tent up, I showered in the warm, well-equipped block. On with my best outfit next, which was identical to my worst outfit, but a lot more creased from being rolled up in the pack for weeks. I made my way to Pentewan village, 400 yards away, and found The Ship close to the old harbour. It was a warm, cosy old pub with a log fire and friendly ambience. A few campers and some locals were inside, featuring no hostilities this time. Mostly it was couples. I ordered stuffed plaice with chips, a chocolate sundae and drank three pints of Tinners ale. At £1.97 a pint it would've been silly not to. I felt quite drowsy in the warm room after my meal and, as I hadn't found anyone to bother by 9.30 p.m., I decided to see what was happening at the campsite Beach Bar, which sounded like a fun kind of place. It was a big mistake and was certainly not a fun kind of place. I was the sole punter along with the most miserable barman, or indeed human being, I'd ever met. Right from the off I disliked him and he didn't like me. In the comedy stakes he made me look like Tommy Cooper. He moaned about everything.

When I mentioned how quiet it was he retorted, "Oh no, they won't come in here, never in a month of Sundays. Last year was the worst it's ever been and this year is even worse, like rats leaving a sinking ship. I blame the government."

I, on the other hand, was already blaming *him* and could see why everyone had left this particular sinking ship. I'd only been in there five minutes and felt like topping myself. After another five or so elapsed I sat in a corner and cried into my Ansells. He prowled the length of the bar, wiping glasses and scouring the horizon for another victim to depress. A couple came in with three noisy kids. After putting up with that racket for ten more minutes I'd had enough.

On the way out the barman glared at me as if to say, "I knew you'd leave early. Thanks a bundle for leaving the sinking ship."

I nodded, muttering, "Goodnight. Won't be seeing you."

I wandered back to the tent in a pensive mood. Nevertheless, it'd been a great day apart from the last half-hour, so I shouldn't moan. I'd leave that to the barman. I was asleep by 10.30 p.m. but woke again at 2 a.m. and spent the rest of the night trying in vain to get back to sleep.

Day 32: Thursday 15 May

I managed a couple of hours but was awoken at 8 a.m. by the sound of torrential rain on the flysheet. No way could I sleep through that. I lay there writing up my journal, listening to my Sony radio. It continued to rain all day, heavier still. What a great decision it'd been to camp here last night. If I'd camped wild I'd be completely stuck, unable to pack away in this. The tiny tent is certainly not the place to spend a whole day, being cramped and uncomfortable, with not even enough room to sit up. At least here I could use the shower block and shop, or run to the pub later, or even the loathsome Beach Bar if I were in danger of drowning. I was listening to 'Mars' again, from Holtz's *Planet Suite* when the rain finally eased after ten hours, marking the longest continuous rain storm so far. I threw off the headphones and bolted over to the shower block. Half an hour later I was sitting – guess where? Yep, the campsite Beach Bar. Would you bloody well believe it? The reason for this was that it was raining so hard again that the pub was too far to run to without a brolly. Yet again I was the only one there, apart from the same barman, now hanging from a rope by the neck from a beam behind the bar. Well he might as well have been! I downed a couple of pints of Cornish Cream (£2.20 a pint), which was like Guinness.

When I asked why there was no food, the barman said angrily, "The season hasn't started yet! What do you expect?"

I told him I expected food, as it was listed in huge letters on every large menu board throughout the entire room. He grunted miserably and, unable to come up with any satisfactory defence, walked away. After an hour of eating endless packets of crisps and staring each other out, I could no longer bear it, so made a courageous dash to The Ship, 500 yards in the opposite direction. I was soaked but at least it was warm inside by the fire. I'd a chicken Kiev, treacle sponge and custard, and two pints of Tinners to drown my sorrows. It was quieter tonight but I got talking to a nice couple – Dave and Andrea – on holiday from Northampton. He looked like Chas and Dave. They were good fun. After they left I drifted into the public bar to kill time for a while before returning through the rain back to my lonely chilly tent. It was now 11 p.m. and it'd hardly stopped raining all day. I must've got through more than £20 tonight in an effort to entertain myself. Hopefully I can get going tomorrow as I can't afford to keep spending at that rate. A shiver ran right through me as I lay in the bag but I fell asleep pretty soon after warming up. At 4 a.m. I was awoken by the pounding of heavy rain again. Would I have to prepare myself for another day in the tent and, even worse, another evening with that bar-steward in the desolate Beach Bar?

Day 33: Friday 16 May

By 8 a.m. the rain had stopped. I was pleased that the heavy black clouds had dissipated and the sky was light grey instead. Over to the shower block next, where I did everything, including some laundry, making good use of the reasonably-priced washing and drying facilities. I walked out of the campsite, into Pentewan village without paying for my second night. I couldn't face all that form-filling again. Besides, the reception area was miles in the opposite direction to where I was going. I'd also spent a fortune on drinks and crisps in the campsite Beach Bar. I'd kept them financially stable single-handedly, so didn't feel too guilty. Before departing I went into the shop where I bought a ham and cheese sandwich, a pasty, and two bars of chocolate from a nice Brummie lady. I kept meeting loads of my fellow Midlanders. Even though it was only noon, I went into her small café and had a cream tea. As mentioned, you can't refuse one when the chance comes up. I chatted to a couple from Hampshire who had a motorhome on the campsite. I felt a pang of jealousy. I expect it was all warm and cosy inside it, but I had to head out on to the freezing, windy cliffs instead. It wasn't fair. Back in the shop I was in time to see an Irishman spend £91.82 on gifts and souvenirs. He must've been loaded. Among his stash he'd got a good-looking black baseball cap (£1.99), which I coveted from right from the start. It was better and much cheaper than the green one from The Minack Theatre. I asked the lady if I could have one the same. Imagine how gutted I was when she replied that his was the last one. I'd always liked the Irish until then. All she had left was a dark blue one. Although it didn't possess the same sense of drama as the black one, I bought it anyway as a sort of consolation prize. Maybe I could dye it or paint it when I got home, or even cover it in matt black fabric. I'm being ridiculous now.

Outside again I'd a quick look at the village of Pentewan. It consisted of The Ship, the post office, and a couple of shops, so not too exciting. There'd formerly been a working harbour, but although the basin was there in front of me, its entrance has silted up over time. Not a lot happens anymore. This harbour used to be linked to St Austell by the Pentewan Railway in busier times. One notable Pentewan resident is guitarist Tim Renwick, famous for his session work with Elton John, Procol Harum, David Bowie, Mike Oldfield, Gary Brooker, Roger Waters, Eric Clapton, and Pink Floyd. I met Tim with The Sutherland Brothers and Quiver back in the "surly evanties", so it was a pity I didn't know which house he lived in. I could've knocked on his door and thrown myself upon his mercy, maybe avoiding two days of lying bored in the tent and those evenings staring-out the nasty barman in the nasty Beach Bar.

It was 1.30 p.m. by the time I got away. The sky was looking ominous as I started the vicious climb up to, and around, Black Head. Once there, the narrow path took me past a 7-foot-high gravestone-like monolith. It seemed like a weird location for something like this with it being so isolated. I turned round to read the inscription that faced the sea, which read: "A.L. Rowse, CH, 1903-1997, poet and historian, voice of Cornwall, this is the land of my content". So this was where the old devil hung out nowadays. Alfred Leslie Rowse was born near St Austell, possibly best known for his poetry about Cornwall, and also works on Elizabethan England. He had a reputation for irascibility and intellectual arrogance, as well as a love of birds and animals, particularly cats. He sounds like a latter-day Bill Oddie.

The hiking was very tough again after being spoiled by a couple of easier days, but I felt physically fit and coped with it well. I couldn't say the same for my boots though. Walking through the soaking grass and mud was taking its toll on them. I started worrying about them breaking down out here on the top. A mile before Charlestown I felt spots of rain that soon became torrential. I stopped in some trees to don the waterproofs before bracing myself to walk through it. I became stifled in them, as the steep ascents and descents required plenty of effort. Once on level terrain again the wind cooled me down and I became comfortable. I presently achieved my first target of the day at the historic Charlestown, which grew out of a small fishing village called West Polmear in 1790. Already looking like a throwback from the old days, Charlestown harbour has been disguised to depict many other historic ports, such as Bristol Harbour, for film and television productions. It has featured in *Poldark*, an adaptation of Jane Austen's *Persuasion*, and various films. The sequence set in Alderney in the film *The Eagle Has Landed* was filmed in and around the harbour and the adjacent beach. The famous Heart of the Ocean necklace from the film *Titanic* resides at the town's National Shipwreck Museum.

After a quick look at three sailing ships "parked" in the old harbour, I pressed on for Par, intent on reaching Fowey by dusk, to make up for my late start. Unfortunately, as I was roughly one-quarter of the way across the windswept golf course above the sands of Carlyon Bay, I was hit full-on by the heaviest rain and gales so far. With nowhere to shelter I'd no option but to soldier on. I was soaked to skin within a minute, despite the waterproofs. I passed three golfers who were squatting low about 40 yards away, cowering beneath their big brollies, trying to protect themselves from the onslaught. My socks and feet were also saturated. The beige-coloured leather boots had practically turned black as they'd become waterlogged in five minutes flat. I felt an uncomfortable squelch with each footstep. I raced on, desperate to get down from this exposed position to look for shelter, and hopefully a B & B. All thoughts of getting to Fowey were now abandoned.

The route descended onto a busy main road and circumnavigated a huge china clay repository, with its docks, hogging a large area of the coast.

There was either smoke, fog, or steam, or all three, swirling everywhere. I couldn't tell which in the depressing gloom. I also had to dodge heavy rush-hour traffic and it was freezing cold. It struck me that this was what it must be like in hell. The only difference was that hell would be warmer. I walked under a small stone railway bridge on the main road and considered sleeping there with it being dry. I forced myself on through houses towards Par, quite worried about hypothermia as I was shivering horribly. I spotted a phone box by another railway bridge and trudged through the deep puddles to reach it. My feet were gone already so no point in pussyfooting around – ha, ha!

Once inside I pulled out my guidebook and thumbed through the B & B section, praying I'd find one nearby that had a vacancy, otherwise I may be sleeping in the phone box with a directory over my head to keep warm. I tried a couple of numbers but got no reply. In this rain and already soaking what could I possibly do if I couldn't find anywhere to stay? The route ahead entailed a lot more cliff work and traversing the monstrous, exposed Gribbin Head, before finally reaching Fowey. It was a good 8-10 miles from Par too, with little or no shelter. I couldn't possibly tackle that tonight. It'd be downright stupid, not to mention dangerous. I dialled another number and asked about a single room, waiting with baited breath for the reply. The woman sounded really nice and said she *had* got a single room I could have. Joy, oh joy! She was my saviour. She gave me directions and said it was £27.50 for B & B. Although more than I like to pay, these were exceptional circumstances, and if she'd said £270.50 I'd probably still have bitten her hand off. I set off along the drab streets of Par for the more upmarket suburb of Twyardreath with my faith in human nature fully restored and with a spring in my step.

I often wonder if the people who run B & Bs know how heartening it is for weary, wet travellers to hear their welcoming tones on the phone and those magic words, "Yes, I can fit you in somewhere," or their equivalent. The relief of knowing that it's all going to be okay after a worrying ordeal it's as good as a big log fire any day. Thank you to all of you that took me in. I really appreciated it. Even the most horrific B & Bs are still better than nothing. Any port in a storm! I'd only walked 50 yards or so when I came to a fish and chip shop. I was starving now. I didn't think there'd be food at the B & B at night so I went in. It was warm, bustling, and friendly inside. As they wrapped my fish and chips I mentioned the guest house for which I was bound, expressing my concern in case there may a problem with takeaway food. If there was likely to be trouble, I'd have to eat it outside before I got there.

The lady serving said, "Oh no, it'll be fine. Mrs Bourne won't mind at all. She's lovely, Mrs Bourne. You'll like her."

Ten minutes after checking my directions with a few locals I knocked on the imposing door of a lovely detached Victorian house fringed by overhanging trees. It was named Polmear House. Mrs Bourne answered the door. Sure enough, I liked her instantly. She had a beautiful welcoming smile and told me to come in and get my wet things off. She'd put them by the Rayburn to dry overnight. I left my boots too, fearing they'd already reached the end of their short working (and walking) life, only four weeks after they'd begun it. My room was tasteful with period features, and most importantly it was warm, and although not en suite, the bathroom was right next door. I started unpacking when the glamorous Mrs Bourne arrived with a steaming mug of tea – despite my room having its own facilities – a plate, cutlery, seasoning for my supper, and a television. She was a very strong woman. I ate my superb fish and chips and felt incredibly tired. It was only 8.30 p.m. but I hadn't slept well for several nights. I fell asleep soon after to the sound of the telly and didn't wake until the Timex alarm went off at 7.25 a.m.

Day 34: Saturday 17 May

Refreshed after a good night I got out of bed fairly quickly, but couldn't get into the bathroom for ten minutes, as it was occupied. I started my packing instead and made a cup of tea. Next time I'd tried the bathroom it was empty. After making myself presentable I went down to breakfast where I joined a lady guest who was staying with her daughter. One was from Horsham, the other from Essex, but they holidayed together. Nice idea, I thought. Our fine full Englishes arrived but after ten minutes there was still no sign of the daughter. She finally arrived with damp hair and sat down.

When Mrs Bourne arrived with the tea, the girl apologised saying, "Sorry I'm late, but someone was in the bathroom for ages."

Mrs Bourne looked at me and, smiling sexily said, "That would be naughty, Overend. Wouldn't it, Overend? He's been a very naughty boy!"

It was the gentlest scolding I'd had since kindergarten. I hoped I might be punished by the gorgeous Mrs Bourne afterwards, but no such luck! I was soon forgiven by all. We chatted and enjoyed our fine breakfasts. Outside was not looking good, with a dark sky and a steady downpour. I'd have to try dragging out my stay to avoid going out. I didn't fancy that horrible huge Gribbin Head in this. As I packed slowly, a cunning plan formulated in my miniscule brain. Instead of heading out onto the wild cliffs in the rain and mud I'd get a train to St Austell, find a cobbler, and get a report on the state of my boots. If they failed their MOT I'd buy a new pair. Depending on the weather, I'd play it by ear from there. It was Saturday so it might be pleasant in St Austell. I may even have the whole day off and enjoy myself. There were sure to be some places of interest to visit. I'd also ask Mrs Bourne if the room was available for that night again, should I need it. Once ready, I went down to the kitchen to collect my sad boots, which had been left by the Rayburn till the last possible moment. Their complexion looked a little healthier now, but the stitching was going on both toes. Mrs Bourne – or

Marion, as I was now permitted to call her, despite my naughtiness – and I chatted by the cosy Rayburn for ten minutes before being joined by her sixteen-year-old son James, who was a really good "bloke". There was no mention of a Mr Bourne and for a minute I thought maybe I should try getting my feet firmly under the table. I'd really like to live here with Mrs Bourne and James. I'd have a lovely ready-made family and we could all live together happily ever after! I wouldn't be too keen on taking in guests though cos they might make a mess in my nice new home. I also might have to get up early. I doubted my plan would succeed anyway so abandoned the idea almost immediately and went up to finish my packing. I packed as slowly as possible, wanting to stay there all day, if only to avoid the heavy rain outside. At noon, however, I bade them farewell and dodged the puddles to Par railway station. It was still raining hard. The fare to St Austell was £1.80, which I thought was extortionate for a five-minute journey.

When I got into the town centre it was horrible. Obviously the rain didn't help, but it seemed characterless and featureless, except for a vile, angular, concrete 1960s eyesore that loomed large in the square – it was Jethro! Only joking, it was probably a car park. NB: I like Jethro very much, and Jimmy Cricket too, though what he has to do with Cornwall I haven't got a clue, unless he's Irish-Cornish. Although it was lunchtime there were few people around, especially for a Saturday. Even at this stage I didn't fancy spending the day in this dump. Apologies again. It's probably lovely on a nice summer's day. I found a cobblers shop and went in. He was a great bloke. I now believe that *all* cobblers are great blokes.

Laughing all the time, he said "Stick your feet on the counter!"

Not being a contortionist, I took them off instead – my boots, not my feet. How could you stick both feet on any counter in any shop without lying upside down on the floor? I found my socks were soaked after only an hour's walk. There was a sharp intake of breath – much sharper than the sharp intake of breath taken in by the Brummie cobbler in Falmouth.

He said sadly, "There's no hope, I'm afraid. They're too far gone. They're very old, aren't they? Is the stitching is rotten?"

I said frustratedly, "No, I've only worn them for four weeks."

"Well that may be so but they haven't been making boots like these for over thirty years now."

That's the last time I buy new boots from a car boot sale! What a waste of three quid! I'd been prepared for the worst, so in a way it was a bit of a relief. I knew in my heart of hearts that they'd come to the end of the road anyway. When I asked where I could buy a new pair, he scratched his chin, narrowing his eyes.

Looking pensive he said, "You won't get any in St Austell. The shop in the market closed down last year."

I couldn't believe my ears or his mouth! This was one of Cornwall's major towns and I couldn't get a pair of boots on a Saturday afternoon! Even though he was a great bloke I left there in downcast mood. I couldn't carry on walking now whatever happened. I strolled around the miserable town centre with two crocodile-mouthed boots in the rain wondering what to do next.

I could phone Mrs Bourne, start crying, throw myself on her mercy, and hope she'd say, "Don't worry, Overend. Even though you've been a naughty boy, I'll come and rescue you."

I found a shoe shop. It was very upmarket and I couldn't see any walking boots at all.

When I asked the assistant for assistance, he said, "That's all we've got."

He pointed to what looked like a pair of brown brogue shoes, completely unsuitable, costing £140! I left there thinking, I'm f*****! After a cup of tea in a grimy café I formulated another plan, which could work and keep me out of the rain for the rest of the day too. I'd catch a train back to Falmouth, where I'd seen that lovely pair of Berghaus Explorers in a sale for £59.99. Being a long journey there and back, including changing at Truro, it'd keep me out of the rain till tea time. An added bonus was that I much preferred Falmouth to St Austell – apologies to any St Austellarians reading this. It's nothing personal. The return ticket cost £4.90, which was a pleasant surprise after the high cost of my shorter trip earlier. Rail fares don't seem to have any logic to them at all. Maybe I could've gone to John o'Groats and back for 65p. Once on the train I felt much more positive and enjoyed travelling in style (of a sort) for a change. I enjoyed another cuppa in the station café at Truro before arriving in Falmouth. As I stepped off the train the sun came out from behind a cloud and it was suddenly a beautiful afternoon. I wandered into the town, passed Trago Mills, where I'd bought my specs last Monday, which seemed an eternity ago with so much happening since. I found the outdoor shop and to my delight the Gore-Tex boots were still on offer. I tried two or three navy pairs and couldn't tell which fitted me best. The problem was that my feet were now completely numb from walking. The helpful owner told me to take my time. After half an hour or so I went for the size 10s, which seemed strange, as I normally take an 11 in ordinary shoes, and boots are supposed to be one size larger. I went with my gut instinct, paying up and wore them out of the shop, along with some dry socks. I couldn't bring myself to throw my old Hawkins boots away, despite the hell I'd endured with them. I gave the chap a fiver to post them home for me. They'd become museum pieces once they'd dried out; a battered worn-out reminder of all the hardships and pain.

I got a can of the kinkily named G Sport waterproof spray in Millets as I wasn't taking any chances, along with another water bladder as a replacement for my leaking one. I had a look round in the sunshine but felt I should get back to St Austell and start walking in my new boots. I'd feel guilty if I made no progress at all, especially now the weather had improved. So I walked to Falmouth Town station. Along the way I picked up the best pasty of the trip; big and amazing. I also bought a lightweight multi-tool for £5.99, which I saw in the window of a girly shop. On the train journey back I noticed that the sky was beginning to look ominously dark again. By the time I reached St Austell it was wizzling down. At 6 p.m. no way was I going to walk now. I needed to decide where to stay for the night. Being in an urban area and in the rain meant camping was out. I could go back to Mrs Bourne at Polmear House, but it would've meant a long wet walk, plus the embarrassment of her knowing I'd failed to walk anywhere all day. I'd feel better if she imagined me struggling bravely with the elements, undaunted by sheer drops, mudslides, gales or rain, determined to reach my objective, in true manly fashion. The only alternative was to find somewhere cheap close to St Austell station, as I'd need to get to Par early to commence walking tomorrow. Heading down the hill for 500 yards I saw a sign hanging outside a Victorian semi-detached house stating, "The Alexandra B & B". Upon enquiring I learned it was eighteen notes, so in I went. My room was small but comfortable, not en suite, but who cares when you're desperate? It had a TV, etc., so it was fine by me, though not as nice as Mrs Bourne's pad. After unpacking I decided to go in search of a tasty treat – namely a curry – that I'd forgone so far on this trip, as the opportunity hadn't yet presented itself. I set off down the hill looking for the Taj Mahal, which I'd heard about earlier. After 600 yards I noticed that the area was not very salubrious, featuring some dodgy-looking people around. Once inside the Taj Mahal everything appeared okay. It was 7.30 p.m. and only two or three tables were occupied. I went to the counter to reserve a table, but was told they were fully-booked for the evening. They offered me a takeaway instead and I had to accept it. They said it'd take forty bloody minutes – it's only twenty at my local back home. I handed over a tenner and two pound coins after ordering a chicken tikka biryani, a lamb bhuna, and nan bread. I'd noticed a grim-looking pub across the road so decided to retire there to wait for my meal. It'd better be worth the money. Crossing the road, I saw a phone box and decided to call Mum and Dad.

As I approached it a bunch of about ten teenagers, who'd been standing around, came towards me shouting aggressively, "Hey you! Lend us a pound!" And: "Have you got any money, mister?" When I said I'd only got enough change for the phone one them said, "Well give us your bag, then."

When I said, "You must be joking!" the smallest member of the gang – a lad who looked about 12 but was probably 15 and the ringleader – fixed me with an insolent stare, swearing quietly but directly at me. I knew this kid had the capacity to be violent and a shiver ran through me. Ten against one is not good odds. I had to keep calm and not show any fear. That would be the worst thing to do. I also knew I shouldn't be confrontational with them either.

I looked at them, said, "Excuse me," quietly but firmly, and walked straight through the middle of them, surprising and scattering them in different directions. I felt I'd partly won the psychological battle with this move, but was still wondering if I might get a knife in my back before I got to the phone box. Once inside I dialled my parents' number and talked to them as naturally as possible, not wanting them to know the position I was in. The kids hung outside, with the little one still staring at me with menace as if to say, "I could take you any day, sucker!" I wondered if he might even have a gun, in which case he definitely could take me. I'd never been intimidated by kids before. Even though I'm a big strong bloke it was quite a frightening experience. After five minutes or so they must've got bored. I saw them run off, probably in search of an easier target. I breathed a big sigh of relief. I still had twenty minutes to kill (operative word?), so I entered the grimy pub.

Inside its scruffy sanctuary I met a drunken Irishman who proceeded to tell me his entire life story, of which I can recall nothing whatsoever, while I sipped a pint of Tinners. That's how interesting his life must've been but it helped pass the time. When it was time to go there was no sign of the kids as I crossed the road and headed for the Taj Mahal. When I got there I was greeted by the sight of a queue stretching down the road. I'd no option but to join the end of it. Having never seen anything like this before I asked a couple of people ahead of me what was going on. They told me that this was the best curry house in Cornwall and was always packed. On hearing this, several others turned round, nodding enthusiastically in agreement. I thought it needs to be after the misery I've endured this evening, simply trying to get a curry. Twenty minutes later I got to the counter and saw that the place was heaving with every table full. I collected my brown carrier bag full of goodies and set off back up the hill to The Alexandra. I let myself in quietly and went up to my room. With the telly on I sat on the bed to enjoy my curry. Halfway through I noticed it wasn't all that great! It wasn't exactly horrid, but it wasn't as good as my local in Hereford. Yet all those people were raving about it. Maybe there weren't any great curry houses in Cornwall, but the locals didn't realise. I didn't even finish it, which is unusual for me. Afterwards I wished I'd eaten a pot noodle and a cereal bar. It would've saved me £14, ninety minutes, and a whole load of aggro.

Day 35: Sunday 18 May

I felt rough upon waking to the sound of the reliable but nagging Timex. I lay in bed for fifteen minutes, thinking I must get out of here today or I'll go mental. I always got this terrible feeling of frustration if I got "trapped" somewhere. I'd been stuck around the St Austell region since Friday afternoon, and also at Pentewan for two days prior to that. Some walkers like to take their time, having a few days a week off to do some sightseeing, or to take things easy, but I'm not like that at all. I like to get on without rest days because I hate walking so much that I'm always desperate to finish and get home to bed ASAP! I also find that I feel fitter if I walk every day. Of course, for various reasons it's not always possible, but

I do start champing on the bit if I can't move on, with the odd exception. However, upon opening the curtains I inwardly groaned, as it was grey and raining again. Not another day in St Austell!

After a soak I went down to the breakfast room. I was the only one there and Tony, the likeable manager, cooked my fried breakfast. We chatted, mainly about the dreadful weather for the time of year. Back in room No. 1, I packed unenthusiastically, constantly glancing out of the window at the glistening road. I thought about staying another night. That way I could at least stay in the room and watch TV all day. After all, it wasn't a bad little room. Or should I risk it and make a bolt for Fowey? I couldn't decide what to do. My brain was hurting from the dilemma. I lay on the bed and snoozed for fifteen minutes and next time I looked out the rain had stopped, the pavements were dry, and the sky was lighter. Suddenly it was all stations *go*! I finished the packing and hurried downstairs to pay Tony. I pushed on quickly up the hill, back to St Austell station. I arrived in time to see my train to Par pulling out. I'd have to wait an hour for the next one.

Alone on the station with nothing to do I sat on a bench, spraying my new boots with a substantial coating of G Sport. It cost £1.80 to get to Par again, where I had to retrace my steps back to the coast path, but I went wrong somewhere and found myself back at the same horrific china clay works. I got a sinking feeling as the conditions were exactly the same as Friday's swirling smoke, steam, or fog. It was cold and raining hard now. I was back in hell, dodging cars. Déjà bloody vu! It felt like I'd never be able to get away from this miserable spot.

The wet suburban streets were deserted as I tried to find my way to the coast path. I'd gone a least a mile before realising it didn't look at all "coast path-y" where I was. I must've missed it somehow. I turned back, searching every house and garden for any sign of a path back to the sea. I was only 300 yards from the china clay works and was beginning to panic. I couldn't face being back there again, when I spied a tiny, almost invisible sign, pointing up a narrow alleyway between the houses. I went through a caravan park. Two minutes later I was on the beach, which I crossed before climbing up the cliffs. Next stop Polkerris.

I slid around in the thick mud, trying to stay on my feet. The poor boots were getting a testing initiation ceremony, but they passed it with flea-ing colours, and my feet remained dry. At Polkerris the rain came down even harder. I rushed into the Rashleigh Arms for shelter. It was warm, cosy, and very busy inside with everyone tucking into their Sunday roasts. The views from the large windows looked out to sea, but also back across St Austell Bay to those damn clay works. Would I never get away from them? I ordered a measly pot of tea. The landlord didn't look pleased, as it was glaringly apparent I was taking up valuable space in his pub because of the rain, and had no intention of becoming a real paying punter. It was hard to find anywhere to sit as it was heaving in there. I hid round a corner with my tea, away from the landlord's line of vision. He'd definitely *not* taken a shine to me, like so many others before and after him. Once the rain eased forty-five minutes later I left before being asked to leave.

Up onto the cliffs, and even though the terrain was not so steep on the green (and brown) Gribbin Head, the rain and gales were getting worse. The new boots were really taking a battering in mud and puddles that were 6 inches deep in places. I was sliding around like a drunken ice skater. A bedraggled walker coming the other way took the brunt of my foul language as he rounded a bend and walked right into my path. We didn't stop to talk. The dreaded Nasty Notemares had returned to haunt me again, plaguing my brain at deafening volume with their solemn repetitive Celtic themes. Struggling around "The Gribbin" – as this headland is known locally – in thick mud was energy-sapping in these conditions, especially with the Notemares pounding away. I finally made it, even having the presence of mind to stop and take a photo of the famous red and white hooped Daymark Tower perched on its tip. This was erected in 1832 as a safety measure, as sailors often mistook Gribbin Head for St Anthony's Head at the entrance of Falmouth Estuary. Many accidents resulted from the confusion until the Daymark Tower was built to distinguish the two headlands.

Once I began to descend from the green headland I was protected from the worst of the weather as I tramped the 3 miles to Fowey. By the time I got there things were looking distinctly better. It'd stopped raining and faired up. Before the town I took a wrong turn up a steep muddy inland track. After struggling uphill for ten minutes I became aware that I'd bungled yet again. I had a wild tantrum before sliding back down to where I'd come from previously. I passed a large, stylish bungalow on the way into the town that'd been one of Daphne Du Maurier's residences, of which she'd had several in and around Fowey. A few people were milling around. A guide told me it was the annual Daphne Du Maurier Festival of Art and Literature this week. I pressed on into the town, thinking I may try for Polperro tonight, not having done many miles today. It'd mean getting another B & B at dusk though, as the ground was sodden. With weather this unpredictable, wild camping was ruled out. It was starting to get expensive, but I didn't have any choice.

In the central square I found a phone box where I got out the guidebook and all my 20 pence pieces, which I always carried in abundance, and laid them out on the shelf in a row. First I tried half a dozen B & Bs in Polperro, none of which had any vacancies. That was £1.20 gone for nothing. It soon became apparent that I'd not be going to Polperro after all, which meant staying either in Fowey or in Polruan across the estuary. I started dialling Fowey numbers but was met with the same answer each time: as it was Daphne Du Maurier week, there were no vacancies in the entire area, yet alone Fowey. For forty-five minutes I loathed Daphne Du Maurier very much. What had she ever done apart from make up a few stories in her head? Stuff like *My Cousin Roberta* or whatever her name was. My granny could've done better with her eyes tied behind her back! I was down to two 20 pence pieces and felt worried when I called the last B & B listed in the book. Oh misery me, no vacancies! However, the gentleman was sympathetic and asked if I'd tried the Tally Ho! He gave me the number and I dialled it with my last 20p. A chap answered and said they had a double room priced at £35. Despite the utter desperation of my plight I stood my ground and told him I couldn't possibly pay more than £25. He told me to wait and when he returned he told me his mother had said she could do it for £30.

I replied, saying it was still too much, pleading, "Can't you do it for £25 seein' as it's *me*?"

"Oh, are you a regular? Do we know you?"

I was forced to grovel again: "No, you don't, erm, know me, but go on, please! Seein' as it's *me*!"

He sounded horrified at my persistence, which was bordering on intimidation now, but told me to hold on again.

When he returned he said frustratedly, "Oh all right! £25 if you insist!"

Overjoyed at the beating down, and not caring one iota about the loss of dignity, I took down the address and directions, said I'd be an hour or so, and set off for a look round Fowey, a favourite town of mine. Most of the shops were shut, as it was 5 p.m. and Sunday. After a stroll round the fabulous harbour area, I located the emporium Odds & Ends where I'd bought some presents on a previous visit, but it was closed now. I went into the Toll Bar café, where I'd had a good cream tea in a previous life. On this occasion I could afford a meal, having saved a tenner on the price of the B & B by grovelling. I ordered scallops, salad, and breasty crud (crusty bread), and a pot of tea for *four*, as I was flush again. I really pushed the boat out and had a chocolate brownie cake, which was nice, but somewhat pricey at £3.00. I decided not to have any more desserts after this, but instead would buy an ice cream, cake, or Yorkie bar at a shop afterwards. I ascended by the church. I asked a few people if they'd heard of Willow Close.

When one of them said it was right up to the top of the steep hill, straight on for half mile, I replied grumpily, "Thanks a bundle, mate! You would have to be the harbinger of doom, wouldn't you?"

Why was it always *up*hill, never *down*? Still unsure of my whereabouts, I caught up with an elderly couple walking up the hill and proceeded to have a row with the exceptionally stroppy old gent. We were like bookends.

I only asked if it was straight on for Willow Close but he started all that stuff about, "No you don't want to do that. I know a shortcut. You want to ..."

My heart sank as he pointed back down the hill to Fowey.

I tried to keep calm as I growled, through gritted teeth: "I don't want to know about any shortcuts. I want to get straight to Willow Close. Do you know it or not?"

He kicked off with, "Well, if that's your attitude I'm not helping you anymore!"

"But you haven't helped me at all! You're trying to confuse me."

Him, tetchily to his wife: "These bloody youngsters are all ungrateful sods and need a damn good haircut too!"

At fifty-six I didn't mind the "youngsters" bit, but realised I was flogging another dead horse. Ignoring him, I said cheerio to his misses.

She turned to me and said, "Don't take any notice of him, he's an old fool."

She politely wished me luck. He was still moaning about me as I hurried ahead up the hill. I came to a modern housing estate thinking, This can't be it! I wandered into it bewildered. I stood and did a 360-degree turn but was none the wiser. I grabbed a passing chap with a dog and asked if he'd heard of The Tally Ho! He pointed to a house 3 yards away saying that was it. The sign was unmissable but I'd missed it. I rang the doorbell and waited.

When a smart-looking lady opened the door I said with a smile, "Gosh this place is hard to find, isn't it?"

"No," was the curt reply. Evidently she'd taken an instant dislike to me. She beckoned me in but before I got as far as the hall she said, "You can take those muddy boots off for a start."

I felt uneasy already but complied without a murmur, unable to risk getting slung out, as I couldn't find anywhere else because of bloody Du Maurier. The house was a family home and nothing like any B & B I'd ever stayed in before. Mrs Stokes showed me my sizeable, comfortable room. It was en suite too with a kettle and accoutrements, but suddenly, to my horror, I noticed there was no television.

When I pointed this out she said politely, "That's correct, we don't believe in television in this house."

You might not, Misses, but I do. It was only 7 p.m. How was I going to occupy myself all night? While on the road, a bit of mindless drivel on the telly is nice after a tough day. I'd sit transfixed in front of the rubbish that I'd never dream of entertaining at home. I suppose you could call it escapism. Even endless boring cookery and property dross programmes would become not only bearable but quite fascinating. She closed the door behind her and I was alone in the silence, all horrible. I unpacked my rucksack, did a bit of laundry, sat on the bed with nothing to do. I only had the guidebook, which was really a reference publication, so became fed up with that after five minutes. I'd already seen enough history to last me ten lifetimes. As I looked round the room for something to do I noticed a long wooden dressing table against the wall in front of the double bed. It didn't look right. The top was suspiciously bare because it looked like something had been on it; something that was no longer on it, but should be on it, namely a *television*! Could it be possible that there'd been a telly there earlier but for some reason it'd been removed?

Had Mrs Stokes flown into a rage and thrown a wobbler when her son had told her, "I've got a dreadful bloke on the phone who'll only pay £25!"

Maybe she'd said to him, "The b******! Tell him okay but we'll teach the swine a lesson when he gets here. We'll get that telly out of his room for a start and take his sausages away at breakfast. Turn his radiator off too."

It sounds unlikely, but it could also explain why she'd taken that instant dislike to me! I don't blame her actually. She was obviously a great judge of character. I pottered around listlessly, hung some laundry up to drip dry in the shower. A black top wouldn't fit on the rail, so I rung it out, put it on a hanger, and looked around for somewhere to hang it. The only place I could think of was a nail, from which a landscape painting was already hanging above the dressing table. I carefully took the picture down and replaced it with the T-shirt. Bored, with three hours to go before bedtime, I decided to brave asking Mrs Stokes if I could borrow some reading material. I went downstairs and called out gently in the hallway. When she appeared I asked if she'd got any Sunday papers or magazines I could read.

Appearing baffled, she said in an offhand manner, "Papers and magazines? I suppose I can find some if you really must read them."

She went into her living room and came out with a pile of the said publications. At least I'd something to do now. Back in my room I ploughed through all the gossip and scandal, plus all kinds of interesting news stories that I'd been unaware of, owing to the nature of my trip.

Whilst reading I became aware of the sound of laughter coming from downstairs, realising that the Stokes family were having fun. As I listened I could make out the theme tune to *Corrie* drifting up the stairs. They'd got my bloody telly on! Everything had settled down by 10.30 p.m., so feeling weary I turned in. Reading made a pleasant change, but wouldn't want to make a habit of it, as it required too much effort.

Day 36: Monday 19 May

I'd set the Timex for 7.30 a.m., but woke up thirty minutes earlier, feeling good. Opening the curtains I was greeted by a blue sky and yellow sunshine. I'd slept well and felt invigorated for the first time in ages. I showered, did most of my packing, leaving the laundry to air on the window ledge. As I was about to go downstairs to eat, I noticed that the black T-shirt was still hanging from the nail, so I took it down and put that in the sun too. I'd replace the picture later. However, as I opened the door I happened to glance at the wall, where, to my absolute horror, there was a black T-shirt-shaped stain! I'd really done it this time. Mrs Stokes would kill me. Running into the bathroom in a blind panic I grabbed my flannel and soap and began scrubbing frantically at the ugly mark. It wouldn't budge! I flew into a rage – a quiet one in case I drew attention from downstairs – but rage wasn't getting me anywhere. Next I became much like John Cleese in *Fawlty Towers* with that "duck surprise", pleading quietly up towards ceiling, begging for someone to help me, but nobody did. Apart from the obvious problem I was also late for breakfast. The previous evening Mrs Stokes told me in no uncertain terms, "8.30 sharp, if you please." To make matters even worse, the scrubbing had started to remove a layer of paint and the white undercoat was now showing through. I groaned in despair.

"Oh God! *Why me?*" I screamed without sound, imagining Munch's 'The Scream', which was fast beginning to epitomise most of the walk.

Not knowing what more to do I buried my head in the sand, simply hung the painting back up over the offending area, slunk downstairs, trying to calm myself down. "Act natural and you'll be all right," I told myself.

Breakfast was in the conservatory where it was as hot as an oven. The matronly Mrs Stokes put me at a table with a very nice lady in her mid-sixties. We got on very well, conversing in the blazing heat. The breakfast was good too, with fresh homemade bread and marmalade. I hadn't had my sausages removed either! Mr Stokes junior, who'd answered the phone, gave me extra portions when I'd eaten the first load. Unfortunately, I'd started with apricots and prunes, which in retrospect turned out to be a serious error of judgement. Mr Stokes had heard that I was an angler. How he'd heard, I hadn't a clue. Maybe I'd yelled out in my sleep and they'd heard me downstairs: "Quick, Rick! Bring the landing net! This fish is a real whopper!" Or words to that effect.

When I said I was a carp angler he stepped backwards with a look of disgust on his face, saying haughtily, "Huh! I'm a trout man myself."

For a moment I thought he may still confiscate my sausages after all, but I got away with it. All through the meal that stain on the wall kept nagging away at me. If I couldn't shift it I was going to have to do a runner sharpish. I didn't have the guts to come clean, being afraid of Mrs Stokes. I feared I'd never get out if the house alive if I admitted it. The nice lady at my table was interested in my walk and asked many questions, which I was only too pleased to answer. She was genuinely enthusiastic about it and chuckled at my yarns. I didn't mention the bedroom wall, though was forced to stop myself blurting it out several times during the course of breakfast. She said she was in Fowey for the Daphne Du Maurier Festival.

She smiled when I said, "I'm sick of that woman! I'll be glad to get away from Fowey."

When she left I continued eating as much toast as I could force down my gullet, in order to save spending any money on food till late afternoon. The Stokes' charming daughter, who was on holiday with them, came over and chatted to me. Even Mrs Stokes changed and became friendly. She was very pleasant under that stony exterior. I got the feeling that she didn't even loathe me anymore. She would've reverted to the loathing immediately if she found out about that stain on her wall. They told me that the lady I'd been chatting to was a famous actress performing in one of the Daphne Du Maurier productions being held that week! She'd never said a word but had let me chunter on endlessly about my walk and moan about Daphne too.

Yes, I thought I knew her face. It must've been from on telly. I felt awful.

After a pleasant ten minutes I went back to my room and the worry returned. I'd have another go at that wall before leaving, so packed the rucksack for a quick getaway and removed the painting again. To my amazement the stain had virtually disappeared. It was apparent that, as the wall had dried out, the colour had lightened up and now matched the surrounding area again. Even the white bits were invisible unless I peered from about 3 inches away. I was over the moon and thanked my lucky stars. With a clear conscience I said thanks and goodbye to the Stokes family and strode off down the hill in the sun towards Fowey.

Before covering the half-mile or so I noticed it wasn't quite so sunny now. By the time I reached the foot ferry the sky was distinctly black and grim. So was my belly! The wide estuary was rough too and I wasn't looking forward to this crossing one little bit. I'd the usual discussion with the captain of the tiny ferry.

"Do you think it'll sink?"

The other six passengers eyed me with disbelief and he said, "Get in, will you? You're holding everybody up."

I crossed myself, said a short prayer, and got in. The crossing took five minutes and was fine. I thanked the captain for not sinking, told him it was well worth the 80p fare, and shook his hand with great gusto whilst he remained impassive. In Polruan my immediate priority was to find a gents' quickly. Damn those prunes! Luckily there was one by the landing stage. I rushed in feeling very rough. I resolved to eat no more fruit on this trip. I'd be better off sticking to fried food, pot noodles, pies, and chocolate from now on. I emerged a few minutes later feeling much better, only to find it was now raining hard. Someone's got it in for me, I thought, sheltering under a harbour-side balcony. A local road sweeper joined me. We passed the time of day chatting whilst waiting for the rain to stop. It was 11 a.m. before I was able to leave by way of a lane that wound up and around the headland to Washing Rocks.

I was travelling west again for a while, which I hated as I wanted to go east. This was a common occurrence though as the whole coastline twisted and turned, going back on itself in many places. I was forced to ask the way every few minutes, but luckily there were people around who knew the way and didn't try to send me on any false shortcuts or wild goose chases. I passed through a little park where people were sitting and reading. Once away from habitation the clouds burst again and it chucked it down. I'd no option but to put the waterproofs on. No sooner had I gone 200 yards when it stopped raining. I removed the waterproofs. Another 400 yards and it started again so back on they went. This was to be the pattern for the next three hours. After changing at least twenty times I kept the hot un-breathable and unbearable Gore-Tex on in the end. I was miffed about it though. I resolved that one day I'd invent my own unique waterproofs. They'd be weightless and transparent to aid ventilation, held at least a foot away from the body by employing large electro-magnets. By utilising 620 10-inch bimetal strips in conjunction with pure plutonium, helium, and hydrogen for extra lightness, rain would bounce off them without even touching the surface – *brilliant!* I wouldn't be able to venture anywhere near a naked flame or anything made of iron, steel, earth, wood, coal, nylon, or anything that sloped. I'd also have to wear a full lead-lined all-in-one bodysuit to protect me from radiation that would be a byproduct of the process. Yes, I'd start work on these magical waterproofs as soon as I got home.

The cliffs were exceptionally rugged today with rough steps cut into the ground on the steepest sections to "assist" us madmen. It was like climbing up a ladder and felt as tough as anything I'd done so far. The rain and gales didn't help either. I certainly wouldn't recommend the SW Coast Path to anyone who wanted a pleasant walking holiday, or to any big girls' blouses, milk-type-sops, namby-pamby wimps, wusses, sensible people, or anyone of a nervous disposition. Near Pencarrow Head I could hardly believe my eyes when I came face to face with the chap I'd passed yesterday on The Gribbin whilst cursing and swearing in deep mud. He recognised me too so I was forced to apologise for my outlandish behaviour. He didn't mind and confessed that he too often let out a few well-chosen words when he believed he was out of earshot. Ice broken, we chatted as the rain had eased again. He was on a walking holiday from Yorkshire and was well-choked about the weather too. He also told me he'd met a tiny Canadian lady a couple of days ago, walking the whole of the SW Coast Path in one go. When the penny dropped I told him I'd seen her a couple of times about ten days ago. Seemingly she and I were both on the same trajectory, aiming for South Haven Point and Poole harbour, the end of our journeys. Travelling on, I wondered how she was coping with the terrain and the elements, apart from all the other hardships and equipment problems that kept cropping up. She must've walked all the way from Minehead. Was she constantly getting lost and going ballistic like I was? Had she overtaken me and gone on ahead after my days off in Pentewan and St Austell?

After several more difficult ups and downs I found myself looking down on another picturesque ancient fishing port, Polperro. I'd visited this beautiful village before so knew what to expect. I came down the narrow path between some cottages and was soon standing in the middle of good old "Pollo". It was sunny and pleasant now that I didn't need it to be, but I felt absolutely knackered. The first thing on my mind was lunch, as it'd been a tough trek from Fowey. My back was hurting from the exertion, so I took the pack off by a table outside The Ship Inn. I was wondering if their food was any good when I saw a chap leaning in his own shop doorway having a crafty fag.

I called across to him: "Is the food any good here?"

He nodded, saying, "Yeah, but if you want a superb meal, walk up to that hanging sign over there. That's *the* place to eat. It's cheap too."

I looked at the sign, at least 50 yards away, before looking at him and said, quite seriously, "It's too far. I'm gonna have to eat here."

I sat at the table, picking up the menu. It occurred to me how tough this walk really was and how I'd do anything to conserve energy. I hadn't walked a single step more than required. It seemed ridiculous in one respect. How can someone walk 630.4 miles (plus detours), yet refuse to go an extra 50 yards and back for food? The answer is that I didn't *have to*. Why waste energy? I soon felt cold and went inside for my plaice, chips, peas, and a pint of Worthington's. I was pretty happy and had saved 100 yards-worth of wear on my new boots too. Putting my new plan into action, I bought a big cream cake from the bakers and ate it outside, rounding off the meal splendidly. It started raining again so I pottered round the shops within my immediate vicinity, bought a few postcards and stamps, and finally got away at 3.30 p.m. The ascent was exceptionally steep again to Downend Point. It wasn't getting any easier, especially with my back still playing up.

Before long I was descending again and could see Talland Bay below. Even though I'd only been walking for an hour I couldn't resist the inviting little café situated near the sea, so I went in for a cuppa, a Yorkie bar, and a rest. I spoke separately with the two owners, as they took turns doing chores and serving the few stragglers who were about in this inclement weather. The chap told me that he and his nine-year-old son had walked from John o'Groats to Land's End two years ago. The lad made it into the Guinness Book of Records as the youngest person ever to complete this long, difficult trek. I was in awe of them both. I followed a couple I'd met yesterday back onto the cliffs and, after passing them, I came to a great sign that made me chuckle. It was situated at the base of an almost vertical stepped climb of 300 feet. It read: "Footpath Only. No Cycling". I'd like to see somebody try! What had possessed someone to go to the trouble of putting it there when it was totally superfluous?

From the top of Hore Stone I saw the lovely sight of Looe Island, my favourite island of the trip, also known as St George's Island. It was a couple of miles ahead and a mile out to sea. Even though it was pouring down and the wind was stronger than ever I was fascinated by the island and couldn't take my eyes off it as I got closer. I took photos and video clips from varying distances, trying to keep the tiny camera dry whilst doing so. It was becoming obvious that I'd not be able to camp in this. I'd have to try and get a room in Looe. It'd be the sixth B & B in as many nights. It was getting expensive, but there was no alternative. I was yet to discover the charm and cheapness of The Youth Hostelling Association, which I finally did two years later. Opposite the island I met a chap named Barry walking his dog and we talked for twenty minutes. The sun was out now and being low down the wind was negligible. He told me about the island and I listened intently. He said it covered an area of over 20 acres and was a mile in circumference, yet it didn't look that big. The highest point is 150 feet above sea level and is designated as an area of outstanding natural beauty. I could see why, as it was very green, partly wooded, and must command incredible views for miles in all directions. Its climate is very mild too with daffodils blooming as early as Christmas. It now provides a sanctuary for birds as it once did for smugglers. The island is normally only accessible by boat but on one or two days a year there's usually a tide low enough for the journey to be made by foot across the rocky sea floor. People are advised not to try it without an expert, as they could easily go wrong and drown, like me if I attempted it. The island's recent history is also fascinating. Two spinsters bought it cheap in 1965 and have lived on it ever since. While we'd been chatting I noticed Barry was holding a plastic carrier, obviously containing something horrid and doggy-ish. When it came time to part company he attempted to shake hands with me.

I rapidly backed away saying, "Sorry, you may be a decent bloke, but I'm drawing the line at shaking hands with you."

He didn't take offence though and we said cheerio instead. After crossing a couple more fields I stepped off the coast path, onto the end of the road to Looe. It was pretty stormy so I wouldn't be going any further. In West Looe, the quieter side of town, I found a couple of empty phone boxes near a small post office. As I went in the nearest one I noticed that most of the panes of glass in both boxes had been broken, but when I picked up the receiver the phone was working. Out came the guidebook again. I flicked through to the "B & Bs Looe" page. In Polperro someone had recommended one particular guest house named Marwinthy. It was only £17.00 in the book too. I found the number and dialled it after laying out no less than ten 20 pence pieces on the shelf before me. I reached an answerphone – oh no!

As it had already cost me 20p I listened to the message anyway: "Eddie Mawby here. I'm in the pub, but you can reach me on my mobile if you need to get hold of me. My number is 07 *********."

Not expecting to get an answerphone, I hadn't bothered getting my pen out. I dialled again and listened to the first part of the message, waiting with pen in hand for the important bit.

"… and my number is 073 –"

Whoooosh! A massive truck roared by 2 feet from the phone box. With the panes broken, it saturated my face and torso in a tidal wave of spray, drowning out the answerphone message. Two birds with one stone! I stood speechless, dripping with brown puddle-water, holding the receiver. I tried to keep calm, wiping myself down with some tissues, and dialled for a third time. Poised for action I listened again.

"Eddie Mawby here … blah, blah, blah … my number is 0734 –"

Whoooosh! A bus roared by, causing another huge tsunami to saturate me, drowning out the answerphone. This time I went *beserk*! I couldn't contain my anger and let it all out in a loud tirade of ugly abuse.

"You ******* bus! Why don't you … I'll … your … head in … you …"

All this whilst wildly waving the moribund receiver about my head, trying to resist smashing it into the shelf, as the filthy brown water and mud poured down my face. In mid-rage I happened to glance to my right where, no more than 6 inches away, trapped in the adjacent phone box, a poor man with sheer terror in his bulging eyes was right in my face. With all the panes smashed my screaming must've deafened him. As I stared at him my high-pitched ranting turned naturally into a kind of low *Exorcist*-style moaning, which he still didn't like much, judging by his contorted expression. It would've been pointless attempting any kind of apology. He was too far gone. I watched the whole scene unfold as if I were an innocent fly on the wall, instead of being the sole cause of the mayhem. I saw him grab desperately at the door to escape, but in his panic he'd forgotten where the door was, so he spun like a top, deliberately banging himself against anything that might give way. I was overjoyed for him when he finally stumbled onto the pavement and slipped over. I thought about helping him, but I'd already done enough. He struggled to his feet and bolted for his life. I did feel awful, as once again I dabbed my face with the same filthy soaking tissues. Right, back to the task in hand with renewed determination. I dialled the number, put in the 20p, and waited.

"Eddie Mawby here ... and my number is 07347 ..."

You've guessed right! All the beserk-ness had now drained out of me. Instead I slumped lifeless over the shelf and tried stuffing the receiver into my mouth, hoping it might do some good, but it didn't really help. Resigned now to only getting the vital number by acquiring one digit at a time, I used up all of my 20 pence pieces over the next ten minutes. After 10,000 gallons of brown water, I finally had all required numbers. Now I realised I hadn't any coins left to call his mobile! I saw a couple walking across the road and quietly accosted them. All was very civil and they produced some change for which I gave them a quid in return.

I half expected them to say, "By the way, you'd better watch out. We've heard there's a madman at large in the area."

Back in the box, which by now had become my least favourite "building" of the trip, I dialled the mobile. A very laidback-sounding Eddie Mawby answered. He did have a room. He told me to cross the bridge into East Looe and he'd be in The Salutation Inn having a pint. I said I could do with one too and would be there in twenty minutes. After only getting lost three times I was there in forty. Eddie was an amiable chap about my own age and, as there was no particular hurry, I downed a pint of Sharp's before we left for the short stroll up the hill to Marwinthy. We were joined by his wife and their dog along the way. The evening was sunny, though there was still a strong wind where there was no shelter. On the way up I decided to check with him that £17.00 was the correct price for B & B. When I mentioned it he said it had risen this year to £20.00. I didn't hit the roof exactly, but at the same time I wasn't happy and proceeded to quibble like mad. He said he'd had to put it up, owing to extra food, wage, and heating costs. I referred meekly to it stating £17 in the book. He said if I wanted to find somewhere else he would understand, to which I replied in an ungrateful and bolshy manner.

"No, can't be bothered. Suppose I'll have to pay the extra three bloody quid, then."

Our conversation was not quite so amicable for the rest of the walk. When I got home in June and studied the guidebook more thoroughly I saw a small paragraph below the B & B section that read: "All prices listed above were for the year 2002 and may be subject to change for 2003." I'd missed this during my trip. I sent Eddie a Christmas card, apologising for quibbling about the £3.

Upon reaching Marwinthy he checked me in and took me up to room No. 5, a large attic room overlooking Looe harbour and the sandy beach. I loved it and immediately felt awful about quibbling. It was a family room with a double and two single beds, with a couple of Z beds hanging about, in case any more kids happened to be born during the night presumably. It had an old-fashioned 1950s look to it, was clean and comfortable, with a sink, TV, kettle, etc. It felt cosy and what I particularly liked was the large array of books on the higgledy-piggledy shelving. There was something for everyone, including some Dickens, Scott, and other major classics. An impressive selection of board games was piled in and on top of the wardrobes. I almost wished I had a wife and kids to enjoy them with, but didn't wish it for long. This all combined to create a magical atmosphere. I felt very much at home here.

As I ate my pasty, chicken tikka sandwich, and salad, I looked out across the roofs to the beach and harbour. It was a lovely evening. I thought about wandering down to the Salutation for a couple of pints but it'd mean shaving and I was too tired to bother getting all poshed-up after another hard day. Eddie mentioned that a Canadian lady was staying there. Surely there couldn't be two of them? It stood to reason that as our paths seemed to keep crossing, we'd meet up sooner or later. I thought about tapping on her door and asking if she'd like to come down to the pub, but didn't want to scare her out of her wits. A woman travelling alone might think I'd been stalking her all the way along the coast path for 400 miles from Minehead! I was knackered too and would probably have been awful company in the pub, nodding off rudely every couple of minutes while she was talking. Instead I prepared for an evening ogling the goggle-box, as I was too far gone to start a book. I'd be leaving in the morning so would never finish it anyway. Whilst watching some soap or other I ate a massive pile of bedraggled, oaty crumbs that had once, long ago, had the nerve to call themselves a flapjack, before being cruelly crushed beyond recognition in my pack. My mind drifted off into a reverie: Wouldn't it be great to book a whole year in this very room? I'd disappear from the rest of the world and read every single classic book on these shelves, leaving the room only to walk the wild cliffs every day at dawn and dusk, and for the fresh seafood that was always available in Looe, and the occasional incognito pint in the Salutation. I must ask what kind of discount Eddie could offer me based on a year-long stay at his joint. None, probably. I might even get barred for life after quibbling over that paltry three quid.

Back in the real world I did some bits of laundry and a few sewing repairs before settling down to watch an interesting documentary about Mary Archer – wife of Lord Jeffery Archer – what a nice lady. Why the hell does she put up with *him*! If she were to play her cards right she might even stand a chance with me, the lucky lady! That could really finish her off. Afterwards I flicked through some brochures on Looe to find out more about the place, which I'd always liked, as it seemed to be an honest working town and not so "chocolate boxy" as some of the other coastal villages. I read in a tourism brochure that Looe is famous mainly for prostitution, lap dancing, and gambling, apart from being a major cocaine importing, sorting and redistribution centre, employing over 2,000 local workers in the three huge factories right next to the pleasure beach. These are open to the public all year round so they can see how it all works and many tourists can partake of the free samples, before buying fun-sized bags of the white powder for special holiday treats. NB: I made up every single word of that last section because I'm fed up with talking about fishing, mining, and tourism all the time. I suppose I'd better tell the truth now or I'm bound to get into trouble with the Cornish Tourist Board, though even more tourists might be attracted if my story were true. Looe is, of course, best known for its boring ancient fishing industry, and also as a holiday resort, dating back over 200 years. Tourism has been relied on more heavily since it's pilchard canning factory closed down in the 1960s, but Looe is still named as the shark fishing capital of Great Britain, though "tag and release" is more the norm nowadays. The town also has a long, attractive tidal harbour, going some distance inland, dividing East and West Looe. These were separate communities in medieval times before a bridge was erected that now joins the two Looes. As far as I could ascertain, there's no prostitution, drugs, or gambling anywhere in the Looe region!

By 11.30 p.m. my eyes kept closing, so I clambered into the double bed and went straight out like a light. Another patchy night followed, waking and sleeping alternately for about an hour each time.

Day 37: Tuesday 20 May

I got up at 7 a.m. feeling rough to start with. After a coffee and a shower I woke up enough to go downstairs. As I entered the breakfast room, several people were sitting around various tables. I spotted the Canadian lady having breakfast, chatting to another guest. When she said hi and smiled I went over and introduced myself. Her name was Janet and, although small in stature, she had a big personality and a great sense of humour. We got on well instantly and discussed our respective adventures. She'd left Minehead one week before me, so I'd been gradually catching her up without realising. I immediately noticed how gutsy and determined she was compared to me, and also how much more positive she was. Her glass was always half full whereas mine was always three-quarters empty! These lopsided statistics kind of cancelled one another out and we struck up a friendship. It was a shame we hadn't met properly until now. Better late than never. She said she would've liked to have gone to the pub last night, had the opportunity arisen! Breakfast over, I went up to pack and had a quick lie down, feeling knackered after a top quality fry-up. Before leaving I wanted to find Eddie to say thanks for a great stay and apologise for the quibbling, however, I was told he was showing some business people around. I'd have to leave it for another time. Janet was fully laden when I came down. I noticed a tiny white "good luck" teddy on her pack. She was about to set off so we had another quick chat, took a few pictures, wished each other luck, and said, "See you later."

I got a few supplies, finished my packing and left as Looe church clock struck 11. It struck *me* that I should've asked for Janet's phone number so we could've kept in touch if we didn't happen to see each other again. The weariness had slowed my brain down and it didn't occur to me until it was too late. It was a hot sunny day and even though it was already late I still expected to cover a good distance if I could wake up a bit. The climbing was severe immediately. That woke me up horridly. I soon caught up with a middle-aged Yorkshire couple who, having made the big move south, were on their way home carrying loads of heavy Tesco's shopping bags along the coast path. After ten minutes we came to some modern whitewashed houses off the path to our left.

Pointing at a Mediterranean-style property, they said, "Here we are. Cheerio, then," and they were gone.

Walking on, I wondered if this was the only way they could reach their house. If this was the case they'd probably paid about ten quid for their property and had no option but to buy lightweight inflatable furniture and carry it the 2 miles along the coast path. Things like fridges, freezers, and washing machines would have to be dismantled in Looe, carried in small sections to the house, and mantled again once inside! It was too complicated to think about so I tried to forget it and move on.

As I was alone again and extremely cheerful for this time of day, I started singing 'Roland the Headless Thompson Gunner' and 'Searching for a Heart', by Warren Zevon, thinking I must work out the chords one day. An hour later I descended from the cliffs to Seaton, and straight into a small café, as it was hot and I was thirsty. Whilst waiting for my mug of tea I took a peek at the menu and suddenly felt peckish again. It had been four and a half hours since breakfast. I must have burned off all the calories by now. I ordered plaice, chips, and peas and, in passing, asked the pleasant woman behind the counter if I could get my water bottle filled up before leaving. She looked sheepish and said she couldn't fill it for me. When I asked why she said she wasn't allowed to fill bottles. I was speechless at first, but pointed out to her that I was about to spend over £10 on a meal, drink, and probably a few items to take away with me afterwards. She looked at the floor, embarrassed, saying she was sorry.

I said, "There's a pound for the tea. You can cancel the meal. I've never heard anything so disgraceful in my entire life."

That was a slight exaggeration. Baffled, I wandered outside with the mug and sat alone at a table. Presently, an elderly couple sat down near me and we began chatting. When I told them about the refusal they couldn't believe it, wondering what sort of person would refuse someone a drink of water.

Pointing to the open café door, I gruffly replied: "That sort!"

When I'd come to terms with the situation and calmed down I decided to pop to the gents' behind the café and fill my bottle there instead. Two guys were digging before I got there. I asked them if the water was drinkable. One of them said he didn't know. I calmly explained what had happened in the café, expecting a sympathetic response, maybe a suggestion about where I could eat instead. The older guy, aged around forty, came towards me with wild eyes, brandishing his spade, shouting aggressively.

"It's my ******* café! I don't have to give water to any of you b******s!"

Stunned, I stepped back, saying, "Are you for real?" and laughed.

This seemed to light his touch paper and the younger one reached out as if to restrain him. Now a potentially dangerous situation I looked at the guy's demented face. He loathed me far more than Mrs Stokes or the landlord at the Rashleigh had, or even the memorable landlord from The Tinners Arms in Zennor. I'd been quiet, polite, and done nothing to antagonise him, apart from saying I'd been refused water in the café. He was obviously a violent man with all the trimmings: shaved hair, muscles, tattoos, earrings, and such like. As I stared at him it occurred to me that the only thing missing was "hate" tattooed across his forehead. After regaining my composure I was determined not to be intimidated by this ageing skinhead and tried to make him see sense.

I said calmly, "I've never been refused water before. Don't you care about your customers or your reputation? I was going to buy a meal and some supplies too, but I certainly won't be doing that now."

His mate pulled him away as he ranted: "I don't give a **** about you! I'm sick of kids asking for water all day long!"

I felt obliged to point out that I wasn't a kid, but a fifty-six-year-old hiker who'd intended spending about £12 in his establishment before asking for any water.

My parting shot was, "I will be telling the SW Coast Path Association and tourist board about this incident when I get home."

And I *did!* They'd already heard about him, surprise, surprise. I didn't bother with the gents' after that but got water and an Orange Juice Burst in another café without problems and left. I thought about the incident as I did some road walking. The thing that really got under my skin was that he didn't give a damn, even about his own reputation, because he knew there'd be another large coach party of holidaymakers along later who'd each spend a tenner in his café. This would happen every day of the season, so he'd no reason to be courteous to anyone. He was a law unto himself and could behave however he wanted and tell anyone where to go with no repercussions. If he'd needed to rely on local trade he wouldn't have lasted a month. I wondered how he'd managed to acquire the café in the first place. I couldn't imagine him dealing with anyone in a civil manner or calmly sorting out contracts and legal procedures. Maybe he got the agents and solicitors by their throats and forced them to sign all the documents!

Whilst walking along the road I became aware of a white van that had passed me on several occasions, alternately travelling in both directions. Although I could only see the driver's silhouette, I could've sworn it was the same guy tracking me. If it was him, what did he want? Did he want to attack me or apologise? Before long though, at Downderry, the path left the road and I set off over the cliffs again, so that was that. If it was him I'd never know what he wanted. The ascents and descents were very difficult and the weight of the pack was hurting again. More steps were cut in the steepest sections, which I always found awful to deal with.

At Portwrinkle there were no shops and I was really hungry. As I climbed up onto a golf course I met a golfer out taking a stroll. When I told him I was hungry he kindly invited me into the Whitsand Bay Golf Club clubhouse for a pint and a pasty. The atmosphere was terrific there. I was treated extremely well by all twenty-something members. The barman was great too. The beer was cheap and he gave me a pasty and two to take away. Quite a contrast to the earlier incident. Everyone was chatting and joking with me. I said I was surprised that non-members were allowed in.

They replied, "That's what they all think, but it's not the case. We like having new faces here but can't get anyone to come in!"

After half an hour it was to time to go, but having such a good time I really didn't want to. As I climbed back up over the golf course for the second time I thought what a great bunch they were. If any of them ever read this I'd like to say "thanks" for their hospitality on that afternoon. You really cheered me up. After that I walked fast and well over more forgiving terrain and, for the first time, I saw Plymouth in the distance. I met two young Dutch guys hiking towards me. We all stopped for a chat and a breather. Pete and Sebastian had come from Plymouth that morning and began relating some hilarious incidents that happened along the way. Our faces ached from laughing. I warned them about the café and they said they'd avoid it. I told many other walkers I met about the "water incident" and where the place was. They were all shocked.

As they turned to walk off one of them said, "Your name isn't Overhead, by any chance?"

"Close; it's Overend, but how do you know me?"

They explained that earlier in the day they'd met a Canadian lady and somehow I'd cropped up in the conversation. She'd written down her mobile number on a scrap of paper and asked them to hand it to me if they happened to bump into me.

"Well I'll go to the foot of our stairs!" as my old granddad used to say.

What a bit of luck I thought to myself as we parted company. After some more road walking, during which I was forced inland for a while by high barbed wire fences and "Danger Firing" signs, I stopped for a breather by the ancient landmark that is Tregantle Fort. My shoulders were killing me. I took off the pack and plonked myself down by the side of the road to have a good look at the heavily fortified Victorian structure a few yards away.

Tregantle is one of several forts surrounding Plymouth that were built during Lord Palmerston's premiership to deter the French from attacking naval bases on the Channel coast. Tregantle is infamous within the armed forces, owing to many of the rifle ranges being located there. They're used mainly by personnel located at HMS Raleigh. They were the reason why I had to take the detour inland. For a few minutes, owing to the nauseating shoulder pain, I became quite despondent about my prospects of re-finishing the walk again. Despite being more than 400 miles into it, I began doubting if I could do it after all. Ten minutes later I struggled to get the pack on and, with all negative thoughts banished, I marched off, aiming for Freathy, Rame Head, and possibly Penlee Point if I could make it before dusk.

After the diversion I came back to the coast road and began a steady climb through the temporary-looking "shantytown" of Freathy, the principal settlement of Whitsand Bay. Quite unique, it's a conglomeration of huts, shacks, and holiday chalets, dotted haphazardly around the long, narrow, undulating strip of land between the road and sea. Every building is different. An intricate maze of access paths connects each one with the road. A posh "shack owner" told me that there are two schools of thought about Freathy. It's either a place of unique charm, or it's an unsightly, ramshackle mess. Indeed, some chalets appeared to be derelict, while others looked very spruce with lovingly tended gardens. I tended to veer towards the former though. I like anything quirky and it was so different from anything else on the entire coast path so far. Whether I could live there is another matter. He also said that property prices were sky high, which I found hard to believe, despite its seaside location. I could see the actual coast path a few yards below me and running parallel, but switch-backing and snaking nightmarishly in all directions. It made sense to stay on the steady incline of the road instead, which ended up at exactly the same point anyway, once at the top of the hill.

At the junction by the former Whitesand Bay coastal battery, the second of many old forts in the area, I left the road and followed the path south aiming for Rame Head in a strong cool breeze. I felt good again, walking quickly and positively. After much zigzagging through woods and green areas I saw Rame Head with the small fourteenth-century chapel of St Michael perched precariously on its tip. It looked dramatic and beautiful. From here I looked back at the long sweep of Whitsand Bay from whence I came. Beyond it I could discern The Gribbin and the distant Dodman. As I approached the chapel I decided against taking the tricky ridge that led to it, as the wind was very strong and I didn't fancy getting blown into the sea. I took a picture and, briefly sheltering by a rock, checked the guidebook. It stated that the chapel was first licensed for mass in 1397, dedicated to St Michael, and is probably on the site of a Celtic chapel. The hermit priest who occupied the building lived in its upper floor and was responsible for lighting a beacon to guide mariners or warn of seaborne threats. Records exist as early as 1486 of Plymouth paying a watchman at Rame to maintain a beacon there to warn shipping and to bring news to Plymouth of important ships. A concrete structure standing on the seaward side of the chapel is the remains of a Second World War radar station. Chilled by the strong wind, I couldn't hang around too long.

After several minutes of energetic walking I felt warm again. Once past Rame Head itself I found myself in a more sheltered position, out of the gale. The path here was flat and green with no buildings in view. To my left were high grassy banks, making it feel remote and tranquil. Time seemed to stand still as I slowed and enjoyed the glorious sea views. Somewhere out there, about 10 miles south of me, stood Eddystone lighthouse, which is among the most notorious of all lighthouses. I couldn't see it from Rame Head but as I strolled along I started to daydream about its strange past. The second lighthouse was built by John Rudyard. With a conical wooden structure around a core of brick and concrete, it was first lit in 1709. This survived for nearly fifty years, but on the night of 2 December 1755, the top of the lantern caught fire, probably through a spark from one of the candles used to illuminate the light. The three keepers threw water upwards from buckets, however, they were driven on to the rock as the tower burnt down. They were all rescued by boat. Henry Hall, who was said to be ninety-four at the time – a few reports say that he was a mere eighty-four, thus making him not as good! – died from lead poisoning 2 weeks later, because he'd swallowed molten lead from the lantern roof whilst fighting the fire. He must've had one hell of a sore throat. A report on this case of lead poisoning was submitted to the Royal Society by the physician Dr Edmund Spry and the actual lump of "congealed" lead (not lard) is now in one of the National Museums of Scotland. It should be in Plymouth really. The present structure is the fourth one built on that particular rock.

Even though I knew Plymouth was getting nearer I still couldn't see it. The only land I could see was looking eastwards to the coast ahead of me. In the distance was Bolt Head and Prawle Point where I hoped to be in a couple of days. I loved this magical stretch and didn't ever want it to end. This was what walking was really all about. It was worth putting up with all the pitfalls, misery, and other rubbish for times like these even though they were few and far between. It was such a pity it was only 7 p.m. as I would've liked to spend the night here. I did see a lovely spot off the path big enough for the tent but it was too early, so sadly I had to walk on. Near Penlee Point I saw five warships a mile out to sea practising manoeuvres. They appeared like pale ghost ships. It was quite an eerie sight as they circled, half shrouded in the sea mists. Next I came to a bench facing the sea, on which was inscribed a memorial to a lady. It read: "Penny Wilson, who died aged 40, and loved this corner of Cornwall". I often felt moved when reading these little memorials. Although it was a bit sad it was nonetheless a lovely spot in which to be remembered. I don't blame her for loving this corner of Cornwall. I loved it too.

At Penlee Point there was a complete change in the nature of the walk. Having turned the corner, I was now heading north into Plymouth Sound itself. The coast path here became sheltered and wooded. I could see tantalising glimpses of Plymouth, and also of what appeared to be the famous Hoe. Below, on the shoreline to my right, was a control post for some of the area's lighthouses. There were several rocky outcrops now and a natural arch nearby. For the next mile to Cawsand the path ran through woodland on tracks and drives. The walking was easy and pleasant. I was starting to feel quite weary, even though it was only 7.30 p.m. I was worried too about the dark and foreboding colour of the sky. Having failed to take advantage of the great little camping spot earlier it looked like I'd be B & B'ing again. I certainly didn't want to camp near Plymouth whatever happened. I always wanted to avoid camping near habitation at all costs. When I got to Cawsand it was drizzling, so I needed to find somewhere quickly. Once in the village, I looked for the local phone box to plan my blanket-bombing campaign of every guest house within a mile, armed only with the guidebook and a mound of 20 pence pieces. I soon found it, but as I prised open the door, I glanced up at a row of small Victorian terraced houses beside me, and to my amazement, I saw a handwritten poster in the window closest to me, which read: "The Hillingdon B & B £18" – a dream come true! Nuff said! I walked the 3 yards and tapped on the door with eager anticipation. When it opened I nearly fainted.

"Oh my God it's Albert Tatlock!"

I was stunned. So this is what happened to him after he left *Coronation Street*. He'd retired and was now running a B & B in Cawsand! I asked if there were any rooms.

He said brusquely, "You'd better come in."

My first feeling was one of relief, my second was one of, "Aarrgghh! I can't breathe!"

I'd stepped straight off the pavement into his living room, which was so thick with blue swirling cigarette smoke that I could barely find my way across it. It was too late to back out now though.

When he offered me a mug of tea I said glumly, "Thanks, that would be nice," and sat at a dining table in the corner.

He immediately appeared with a menu and notepad, asking me what I wanted for breakfast. I was slightly taken aback, not expecting a menu for £18, plus I'd been in the house less than two minutes. I scanned it while he stood over me, pen at the ready, and was forced to make a hurried decision that I'd later regret. I was told in no uncertain terms that I was to be at the table for 8.30 sharp. He brought the tea and whilst sipping it I wondered if I'd done the right thing here, partly because when they offer to make you a tea on arrival it generally means there're no facilities in your room. Sure enough, when I was escorted upstairs the room had no kettle, no TV, and no bed (I lied about the bed). It was Spartan to say the least but it was clean and neat. I wished I'd spent ten minutes in the phone box and found somewhere for £20 instead with all the trimmings! After the gruff old Albert (Henry Yarwood actually) left me, I unpacked, did a bit of laundry, and realised I couldn't spend the whole evening in here with nowt to do. (I found myself lapsing into the "*Corrie*" vernacular there.) I went downstairs where I could just make out the shape of Albert through the haze of smoke. He was sitting watching his telly with 2 inches of ash hanging off the end of his ever-present fag. He told me there was a pub in the village so I decided to spend the evening there.

As I went in search of it the drizzle had stopped but the sky remained decidedly dodgy. I came to a small supermarket where a lovely Border collie was tethered to an ice cream sign outside. Inside I bought a carton of cranberry and raspberry juice for tomorrow and two cans of Worthington bitter. I got talking to a pretty girl working there who seemed fascinated with my journey and plied me with many varied questions for over ten minutes. She was good fun, but I'm not sure if her boss was too happy. As we talked there was a loud kafuffle coming from outside. We headed for the door to see what was going on. It appeared that the poor old doggie, having become bored, had dragged over the ice cream sign and proceeded to tangle himself up with his lead. As a result he'd become hogtied, but with his one free leg was dragging the heavy sign around in the road, howling in despair and panic. It was a sorry sight and potentially dangerous too, his owner being unable to get close enough to free him, owing to the poor woofer's fright and confusion. Struggling hard, he managed to free another leg. I managed to grab the sign whilst the owner grabbed the doggie. A minute later the story had a happy ending with the doggie getting treats from everyone present. Afterwards I wondered if he'd set up the situation himself knowing he'd benefit from it eventually. Perhaps he did it all the time and maybe his owner was in on it too! I made my way up to The Rising Sun, wondering if I should go back and ask the nice girl if she'd like to join me for a meal. I soon changed my mind, realising it could prove expensive, plus she was around twenty-five and most probably married to some local hard case who'd beat me to a pulp after she'd told him some bloke asked her to go up The Rising Sun with him. It'd mean certain death, preventing me from completing the walk, so I didn't ask her.

Inside the pub it was miserable. Well, what can you expect on a rainy Tuesday night in Cawsand? I ordered a chicken tikka with rice and a pint of Courage bitter. Sitting alone in the empty room I thought about risking a beating-up by going back and taking the bull by the horns – the same bull as before but different horns – but no, it's not really my style. I'm not good with bulls either, as you may recall from Coverack and Portscatho. Besides, the supermarket would probably be closed by now, so no point really.

On the bright side, I'd definitely not get beaten up, unless she told the hard-case husband, "I'm sure this bloke was going to ask me to go up The Rising Sun with him."

Whichever way I looked at it I couldn't win. I prepared myself for the worst but luckily it never came. The chicken tikka did though and I wished it hadn't! It cost about £7 but was reminiscent of those microwave curries with rice that you get from Mozzers (Morrisons) for a quid each. I should've got a few snacks from the supermarket instead. I was pleased I'd implemented my new no-puddings policy though, which saved me another £3, but having spent over £9 already I thought I'd better get out, lest I should be tempted to buy another pint if only to cry into. It was obvious that nothing was going happen all night, so I wandered back to The Hillingdon despondently at 8.30 p.m.

Uncle Albert opened the front door, fag in hand and ash all down his patterned cardy, gesturing, "You can sit over there and watch the television but I don't want to hear a single peep out of you."

Charming! I thought, sitting down halfway through an episode of *The Bill*; a programme I can't stand if ever there was one. I took out my cans of beer and quietly offered him one.

He curtly replied, "No, and I told you to shush, so pipe down."

I pulled the ring off my can as quietly as possible, fearing it may drive him crazy, and sat in silence sipping it while a daft rooftop police chase ensued through the blue smokescreen haze and onto the television screen! After five minutes I was bored out of my mind and could stand it no longer. I was afraid to move though, knowing it'd incur Uncle Albert's wrath again. He was engrossed in the story, so I remained seated and depressed. A gift from heaven – "End of Part 2" – appeared onscreen. I jumped up ecstatically and, faking a yawn, said that was me done for. I'd see him in the morning. He grunted without looking up, seemingly transfixed by the adverts. In my room I still felt the effects of all the smoke, and to think I used to be a smoker myself, I can't imagine how. Thank goodness I'd packed it in twenty years ago. I could never have done this walk if I hadn't, that's for sure. I took advantage of the big bathtub by having a lengthy soak. My feet had been aching today, along with my back and shoulders, so this did them a lot of good. I must've done over 25 miles today and it'd been another tough one. The bath relaxed me and I soon drifted off into what was to be my best night's kip for ages.

Day 38: Wednesday 21 May

I was awoken by a loud thumping and splashing noise, sounding like somebody having a bath next to my bed. The reason for this was because somebody *was* having a bath next to my bed! I sat up boltright (another of my own). I panicked before realising there was a paper-thin "wall" separating the bather, who was all of 2 feet away. It was disconcerting being able to hear everything that went on in the bathroom quite clearly. The sooner I could get out of my room the better. I found another bathroom and showered before doing most of my packing. I went down for breakfast at 8.30 sharp. Halfway down the stairs I heard the lilting tones of a well-spoken woman's voice. She sounded like a female version of the actor Leslie Phillips in the *Carry On* films. Before reaching the bottom step she appeared below me and, upon seeing me, spoke with great affectation.

"Oooohh, he-ll-oo! I'm Hermoine. And what, pray, is *your* name, young sir?"

Whilst speaking she held her hand out theatrically towards me, after first performing a graceful swooping flourish with it, presumably for me to kiss. She was like a combination of Dora Bryan and Beryl Reid, with a tinge of Irene Handl thrown in for good measure. It was as if she was acting the part of a debutante in a 1960s farce. She wore a "kind" of evening gown, with a 1920s bob hairstyle, large dangly earrings, and a long cigarette holder. She was at least ninety.

Confused by the vision before me, I mumbled, "It's Overend," and shook the hand on offer in a limp offhand manner, not really knowing what else to do. It didn't seem to go down too well but it was all I could manage.

Not to be deterred though, she laughed gaily, coming back with, "And tell me, Everard; are *you* on the stage?"

After getting up off the floor I confirmed I wasn't. She gave me a look of disdain, seemingly losing interest in me. She barely spoke to me again. I thought what an incredibly odd couple: the gruff Albert Tatlock and the gushing Queen Mother! I was ushered to the dining table where I was introduced to the other house guest, "The Wonderful Mr Brown". He was a large decent chap in his mid-sixties, lodging at The Hillingdon for a few weeks while he was overseeing some building work on property he owned nearby. Being an imposing, quietly-spoken, professional man, Hermoine (or Mrs Yarwood) was in total awe of him and flirtatiously fawned over him like a bee around a snapdragon, overwhelming him completely.

"Are your eggs cooked correctly, Mr Brown? Would you like some more sausages, Mr Brown? More tea, Mr Brown? Did you sleep well, Mr Brown?" Calling out: "Henry! Have you got Mr Browns kidneys?"

"Your kidneys are coming, Mr Brown."

The poor chap got no respite at all. He managed to get in a couple of quick mouthfuls as she disappeared into the kitchen briefly, where "Albert" was doing all the cooking.

She soon bounced back out though, exclaiming, "I've brought you some extra toast, Mr Brown. Is there anything else I can get you, Mr Brown?"

He didn't speak but gave me a look that said, "It's all right for you. You'll be out of here in an hour."

When she'd run out of things to offer him she turned to me and proudly stated, "Mr Brown used to be on the stage, didn't you, Mr Brown?"

Looking embarrassed, he mumbled, "Well not exactly ..."

He was overridden immediately: "Oooohh, nonsense, nonsense, Mr Brown! You're being bashful now." Addressing me: "Isn't Mr Brown wonderful?"

I sort of nodded, not wishing to offend either of them. Both he and I were cringing but there was no escape. The one saving grace amongst all this was the size of the breakfast. Mr Brown must've been presented with enough food for at least six hungry people and now I heard old "Albert" serving up mine at last. Hermoine came out of the kitchen, permanent red lipstick showbiz leer still intact, carrying a tiny plate and plonked it unceremoniously in front of me and, without a word, ran over to attend to the needs of Mr Brown for the umpteenth time. On the tiny plate was an even tinier breakfast that wasn't even a fry-up. Not a single sausage was in sight. In my haste to order breakfast the previous evening I'd opted for the smoked haddock with a poached egg, as I thought it'd make a change – it did; a bloody horrible one! I could've plumped devilled kidneys, or a full English like I usually did. I looked at my plate and looked at Mr Brown's plate. For a moment I hated him. It also occurred to me that it was Mr Brown in the bath that'd woken me up. I really hated him. I chewed on the measly dried-up piece of fish, wincing at the same time. After a thirty-minute wait it took me one minute to polish off the lot.

After slurping down my mug of tea in one go, sloshing it all over my freshly-laundered wicking top at the same time, I exited rapidly, back to my room, to the strains of "Oooeeer, can I get you another napkin, Mr Brown? What time would you like your dinner, Mr Brown?" and "Three bags full, Mr Brown?" When Hermoine caught sight of me standing she said joyfully, "Oh you're off now. Well, have a nice walk." After saying I still had to pack and wouldn't be leaving for another twenty minutes, she moaned, "Oh dear," becoming very downcast, and ran back to the wonderful Mr Brown.

After finishing off my packing I came down for the final time. By now Albert was clearing the table in his apron, ash all down the front, and lighted fag glued to his lip. He became quite friendly towards me now, probably because he knew I'd be leaving in five minutes. When I mentioned the varied breakfast menu he told me that he used to be a chef before retiring. I felt like saying it was a pity he'd forgotten it all, but bit my un-fagged lip instead. As we spoke a "not well" greyhound ran into the room. He began circling whilst stopping to do his runny business on the carpet every three seconds.

Hermoine followed behind in its most unpleasant tracks with bucket and mop uttering, "Ohhhh it's no use, Henry, we'll have to call the vet."

It was definitely time to go. I said goodbye and shook hands with the wonderful Mr Brown, wished him luck, and bolted pell-mell for that front door. On the street I breathed a real sigh of relief. Ah, fresh air! It'd stopped raining too. I looked around me, wondering which way next. Cawsand and its neighbour, Kingsand, are effectively one village, but up until the mid-nineteenth century Cawsand was in Cornwall and Kingsand was in Devon. Nobody seems to know why this was. The only clue to the meeting point of the two is a little house named Boundary Cottage near the post office. Today the county boundary follows the centre of the river Tamar, which I'd hopefully be crossing later on the ferry – if it didn't sink – from Cremyll to Plymouth. Cawsand and Kingsand together provide the last example on the SW Coast Path, of Cornish "quart in a pint pot" architecture, in which cottages are crammed and shoehorned together among steep, narrow lanes, like they'd been in previous villages I'd walked through. I could see a maze of lanes and alleys, but unfortunately couldn't find any obvious path out of the area. It stated in the book that the coast path was only way-marked once, and so discreetly that the sign was easy to miss, which of course I did. I stood baffled in the main square. To my right was a harbour and beach, but according to the guidebook, the coast path followed a steep lane uphill before rejoining the shore itself.

Somehow I eventually found the route without going ape, and set off hoping I'd find Mount Edgcumbe Country Park a little more easily. I came to a grassy stretch with plenty of bench seats with good views across Plymouth Sound to Staddon Heights and Bovisand Bay opposite. As I rounded a corner into a small woodland dell, I saw a woman sitting on a log, lacing her boots. It was Janet! She'd been resting for a few minutes. It was lovely to see her again and we walked together, jabbering away about our adventures since Looe the previous morning. Much had happened since then. I told her about the skinhead café owner, the golf club, and the hilariously tragic Hillingdon. She told me that she'd stayed on a brilliant campsite at Whitsand Bay with a great swimming pool, costing her £4 for everything! I was insanely jealous but had to hand it to her. She was no mug and had done a lot better than me. We laughed as we walked the few miles to Cremyl. Janet had arranged to meet a family friend there so would be staying in Plymouth for a couple of days for a rest and a bit of sightseeing. The path was still undulating in parts, but both being fit we coped with it easily, looking at the panoramic views. There was also some mature woodland walking with bright bluebells still blooming under the branches. We arrived at a road near Hooke lake Point uphill over a stretch of heathland, before traversing another broad, flat area with colourful rhododendrons all over the place. It was lovely around here although the sea views were blocked for quite a while by the dense woodland.

Somewhere below us was Picklecombe Fort but we couldn't see it. We eventually came to a flat open area. We walked through a lovely Victorian orangery with a large stylish conservatory and a café. We didn't stop though as we both wanted to get to Cremyl. Once there we met up with Janet's friend who kindly bought us both a polystyrene mug of tea from a refreshments van. After a ten-minute chat I left to climb aboard the ferry to Plymouth whilst they left by road. Waving goodbye I realised I probably wouldn't see Janet again, as I was travelling much faster and she was having two days off. I felt quite sad. I didn't like the look of this ferry either (I never do). I was too afraid to ask but I think it was only a set of chains that pulled the thing across the Sound with no actual engine – very dodgy! We landed safely anyway, at the quay named Admiral's Hard – don't tempt me – at 11 a.m. where there was an impressive hefty cast-iron SW Coast Path marker post. Soon after I left the ferry slip I was at the start of the recently created and imaginative "Plymouth Waterfront Walkway". The route immediately launched into a celebration of Plymouth's history and heritage, from the vinegar works to views of the docks. I came to the larger than life famous figures who'd sailed from Plymouth: Drake, Lawrence of Arabia, Isambard Kingdom Brunel, Robinson Crusoe, and Sir Arthur Conan Doyle, all created by the artists of the Why Not Associates. The path took me along Durnford Street, where Sir Arthur Conan Doyle once worked as a doctor, and where I spotted some quotations from Sherlock Holmes set into the pavement, which was a nice touch.

After that the path stayed with the coast as much as it could but there were some more inland detours where this wasn't possible. The route went around the front of a small circular building, along "Rusty Anchor Seawall", which was 4 feet high on its seaward side, and on the top of which were "embedded" about ten models of different seafaring vessels placed every 3 feet apart. Being in a public place, my first thought was how come they don't get nicked? Yet when I felt their thick, knobbly superstructure, and pulled at them slightly – like a bashful vandal – I realised they were immovable, probably held in place by concrete, reinforced with steel pins or something similar, with no fussy intricate bits. Later there was the wall of stars, a golden scallop, and a ten-ton rhino. It was obvious that everything in Plymouth was naval related, either to current naval matters, or to its naval history, making a refreshing change from fishing. There were great views across to Drake's Island from this area too. I quite fancied living there, but it'd only be my third choice with Looe Island being No. 1. I'll tell you what No. 2 was later.

I walked away from the water, up a long straight road, passed a massive old building used as barracks, probably for marines or sailors. As I walked by, a sentry holding a large machine gun horridly grimaced at me. This could be the end of the road, I thought, hurrying on, waiting for a burst in the back. I was lucky; he must've changed his mind. When I got back to the water again I took what looked to be a wide *tarmac* promenade, hoping it'd lead to the town, but instead, after 500 yards, it led to a dead end, forcing me to retrace my steps. As I turned back I saw a warning sign which read: "DANGER FIRING". I glanced over a wall with a barbed wire fence on top and saw half a dozen soldiers aiming machine guns at targets. Suddenly they fired. The noise was deafening. Apart from the terrifying cacophony I could also see the multiple muzzle flashes too. I thought it was most peculiar that this could be allowed in full public view. It struck me that I was probably trespassing on private MOD land without knowing it. I dashed back the way I'd come, onto the road, having survived being shot for the second time in ten minutes.

After a while I came to the famous Hoe and walked its length with the coast on my right. I'd been here before so knew what to expect. I passed Smeaton's smart red and white hooped third Eddystone lighthouse on my left. It looked very much at home in its new safer setting. Once at the Barbican I wanted to find the ancient steps from which the Pilgrim Fathers had embarked before making their historic voyage to America on their ship *The Mayflower* in 1620. I asked lots of people who were milling around but nobody had got the slightest clue. I ran into a nearby newsagents and begged the owner to tell me where The Mayflower Steps were.

He ambled to the door with me and, waving in no particular direction said, "I think they must be somewhere over there, mate."

It was where I'd come from. Even *HE* didn't know, so what chance had I got? I pottered about and did find some insignificant-looking old stone steps, but whether they were the actual ones, who knows? Not to be thwarted I pretended they were the real deal and took a photo before going in search of the ferry point from where I'd have to get across to the Mount Batten peninsula to get back on the coast path itself.

It started pouring down miserably again, which was a mixed blessing in a way. Although it was hateful, at least I didn't feel guilty about leaving Plymouth so soon. Sightseeing in a downpour wouldn't have been much fun and I'd done some of Plymouth before, so it was better to push on. I sat sheltering from the torrential rain in a small hut waiting for the ferry to arrive, not looking forward to walking in this once on the other side. The crossing was short and not too rough, but the rain was going to be a problem. Once I stepped onto "wet land" again I began looking for shelter, being too much of a coward to endure this if I wasn't forced to. The only refuge I could see was the large, imposing Mount Batten Hotel near to the pier, which looked very welcoming. There were many visitors in the large dining room, which had a bustling, friendly atmosphere, and good views over the surrounding coast and back to Plymouth. I wasn't much interested in views at that time, feeling like a drowned rat and weak with hunger to boot. The menu prices were reasonable so I ordered Cumberland sausages with mash, peas, and gravy, and the now obligatory pot of tea for two. The young amiable barman helped me with the *Yellow Pages* with regard to finding some potential B & Bs for later on. I jotted down a few numbers. I certainly wouldn't be able to camp. How much longer would the weather stay grim? It was mid-May after all. After finishing my meal I remained slumped in my chair and soon started to nod off in the warm, cosy room. Sometime later I came to with a jolt, realising I couldn't allow myself to get too comfortable, as I'd need to move on as soon as the weather changed. I'd surely get slung out if I outstayed my welcome, which I'd done by half an hour already. It was a real low point as all I really wanted to do was climb into a soft bed and drift into a much needed long slumber. I knew without even asking that The Mount Batten Hotel would be way out of my price range, so instead I staggered to the well-equipped gents' to slap cold water on my face to try waking myself up. I almost nodded off standing up in there. Things were bad! Still knackered, I came back to the bar and saw that the rain had stopped at last. I'd have to leave immediately. The pack felt like lead (not lard) now, as I struggled to pull it on in front of the other diners. I got a few comments like, "Rather you than me," "Don't overdo it," and "Nice weather for ducks." I smiled back benignly, unable to muster up enough enthusiasm to answer with my usual wisecracks.

It was horrible stepping out of the warm bar into that wind again. A shudder ran through me. It was 3 p.m. so I had four or five hours of walking to do. As I looked to the lofty cliffs ahead I was dreading it. First, after a short section of road walking, I had to ascend Jennycliff. I really liked this name as I'd once had a lovely girlfriend called Jenny in the 1970s who I'd been very fond of. This cliff somehow reminded me of her; not visually, but the name. Imagine being attracted to a girl whose face resembled a cliff face? You'd have to be pretty weird. I thought about Jenny for most the steep climb and wondered what she might be doing this very moment. I felt sad to think that there was little chance of us ever meeting again, but I guess that's life. By the time I was halfway up I was in thick low cloud and, for a time, could see nothing in any direction. On the top the terrain was ruggedly undulating and through gaps in the cloud I caught glimpses of boats and jetties way below.

From near Staddon Point I could make out bits of the impressive mile-long man-made Plymouth Breakwater. Before the freestanding breakwater was built, complete with Shovel Fort lighthouse (or even Fuvvel Lort Shitehouse) at the western end, and beacon at the eastern end, Plymouth Sound was open to storms from the south-west, which made it a dangerous anchorage. I was so transfixed by the sheer scale of it that I tripped and almost fell off the cliff. Maybe I would've landed on it and it would've saved my life – no chance. Although grey, there was no more rain and I started to get into my rhythm. It was nice to be striding forward after the sluggish day I'd had so far.

Walking due south for a couple of hours I came to Heybrook Bay. I'd previously read that somebody famous had written something important whilst staying at the Heybrook Bay Hotel but couldn't for the life of me remember who or what it was. Maybe it'd come back to me later. Hurrying on without stopping to Wembury Point, there were a cluster of gloomy grey derelict MOD buildings, slightly above me and to my left. I expected to see shadowy figures with lifeless jet-black eyes peering from the smashed windows as I passed by. I was glad to leave them behind, but unfortunately their gloomy presence brought on another attack of the insidious Nasty Notemares. As I descended a steep slope I felt slightly faint and shaky. Not being a good place to collapse, I stopped, took off the pack, and sat on a large rock. I'd had this feeling before but not for a year or two. I also knew the cure. I reached into the pack and pulled out a Boost chocolate bar and ate it in about three mouthfuls. Within a minute or two, with blood sugar levels fully restored, I felt fine again. I pulled on the pack and was off. Having seen nobody since Mount Batten I met two sisters around my age on the path. We chatted for five minutes about the weather, walking – the usual.

Back up to full speed I soon arrived at a large Holiday Park consisting of static caravans. In the small kiosk at the entrance barrier I was confronted by the second best-looking woman of the trip. She looked about thirty, very classy, with well-cut blonde hair, nice clothes, and a great set of white gnashers to round it all off. I wouldn't have been surprised if they were all her own too. I'd to walk through the site but it seemed a bit strange to have to pass through the barrier on foot, as it was intended for cars and caravans. She told me there was an onsite café still open. I was desperate for a cuppa and a rest as it was 6 p.m. Before going though, I thought I'd tell her about the fantastic brainwave I'd had walking earlier in the rain. It might impress her too. I told her that my idea was to buy a load of ancient beaten-up caravans for twenty quid each, put them in a field, with no facilities apart from a single water tap and a shovel, let backpackers use them for five quid a night, no questions asked. It'd be better than putting up a tent in the rain. It could even be quite cosy once inside your sleeping bag, especially with a hot brew bubbling away on your own camping stove. She looked at me blankly without "eyeing a batlid", but I'd the distinct feeling she wasn't impressed. All right, you wouldn't be in the lap of luxury, but when you're down and out any port in a storm will surely do. On reflection though, she didn't really look like the calibre of woman who was used to "roughing it". I probably made an error of judgement by confiding in her.

It didn't help when I asked, "I don't suppose you've got anything like that here, have you? Or even an old shed or dog kennel I could doss down in for the night?"

She politely said that the site was family based and she was afraid she couldn't help me. I couldn't help thinking, as I slunk off, that I hadn't exactly shown myself in my best light. In retrospect, I should've used more of a James Bond approach. That would've definitely worked with a classy chick like her. If she hadn't been on duty I'd still have asked her to join me in the café. (Who do you think you're kidding, son? No you wouldn't because you're a spineless jellyfish!) The Beachcomber Buffer Café was only a couple of hundred yards away in the middle of the site. Four workmen were sitting at a table looking like they done a hard day's work in the rain. They eyed me with suspicion from the start, despite me offering them a cheery "Afternoon!" Apart from them there was a couple of friendly staff on duty. I ordered a pot of tea for 3.879 people, plus a ham salad baguette to take away for Ron (later-Ron). I sat at a small table, studying the guidebook. Wembury village itself was no more than a mile or two. I'd try to find accommodation there for the night. Being a holiday park I asked the waitress if she possessed a ferry timetable. I'd need to cross the river Yealm beyond Wembury first thing tomorrow morning. She said she hadn't but called across to the workmen. Did any of them know what time the ferries ran tomorrow morning?

They looked blank, before one of them, after a long pause, answered her firmly: "Ain't no ferries around these parts."

Holding up the guidebook, I politely pointed out that there was definitely a much-used ferry over the river Yealm. It was listed in the book, plain as the nose on yer face. The times weren't listed, as they were susceptible to change. They looked at each other.

"You ever heard of a ferry, Jack?"

"Nope! There ain't no ferries round here, like you said, Kev."

Another one chipped in with, "I've lived here all me life and I've never heard of any f***** ferry."

"That's cos there bloody well ain't any! Ha, ha, ha!" interjected "Kev" without even acknowledging my presence.

They'd decided to play silly buggers with me, obviously their insolent way of intimidating unwelcome outsiders in their territory. It was reminiscent of an old cowboy film and they were the black-hatted baddies! I was, of course, the cool Clint Eastwood figure. I felt like pushing it and telling them not to be so ******* stupid but what would be the point? It was better to ignore them, which is exactly what I did, until they swallowed their shots of "red eye" down in one slug and left without speaking. The staff, on the other hand, was terrific and extremely kind too. It was a family-run business and nothing was too much trouble. When I mentioned about B & Bs the lady owner offered to call a few for me on the café phone, so I wouldn't run down the battery on my mobile. Now that's what I call consideration. After a couple of failures she handed me the receiver saying that there was a room available and would I like to speak to Mrs Potter? A well-spoken but quite vague-sounding lady was on the other end.

After introducing myself, I bluntly asked her the vital question, "Have you got a room and if so how much?"

"Oh, eeerrr, I don't really know. I suppose ... I suppose ... you could, eeerrr, have my son's room. It'd be, eeerrrr, £20."

I liked the price but was slightly concerned about the whereabouts of her son in all this. Was he going to be in the room with me? Or was she going to pack him off to his mate's place for the night? From my point of view it seemed like a funny thing to say. As mentioned before, you can't look a gift horse ... I said okay and asked for directions, which was a mistake. *She* obviously knew where she was but was totally unable to convey her whereabouts to me. She began vaguely and the vagueness got even vaguer until she gradually ground to a complete halt like a spent battery before my blunt pencil even touched the paper. I butted in, asking her to give me the address and I'd find her somehow. She did this quite vaguely but I took it down successfully. It was Glebe House, Chapel Road, Wembury. Sounds pretty straight forward, doesn't it? As I was now fixed up for the night, and with Wembury only half an hour away, there was now no rush. I had more tea followed by a big choc and toffee double scoop ice cream cone – you're only young once! I chatted with the lovely family. We joked a lot and they had felt embarrassed by their behaviour of the Devonshire cowboys. They apologised for it. I said there was no need. During the conversation I couldn't resist slinging in an old chestnut they must have heard 1,000 times before.

Me: "Where's the stadium, then?"

Them: "What stadium?"

Me, impersonating a gentleman of Oriental origin in a non-racist way: "Wembury Stadium, of course!"

They groaned politely. Time for me to be off before the rain started again. It was spitting as I approached Wembury beach with its many rock pools where there were still a few hardy tourists milling about prodding at things. I picked off any stragglers to ask if they'd heard of Chapel Road. Unsurprisingly nobody had. All I'd managed to decipher from Mrs Potter was that her bungalow was inland and up a hill towards Wembury itself. I finally got talking to a great couple who were possibly a little older than me but in far better nick. Mike was an old teddy boy who still sported, on his bonce-top, the crumbling ruins of an obviously once mighty quiff. They both still had "the look" too. They were on holiday, hence they didn't know the area too well either. They were a real laugh and even though they'd never heard of Chapel Road, I no longer cared, as I was bent double, almost crying with laughter after three minutes with them. After fifteen minutes I'd to drag myself away as it was nearing 7 p.m. I'd said I'd be there before then. They wished me luck. I took a lane inland hoping for the best. I didn't get the best. I was lost after a short distance, finding myself in a flat rural setting surrounded by meadows, hedges, cows, and all the usual trappings you'd expect to find in a normal countryside. This couldn't be right. For starters I should be going up a hill with houses on both sides according to the sparse directions given by Mrs Potter. When I was right on the edge of becoming irate I spied a red phone box completely alone amongst the greenery, looking out of place, but it must've been an omen. Once inside, after establishing it was in working order, I dialled Mrs Potter's number. When I told her I was in the red rural phone box she became very vague again. Although she knew the location of the phone box she couldn't tell me how to get from it to her bungalow.

All she could manage was, "It's not, eerr, far … honestly." To try making my task easier I asked how far she thought it was in yards or metres. Obviously boggled by the multiple choice question, she uttered, "Eerr … I, eerr … don't really … know … I'm afrai …" Her words petered out tragically.

I said not to worry – even though I was worrying – and I'd find her somehow but may be two hours late! Before I hung up she muttered something about keeping an eye out for me. I said that'd be most helpful should I arrive in the vicinity. While the opportunity presented itself I rang Mum and Dad, my old mate Rick, and all were fine. When the coins ran out I stepped outside, where to my amazement, 10 feet away from me in the meadow, stood a beautiful red fox. The sight of him really took me by surprise, whereas he remained quite unruffled, casually looking me up and down for at ten seconds before turning round and trotting off towards some trees. I quickly tried to get the camera out but in my panic dropped it in the long grass. By the time I'd retrieved it my friend had gone. Never mind, I'll always have the memory of that fine South-Devon fox. I was glad about getting lost as that lovely encounter wouldn't have happened otherwise. As I stood there plotting which way to go –"Eeny, meeny, miny, mo" – a red car pulled up next to me on the narrow lane.

A voice called out: "Haven't you found it yet?" It was Mike the ted and his good lady (whose name escapes me, sorry), and we all started laughing again for no particular reason. He said, "For God's sake get in and we'll find the place together!"

Considering I'd been walking in circles since I'd last seen them an hour ago I deduced that I'd not be cheating if I accepted a short lift. Besides that, I knew that there was very little hope of me finding the place any other way. I sat in the front as he drove back to the harbour and found a hill to go up. We went slowly so I could look out for street signs or, failing that, people to ask. After ten minutes we still weren't getting any nearer to finding Chapel Road, when I suddenly spotted a young chap on the grass verge ahead who was peering anxiously at our car.

I said to Mike, "That must be her son. She said someone would keep an eye out for me."

Mike pulled up next to him. I got out with my pack, said thanks and cheerio, and went over to the chap.

He said, "Hi. I was beginning to wonder if you were going to turn up."

"Yeah, sorry, I'd a lot of trouble finding the place that's all. Where is it? I'm totally exhausted."

He looked puzzled, pointing to a knee-high cardboard box at his feet, saying, "Here it is."

I looked at the box in amazement and blurted out loudly, "I can't sleep in *that!*" He looked baffled. I mumbled "What the hell is it anyway?"

"It's the Porta-Potti, isn't it?" I stared at him in disbelief. The man was a fool! He elaborated: "It's the chemical toilet you bought off me over the phone earlier. I arranged to meet you here outside my house at 6.30. Surely you remember?"

For a moment I thought it was true; I must have bought it, but somehow forgot all about it. The walking was making me delirious. Oh God, I'm losing my marbles!

Logic took over and I yelled in frustration: "I'm a backpacker! Here's my rucksack to prove it! *How* exactly am I supposed to carry a bleedin' Porta-Potti along the South West Coast Path!" Immediately after my outburst the penny dropped. I said, "You are Mrs Potter's son, aren't you?"

"No, I've never heard of any Mrs Potter. I'm Paul Higgins. I don't like people messing me about, so do you want this Porta-Potti or not?"

I twigged it before he did and collapsed into a fit of hysterics at the ridiculousness of the situation, stuttering, "No I bloody well don't, thank you very much!"

I explained we'd been talking at cross-purposes and I wasn't, in fact, the chap he was supposed to meet. When I told him I was looking for a B & B he began laughing too. I turned back to Mike, who was still there, studying a map. Soon we were all cackling. What were the chances of that happening? We wished Paul good luck with his Porta-Potti and bade him farewell after he'd told us how to find Chapel Road. It hadn't been a total waste of time. Back in the front seat we slowed every time we reached a turning.

At last I cried out with joy: "There it is! There it is! Chapel Road!"

Mike swung the steering wheel right, into the lane. We soon saw a drive in front of Glebe House and went straight up it. Mrs Potter was gardening and sauntered over to Mike's door, trowel in hand. She was a pleasant-looking lady in her 50s. Mike began quipping and she was highly amused by his charming banter. Meanwhile I'd got out on the other side and was pulling my pack from back seat with the help of Mike's wife.

At the same time I heard Mrs Potter laughing, saying to Mike, "Oh you are awful! Don't be so cruel, it's lovely around here. You really are wicked fellow!"

It was obviously going to be a lot of fun staying here, despite the trouble I'd had trying to find it.

Mike backed out of the drive, quipping, "Watch yourself on that trowel! You could have a nasty accident if you sat on that by mistake!"

As they drove off, Mrs Potter was still giggling like a schoolgirl. She took one look at me and her mood changed instantly! It was apparent that she too had taken an immediate dislike to me. I wondered what was so abhorrent about me. I didn't possess the boyish charm or cheeky grin of the "Jack the Lad-ish" Mike, but I was hardly Adolf Hitler, Saddam Hussein, or even Sid Vicious.

"Bring that rucksack in and take off those muddy boots immediately. I don't want my carpets ruined," she said, not at all vaguely.

Once inside the plush house, she led me down a corridor in my stocking feet, to a small room built right at the back; a kind of one-storey lean-to extension. Inside it was cluttered with clothing, tracksuits, loads of magazines, books, and baseball caps scattered hither and thither. There was a PC 2 feet from the single bed. It was her son's room but where was he? Under the bed? She told me, in a vague fashion once more, there was a bathroom next door and breakfast was at 8 a.m. *sharp*! She wasn't remotely vague about this, which I thought was below the belt. She left me to my own devices. I sat on the bed and within two minutes I was shivering. Quite often after finishing walking for the day I'd cool down rapidly. In all the earlier excitement I'd forgotten to put on my warm fleece and this time I'd left it too late. The room felt very damp too. I pulled a blanket over myself but was still cold. Time had come to pluck up courage and ask Mrs Potter for a fire or some other form of heating.

When I tapped on her living room door and said, "Sorry to bother you, but it's a bit damp in there. Could I borrow an electric fire?"

Tutting grumpily, she moaned, "It's not damp in that room. Couldn't you have a shower instead?"

She closed her door on me. I didn't want to get into an argument so held my tongue – above my head for extra warmth – and shuffled back to the room to sit there shivering again. Five minutes later I heard a metallic creaking noise and reached over to the radiator next to the bed. She did have a heart after all. The room soon warmed up so I began unpacking the rucksack. The main problem was that I was worried about mixing up my gear up with her son's gear that was everywhere. I was forced to clear a small space on the floor for mine, which was hardly ideal, but with no alternative that's what I did. I uncovered a hidden dehumidifier at the same time. Game, set, and match – it *was* damp! More comfortable now, I spent the evening watching his portable telly, reading one of his books on New Zealand, wearing three of his baseball caps, smoking his cigars, drinking his Jack Daniels, and listening to his favourite CDs. I called a few of his mates on his mobile, checked his emails, replied to a few of them, and ordered a cool designer suit and DVD recorder from Amazon using his credit card. After enjoying myself all evening at his expense I got into bed at 11 p.m. wishing that his girlfriend had been left casually lying around too! I also wondered if I should leave the big light on in case his mother had forgotten to warn him. He might arrive home at 3 a.m. and unwittingly climb into bed with me. As a result I had an uneasy night but managed about five hours.

Day 39: Thursday 22 May

It was painful but I did make it down at 8 a.m. Mrs Potter was cooking my breakfast and was like a totally different person now. Full of the joys of spring and chatting away, I could hardly get a word in edgeways. Maybe she was a "morning person".

She asked, "Were you warm enough in the night? I was worried, as that room can be a little damp."

I felt like asking her if she's got a twin sister. This was not the first or last time I experienced this kind of change of heart, making me wonder what could possibly bring it about. I pondered on it whilst Mrs Potter took a phone call. Question: *why* did they loathe me on arrival, have an offhand attitude, would not speak, be rude, yet the next morning they were all sweetness and light, kind, friendly, and talkative? Answer: this came to me in a flash. When I arrive at their establishments the previous evening they're panic-stricken, as I appear shifty, common, and scruffy. They figure I could be a murderer, a thief, a conman, an arsonist, a rapist, a pillager, a sleepwalker, a true-age navveller, a bed-wetter, a member of NWA or the Daniel O'Donnell Appreciation Society, or simply a madman who's going to go berserk and run amuck in the night with an axe! This is what they imagined. So when they wake up in the morning and realise that they are miraculously still alive, and haven't been garrotted during the early hours, their house hasn't been razed to the ground, all their Royal Worcester is still intact in its glass display cabinet, and the family pet hasn't been roasted in the microwave, they begin warming to me! By the time I arrive downstairs for breakfast freshly showered, shaved, and wearing clean clothes, they all can hardly believe it, thinking, He must be human after all! Knowing I'd be leaving immediately after breakfast would, of course, be very heartening for them too. Issue solved!

Mrs Potter and I chatted away nineteen to the dozen over breakfast. She was a very nice lady and not the slightest bit vague any more either. It turned out that she was a keen rambler herself and knew the area well. She was also interested in my walk. Her son was away at college. He was a classical musician. She proudly showed me photos of the good-looking chap. I felt like saying, "You could've got him to clear up his room before he went," but resisted. She never mentioned a Mr Potter and I didn't ask. Unfortunately, the full English was only "fun-sized", but I should've expected it, as Mrs Potter was a slim, healthy-looking lady and probably only ate muesli or porridge with fruit in the morning. Heavy rain was now running down the glass panes of the conservatory. I'd have to embark on a "go-slow" once back in my room and drag my departure out as long as possible. Unfortunately, she put the mockers on my cunning plan, informing me she had an appointment and we'd both have to leave in fifteen minutes. I had to hurry with my packing instead and walked out of the door at 9.15 a.m. after a cheery goodbye from Mrs Potter. Rather worryingly, she'd never heard of any Wembury ferry either. I made my way quickly back down the hill in the waterproofs without getting lost once.

From Wembury beach I saw the distinctive feature known as The Great Mew Stone. A mile out to sea from here, it's a triangular island, currently uninhabited. In bygone days it served as a prison and a private home, as well as a refuge for local smugglers. Its most infamous resident was Sam Wakeman, who avoided transportation to Australia in favour of the cheaper option of transportation to the Mewstone, where he was interred for seven years. After his internment on the island he remained there paying his rent by supplying rabbits for the Manor House table. It's said Ray the shopkeeper is responsible for carving the rough stone steps to the summit of the Mewstone. The Mewstone and Little Mewstone are now bird sanctuaries and access to visitors is now barred. The sods are taking over the whole world, aren't they? This was my fourth favourite island, but they'd have to get rid of those birds before I'd consider moving there. I could tolerate a few little budgerigars, maybe a parrot at a push, but not thousands of those big ugly things.

Up the cliffs again it was cold, damp, windy, and grey on the top, typical weather for May these days. After a miserable half-hour I arrived at Warren Point where I'd somehow have to take the non-existent ferry across the Yealm estuary to Noss Mayo. Having looked at the ferries in the guidebook last night I was very concerned, as I'd have to negotiate three or four estuaries in the near future. None of them seemed to be regular or reliable according the book. It seemed travellers had to take pot luck and hope for the best or wade them!

Down at sea level again the rain had eased, but it was still cold and windy as I stood looking across the Yealm, packed solid with yachts, cruisers, and small watercraft. They appeared to be moored up. The owners obviously didn't wish to risk the savage waters beyond the shelter of the estuary. Next to me on the tiny landing stage was a black circular board, a bit larger than a dartboard, with some instructions alongside. Following these I undid a catch and lowered the black hinged "lid", revealing a pure white board underneath. I thought this was extremely racist but could do nothing about it. Apparently though, the white board shows up better on the opposite side of the Yealm and acts as signal to the ferryman who knows that his services are required, and in theory hopefully makes the five-minute trip across. Of course, nothing happened and after ten minutes I was freezing and screaming "Help!" to anyone who might hear me. I flicked through the book and found a mobile phone number belonging to one Bill Gregor, the elusive ferryman. When I dialled it rang and rang. I let it go on for five minutes, but fearing for my battery, gave up and switched it off. What a bloody disaster! I was trapped in a very exposed spot too, so was forced to don every item of warm clothing I could get at.

After half an hour I was still alone on the landing stage. Maybe those nasty workmen were right. Perhaps the white board was meant for some kind of private enterprise, not for the public. When my spirits couldn't sink any lower I heard a worrying dripping sound. Looking down, I saw my Platypus bladder was pouring yesterday's cranberry juice all over the floor. I must've dislodged the hose cap while rummaging for the extra clothing. By the time I got to the loose cap, all the juice was gone, hoisted with me own petard! Suddenly I heard a lawnmower going flat out. I looked up, spying a small ferryboat right in front of me, with a smiling captain standing alone at the wheel.

"Sorry to keep you waiting," he said. "I'd a few jobs to do first."

I forgave him instantly, delighted that he'd bothered to come at all and that the ferry actually existed! When I asked if he was Bill Gregor he confirmed he was. I told him I'd been trying to ring his mobile.

"You won't get me on that, it went overboard last year. I haven't got one now!"

The crossing only took two minutes so I was horrified when Bill asked me for £1.50. I tried pleading desperately – "Chris De Burgh definitely told me not to pay you" – but it was in vain. I forked out. Most of these tiny ferries were about 80p.-£1. Safely on dry land at Noss Mayo I set off through oak woodland on a winding path going in a westerly direction. Yes, I was forced to walk the wrong way again to get round the bleak west-facing Gara Point, with an icy wind blasting right in my screwed-up fizogg. The next few hours were very lonely with no coastal settlements and only the odd solitary house visible. At least I was going eastwards now and the rain had about kept off. After a slight navigational mishap I arrived at the coast by the ruined church of St Peter the Poor Fisherman, on to Revelstoke Drive. This is an unexpected old carriageway round the cliffs, constructed by unemployed fishermen. Originally intended as a scenic footpath to impress his guests, history relates that when Lord Revelstoke inspected the almost completed work, the men looked distraught as there was no more work for them in the area.

"Very good," he said. "Right, now make it 3 feet wider, please."

So the path became a carriageway. The terrain was hideously strenuous again, but I pressed on regardless. Beyond Beacon Hill the path wound round a succession of tiny coves near the hamlet of Mothercombe, overlooking the River Erme, to which I descended wiped-out. When I came to its banks there was nothing whatsoever, apart from a small deserted landing stage. On the opposite bank a few hundred yards away I could also see nothing. I groaned in despair, as I could see no way of getting across. In the book it stated bluntly "no ferry." I contemplated wading across it, as the guidebook implied this was possible at low tide, if great caution was exercised, owing to the terrible danger and ghastly peril! The estuary, however, reminded of the deadly seas around Cape Horn with gigantic waves crashing on the shores. No way was I going to step into that. Low tide was probably several hours away and I couldn't possible hang around for that long, unless I put up the tent, which I really didn't want to do in the wind. Besides, it was only 2 p.m. I'd intended to get a lot further than The Erme today. I wandered inland, up a hateful hill (is there such a thing as a nice one?), 100 yards or so to regroup, where according to the book, there was a café, but when I got there not only was it closed down but it'd also been vandalised. The phone box beside it was in a similar condition with four-foot-high grass and weeds growing inside it. My lifeline gone I ambled solemnly and aimlessly, without a spring in my step, in no particular direction kicking wildly at tufts of grass in frustration, muttering to myself.

"You've really done it now, yer big pranny! 400 bloody yards across but nobody will bail you out this time. You're on yer own now and it f****** well serves you right too! Let's face it, you really have blown it!"

I came to a small, flat grassy area where two cars were parked. Three wet-suited young surfers were emerging from the first one, so seeing a glimmer of hope, I asked if they knew if there was a ferry after all. They said there definitely wasn't one, meaning I'd have to take the inland diversion right around the estuary, walking 9 extra pointless miles – well, pointfull miles really, as I'd eventually get around the vile estuary. It'd take me about three hours. I came to the second car where an older gentleman appeared and was opening the boot having taken his dog for a walk. Explaining my predicament I asked him if he knew of any buses that I may be able to catch to get round the Erme.

Pausing briefly, he said, "I'm not doing anything this afternoon. I could run you round if you like, it's no trouble."

I wanted fall to my knees and kiss his feet in gratitude but drew the line at that, instead saying generously, "Oh thank you! Thank you so much! I'll pay you *anything* you want."

Dangerous talk in retrospect. I must watch that in future. He laughed and said he didn't want any money and told me to get my pack into the boot. Sitting in the front seat of his car with the poor doggie relegated to the back seat I instantly went from "0" to "10" on a happiness scale of 0 to 10. His name was Bob Bridger and he was a retired lecturer in mechanical engineering, exactly the same as my dad, and also the only other one I'd ever met in fifty-six years. I'd always believed that my dad was the only one in Great Britain.

After a pleasant twenty-minute trip along minor roads and lanes we came to the shore on the eastern side of the estuary. I tried to force an Uncle Ivor (a fiver) into his hand but he was having none of it, refusing pointblank to take a single penny from me. I thanked him profusely, we shook hands, and I set off on the mile-long walk south towards Beacon Point before I could resume walking east again. Within a minute I was lost and screaming in a mixture of tall wet stinging nettles and long soaking grass. After five minutes of this I went back down to "0" on a scale of 0 to 10. I also sank up to my knees several times in thick stinking mud and slime, which drenched my boots and socks. After another five minutes of getting stung and beating down the undergrowth I emerged, quite vexed, onto some sand-flats where Bob was casually strolling with his dog! I asked him how the hell he'd got there. He pointed straight towards a path right through the jungle that I'd obviously missed. We had another five-minute chat. He told me about the estuary, while the dog played with bits of flotsam and driftwood on the beach. Being a bit of a bird watcher, I hesitate to say "twitcher", he told that the estuary was rich in birdlife (groan, groan), providing food for redshank, dunlin, oystercatchers, curlew, and turnstones on the sandflats. On the cliffs stonechats, whitethroats and linnets could be found. I don't know about mechanical engineering but he had a good knowledge of mechanical birdlife. We shook hands for the final time and I begrudgingly headed south again (I only ever wanted to walk east). Back on the 300-foot cliffs yet again the going was now horrific.

As well as all the steep stuff I was also fighting against the freezing gale that was hitting me head-on, causing my face to contort as if I were experiencing G-force in a spaceship. At times I could hardly move forward at all, having to lean hard into the wind. I needed to be very careful otherwise I might go over the edge if the wind were to suddenly drop. This was as gruelling as anything I'd experienced in the last five weeks, sapping every ounce of my energy. I knew I wouldn't be able to walk until dusk tonight. To add to my despair I was also suffering my worst bout of Nasty Notemares since Tintagel. This time it was a bit of everything, including 'Mars' from the *Planets*, plus endless mind-numbing, nondescript Celtic airs played flat-out on bloody bagpipes!

After what seemed like an eternity my spirits were lifted, as I spotted the famous Burgh Island a couple of miles ahead. This meant I was almost at Bigbury-on-Sea, where I'd look for somewhere to stay. The wind mercifully dropped as I too dropped but only into Challaborough Bay, which was an average-looking holiday park centred around its sandy beach, with chalets, static caravans, and the like. I went straight into a small supermarket and bought a pile of chocolate and a beer for later. This was the first shop I'd seen since the Beachcomber Buffer Bar thirty hours previously. Walking along the edge of the beach towards Bigbury, I saw the long Regatta Bar, and went straight in the side door for a drink and a rest. Inside were the barmaid and a lone punter. As I approached the bar to order a drink they hadn't seen me coming but I overheard her speaking to him.

"Oh it's awful! I keep getting this terrible recurring nightmare." Bang on cue, I stepped right in between them, interjecting with, "– And here it comes again!"

Surprised at the unexpected intrusion, they looked at me and we all began laughing. I ordered a pint of Worthington's to quench my thirst and a pint of tea to warm my hands, which I could no longer feel, owing to the iciness of the gales. Within minutes I began to shiver and quickly dug out my warm camo fleece from the depths of the pack. Even though it'd been freezing on the cliffs I still only walked in my short-sleeved wicking top. I found it more comfortable than wearing heavy clothing that'd make me sweaty and clammy. I was warm enough as long as I kept moving and expending energy. Once I stopped I soon began suffering from the cold shivers. This time it was particularly bad but after fifteen minutes, recuperating in the warm bar, I was okay to carry on again. It was only 4.30 p.m. when I left to walk up the hill 500 yards to Bigbury, but I was ready to pack it in all the same. I knocked on a few doors but no rooms were available. They all said I'd find it difficult as the season had started now. I quipped to one landlady, "Yeah, the winter season."

By the time I reached the phone box opposite Burgh Island the weather had taken a turn for the worse. I was glad to shelter in there. I pulled out the guidebook and looked under "B & Bs Bigbury." Of the few listed, the first to draw my eye was Warren Cottage, chiefly because the price was £18 and it was central too. Someone had mentioned this one to me yesterday. I dialled the number as the rain bucketed down and gales howled. It rang and rang so I hung up, waited five minutes, dialled again – still no reply. I tried the other Bigbury numbers but no rooms were left. I repeated dialling Warren Cottage for another half-hour but still got no reply. Between the calls I peered across the causeway through the rain to Burgh Island – my second favourite island – wondering if I'd be spending the night in the phone box. I turned to look for anywhere nearby that may have accommodation. To my amazement, 10 yards across the road, was Warren bloody Cottage! The sign was clear for all to see, but in my haste I hadn't seen it!

Leaving my pack in the phone box I ran over and up the drive. It looked like a café too – superb. Reaching the front door, I realised it was completely empty, with no curtains, furniture, fixtures – nothing. It must have closed down recently, but why was the stupid phone still connected? Bunch of pigs! Back in the phone box my options were running out. There was only one B & B that I hadn't tried, mainly because it was back in Challaborough Bay. The last thing I wanted to do was walk all the way back there again, as it'd also mean walking back up the hill the following day. I'd have to walk more than a mile in total, backwards and forwards, three times over the same ground. Not my style, I'm afraid, squire. Down to my last 20 pence I dialled "Follyfoot" back in Challaborough Bay. A friendly Irish chap told me there was a room for £22.50 if I wanted it. I was peeved at the price but so weary that I couldn't be bothered to tell him that it stated £20 in the guidebook. The top half of me was ecstatic with joy at finding somewhere, while my lower half was distraught at the prospect of all the extra walking, but it was no contest really; the top half won hands down. I told him I'd be there in twenty minutes. So back down the hill again where I stopped at Steve's chip van for a good portion of chicken and chips to fortify me before walking the remaining 20 horrendous yards to Follyfoot. It was a smart modern bungalow with plush light-coloured carpets. It was no surprise when Peter asked me to take off my filthy boots in the hall. On this occasion it was somewhat embarrassing, as the stench from the horrid black bog by the river Erme was quite overwhelming. I tried explaining that it wasn't my feet, but I don't know if he believed me.

My room was warm and cosy. I was so glad I hadn't quibbled about the extra £2.50. I ate my takeaway with my can of beer followed by three Twix'sisis' and plenty of hot tea. Although worn out, I diligently did my laundry, a double wash for the socks, and hung it up to dry before lying flat-out, snoozing in front of the box. I briefly considered an outing to The

Regatta Bar, situated 50 yards away, but even that was a bridge too far tonight. I left a message on Janet's mobile warning her about the estuary crossings that she'd have to negotiate and told her how I'd done it. I was concerned for her, particularly the Erme estuary, as I didn't imagine that old Bob Bridger would be hanging round waiting to drive her inland and back, as he had done for me. I guessed she'd have to walk round or risk wading at low tide. I glanced at the guidebook to see what fresh horrors tomorrow might bring and saw that the first was to be another difficult estuary. I'd have to get over the river Avon to Bantham, hopefully by ferry tomorrow morning. I closed the book and was asleep by 11 p.m.

Day 40: Friday 23 May

I was at the large communal breakfast table for 8.30 sharp, all ship-shape and Bristol Cream. Why don't B & Bs serve breakfast until midday? A young couple was sharing with me but for once I didn't mind. They were really easy to talk to. The only – and therefore the best – Full *Irish* of the trip was exquisitely served by Peter, who'd cooked it himself, assisted by his lovely wife, Carol. It all went off in a civilised manner with nobody getting out of hand or starting a fight. I collected my rucksack and sat in the hall lacing my cleaned boots. I took a photo of Peter and Carol. He told me it wasn't raining outside and not to worry about missing the Bantham ferry, as it was only a twenty-minute walk away. I closed the door behind me and noticed it was pouring with rain despite what Peter had told me seconds earlier. I ducked into a doorway and put on the WPs. A trip to Burgh Island would've been nice, but apart from the weather being grim, I needed to get to the western bank of the Avon near Cockleridge by 11 a.m. or I'd miss the ferry. I couldn't risk that. There were only two a day, the other being at 4 p.m. I stopped for a good look at (Chris de) Burgh Island a short distance across the causeway.

Once out of Bigbury I'd some road walking to do, uphill, naturally. I glanced at my watch: 10.25 a.m. No worries. I'd still be there fifteen minutes early. I walked quickly up the hill for twenty minutes but couldn't see anything resembling an estuary. I saw a small finger post a few yards away that read: "Ferry To Bantham 1¾ miles." Oh my God, no! I hated that Irishman so much that if he'd been standing next to me I'd have gladly "throated" him very badly. In a rage I ran willy-nilly (and hilly) in any direction until my brain kicked in again and I fell towards the path indicated by the post. Needless to say it was uphill again. I was sweating like a huge fat bloater by now but didn't have time to stop and remove the stifling WPs, even though the rain had stopped. Fourteen minutes remained to cover the 1 and three-quarter miles. Roger Bannister could've done it in seven minutes, I told myself, but he probably wasn't fifty-six and carrying a 45-lb. pack uphill after a Full Irish breakfast at the time. The path veered off to my right, through a deserted farmyard, onto a piece of waste land with no path, signs, or anything else. I went into a screaming fury spinning rapidly in circles. The air was psychedelic-blue by this time! I'd blown it without a doubt. My first thought was to throw off my pack, leave it there, rush back to Challaborough, and have it out with the Irishman! Whilst considering what to do, I looked around and saw a middle-aged couple walking up a grassy hill towards me. I careered drunkenly down the hill yelping wildly to attract their attention.

When I'd almost reached them, breathless, I blurted out both rudely and hysterically, "Hey you! Where's the ferry? Come on, where the hell is it? Quick! Quick!"

Taken aback and frightened they retreated a few feet as he asked nervously, "Which ferry do you mean?"

I exploded: "The Bantham bloody ferry, of course! What else?"

I felt like lunging wildly for his lapels and shaking the directions out of him, but managed to hold myself back, realising, somewhere deep inside, that it may not be the best course to take.

He pointed down the hill saying, "It's, erm, it's, erm, down there at the bottom. We've come over on it. If you hurry you might catch it."

I bolted down the slope like a greyhound out of the starting blocks shouting hysterically back over my shoulder: "Sorry, sorry! Thank you, thank you! I'm so very awfully sorry!"

I ran the remaining half-mile like a mad March hare until I could run no more and was forced to slow down to walking pace. I'd arrived at the bank of the estuary but there was no sign of any ferry or of anything. I walked inland along the grassy estuary bank with my eyes peeled for any signs of life but the scene was devoid of anything to do with the human race. I began cursing again. This time in a series of short, sharp, high-pitched, vixen-like shrieks, thinking to myself, That's a new one. I'll have to make a note of it and use it next time I have a tantrum. It always amazed me how I was able to detach myself from these tantrums and see things from a bird's-eye point of view, often *while* the tantrum was in full flow. I reasoned that I must possess very special qualities to be able to disassociate myself from it in this way. Maybe I should become a psychiatrist when I get back? I kept on raging at the same time though. I quietened down after a few minutes and sullenly skulked along the bank, knowing it was all over and I had a five-hour wait until the next ferry. When I looked down there was a lovely black Labrador ambling along happily by my side. It must've been the vixen-like shrieks that had attracted him. He didn't seem to have a master, so must've figured that I'd do till someone better came along. I spotted a rowing eight about to overtake me 100 yards out into the estuary. I waved, pathetically shouting help. Politely ignoring me, they looked the other way as they sped by. I suppose I'd have done the same in their shoes, or should I say their "rollocks"? Besides, how would I possibly fit into a full eight-seated boat with my pack?

I sat despondently on a rock wondering what to do. I watched the doggie wander away sniffing at the grass, which was obviously more interesting to him than I was. To make matters worse, the guidebook issued a dire warning to anyone considering wading the Avon, very strongly advising an inland diversion of 8 miles instead. Not only was the water itself treacherous, but there were many reports of weever fish stings here, which are reputedly agonising. Looking up I saw a small boat crossing the water about 100 yards upstream. I heard the putt-putt of its tiny outboard motor and saw just one man in it. I ran towards it as fast as possible, praying that I may be able to beg a lift across. I'd pay *anything* and meant it this time! The boat stopped about 10 feet away from the bank, unable to get any closer or it'd be grounded. I asked if there was any chance of lift.

The thirty-five-year-old rugged-looking chap answered with a smile: "Well seein' as I'm the ferryman there's every chance of a lift, but you'll have to wade out to her I'm afraid."

Yippee! I hadn't missed it after all. What a miracle! I felt like rejoicing: Oh thank you, God, thank you so much! And those nice people that I frightened out of their wits too! And poor nice Irish Peter who only tried to be helpful, but I'd wanted to strangle ten minutes earlier. I didn't mean any of it, honestly. Sorry everybody! Unfortunately, after wading the 10 feet out to the boat, my boots and socks became saturated again. A violent gust of wind lifted my Tilley hat clean off my head and deposited it 20 feet away in the mixture of mud and water that the boat had stirred up. I slipped as I ran and grabbed at it and went straight over in a foot of sludge. I got up cursing and dripping all over with the thick brown mud and turned to see the horrid ferryman laughing at me. I slapped the hat back onto my bonce, unaware that it was full of mud, which ran all down my face and front, much to the amusement of the ferryman. I yelled semi-angrily, but also chuckled at my own misfortune.

"I ain't paying you now!" Despite being in a disgusting state I was forced to see the funny side of it, and even began singing 'Mud, mud, glorious mud' to my companion as we chugged across the estuary. The cost was an extortionate £2 but he wouldn't lower it, despite protestations like, "Look at the state of me! That's all your fault, that is! I'll sue the ferry company. That's an expensive hat."

Once at Bantham I wasn't quite so het-up as I'd done the three worst crossings now. I was feeling Natalie Tokered again from all my exertions and needed a rest, not to mention a good scrub down. I saw The Sloop up the lane. It looked like a fantastic old character pub. I walked in to find it empty, thank goodness. The barman appeared and looked at me with disgust.

"It's not my fault, honestly. I fell in the mud. The ferryman will tell you it was all his fault, honestly."

He refrained from slinging me out so I ordered a pot of tea for 6.31 people and sat down to recover before monopolising his gents' for a good ten minutes, using up all the liquid soap and every single Cresco paper towel in the place. After half an hour sitting alone I had got over the morning nightmare and felt ready to go off in search of the next one. I made my way north-west, which really got my goat again, walking in the wrong direction in order to get around another stupidly-shaped headland. At least the landscape wasn't so severe now. It took around an hour and a half to reach Hope Cove, without incident too, which I was very pleased about. I didn't like "incident" at all anymore. Hope Cove was a charming little place with attractive thatched cottages nestled in the shelter of the mighty Bolt Tail, which protects it from much of the bad weather. It has a long, fascinating history, first mentioned in the Assize Rolls for 1281, consisting of two tiny villages – Inner and Outer Hope – that are linked by a road and footpath.

I stopped at a snack van near the beach and got myself a hot mug of slop and a bottle of Irn Bru for later. I'd never had it before but with a name like that I'd always assumed it to be a fierce, lethal alcoholic drink, but Rocky the Scotsman burst his sides with laughter when I said I hoped I could handle it, as he encouraged me to buy a bottle. The tea and the conversation were both good. Rocky, who was a really good bloke, not only gave me directions but also a free top-up of tea that was most welcome. I always kept a watchful eye on the sky at all times now, and could predict quite accurately what was going to happen weather-wise, and it wasn't looking good right now. I got myself a pasty and a rose cheel (cheese roll) for later and set off apprehensively for the tough climb up to Bolt Tail. Next stop Salcombe.

For half a mile I was travelling west again, much to my annoyance. I made a mental note that if I ever decided to do another walk I'd at least pick one that had got the common decency to go in a straight line, like Offa's 'Orrible Dyke or John's End to Land o'Groats. As I neared the top the inevitable happened but this time I was ready for it. In an instant I pulled on the WPs. The rain was even worse than Carlyn Bay golf course two weeks earlier. I was being hit full-on by large, hard hailstones, driven by the severity of the gale. I struggled through it, drenched and feeling low again, with the Nasty Notemares bugging the hell out me. Those damn bagpipes were blaring away in my head. I didn't know how much more of this I could take and really felt like packing it in. I was losing the will to live. I knew I couldn't fail at any cost. I kept telling myself and drumming it in over and over again: I will not give in! I will not give in! There was no shelter or habitation after Bolt Tail, only rocky outcrops and ups and downs in between them. I tried blocking out the misery by imagining I was somewhere pleasant like in my bed at home or in the foetal position with the duvet pulled over my head!

After two hours of wishing I was dead the sky suddenly cleared. That yellow sun came out and shone beautifully. What a welcome sight! Someone up there must've heard me even though I didn't believe in him! Everything around me began to dry out in the warmth. Six human beings appeared ahead of me after I'd begun thinking I was the only one left on earth. I even managed a smile and a joke as I overtook them, although the going was tough with great pinnacles of rock surrounding me. I enjoyed walking in the sun and became quite optimistic until getting lost when nearing Bolt Head. As usual I didn't know where I'd gone wrong. I'd taken what appeared to be the obvious path at every junction. The guidebook had stressed that it was easy to go wrong here and how correct they were – for once. Unfortunately, they hadn't stressed what you had to do in order to go right! They'd advised the reader to stay on the coast route and not to divert inland. Call me silly, but I would've thought that they were stating the bleedin' obvious, considering I'm walking the coast path. Anyway, I was lost yet again and horribly this time. I was sort of inland, but how? I started going to pieces for the second time that day.

Before long I was yelling for help again. It was to no avail. Not a soul was about in this wilderness into which I'd unwittingly wandered. Why hadn't I latched onto the six walkers I'd overtaken an hour ago? I bet they weren't lost. I should've followed them from a safe distance, hiding behind boulders, and everything would've been all right, but no. I knew it all, as usual. Not having enough energy left for an out-and-out tantrum, I tried repeating the vixen-like shrieks from earlier, but that took a fair bit of lung power. I gave up in favour of a kind of a continuous low whining wail that gradually rose in pitch to a great height according to my level of anger at any precise given moment. It was reminiscent of a banshee suffering from terrible piles. This worked very well as I was also able to regulate the pitch according to my expenditure of energy. On a steep ascent I'd lower the pitch, whereas on a descent raise it right up to number 11 on a scale of 10. On one particular descent I was letting rip at full volume, simultaneously improvising a tragic sobbing noise. As I rounded a corner I saw a terrified family sitting on the grass not 20 yards in front of me. They must've heard me coming for miles! I noticed they hadn't yet spotted me, so without even breaking my stride I cut the unearthly wail stone dead, and when they looked round with abject terror in their eyes I was already smiling and greeting them. They looked bewildered and without speaking nodded in the affirmative.

Smiling pleasantly, I said, "Have you heard all the wild cries of the seabirds this afternoon? Fabulous, aren't they?"

I received no reply. I strolled past them full of the joys of spring until I got about 100 yards beyond them. Once out of sight I could no longer hold it in a second longer, so roared and bellowed with all my might, not caring anymore about what they nor anyone else might think, while pleading with any greater force to please put me on the correct path or I'd top myself! I'm sure a miracle occurred because almost immediately I saw a sign pointing down towards Salcombe. After this I could see I was going to have to start believing in something major. My rage subsided and I made my way down the grassy slope in the warm sunshine. I came down to sea level at the picturesque, sheltered, quiet South Sands beach.

Time for a rest, so I bought an ice-cream and sat down at a table. Doing so, I spotted a sea tractor similar to the one at Burgh Island, standing in the nearby shallow water. A couple of local lads got chatting to me, explaining that the sea tractor was used for getting ferry passengers through the shallows and onto the boat as it couldn't get in close enough to load them from the shore. They said a ferry was due in ten minutes, which would be going up the estuary to Salcombe proper. Although not being much of a sailor this was too good a chance to turn down, plus the water in the estuary was very calm on this beautiful afternoon. I waited for the ferry to arrive. About six of us boarded the old sea tractor and it conveyed us very slowly and safely the 30 yards or so to the waiting boat. We pulled out of the small bay and set off up the Kingsbridge estuary, affording us beautiful views, not only to the lovely old buildings of Salcombe on the steep Western side, but also out to sea and east across the water to the village of East Portlemouth opposite. I enjoyed the ride greatly and decided to have a quick look round Salcombe before continuing walking well into dusk, as I wasn't prepared to waste an evening as pleasant as this.

High above I spotted Overbeck's elegant Edwardian house and museum set in enchanting sub-tropical gardens with mesmerising views, now owned by the National Trust. I'd visited the house before and had a super cream tea and a mad race around the gardens. In the house are inventions of Otto Overbeck, a mad scientist who made his fortune by inventing gadgets, the most notable of which was his "Rejuvenator" – a device that uses electrodes to "practically renew youth" – patented in 1924. In reality it had no effect whatsoever, but with electricity being all the rage, he rode the gravy train and cleaned up! He was also a pioneer in the world of carp fishing, being the first man to catch large carp intentionally, rather than merely by chance, which had been the only method until he formulated new successful techniques. There're many large cased fish in the house bearing testament to his success. He was also known for his good work helping underprivileged youngsters.

I alighted in Salcombe at 6 p.m. and pottered up the almost deserted main street. Everything had closed. I should've got here earlier and would've done if I hadn't got horrifically lost. My big priority was to find a cash-point as I was now down to less than my £50 danger level. I slipped my card in with baited breath, as the crack in it had got worse, but all was okay. £200 pounds came sliding out, much to my relief. Having got that out of the way, I sauntered around looking in shops, estate agents windows, clothes shops, and art galleries. Salcombe was a pricey place, certainly the most up-market village since St Mawes. Property prices are second only to Poole Harbour, with waterfront sites commanding millions of pounds. I doubted if I'd find a B & B for eighteen quid here. According to my quick calculations, based on the above weekly rental figure, it'd cost me exactly £1,714.28 for one night's accommodation in Salcombe. I decided to get going while the going was good.

I took the small ferry to East Portlemouth at 6 p.m. Three of us were aboard. More sandy beaches were in evidence on the other side, which, like Salcombe, is designated as an Area of Outstanding Natural Beauty. I didn't hang round in the village though. I was anxious to cover a good distance before finishing for the day. I walked through cool evening woodland, gradually climbing again. I was walking south-west, back on myself again, in order to reach the head of the estuary and I would turn left for Prawle Point. This time I didn't mind so much, as no gale was blowing in my face and there was a golden evening glow washing over everything in sight – me included. The stunning views of the estuary, Salcombe, and beyond made me feel relaxed and positive. Always better in the evenings, I got into a good rhythm and was soon flying along. The sky was a little darker in places by 7.30 p.m. I didn't think it'd rain though so wasn't unduly worried. I was back in the zone again with all my senses on red alert, floating on air, appreciating every sight, sound, and smell around me, exactly how I like it. I wished this would happen more than twice a week, as it's stupefyingly wonderful.

After many more ups and downs with fabulous sea views I saw the old coastguard hut perched on the end of Prawle Point. I passed by the eerie empty little building and turned the corner to walk north-east towards Start Point, which I knew I wouldn't reach tonight. I passed Langerstone point, a row of cottages 50 yards away on my left near East Prawle, and came down to sea level again. Now alongside the shore on the grassy path, I was beginning to worry about camping, as it was almost dusk. I came to a narrow fenced-off strip of grass next to the path and decided to risk it. I climbed over a low wire fence and pitched quickly, hoping that darkness would descend rapidly so nobody would spot me and move me on. It must've been fenced off for a reason. I ate my pasty and roll in the dark, not wanting to draw unwanted attention by using any artificial light. I fell asleep quickly and slept through till morning without incident.

Day 41: Saturday 24 May

I woke up feeling exhausted and lay still for ages, not caring if I got caught now. They couldn't take my sleep back, so what could they do now that would upset me? I performed the hour-long chore of packing slowly to the lapping of the gentle waves on the nearby shore, saw nobody and left at 9.30 a.m. It always felt fantastic to walk away the following morning after camping, to be on the move again without any major traumas in the night. I always checked and double checked the site in case I'd left anything behind. The route was still flat, for which I was grateful, as there's nothing worse than a horrific steep gradient first thing in the day. It could finish me off for the whole morning. I soon passed a beautiful solitary house, 50 yards inland to my left. I wondered who might live in it, imagining a picture of it in a Salcombe Estate Agents' window:

A substantial Victorian Property in secluded, stunning coastal location, enjoying extensive sea views, 40 acres including gardens, pasture, paddock and woodland, swimming pool, tennis courts, stable block, vineyards, garages, outbuildings, original interior, only 2,000 genuine miles on the clock, never raced or rallied, only one lady owner. Price £8,500,000. No time wasters!

I almost tripped up looking at it. I was transfixed as I walked by, and horribly jealous too. I was starting to get concerned about my remaining water rations, being down to my last half-pint, and the weather was looking good, i.e. hot. I'd need a refill before long. Until this trip I'd never known what being really thirsty was like and how it could affect the human body. Previously I'd hardly ever drunk water by itself, always finding it boring without whisky added. This notion had been turned on its head now though. I drunk it rapaciously by the gallon, mostly via my hose, and had enjoyed every drop of it on this trip. This is on top of all the numerous pots of tea, soft drinks, and beer of course. I was probably drinking twelve-fifteen pints of liquid per day, more when very hot. Thirsty work, this backpacking lark.

Somewhere before Lannacombe Beach I came to another solitary house, overlooking the path and sea. Although not built on such a grand scale as the previous mansion it was still a beautiful Victorian house, red brick combined with grey roughcast with three attic windows. Its green lawn sloped down towards a 3-foot-high stone wall. On the other side of it a lovely black woolly bulstrode sat looking at me and I saw a man about my own age pottering by a shed 30 yards away. I was loathe to disturb him in his garden on this quiet Saturday morning, but being desperate for water I nervously called to him and he came over. He gladly took my two bladders and filled them from his own well before we got chatting. A real Devonshire countryman, his name was Bill Langham, and he'd an air of contentment and calmness about him. I hoped some of it would rub off on me! It seemed he'd lived in this lovely house for many years. He was at one with it and the surrounding land and seascapes. His appreciation of the hand that life had dealt him was obvious. I envied him his contentment. I drank the pure, cool water from my Platypus, realising this was the best thing I'd ever tasted in my entire life; a kind of "eureka" moment. I guzzled down the whole two litres straight from the bladder, simply raving about how great it tasted. I hate "litres", but the bladder capacity was in litres, so I was stuck with them.

He chuckled, making the understatement, "It's not bad, is it?"

I asked if he'd mind putting pints into the bladder next time as he went back to refill it for me! This time I held back, only drinking a little of it, before screwing on the hose and putting it carefully into my rucksack. We

talked for another ten minutes before I took a photo of him holding his
lovely cat, named Willow. Now it was time to go. I really didn't want to. It'd
been one of those perfect interludes where you wish time could stand still
forever. When I think back over the whole walk, this special fifteen minutes,
although not dynamic or exciting by any means, is still one of the most
beautiful. Good luck to you, Bill. Thanks for your time, your kindness and,
of course, that magical water.

Reluctantly I said goodbye and set off to begin the climb up to Start
Point. I wondered if Bill often got bothered by walkers asking for various
favours. If he did it hadn't turned him against us yet, thankfully. Unlike the
thug at the café in Seaton, I can't imagine two people any more opposite. It
was a beautiful morning by now. I took my time, taking it all in. I met a
great elderly couple near Sleaden Rocks. We stopped for a chat and a sneaky
rest. They were on holiday, revisiting places where they'd spent their
honeymoon in 1940. They'd picnicked near the spot where we were
standing. This was the first time they'd returned in the intervening sixty-
three years. I said I felt like I was intruding on their memories but they just
laughed.

"Don't talk nonsense! It's nice to be able to share the memories with
someone else up here after all these years."

I didn't feel so bad after that, so we carried on chatting for ten minutes
before bidding each other goodbye. I'd climbed to around 300 feet by now
and was fast approaching Start Point where I'd soon swing north after
rounding the tip of the headland. When I turned that corner I could hardly
believe my eyes. Wow! I stopped dead in my tracks, my jaw dropping, taking
in the breathtaking panoramic vista that spread itself out before my eyes. I
don't know why but I hadn't expected anything quite like this, and after all
the stunning stuff I'd already seen it came as a real shock, probably because
I didn't have a proper map. I stood mesmerised, gawping at the huge sweep
of coastline. Immediately ahead was Start Bay followed by Torcross and
Slapton Sands. Beyond that I could clearly make out the Dart Estuary.
Further to the north-east were Lyme Bay and the Jurassic coasts of Devon
and Dorset. Further round still was the peninsula of Portland Bill. Seeing
this gave me a real buzz, as I knew that Poole harbour, and therefore the end
of my journey, was only about 40 miles beyond its tip. I could also make out
a faint shape way beyond that. Surely it couldn't be the distant Isle of Wight?
The sun was shining brightly on the whole scene, making it the most
awesome, welcome sight in the six weeks I'd been on the trail. I continued
slowly along a smart broad gravel path that skirted the cliff whilst heading
north. Several day walkers were enjoying the views too. I stopped to pass the
time with many of them, feeling no need to rush now. I saw a sturdy sign
post that gave me a feeling of confidence. Maybe I could finish this walk
after all! The sign stated: "Minehead 468 miles/South Haven Point 158
miles". This meant I was three-quarters of the way round, with the toughest
sections hopefully behind me. I started feeling great. It'd been a long time

coming, apart from the odd ecstatic hour, but this was different. It was a quiet belief that I really could do it, providing my feet, body, and equipment held out for another ten days or so. I was so engrossed in my thoughts that I hardly noticed the ominous black clouds that'd gradually crept up on me from behind. They looked set to tip their billions of gallons – definitely not litres – of water directly onto my unsuspecting bonce. Strangely, this time I wasn't too bothered. I didn't welcome the prospect of getting soaked to the skin, but it didn't seem so terrible anymore. Despite all I'd endured, the rain hadn't got through my skin as yet, so why worry?

I came to Trout's Apartments and faced a café-kiosk, boasting a good-looking menu. A well-spoken middle-aged gentleman inside told me that food was available if I wanted to eat. I chose scimpy and chaps, peas, plus the mandatory pot of tea for two. I sat on the lawn in front of the apartment block that'd formerly been The Trout Hotel, built by former residents of the ruined village of Hallsands, which lay directly below the cliffs here. It's said that some of the compensation money from its destruction helped build the hotel. Although there's no longer any public access to the village it can be seen from a viewing platform placed on the cliffs here at the Trout. The small fishing community had been in existence for around 400 years, eking out a living from the sea, mainly crab from the Skerries Bank. My meal was served to me on the lawn, butler-style, by the aforementioned posh gent and it was delicious. The sky, however, was the complete opposite of delicious, forcing me to grab my tray and bolt for the sanctuary of the Trout Apartments' lounge as the heavens opened. I made it indoors in time to save my food, the rain being so heavy that visibility was reduced to almost nil across the lawn where I'd been sitting happily two minutes earlier. Within minutes four bedraggled, dripping walkers pushed open the door, coming in for shelter and tea. It took forty minutes for the rain to stop and allow me to carry on.

I set off through the puddles, passed Tinsey Head, and down to the pleasantly named village of Beesands, which consisted of one row of cottages and houses spread out in a long line behind, parallel to the beach. It seemed Beesands had been quite fortunate compared to its neighbour, as some dredging had taken place near here too. I liked this village so much that I stopped to buy an ice cream (I do like my ice cream, especially after a meal), plus a couple of "sad-looking goom-wiches" for later on. I climbed up through some trees where the rain started again, so I tried pressing myself against a large trunk to stay dry and it worked. Ten minutes later I was on my way again. By the time I reached the uninspiring Torcross it was drizzling again. I found a hotel café and went in for some more tea and a break. The staff was not the friendliest of people, but as long as I was out of the rain I didn't care, especially with only 150 miles to go. A nearby couple eyed me with suspicion as I fiddled with the contents of my rucksack, which I deposited all over the floor in order to try organising them better. I threw out loads of wrappers, empty bags, deceased black bananas, bottles, and other accumulated rubbish. A family sat at the next table. They were nice and friendly, making up for the other pork pigs that were horrid to me.

I began to route march the 2 miles of busy main road alongside the shingle causeway between Slapton Sands and the Slapton Ley freshwater lake and nature reserve. It was here off Slapton Sands where a tragic incident occurred during World War II. In the early hours of the 28 April 1944 eight Landing Ship Tanks, full of American servicemen whose purpose was to take part in "Exercise Tiger" (the realistic rehearsals for the D-Day landings in Normandy) met with disaster. The night turned into tragedy as a group of patrolling German e-boats discovered and attacked them. By the end of Exercise Tiger 946 American serviceman had lost their lives. As a tribute to all these lost American servicemen, a 32 ton Sherman tank lost in the exercise was later recovered from the sea bed and is now displayed at Slapton Sands in their memory.

I walked on the grass for most of the way along the edge of the freshwater lake, which was far more pleasant and much safer too. I could see people with butterfly nets near the lake and a few others milling around with binoculars, obviously trying to pry into windows of the nearby houses. The sky was bright blue again with not a black cloud in sight. I prayed it'd stay like this for the rest of the day. At Strete Gate I left the road and took a grassy path up to my right towards the sea. I was enjoying this little path until I saw a sign that read: "Beware Adders". Oh no, not again! I've nothing against adders, but it meant closely concentrating on the green floor and surrounding areas instead of letting go and ambling without a care, which I really felt like doing now. One or two cottages were on my left. I spotted an old maroon railway carriage to my right, hoisted up into a fantastic position overlooking the sea. I wanted to buy it and live there immediately. I crept up to it and peered through a window, hoping I wouldn't be caught trespassing. Inside it was like a great mini-home. It looked like it was used as a holiday retreat. I wondered how someone had got permission to do this, as it wasn't a private garden. Could I buy a similar carriage, plonk it down somewhere on the coast, and live in it or rent it out for a small fortune? I was always intrigued when I saw these unusual "follies" and wanted one for myself. It's not fair!

I was forced to return to the main road at Strete, as the coast was inaccessible for the next seven or eight miles, owing to ongoing negotiations with local landowners not keen on opening up their land to poor old walkers like me, preferring us to risk life and limb on the main roads instead. I walked past a roadside sign that read: "Strete". Once there it looked easy, but was a veritable maze of horror rather like the Hampton Court maze but worse. I found myself in a modern housing estate knocking on doors for directions to the SW Coast Path which, of course, nobody had ever heard of, even though they practically lived *on* it. I wandered back out of it knowing I'd have to rely on my wits; those very same wits that had already let me down 10,000 times during the last few weeks. I took various logical turns for the next fifteen minutes and really felt I'd cracked it, until I came upon a roadside sign stating: "Strete". It was the same one I'd passed twenty minutes earlier. So much for my wits! I needed to get out of this godforsaken dump. After a game of "eenie, meeny, miny, mo" I took any path I could find that was going anywhere vaguely resembling a northerly direction. Apologies to any irate residents of Strete. It wasn't really a dump but it was to me that afternoon. After a load of inland ups and downs I came down to an old, picturesque hamlet, which I presumed was that of Blackpool, but as it was inland and I could see no Eiffel-type tower, I must've been wrong. Slightly disgruntled, I sat on an ancient stone bridge to check the guidebook for signs of the path to Stoke Fleming, when a car pulled up on the bridge beside me.

Winding down his window, a chap said, "Excuse me. Please can you tell me the way to Warfleet?"

What the hell is wrong with people? A backpacker is surely the last person in the world you'd ever ask for directions, however desperate you may be. By definition he can't possibly not know any local area well, as he's merely passing through, as is the nature of his trip. His rucksack is usually the giveaway. He's also, nine times out of ten, struggling with routes and directions himself, desperate to find someone local to ask.

I rolled my eyes before replying bluntly: "No, I've never heard of it or anywhere else round here."

I didn't elaborate and they drove away no better off in search of Warfleet. I took a rural lane north for half a mile, followed by a path east up yet another bloody great hill. I was slipping and sliding down on gravel through some woodland that was tiring me out. I decided if I was ever able to find Stoke Fleming I'd definitely stop there for the night. Finally, at the top of the hill, I came to a flat lane and walked into Stoke Fleming.

It was after 7 p.m. when I strolled past a few houses and straight into the ancient pub for refreshment and advice on where to stay. The Green Dragon pub dated back to the thirteenth century, according to the local couple I got chatting to, as I sank three halves of Flower's bitter. She was all right but he was strange. I didn't like the way he kept looking at me, so I turned to the owner Peter; a decent cove, and talked to him instead. Amazingly, he told me that he'd once sailed across the Atlantic solo. I asked if he'd kept getting lost like me, but he said he couldn't really tell, as it'd all looked the same! Martin, a rugby player, joined in the conversation. Soon I was simultaneously chatting to all eight people in the bar, also trying to ignore the strange bloke who kept looking at me. They were a nice crowd – apart from that strange bloke who kept ... When I mentioned I was searching for somewhere to stay, someone pulled out a mobile and called the cheapest B & B in the village, saying it was very good, before handing me the phone. Unfortunately, although it may have been the cheapest in the village, it was far too expensive at £35. I felt rather stupid turning it down with everyone listening, looking at me agog, especially that strange bloke who was even stranger now. I really hoped he wasn't going to invite me to stay at his place. Somebody mentioned there was a campsite 50 yards away, above Leonard's Cove, so that was it. I toddled off slightly tipsy towards the old church of St Peter where the site was located. It took a long time to pitch the tent after one and a half pints on an empty stomach, but I didn't care, as I now had a good place to stay, the weather was fine, and The Green Dragon was 50 yards up the lane. They did evening bar meals too. This was better than lying out on the wild cliff tops alone, eating cold pasties with water. I visited the campsite shower block and prepared myself for a pleasant evening.

Back at the tent a young couple was setting up their gear next to me. Their names were William and Carol. He'd returned from Iraq after spending several months on duty in a submarine. They were lovely people. We got on like a house on fire. I greatly admired them both for the sacrifices they'd chosen to make in their young lives. I eventually dragged myself away after they'd promised to meet me in the pub later for drinks on *me*! I must've really liked them! I walked to the pub, pushed open the door, finding it was packed solid inside. Where had they all come from? It was about 8.30 on a Saturday night so, apart from the campsite and the locals, I guessed the rest had probably come from Dartmouth. Fortunately there was no sign of the strange bloke from earlier. I fought my way to the bar where Martin the rugby player – a really genuine guy – immediately bought me a pint, congratulating me on my walk.

I replied, "I haven't finished it yet. Perhaps I should only drink three-quarters of it tonight and come back for the rest if I do complete it."

Shortly afterwards we shook hands as he had to go to bed early, having a big match at Twickenham the next day: England versus the Baa-Baas; The Barbarians for the uninitiated. I wished I'd asked what his surname was afterwards. Not Johnson, surely? I ordered Moroccan Chicken with rice, which was superb, and only £6.20. We were all packed in tight like sardines. I got chatting to another local couple – Patti and Gordon – whose faces were 6 inches from my own. Luckily they weren't too ugly. He was a local potter and reminded me of the actor Robert Lindsay, who, incidentally, used to be a regular in my Chiswick antique shop in the 1980s. It was hot in the room. We were drinking quite heavily, with Gordon buying me a pint for doing the walk, me buying him one for not doing it – any excuse to get them in. As we descended into a tired, drunken stupor we began talking about man-things, such as football, about which I know absolutely nothing but still voiced my uninformed opinions. We also discussed motors, carp fishing, cricket, the Iraq war, the government (of course), and rock music, which was better. At one point we were trying to decide who was the world's best ever guitarist.

Gordon slurred, "What about Weedon?" at which point I fell off my stool laughing. "All right, all right, he was crap, but Clapton was God in the '60s of course."

I quipped, "Oh yes, Gopton was clad all right, but you've got old Jeff, who's still brilliant now."

"Oh yes, pure class, old Jeff. What about Pagey?"

"Yeah, but I think he's past his peak now. What about the metal boys? Vai and Satriani?"

"Slash ain't bad, and there's old Jimmy Hetfield from Metallica; huge rhythm player, him."

I mimicked "huge rhythm" on air guitar, accidentally elbowing a woman on the next stool right in the chest. My humble but drunken, longwinded apology was accepted, thank Clapton!

"Then there's King, of course."

"Yeah, good point. Old BB, or d'yer mean Albert, Freddie, or Jonathan? But the guvnor has to be Hendrix, surely?"

"Oh without a doubt. Jimi will always be *the king*."

"No human being could ever equal that. *Never*, no *never!*"

We drunkenly concurred whilst attempting to "sing" his 'Star Bangled Banner' from Woodstock. Gordon, almost sobbing into his pint, cried out passionately for all around to hear.

"Yeah, and the silly bastard went and killed himself!"

Everyone in the pub fell silent at this heartfelt statement. You could hear a pin drop. I too was taken aback by his emotional outburst, unsure how to respond. I put my arm comfortingly around his shoulder, sighed, and while shaking my head knowingly, spoke with great sadness.

"Well, that's Jimi for yer." I solemnly added, "He's gone to a better place now, playing in that great band in the sky along with Brian, Buddy, Jim, Elvis, Janice, and Johnny."

Who the **** was Johnny? I inwardly cringed at my own inane comments. It was definitely the drink talking, but it seemed to calm Gordon down. Everything started up again and normal service was resumed. He went on to tip most of his pint all over my "best" trousers when someone barged into him. I bought him a pint and he bought me another one. I wasn't quite as gone as him and was beginning to wonder what had happened to the nice young couple William and Carol from the campsite, as it was after 10 p.m. already. More and more people packed into the pub as the evening went on. Meanwhile Patti had got bored and disowned us half an hour earlier. She was talking to another nearby couple. Some bloke in a Tilley hat like mine waved frantically to me across the room. I gave him the "Tilley Owners' Club" thumbs up before ignoring him to discuss the more important subject of 1950s' chocolate bars that you never saw anymore, and how much bigger Mars Bars used to be when they cost 4p. in old money, and inevitably whether a normal-sized Snickers is only a fun-sized Snickers to a giant, though the riddle was totally beyond us in our woeful condition, causing us to abandon it after five minutes of bickering. Eventually it was chucking-out time. Gordon and I hugged each other as if we'd been lifelong mates. I shook hands with his wife and we all swapped emails and phone numbers, vowing to keep in touch before saying our goodbyes. Needless to say we never kept in touch.

I staggered back towards the campsite, hoping I'd be able to find it in the dark. I spotted the village chip shop and reeled in its general direction, half starving, as it was a three hours since my pub meal. I wrenched at the door but it was locked. The lights were on though so I persisted. After a few minutes an upstairs window opened. A bloke called down to me.

"Sorry, mate, we close at 11."

I couldn't believe it and shouted back: "I only want some chips ... with peas ... fish ... and gravy ... and a mushy drink."

"Go away! It's half past eleven. I told you we're closed!"

Not being a violent man I slurred back: "I'm hungry! I'm not coming here again! It's *not fair!*"

I sloped off grumpily. Finding the campsite was not easy, but once there, finding my tent was nigh on impossible. The first thing I did was trip over the guy ropes of a huge tent causing it to shake dangerously, provoking cries of "F*** o**!" from the ten campers inside. I hadn't had the foresight to take a torch to the pub, so I was literally in the dark now. I tried lining up the silhouette of the church with the shower block. This way I should be able to locate my tiny pitch more easily. Somehow I ended up on my hands and knees crawling and feeling gently for guy ropes. I felt like a bomb disposal expert.

I heard a voice directly above me: "Overend, what the hell are you doing down there?" It was William. I explained I was a bit lost, to which he replied, "You've crawled right past your tent. It's 10 feet behind you." I thanked him, standing up with as much dignity as I could muster in my drunken state. When I asked why he hadn't come to the pub, he said, "I did! I waved to you like mad but you were chatting to somebody else and I didn't want to bother you." When I said I hadn't seen him, he said, "I was wearing a Tilley hat like yours."

The penny dropped. I felt awful for not recognising him in the hat. I apologised profusely, saying I'd really looked forward to chatting to him and his wife, and it was a real shame they hadn't barged in on Gordon and me. As we whispered in the dark we were deafened by the noise of the church clock, situated 20 yards away, striking midnight. Boing! Boing! Boing! Surely it wasn't going to strike all night! We said goodnight and retreated to our tents. Once inside I got into the bag without messing about and curled up. I was aware of chattering coming from some of the other tents, but I was beginning to nod off when, twelve minutes later, the clock loudly chimed the quarter. This went on all night. I barely slept a wink. Stoke *pigs!* Fleming bacon *pigs!*

Day 42: Sunday 25 May

I say I "woke" at 8 a.m., but what I really mean is that I gave up trying to sleep at 8 a.m. What a dreadful night! The worst kip ever, and besides that, I'd got a nasty hangover and felt like death on wheels to boot. I'm not a heavy drinker so the six or seven pints I'd sunk had quite an adverse effect on me. Despite this, it'd felt like time to unwind last night and go on a small bender. It helped get over the memories of the angst-ridden, rainy fortnight since Mevagissey. It'd been a great evening. I needed it and it'd come at the right time too. After a drizzly start the weather had come good again as I ambled to the shower block and spent a long time under the lukewarm jets at a cost of 40 soddin' pence. I almost felt human again by the time I got back to the tent, with headache subsided and all other ill effects appeared to have gone too. Strangely, I didn't feel particularly tired either. I was delighted by this, as I couldn't face walking the cliffs with a hangover. I rang my lovely accountant Sandy, who'd told me she may be sailing at Dartmouth during May. If the timing was right we might be able to meet up for a meal or at least a drink. Unfortunately she told me she'd sailed down to Salcombe, so we'd missed each other by a day or two. It was a pity, but maybe it was for the best, as another evening of drinking and partying with Sandy and her friends may have been too much for my already frail metabolism. I was wondering what to do about paying, having not seen anyone since arriving on the previous evening.

Suddenly, as if by magic, a bloke appeared from nowhere, smiled and said, "That'll be £8, please."

Horrified, I replied, "Have a heart, will you? I haven't slept a wink because of that church clock. Let me give you a quid instead." He was having none of it and said it was exactly the same for everyone, to which I replied, "What, nobody who's ever camped here has slept a wink either?"

After a lot more pleading he obviously felt sorry for me and said, "Oh give me a fiver and don't tell anybody else."

It was kind of him but I made a mental note never to stay there again, despite its proximity to the pub and chip shop, unless they agreed to demolish that horrid church.

I said goodbye to William and Carol and left along lanes at the ludicrous late hour of 11.15 a.m. bound for Dartmouth. It'd taken me three and a quarter hours to leave. *How?* Owing to the ongoing land disputes, I was still walking inland, but managed to regain the coast again at the charmingly named Dancing Beggars rocks. After a couple more miles of high stuff I came down to catch the little ferry up the estuary for a mile into Dartmouth, where I saw a sign for Warfleet. So there was such a place after all. I wondered if they'd managed to find it yesterday. This was a short but lovely trip with about six of us aboard the twelve-seated ferry. To our left was the attractive town of Dartmouth, strung along and above the waterside. To our right was the smaller community of Kingswear. I scrutinised the cliffs on the eastern side of the estuary to see how steep they were, as I'd be scaling them later, and although heavily wooded they looked horribly severe. I don't know why I was surprised by this once again.

As I stepped off the ferry the centre of Dartmouth was bustling with activity, with all manner of boats coming and going, people lunching in and outside restaurants, while others milled about shopping and sightseeing. I'd never seen the town any other way. It seemed it was always sunny here and I loved it. My first priority was to get a good square meal inside me – no, not a cream cracker – as I'd only eaten two cereal bars that morning with nothing else being on offer. I found a nice café up a side street named The Spinning Wheel and ordered a cold smoked fish salad, with salmon, crab, prawns, crusty bread, plus a floral print pot of tea from the pleasant waitress. It'd make a nice change from all the full Englishes of which I'd partaken over the past six weeks. I sat with about a dozen other diners in the small courtyard outside in the sunshine. After five minutes nothing had arrived. After fifteen minutes nothing had arrived. After half an hour I realised I'd made a grave mistake, but it was too late to cancel the order. I was wasting so much valuable time and was not a happy bunny. I'd only ordered a bloody salad! How could it take this long to "cook" that? Were they out trying to catch the fish? Finally, after three-quarters of an hour, my salad arrived along with apologies for the delay. I hadn't got the energy to complain on this lovely day so ate the food, which I must say was very good, but still not worth a forty-five-minute wait.

After finishing the meal I became aware of a loud commotion above us. Looking up I saw about five large gulls swooping down over the courtyard, no doubt checking out the food. As they dive bombed us they deposited their large "calling cards" all over the four diners on the next table. They were all covered in white mess; their clothes, hair, food – it was everywhere. They all jumped up shrieking in disgust. Poor devils, I thought, while being secretly overjoyed that it wasn't me. I, it seemed, had escaped unscathed. As if they'd been expecting it to happen, the waitresses all came running out with bowls, damp cloths, and all manner of cleaning materials, causing me to wonder if this was a regular occurrence around these parts. I took this as an omen and ran inside to pay my bill before I became another victim. I would've loved to loiter in the sunshine in fabulous Dartmouth all day, but couldn't afford the time or money to do that. I allowed myself half an hour to stroll about gawping at things, such as the tall, ornate, elegant gabled buildings beside the quay, before nipping into Somerfield's to get some supplies for the rest of the day. When I came out onto the street my mind wandered back to the last time I was in Dartmouth, on a warm evening about five years earlier. I got very excited as I walked past Somerfield's with my friend Roberta.

She nudged me and said, "Isn't that bloke over there in *Emmerdale Farm*?"

I exclaimed at great volume: "Where! Who is it! Where is he!"

My loudburst (there's another) caused people to turn and stare at me. I couldn't see anyone at first, but when she pointed him out I said I'd never seen that bloke in my entire life. She persisted, even though she never watched the programme. I recognised him. Yes! She was right! It was none other than *Frank Tate!* – actor Norman Bowler – the rugged, gritty, northern, self-made multi-millionaire! He was going into Somerfield's for some last-minute knock-down bargains!

Not being an *EF* fan herself, I excitedly informed Roberta that, "He's supposed to be dead. Kim – his beautiful but evil wife – finished him off last year by refusing to give him his heart-attack pills when he collapsed in front of her, begging for them, and now here he is in Dartmouth, as large as life and as bold as brass, doing his shopping!"

Well I should co-co he wasn't dead after all. I became very exuberant and insisted that we had a cup of tea in the café opposite Somerfield's so we could watch him come out again.

Roberta was not particularly enthusiastic, but I said, "You don't see old Frank Tate every day of the week, do you?"

"No, thank God!" (Or words to that effect.)

I had a brainwave. I set up my large video camera on our table facing the supermarket door – this was before mobile phone cameras were around –without regard for the Data Protection Act, and put it into "record" so I could show him to Mum and Dad when I got home. When he came out, however, he was gone in the blink of an eye. My brainwave wasn't so brilliant after all. On playback Frank was an unrecognisable blur, lasting for one-quarter of a nano-second! Still, it's the thought that counts.

Later when we were leaving Dartmouth in the car, we rounded a bend and there he was again, walking on the pavement. Roberta, now getting into the spirit of things, wound down her window at the same time as me and we both yelled out at the tops of our voices.

"Frank! How're yer doin'? Good old Frank! Great to see you're still alive and kicking!"

Good old Frank never acknowledged us and kept on walking. I could guess what he was probably thinking. I thought afterwards that maybe we should've offered him a lift, but Kim might have tracked us down and killed us, so it was lucky we didn't. He certainly made my day though. So, if you ever read this, thanks, Frank, old mate!

Back to reality. My next port of call – literally – was the smaller town of Kingswear across the estuary. I'd have to board another foot ferry to get there. The growing number of ferries I was taking was worrying me greatly, as the odds were shortening with every trip. Sooner or later one of them would sink. If I knew which one I wouldn't get on it. Carrying my weighty supplies in carrier bags I made my way to the crowded quay to find the ferry. I spied the larger boat that we'd travelled on when we'd done the Round Robin day trip up to Totnes on the beautiful River Dart last time – a trip I'd definitely recommend. I boarded the ferry and it didn't sink once during the five-minute crossing, thus further shortening the odds for my next ferry ride, which I'd calculated would be from Brixham to Torquay in one or two days' time.

Once safely in Kingswear I passed the old railway terminus where the same steam engine on which we'd travelled from Paignton to Kingswear five years earlier was standing hissing steam beside the platform with its round iron face grinning at me. Talk about a trip down memory lane. It was like a time warp. I felt very nostalgic. Oh happy days! An ice cream was called for immediately. I'd deliberately forsaken the pudding again and now needed to fill that gap to feel fulfilled. I climbed the steps from the ferry, went into the post office, and bought myself a Magnum. I sat on a stone wall to eat it whilst looking across the water to Dartmouth. The buildings looked splendid from here, like the Britannia Royal Naval College, where all officers from many navies are trained. Looking across the water at Dartmouth for the final time, I felt quite emotional, as it'd been a very special place for me over the years.

Not wishing to start blubbing like a toddler, I pulled on the pack and set off briskly for the climb ahead, which I'd heard through the grapevine was going be absolutely gruesome. The grapes themselves are not particularly gruesome, unless they've gone mouldy. It was 3.30 p.m. as I ascended through woodland with golden shafts of sunlight dancing through the leaves on the trees ahead of me, as the breeze caused them to rustle gently. I met several walkers, including a nice couple from Totnes, who I chatted to about the horrors of walking and how great Totnes was in real life! Soon after that I changed into my wild shorts for the first time in two weeks. It was great to feel the sun again. My whole demeanour had changed since I saw that lovely mile post at Start Point. I didn't feel at all "Eltonic" (tantrummy) either. I passed the World War II gun emplacements, the old castle, and came to an awful series of steep up and down zigzags. This was a nightmare that took forever. After an hour of walking I'd only travelled one mile, such was the stupidity of these switchback paths that constantly went back on themselves, while simultaneously descending and ascending from sea level back to the top and back again. Whoever it was that told me it was gruesome, I wanted to throttle them, because they were right. It reminded me of one of those dreams where you can't run away no matter how hard you try. I couldn't get away from there. I thought about ranting but it would've taken too much energy, which I couldn't afford to expend, requiring every ounce for this ridiculous terrain. I felt plum-tuckered by the time I got onto a reasonable path again. I met a couple coming the opposite way, called Tiffany and Roger. They were very excited, having seen a seal in the sea at the base of the nearby cliffs. Not wishing to miss out on this sighting I begged them to tell me where it was. I'd yet to see *one* marine creature since leaving Minehead. They looked at me in disbelief.

"What, *nothing* in 500 miles of coastal walking?"

I'd seen no whales, dolphins, or porpoises, nor basking sharks or seals off Zennor, where they're all supposed to hang out for tourists who go by boat to watch them. I'd heard in The Tinners Arms that nothing had been seen for several days before I passed through there.

After they left I ran like hell to the spot they'd described in the next bay and peered over the cliff – nothing. I took out my monocular and scanned the rocks way down below, spotting it a teeny-weeny head poking out of the water. I could barely make it out and wouldn't have done at all if the couple hadn't told me about it. In the blink of an eye it vanished, never to be seen again, but it was hardly the Mockless Non-ster anyway! So not a spectacular sighting but was still better than nothing. As I walked on I thought about how strange it was that I hadn't seen anything in 500 miles. The only creature I'd seen was that lovely red fox near Wembury, apart from a rotting crab or two on a beach somewhere. I had wondered if something was wrong with my eyes or if I simply give off the wrong pheromones? Yes, that must be the answer. My pheromones were obviously all wrong and horrible, thereby causing all animals and fish to flee in horror as soon as they sensed my imminent arrival.

Riddle solved, but what could I do to rectify this situation? I'd love to see loads of fabulous creatures on my travels. Maybe a strong aftershave lotion could help or maybe women's perfume, like Chanel No. 5? I remembered that in salmon fishing circles it was always women that seemed to catch all the huge fish. Miss Ballantyne still holds the British record at 64 lbs. with a fish she caught in 1922 on the River Tay in Scotland. The English record of 59 lbs. from the River Wye is also held by a woman. Experts always put that down to pheromones. For one crazy moment I considered having a "gender realignment" operation (a sex change, for the layman), but realised I'd have to buy a whole new wardrobe and change my name on my bank accounts, driving licence, and all the household services bills. Plus the milkman would probably think I'd got myself a fancy woman, especially if he saw me through the window hoovering in a pink flowery housecoat. It would also be tricky breaking the news to Mum and Dad, plus me old muckers Rick, DR, Mark, Phil, Michelle, Moshe, and the rest. They might think I'd gone a bit funny, so I abandoned that idea before it got off the ground. I felt slightly peeved though, as it would've been nice to catch a record salmon. I'd have to live with the pheromones that I'd already got and put up with all animals hating me forever. Maybe my own substandard pheromones might come in useful in other ways. For example, I loved the sound of that pheromone doing the high wobbly bit on 'Good Vibrations' by The Beach Boys. Maybe mine were that type, which couldn't be bad. I rehearsed that high wobbly bit as I walked and I could do it!

It was remote, rugged, beautiful coast again. I was captivated by the sea views, and started to get that special feeling I loved so much – complete freedom; the reason that I walked. High on the cliffs around a corner near Outer Froward Head, right before me, were some gorgeous ponies grazing. There were about eight of them, coloured black, white, and grey (without wishing to sound racist). As I approached I expected them to run off, owing to my pheromones and the sight of my enormous frightening lardbulk, but oddly enough, quite the opposite happened. They walked purposefully towards me without trepidation. Having arrived right next to me, they proceeded to pull and nibble at my shoulder bag, plastic drinking hose, bare arms, and anything else they could sink their teeth into. I stood laughing, surrounded by them, as they tugged roughly at me and my belongings. One cute little white one (racist again) kept nipping boldly at my shins and ankles. It tickled more than it hurt and I videoed him as he boldly nipped where nobody had boldly nipped before. I tried shushing them down though before they got too carried away and pushed me over the cliff. So much for the wrong pheromones now!

By 7.30 p.m. I came down to another small cove and was beginning to think about pitching up, but it was still a bit too early. The evenings were starting to stay noticeably lighter. I was near Scabbacombe Head when I looked onward only to see a monstrous great hill, which I'd have to climb sooner or later, or find a way around, but this was like no other hill I'd seen. It went up and up forever, making me all giddy merely looking at it. After some thought I decided it'd be better to tackle it immediately, as if I camped now I'd have nightmares about having to attempt it tomorrow morning whilst half asleep. I sauntered nonchalantly towards the base. Hoping to take it by surprise, I rushed at it like a bull-at-a-china-gate! Up and up and up the bare grassy incline and I still hadn't reached the top after forty-five minutes. This was unheard of. I moaned, leaning on my pole to rest for the tenth time. I could see for miles in every direction and not seawards as was the norm. I couldn't appreciate the views, owing to my altitude sickness! Most hills so far, no matter how daunting they may have looked from below, had only taken fifteen minutes max to climb. This, however, was a different kettle of hill. After almost an hour I finally got there, out of breath and exhausted, realising that I'd almost had it for the day. I prayed that this was a one-off and not the beginning of a terrible series of mountains that the guidebook hadn't bothered to mention, lest it might put walkers off coming to South Devon. It would certainly have put me off. I can honestly say that I'll never climb that hill again if I live to be 1,000 years old.

I began the long descent from the summit on a wide green path. I coasted down quite easily as it wasn't too steep, and arrived on a low flat section some 500 yards long and 40 feet above sea level, bridging the gap between the higher cliffs. Roughly 100 yards away several chimneypots were poking up above the low cliff top, which must've belonged to a large house. Looking at the short grass it was apparent that this would be a good spot to camp. Whilst unrolling the tent I became aware of a fairly strong, cold breeze blowing in from the sea. The spot where I was about to camp was covered in sheep muck. I kicked all the offending articles away in a couple of minutes and reached for the tent but it was nowhere in sight. I managed not to panic, knowing it couldn't have gone far, because the breeze was blowing from a seaward direction, so it couldn't have gone over the cliff. I soon found it 30 yards inland behind a low bush trying to hide from me.

After a beating I dragged it back to the freshly prepared spot. Unfortunately this wasn't the end of the story. Whatever I did I couldn't pitch the damn thing in the now stiffening breeze. It had a life of its own and kept escaping from my grasp, heading for that same bloody bush every time. I had a tantrum-ette, cursing as loudly as I dared. I was too near the house to have an out and out belter. They'd be bound to hear me if I did. After about twenty minutes I'd managed to secure the main guys and scrambled inside, relieved, after another five minutes. What a horrid half-hour that was after what could only be described as a fabulous day's walking. I ate the remainder of my sandwiches, mesmerised by the sea views from my tent flap, with the sun's dying red rays coming from behind the tent, shining over the stretch of water before me, giving off a rich deep-pink glow. It was 9.30 p.m. and it'd become chilly. I felt a cold shiver run right through me. Someone was walking on my grave again. I fell asleep quickly but woke at 2 a.m. for two hours before getting off again. I still wasn't sleeping well, despite being exhausted.

Day 43: Bank Holiday Monday 26 May

At 6.30 a.m. I was woken by hot sun on the nylon walls. This made a change. It would've made a much pleasanter one had it been 8.30 a.m. instead. Still, I shouldn't complain, as this boded well for the long day ahead. I hoped to reach the "English Riviera", or Torbay as it's more commonly known. I'd holidayed there several times previously and had some great memories, particularly from in and around Brixham. Torbay itself is a sheltered, semi-circular, east-facing bay, over 4 miles long in a direct line from north to south. It's protected from the worst of the weather by the two large, prominent headlands of Berry Head in the south, and Hope's Nose in the north, both of which protrude out some distance into the English Channel. Torbay includes the towns of Torquay, Paignton, and Brixham. The sun on the tent made me feel drowsy again. I dozed intermittently until waking properly at 9.15 a.m., furious that the sun had gone in and been replaced by the familiar rain clouds, right in front of my back! It can't be *behind* my back because, logically, the only thing behind my back is my front, if you see what I mean. It'd also gone quite cool. A "scorcher" was no longer on the cards.

I left at 10.15 a.m. determined not to let the weather get me down this time. Although there were more strenuous ups and downs, I made good time to Sharkham Point without getting wet. Having only eaten one chocolate bar so far I took advantage of the large campsite café/supermarket and got myself another load of cheap chocolate bars, an ice cream, and a quick pot of tea for two, as I planned having a proper meal later in Brixham. All this chocky and I'm still losing weight. It's brilliant. As I made my way back to the path I bumped into another walker coming towards me with a fair-sized pack. We stopped to chat. He was only about the sixth long-distance walker I'd met on my journey. In his late-thirties, long-haired and bearded, he was a fascinating, intelligent, extremely laidback guy. In fact he was so laidback he was almost horizontal, as they say. His name was Sean and his "backpacking techniques" were the exact opposite of mine. For starters he didn't appear worried about anything. He didn't seem to know or care where he was going or what the weather did! He'd been backpacking abroad in the Far East with a mate who'd broken a leg, so he (Sean) returned to England and continued backpacking alone, going anywhere willy-nilly. No poncy guidebooks or maps for him, nor a compass or time limit either. He'd wandered from somewhere up north and was now heading towards Land's End intending on going north again once there. Well he could hardly go south, could he? He reckoned he'd probably do about six months or so on the trail, taking him through to the winter.

When we got onto the subject of rucksacks I asked what kind of weight he was carrying. When he said around 10 lbs. I was dumbfounded and asked how. It was about 40 lbs. less than me! It seemed he'd virtually nothing in it. No tent (no f**king tent!), no airbed, very little clothing, no gadgets or gizmos, no pocket knife apparently, so what did he do about camping? He said he'd been kipping down in churchyards or church porches if it rained. If forced, he'd sleep in woodlands (woodlands!), fields, or anywhere else. He simply slept in a lightweight sleeping bag placed on a small plastic sheet! I'd definitely have died of exposure had I attempted this. He camped in town centres, on park benches, or on odd bits of grass. When I asked if he was afraid of being murdered by yobs, thugs, or hoodies he smiled and shrugged, saying he never got bothered by anyone. I found this unbelievable after my own experiences, which luckily had been few and far between, but had nonetheless been worrying. I told him I'd avoided camping near any kind of habitation at all costs, urban or rural. Don't forget that I hate people and they hate me, but Sean may have had a different perspective. Regarding clothing, he bought all his in charity shops or markets (socks) as he went along, chucking them away when they were wet or dirty before buying new ones! Surely this must be a far more expensive and troublesome way of travelling than mine in the long run, plus you'd be limited to whatever was available on the day.

As we chatted I noticed he was wearing a patterned bath towel around his neck like a scarf, plus a heavy pullover and an anorak, yet it wasn't that cold. He said he'd rather wear them than carry them in his pack. This bewildered me. Surely they'd still weigh the same whatever he did with them, so why endure the discomfort? It would've been pointless trying to tell him anything, as he was quite content with his methods, whereas I, not being the slightest bit laidback, was constantly trying to find better ways of doing things regarding my gear, as well as fretting over everything else. The difference in our approach to every single thing was astounding. I couldn't live that way and he probably wouldn't want to live my more complex way. When we shook hands after twenty minutes his hands were hot and mine were freezing cold. This probably was because he was wearing every item of clothing he possessed, whereas I had on a thin short-sleeved wicking top, which was all I ever wore unless there was heavy rain. I really must put on my fleece when I stop walking from now on though. Trouble is I keep forgetting I'm cold until I'm frozen. When we went our separate ways I wondered what buzz *he* got from walking and backpacking compared to me. He obviously cared far less about his comfort levels than I did. I couldn't imagine him having anything vaguely approaching a tantrum.

If something horrible happened he'd probably say, "I'll have a little sleep and see what happens."

I'd go apeshit, rant, and smash things. That said, my anger is always directed at myself, usually because I blame myself for any problems that crop up. I have occasionally shouted at innocent bystanders in frustration, but 99 times out of 100 they seem to understand why I'm all grim. I'd like to have walked with Sean for an afternoon to find out what really made him tick. I really liked him all the same and wished I possessed some his laidback qualities. Good old Sean!

Back on the path I soon rounded St Mary's Bay and Durl Head before seeing the lighthouse on the tip of Berry Head half a mile ahead. Once there I wandered round looking at the stumpy little beacon and the ancient fortifications that included an Iron Age fort. I soon felt spots of rain on my bare arms, so headed for some buildings in search of shelter, should it get heavier. I was in luck. One of these buildings was a café that'd never been open on my previous visits. Today it was. Off came the pack and in I went. It was great inside and had a decent menu featuring decent prices with a friendly atmosphere. It was a family-run concern, which was often a good omen, as it proved to be in this case. The rain belted down outside as I tucked into my large plaice, chips, and peas. After I'd finished my meal it was still raining, so I decided to hang around and order another pot of tea, which the nice owner let me have for a quid, understanding my predicament regarding the weather.

I left at 2.30 p.m. for Brixham, which was only a twenty-minute road walk away, all downhill for a change. As I came down the final hill I saw crowds of people thronging about by the old harbour under the ominous-looking sky, and could make out the strains of a live band playing jazz. Before joining them I popped into a phone box to call my parents. When I dialled their number The Herefordshire Porkers were *out!* Disappointed that I couldn't reach anyone, I left the box, pulled on the pack, and walked away. Before getting 10 yards the phone rang in the box behind me. I pulled the door open and answered it – it was *Dad!* They'd come in, heard the phone, and dialled "ringback". We had a lovely half-hour chat and a laugh. They were well and told me all of the juicy gossip back home, including the latest dramatic developments in *Emmerdale Farm*, which I'd desperately been trying to wean myself off during this trip until now, owing to the fact that it's complete drivel. The only reason I watched it at all was that it happened to coincide with me sitting down with my dinner on my lap at 7 each evening when there was nowt else on. My lovely bulstrode BB was enjoying herself, getting spoiled rotten, knowing Mum and Dad. It was always reassuring talking to them. They took great interest in my progress, tracking my journey with maps that I, of course, didn't possess, despite that it was *me*, not them, doing the trek!

Feeling very cheerful afterwards I sauntered down the hill to the harbour, the crowds, and the lively Festival of Jazz. I spotted "The Golden Behind" – the replica of Sir Francis Drake's famous ship that's permanently moored here as a tourist attraction. I'd been on it before but was rather upset, as I'd hoped there might be an exact living replica of Sir Francis Drake himself on board to make things more realistic. You'd think scientists would've cloned somebody as important as him and realistically they should've done *him* instead of Dolly the sheep. It'd been deserted on board apart from half a dozen boring, seasick landlubbers. I didn't bother this time. The party atmosphere in town was wonderful. I took in all the sights, sounds, and smells. They were obviously gutting fish in the large buildings across the harbour. Brixham is also famous for being the town that inspired the famous song, 'Red Sails in the Sunset', written aboard a local sailing trawler called the *Torbay Lass* (well blow me down if you live and *don't* learn). The colour of these distinctive red sails was derived from the mineral ochre that was daubed on the sails after treatment to protect the canvas from sea water and prevent them from rotting. This ochre was obtained locally as well as limestone and iron.

I'd always felt very much at home in Brixham. It was high on my list of possible places to retire to when the time came. After all I'd been through lately it felt like that time had come now. It was good to be here on a busy Bank Holiday after spending so much time alone over the past few weeks, apart from The Green Dragon at Stoke Fleming. The only thing worrying me was the colour of the sky, which was now not so much of a worrying dark grey, but more of a terrifying light black. I passed my time with some of the more "debonair" revellers. I thought about what to do about accommodation, as it wasn't really feasible to camp in Torbay itself, especially with that sky looming ominously. It was a bit early to stop, so I decided to check out the ferry to Torquay and look for somewhere there instead. I needed to do some shopping first. I found a Co-op where I bought sandwiches, pies, orange juice, a banana, and an apple. Time for some health foods. I looked for a pack of Wilkinson's FX razor blades and was amazed when I couldn't find any in the whole of Brixham. Something as serious as this could prevent me from retiring here one day unless I decided to be a groward (grow a beard). The fruitless search slowed me down considerably, so I grabbed some shaving oil and antiperspirant before hurrying back past the terrific Beamers restaurant and down the opposite side of the harbour, getting there in time to miss the Torquay ferry. All was not lost though. Another was due in half an hour, which I couldn't afford to miss, it being the last one of the day. I de-cluttered the pack again, chatting to Barnacle Bill the sailor, a craggy old white-bearded seadog.

Brixham, which is surrounded by hills, was once two separate communities with a boggy track connecting them. Cowtown was the area on top of the hill where the farmers lived, while Fishtown was a mile away in the harbour where the seamen lived. There's much to say about lovely Brixham but I can't mention it all here as "Tim waits for no man" (Tim Higgins from Basildon who repairs clocks for a living). I shook hands with Barnacle Bill, grabbed my pack, and made for the small ferry that was about to leave. I had an animated yet humorous discussion with the captain and stewards before boarding with regard to the chances of the boat making it across to Torquay in the choppy waters of Torbay, much to the amusement of the other passengers waiting for me to make up my mind.

Looking at the old boat I commented, "It looks a bit old and rusty to me."

A steward replied, "She's a fine, sturdy boat. She's worked these waters since before the war and hasn't sunk yet."

"Yes, '*yet*' being the operative word! Which war do you mean? The Crimean?"

They explained that she'd been built as a minesweeper, or something similarly impressive, and a notable feature was her stability. Unimpressed, I started on about the *Titanic*, the *Bismarck*, the *Mary Rose*, and other supposedly unsinkable boats whilst the passengers looked on, their patience beginning to be tested.

The captain said, "Look, I haven't got all day. Are you boarding or not?"

I meekly replied, with an air of resignation, "I suppose I'll have to."

I still had a hangdog expression on my face as I took what may have been my final steps. Once aboard, I was determined to make the best of it, no matter how awful the outcome may be. I ordered a hot mug of tea to drown my sorrows. The sea was choppy as we left the safety of Brixham harbour for the twenty-minute crossing. There was also a strong wind, but nobody apart from me looked in the least bit bothered. Two ten-year-old girls were rushing about giggling, leaning over the side pretending to be seasick, causing much mirth among all the passengers. I could see the town of Paignton, its pier, and its suburbs to the west, but owing to the built-up nature of the shoreline here, SW Coast Path walkers generally adopted the same policy as me and took the ferry across Torbay to avoid this mainly urban sprawl. This is recommended in the guidebook, so it's *not* cheating. The sky was so black now that rain couldn't be far off. I prayed it wouldn't come until I'd found somewhere to stay. A wave of relief swept over me as I alighted on Torquay harbour. I'd made it this time, but that's another life gone! I walked towards the town wondering how to set about finding somewhere to stay, when within 50 yards I spied the Tourist Information Centre. The chap behind the desk was most helpful. He started ringing cheap B & Bs for me, free of charge. They were all full, however, as it was Bank Holiday, plus the season was truly underway now. Was I going to have to spend the night in a churchyard at last, with muggers and murderers all around me, like old Sean? After trying about a dozen more without success he said, sort of reluctantly, that there was one more he could have a go at, as they usually have rooms available at The Petunia Guest House. It struck me as a bit odd that he hadn't called it already if this was the case. I listened as he got through.

Nodding his head, he covered the receiver with and told me, "There's a room for £35 if you want it."

I shook my head vigorously, mouthing, "too expensive."

He tried again: "They'll accept £30 on this occasion." I said I couldn't possibly pay more than £25. Seconds later he gave me the thumbs up whilst speaking into the receiver: "£25 it is, then!"

After getting complicated directions from him, I thanked him for his time and the phone calls, and asked how they could provide this great service free of charge. He said it wasn't free, but it was to *me*. Their 10 per cent fee would be paid by commission from the B & B, so I'd pay the Tourist Board £2.50 and the remaining £22.50 to the B & B. This seemed like a brilliant idea to me, and probably pretty damn good to the Tourist Board, but I wasn't sure if the Petunia Guest House would agree having been beaten into the ground on the price before that fee, by none other than naughty old Overend. After leaving the bureau and heading around the corner, I came to the famous Princess Theatre, whereupon looking in the window I saw a poster for "A Kind of Magic"; a Queen tribute band who were on for one night only – last night! I hated that bloody group! Every single time I'd been on holiday in the south-west over the years I'd managed to arrive somewhere one night too late to see them. It was "kind of tragic" and I reckoned they'd "a kind of grudge-ic" against me, evading me on purpose. Bohemian pork chop Rhapsody *pigs*! Of course, there was nothing on tonight whatsoever. Mind you, I wouldn't have paid more than three quid to see them, assuming I'd failed to blag my way in for free.

Although "A Kind of Magic" isn't a particularly good example, I've always liked the appropriate and hilarious names that tribute groups manage to come up with: Think Floyd, The Ebay City Rollers, Alice in Cooperland, T-Rextasy, Hay Seed Dixie – a bluegrass AC/DC, Beatallica – Beatles songs done Metallica-style, although I'd quite like to do the opposite and form The Meaticles, who'd obviously play Metallica songs Beatles-style! Also, Nowaysis Oasis, and my favourite of all, four fat blokes called Obesis! There was a tribute band to my own band called Not The Hoople and they were better than us! Over the years I've come up with a few of my own, in case things get tough and I'm forced to go back on the road. How about Poxy Musac for Roxy Music, Diarrhoea Stains for Dire Straits, Status NO, The Six Pestles, Fairport Convulsion – a folk/punk tribute – and Fairground Atrocious instead of Attraction, which they were, and finally there's my favourite punk band, The Anti-Nowhere League. My own tribute band would obviously be named The Anti-Kneewear Logue.

As I trudged through the drizzle looking for Belsize Avenue I wondered what kind of reception I'd get, bearing in mind they were losing out on £12.50 through me being a cheapskate, beating them down. If I'd been them I would not be happy. After walking ten minutes on main roads and up a few hills I found it; a sizeable red-brick Victorian terraced house set back off the main road, bang in the middle a similar row of guest houses. It looked pretty good. When I rang the bell a large dog appeared through the frosted glass, barking at me. A second later the door was opened by a timid middle-aged, middle-class man, timidly holding back the un-timid dog by his collar.

"This is Woody," he said through the racket. When I asked if he bites the answer was a perturbing, "Well, not normally." I was waiting for the punch line, "... but in your case he might make an exception," but luckily it never came.

The chap, named Julian, was not capable of a two-way conversation. He was most odd, fussy, and old-womanish. He was definitely a "Spuckman" too. "Spuck", who'd once been a "friend" of mine, was often mistaken for the character Trigger from *Only Fools and Horses*. Spuck was definitely more abnormal, making the vacant Trigger look more like Jeremy Paxman. Anyway, this chap's mannerisms were most Spuck-ish, plus he had a kind of homemade, basin-cut, Beatle hairstyle, which somehow didn't sit right on a guy of forty-five. This unnerved me so much that I kept staring at it, mesmerised. Was it a wig or was he simply a secret member of The Meaticles? He seemed very insecure and when I spoke to him he heard nothing, but as we ascended the stairs he began dictating rule after rule in a monotone, as if he were reading blankly off an autocue.

"In this hotel we don't believe in smoking. In this hotel we don't believe in takeaway food. In this hotel we don't believe in pets." That's poor old Woody straight down the vets for the jab, never to return. He continued the relentless barrage: "In this hotel we don't believe in coming in after 10 at night. In this hotel we don't believe in allowing visitors of the opposite gender in our rooms. In this hotel we don't believe in smoking." His brain had got stuck on this one and he repeated it every thirty seconds or so. "In this hotel we don't believe in sleeping. In this hotel we don't believe in disobeying the rules."

Had I taken a wrong turn and wandered into Nazi Germany? Not too far from the truth, as it happened, as I remembered that the 1970s sitcom *Fawlty Towers* was based on a real hotel in Torquay, namely the notorious Gleneagles Hotel and its owner, the inspirational Donald Sinclair. Anyway, I recalled that Basil had a bit of a thing about Nazi Germany. To try and shut him up I did finally tell Julian I was a non-smoker. Ignoring me, he persisted with, "In this hotel we still do not believe in smoking," every thirty seconds or so, like a malfunctioning robot. As he did so he also pointed at several printed framed signs, boldly displaying in capital letters: "IN THIS HOTEL WE DO NOT BELIEVE IN SMOKING." They were dotted about on various surfaces to make sure that the message definitely went home.

The poky room was on the top floor at the front, looking out onto the busy main road. The small en suite was better than nothing but only just. The room was clean and tidy but well past its sell-by-date, also being depressing, brown, and drab. Still, it was marginally better than the churchyard, I kept telling myself. It did at least have a kettle and a telly. Suddenly, Julian became quite animated as he pointed to a hideous, ancient, wooden contraption behind the door, which he proudly announced was a trouser press! That was going to be very useful, I must say. I'd seen loads of these useless moribund 1920s "collectors' items" down Gloucester car boot for 20p each or ten for a quid!

As he repeated, "In this hotel we don't believe in smoking," for the twentieth time I could no longer hold it in.

I blurted loudly in his face: "Look, I've walked over 500 bloody miles! Do you think I could do that if I smoked sixty a day? Unbelievable!"

I knew he wouldn't have the courage to stand up to me. He was momentarily fazed and cowered silently for a few seconds before resuming, but more apprehensively.

"In this hotel we don't believe in being late for breakfast."

It'd been five minutes since we'd entered the room and he was still spouting the rules. How much bleedin' longer? I was thinking, wishing he'd leave. Finally he'd used up his whole repertoire and made for the door, closing it behind him after saying goodnight. Thank God for that! I thought, but as I did so the door slowly opened again.

He stuck his head around it gingerly and said meekly, "There's an ashtray in the bedside cabinet and another one in the bathroom. Well, goodnight then."

He closed the door behind him for a second time. I fell onto the bed kicking my feet wildly in the direction of the ghastly trouser press, before grabbing the bakelite ashtray and wedging it hard into my mouth to prevent myself from going berserk whilst cackling hysterically. This had got to be the weirdest B & B ever! I'd never forget this one and I still had the breakfast session to come yet. What new joys or horrors would that bring? I couldn't wait – Yippee! I did get a kind of masochistic pleasure from these situations. In fact I revelled in them. There was always the feeling that these outdated, regimented, ailing dinosaurs were living on borrowed time and would, within a few years, become extinct. I felt that in a way I was privileged enough to be a proverbial fly-on-the-wall, observing their inane eccentricities firsthand before it was all over and they were gone. Today, with a far better variety of accommodation becoming available, albeit at a price, the 1950s-style "Boarding House" was now a part of an old fading Britain. It was "kind of sad-gic" in a way but time marches on. Not yet though.

It was 9 p.m. by the time I'd done my laundry, showered, sorted out more stuff to post home, and settled down for the evening. Being very weary I couldn't be bothered to go out to eat so I used up my old prawn sandwiches, pies, and cakes, praying Julian wouldn't find and scrutinise the packaging in my bin for I feared it may result in The Petunia imposing a large fine upon me for breaking the hotel rules. "We do not believe in takeaway food in this hotel." I was pleased that A Kind of Magic weren't on after all, as I couldn't have faced the 2-mile-long walk there and back in the rain, especially if it was going to cost me three quid, no matter how good they were. Peering out of the window into the drizzly darkness, my mind wandered back to that classic scene in *Fawlty Towers* where Basil is speaking the stroppy old woman guest, who complained about her view.

"Well may I ask what you were expecting to see out of a Torquay hotel bedroom window? Sydney Opera House, perhaps? The hanging gardens Babylon? Herds of wildebeest sweeping by majestically?"

What brilliant stuff! I watched a *Timewatch*-style documentary about Cleopatra and the Queen of Sheba – and a pair of right old birds they were too! How un-PC can you get? Nothing to do with me though. That's how they were referred to in the documentary. I was so incensed that I thought about complaining about it myself!

There is a strong literary tradition in Torquay, with two classic pieces of English literature. Oscar Wilde's *A Woman of No Importance* and Sir Arthur Conan Doyle's *The Hound of the Baskervilles* are reputed to have been written whilst their authors were staying in Torquay. Agatha Christie (1890), satirist and comedian Peter Cook (1937), actress and comedienne Miranda Hart (1972), and Wishbone Ash's bass guitarist old Martin Turner (1947), were all born in Torquay. Martin, incidentally, once bought one of my beautiful original Gibson Thunderbird basses from me. Torquay also has an unusually prolific history of providing models for the glamour and erotic industries, with glamour model Lauren Pope (that's more like it), popular lads-mag pin-up Natasha Mealey (positively fascinating), who has appeared in publications such as *FHM* and *Zoo*, and also erotic actress Layla Jade (it doesn't get much better than this), all having being born in the town, along with international catwalk model Lily Cole (elegant daughter of Lily Allen and Nat King Cole possibly?). All in all Torquay got pretty interesting, especially towards the end, didn't it? Finally, after writing up my journal, I turned in exhausted at 11 p.m., praying for a decent night's sleep and fine weather tomorrow.

Day 44: Tuesday 27 May

The Timex woke me at 7 a.m. I'd slept okay but could've done with another four hours to catch up. As a result I dozed off again in the warm room only to wake with a start at 8 a.m. Oh dear! I needed to get downstairs fast for breakfast. I wasn't going to forsake that, meaning I'd have to shower and shave afterwards, which was fine, as I showered off the trail dust last night. I pulled on some clothes and a baseball cap as my hair was everywhere after sleeping on it while still damp. As I got to the bottom of the stairs I was confronted by a big blonde woman, who introduced herself as Pam the landlady, Julian's much larger other half. It was immediately obvious who wore the trousers in this establishment, as she complained to me about the state of everything these days, but specifically the guesthouse business. She seemed nice enough as she continued to moan, but scolded Julian every time he squeezed past us carrying a tray.

"No, Julian! Take that back to the kitchen quickly! Can't you see I haven't put any sausages on it yet?" She rolled her eyes at me and I thought she might clip him round the ear if he did it again. She was like a big black widow spider that eats its smaller male mate when she's sick of him. I wouldn't fancy being in poor old Julian's shoes! "Get back in that kitchen *now* and take that pot of coffee to table 6! Hurry up! *Pronto!*"

I found it all quite uncanny as the comparisons with *Fawlty Towers* were again spot on. Like Manuel, Julian had to jump when Pam said "Jump!"

The breakfast room was a fair size and empty apart from a party of half a dozen people in their late-sixties seated at a large table 20 feet from mine. As I sat down I nodded and they nodded back. We exchanged a few words during which I ascertained they were here for some kind of AGM, being members of an organisation similar to the Freemasons, but if I remember correctly, something to do with moose's or bulls horns! Maybe it was wildebeests. As I sat at my table it became evident that Julian couldn't cope with distributing seven breakfasts at the same time. At one point he barged through the swing doors with a cooked breakfast in each hand. Stopping suddenly, he looked first at one breakfast and then at the other. Pausing for a moment, obviously bewildered, he ran back into the kitchen for further instructions from the Führer! I remembered Manuel performing exactly the same manoeuvre. I'd no further contact with the party of guests as they chatted between themselves but couldn't help noticing that one of the older men looked particularly scruffy. He was wearing a tatty, open-necked, creased-up, "white" shirt, the tail of which was hanging out. It was so long that it was dragging on the floor behind his chair. He wore red braces over the top. Maybe he'd had to rush to make it down to breakfast too. It seemed an eternity until Julian plonked down my meagre "half-full English" in front of me. It was hardly worth getting up for. Another thought occurred to me as I'd been waiting, regarding the never-ending list of hotel rules. I kind of pre-empted what was about to happen. Call it women's intuition if you like but I *knew* it! As Julian put down my coffee pot he leaned down towards me and spoke timidly.

"My wife says would you mind removing your baseball cap in case anyone complains about it?"

In case anyone *complains* about it! Who the f*** is going to complain about it? Surely not the party of six who were engrossed in their own conversation and had forgotten I existed? Besides, if they *did* have the audacity to complain, I would've immediately pointed out to all and sundry that I was most distressed by the presence of the man whose horrid shirt was hanging out in a most unsatisfactory, displeasing manner! With them ruled out, that left only Julian or his wife Pam, who'd not left the kitchen since I'd seen her half an hour earlier, so *she* definitely hadn't had to endure the unadulterated vulgarity of my vile, grossly offensive baseball cap. So who was left to complain? It only left Woody the dog! I found this ludicrous request completely out of order. I doubted very much that it would ever happen at The Dorchester either, as in my experience the more up-market establishments seemed far more tolerant in general than the mid-price range, snooty guesthouses. Strangely, it always seems to be the second-rate (£30-£40) guesthouses that are the worst. They tend to be run by "Hyacinth Bucket-type"s, giving themselves airs and graces, whereas the third-rate (£15-£25) ones were normally less fussy and more easygoing, apart from Albert Tatlock telling me to be quiet while *The Bill* was on, that is. Anyway, I was ready for Julian, as this was exactly what I'd anticipated. Following his idiotic request I beckoned him with my finger. When he leaned towards me I spoke quietly in his ear.

"You might like to know I've recently had a serious brain operation and I'm afraid my cranium looks very disturbing as a result; blood and awful scars, you know the kind of thing, and I wouldn't want to upset your other guests, so I put the cap on deliberately to stop them from fainting at the gruesome sight of it. I thought it would probably reflect very badly on your guest house too."

Julian jumped back in horror so violently that he almost fell over, having to grasp at another chair to stay upright.

He blurted out: "Oh right; right! K-keep your c-cap on! D-don't take it off! P-*please* don't t-take it off!"

He made straight for the kitchen, obviously to break the worrying news to his wife, while I chuckled to myself. Naughty old Overend, but I really didn't see why I should be dictated to for no good reason. When he appeared a few minutes later with more toast and coffee no more was said. I ate about twenty rounds of toast and marmalade to make up for the meagre breakfast.

As I rose to go to my room, I said to Julian in earnest, "Was it all okay about the cap?"

He nervously replied, "Oh f-fine, yes f-f-fine, perfectly f-f-f-ine!"

He hurriedly backed away from me. I'd really got him going now. Hee, hee! I felt like a real little devil! Packing done, I came downstairs for the final time to find Julian and give him the agreed £22.50. I asked him if he knew where there was a chemists. He stiffened, obviously thinking it was something horrid to do with my head, like maybe my skull was about to split open and my brains would spill out all over the nice carpet right in front of him and all of the guests. In reality I needed to find those elusive FX razor blades.

There was a small parade of shops nearby, so I left my pack taking only a carrier bag containing the stuff I intended to post home, including three unworn T-shirts, two pans – I wasn't cooking so only retained my kettle – a pile of receipts, booklets, brochures, and other priceless debris I'd acquired along the way. After purchasing the blades, I found a post office, where I cadged a cardboard box and got rid of another 5 lbs. of junk at a cost of £4 postage. I collected my pack, shook hands with Julian – he wasn't such a bad old stick after all – and set off down the hill towards the town centre. It was grey but thankfully not raining. My first priority was to buy some more shorts, as my wild ones, being made from cotton, took too long to dry when I washed them, rendering them un-wearable for several days. I came to the main shopping area and began looking for clothing or sports shops, having decided I wanted black ones to match my wicking tops. The first shop I saw was The Officers Club, but the window was full of normal clothes, so I passed it by. After an hour I'd tried about twenty pairs of shorts in fifteen different shops and hated them all. They were either made of shiny, brinzely-type satin-y fabrics, were too tight, or hideously baggy. Who wants to look like MC Hammer? By now it was noon and I needed to leave Torquay. I had to move on without finding any shorts. As I passed The Officers Club on the way back I thought I'd check it out and of course immediately found a great pair of black shorts for the princely sum of six quid. If only I gone there first I would've saved myself an hour.

I made my way back to harbour before relocating to the coast path near Peaked Tor Cove, walking past Daddyhole Cove, and eastwards through Torquay's suburbs towards Hope's Nose. Somewhere above Meadfoot Beach, while passing through a posh, leafy, residential area, I met a large friendly chap named Mick walking his two dogs. When I told him what I was doing he became quite excited, wanting to know everything there was to know about the walk.

He said, "I've always wanted to walk The South West Coast Path. What's it like?"

After firmly telling him, "*Don't* do it! It's like hell on earth!" I said there really wasn't a short answer to that question.

"I do admire you. I wish you would come back to my house, meet the wife, and spend all day telling us about your adventure."

He was a very sincere, likeable guy, and was obviously overjoyed at meeting this apparently super-human being who was attempting "the impossible". Chuckling, I told him that if it were 8 p.m. instead of 1 p.m. I'd gladly have taken him up on his kind offer in exchange for a good meal and somewhere to camp, like in his garden. We shook hands and I was off with another spring in my step. Surely I couldn't fail to finish now? I was noticing the different reaction I was now beginning to get at this later stage of my walk, compared to what I'd been getting earlier on. Back then, when

I told people what I was doing, they'd simply say unenthusiastically, "Oh right."

As I climbed up I came to a lovely deserted park near Hope's Nose. The rain started and I was forced to take cover in a large shelter that'd been vandalised, with mindless graffiti scrawled all over the walls. It saddened me to see this mess in such a beautiful park. I couldn't imagine anybody (except vandals) coming here to enjoy themselves anymore. It shouldn't have come as too much of a surprise though, as Torquay has higher crime figures than the national average, with drugs being one of the main problems. After five minutes I was able to continue on my way, soon turning north for Babbacombe. As I walked along the familiar promenade towards Petit Tor Point I saw a cute white terrier ambling casually towards me. As I looked down and said, "Who's a gooboy?" I noticed, to my amazement, that he was smoking a pipe! My eyes were out on stoppers. Was it an optical illusion? No it wasn't. As I leaned down to investigate, two large dogs appeared and the funny little chap dropped the pipe, ran and saw them off. He immediately returned to pick the pipe up again, the right way up, to resume his smoke. I took some video of the wonderful sight before his owners arrived, explaining that he loved his pipe and would simply not leave the house without it. Apparently he'd taken a shine to it one evening when it was lying about and stole it from his master on a permanent basis. In fairness it wasn't lit, but he seemed to be enjoying it all the same. It was better for his health that way too. This really cheered me up as I continued around the rocky curve of the shoreline. The weather was looking much better too, which was most welcome.

When I came to the bottom of the high tree-lined red cliff at the end of the beach I spotted the cliff railway. With a feeling of great joy, I realised this could save me a tough climb, not to mention some precious time. I approached the chap in the ticket kiosk, who wore a uniform and cap, to ask how long I'd have to wait and what was the price. Close up he looked like a cross between Blakey from *On the Buses* and Adolf Hitler. When I started speaking I realised he was worse than either of them and not as funny. He was another one of those people from the planet Zog in that he failed to understand anything I said. Although he was English he may as well have been Russian. He was also a humourless old jobsworth to boot.

Pointing to the cliff railway I simply asked, "Is this the quickest way to the top?"

Looking blank, he replied, "Well, if you go back the way you've come for half a mile there's a steep path up the cliff there."

"No, I don't want to go back half a mile or find any steep path going up anywhere. I want to get on this cliff railway here and go up to the top now. Does it go there or not?"

He amazed me by saying, "No. Well it does go up but not where you want to go. You need to go back half a mile and then ..."

I only wanted to go *up*. I didn't care about where it came out, as long as it was somewhere at the top. So why, not knowing where I was going, did he assume it'd be wrong for me?

I butted in with: "*Look!* I told you I'm *not* going back! I want to get in a rail car *here* and go to the very top. I couldn't give a toss where I end up! So when does the rail car arrive?"

He mumbled grumpily, "Well it varies according to the time of day, so I can't tell you."

We were at quite aggressive loggerheads by now. I groaned inwardly. Apart from having to wait for an indefinite period, I couldn't face being anywhere near him whilst doing so. We didn't like each other and there was nobody else waiting. He was incapable of grasping anything I said, the belligerent fool. How do people like this get jobs when other more intelligent people can't? It's unfathomable. How did he ever get through the interview when he had *no* communication skills whatsoever?

Having seen a tiny winding path about 50 yards back, I decided to try that. When I found it there was a tough climb, almost vertically through the trees, causing me to puff and pant immediately. After a couple of minutes I was exhausted. When I came out right next to the upright iron girders of the cliff railway I couldn't believe it. Sweating profusely, I paused to rest, leaning heavily on a concrete pillar. The fool had tried sending me on a wild goose chase. This was obviously the most direct path to the cliff top, as it climbed alongside the cliff railway. To add insult to injury, as I stood there gasping for air, the rail car appeared from below and, as it rattled past 6 feet away from me, I saw half a dozen faces staring smugly at me from inside it, while their attached bodies were being transported in complete comfort to the top of the cliff, where they'd arrive a good ten minutes before me. I hated them. I hated that bloke down below even more. It was no more than three minutes since he'd told me he didn't know what time the car would arrive. Talk about bringing tears to my eyes! In reality it brought a punch to my fist! I wanted to rush back down the cliff and sort the fool out, but had no energy left. Besides, what would be the point? If I shook him by the throat he wouldn't be able to understand that either! When I finally clambered out of the trees, on to the top, I saw the other ticket kiosk about 20 yards to my left. I fell on the grass, worn out, lying there in a silent rage for ten minutes before getting myself together and moving on, trying to put the half-hour nightmare behind me. Following a short spell of flat suburban walking the path became green and pleasant again. The sun came out to keep me company, proving most welcome. There was some good woodland walking on the way to Watcombe Head. After passing this I was on the exposed cliff tops with glorious sea views, but this time there was fabulous sunshine and no horrible gales.

My thoughts wandered to the old Watcombe Pottery that'd produced much of that novelty brown and cream coloured "motto ware", each item of which carried an appropriate handwritten, yokel-ish slogan, such as "Du'ee zit down an' 'ave a cup a Tay", which could be found, for example, on a teapot! The factory utilised the distinctive local red clay. The pottery was very popular from the late-nineteenth century onwards and is still collected today. I couldn't help thinking that if I'd a penny for every piece of motto-ware I'd ever sold over the years I'd have at least 25p by now. I met three Scout leaders coming the opposite way, accompanying fourteen uniformed lads on a trek.

We got chatting and soon the leaders were telling the lads, "This chap's walking the whole of the South West Coast Path. *He*, and people like him, should be your role models."

I couldn't help thinking that if they'd seen me throwing "an Elton" or two they certainly wouldn't be saying that. The lads were suitably unimpressed, having probably never heard of the South West Coast Path anyway. After a few laughs we parted company. I passed Maidencombe heading for Shaldon, where I'd need to take yet another ferry (oh no!) across the estuary of the River Teign to get into the town of Teignmouth. It stated in the book that this ferry has operated for over 1000 years – without sinking once – since before Saxon times, making it the oldest working ferry in Great Britain. Surely it wouldn't be too much to ask for it to make one more successful trip with me on board. There was an old ferryman too, named "Shrimpy" Mole. I liked the sound of him but seeing as he was working in 1890 I doubted he would be working there. From the top of a particularly high green hill – Beacon Hill I think– I got the most brilliant views ahead over the red cliffs to Shaldon, the estuary, Teignmouth, and the coastline to the north and north-east.

I stopped to lay down for a rest with the magnificent view spread out before me, being in no hurry, as the ferry ran until dusk. I descended into Shaldon at 6.45 p.m. and started looking for the passenger ferry, with the intention of crossing over the water, getting some kind of takeaway, before aiming for Dawlish tonight, where I'd camp either this side or the other side of the town, depending on how rapidly I progressed. When I found the ferry point there was no sign of life. I asked a local chap walking a pooch if he knew what time the next ferry left. My plans were totally scuppered when he told me that the last one left ninety minutes earlier! I couldn't believe it! I showed him the timetable in the guidebook. He remarked that the timetable had changed for 2003. The ferries no longer ran until dusk. Shaldon pigs' trotters! I could have cheerfully killed them, and him, along with the guidebook people, and all of the town's inhabitants too. That was it. I'd no alternative but to make the long trudge west, inland through Shaldon, across the long road bridge over the River Teign, east again, and back along the estuary to Teignmouth. It'd take at least an hour. I set off heavy hearted, which was a great shame, as my pack was heavy enough without any extra weight.

Shaldon looked like lovely old seafaring town but I couldn't enjoy it because of those horrid ferry porkers. I walked through tiny lanes with ancient names, such as Salty Lane and Horse Lane, and passed pretty thatched cottages like Sea Peep, Salthaven, and Forever Cottage. It was all rather quaint, reminiscent of an old English village with a green, where bowls are played. The clock tower on this particular green was dedicated to the memory of local men who died during the world wars. I came to a tea shop that advertised Devon cream teas. Although I was starving I was two hours too late to get one. I crossed the long bridge turning right at the far end and back along the estuary towards Teignmouth, where I'd visited briefly before and liked it very much. All members of the rock band Muse attended school at Teignmouth Community College. I can't imagine any of them having a desperate financial status! Feeling tired and grumpy I stopped at a supermarket for some chocolate bars and a couple of cold drinks. I didn't buy any food as I wanted to find a hot filling takeaway whilst in a town.

At 7.30 p.m. I was getting worried about camping. I'd need to pitch in an hour or so and hadn't eaten yet. I hurried into the town centre where I found a busy chippy. I joined the queue of a dozen people after ordering and paying for a large portion of fish and chips. As I stood there I became aware of loud rap music emanating from a tinny-sounding pair of speakers high up on the wall. It was gangster rap, the "lyrics" of which – if you could call them that – were totally disgusting. It was all the usual "c-rap" about guns, shooting cops, and abusing women, with bad language liberally peppering every line. I couldn't believe it was being played in an otherwise perfectly normal fish and chip shop. The smiling fifty-year-old manager behind the counter looked like Mr Average; the sort of bloke who might like Des O'Connor or, if he was feeling particularly wild on a Saturday night, maybe Tom Jones. He seemed oblivious to the vile offensive racket, as did the other customers, some of which were eight-year-old kids. I felt like asking him if he knew what the words were about, but as nobody else looked the slightest bit bothered I put up with it, not wishing to get into an argument.

Although I've been known to curse occasionally, I'd never do so in public or to this severity either. Predictably the food took forever as the chips had run out of the shop, no doubt to escape the rapping, so not only did I have to endure the horrible row for another ten minutes, but I was glancing at my watch every few seconds, thinking, Come on! For God's sake, come on! It was a relief to finally get out of the noise. Leaving with my large parcel of grub, I thought, Maybe I'm getting old? I'm afraid I did find that kind of mindless row offensive and always will. I also wondered if that rap album may have been Des O'Connor's latest offering. Until now I'd been unaware of his musical change of direction. I soon dismissed that idea as ridiculous though. I hurried on to the deserted sea front. I sat on a bench and ate my food as quickly as possible, unable to really enjoy it, owing to the time pressure. Before leaving I rushed into the gents' to fill my water bladders, panicking because I'd left my Leki pole by the bench by mistake, and was worried about it getting nicked. It was still there when I returned so I grabbed it and ran along the promenade. It was after 8.30 p.m. I was desperate to leave Teignmouth and camp.

I came to a sort of fork and took the lower seaward path, which naturally turned out to be the wrong one, as I realised when arriving at a dead end five minutes later. Retracing my steps, I hurried back, cursing under my breath. I used some of the rap lyrics to make a change from the norm. I took the other fork up East Cliff Road and ascended until I was high above Teignmouth. It was dusk now. I'd got about fifteen minutes max to camp. I came out on the edge of a lovely, large park; Eastcliff Park according to the book. There were some clumps of trees and some housing estates down the grassy hill about half a mile away. I stopped momentarily to survey the scene. All was quiet and would soon be dark. This would have to do. I found a secluded spot behind a small clump of trees and pitched the tent quickly in the long grass, making a note of where each peg was placed so I could locate them easily in the morning. Relieved at finding somewhere, I crawled inside, got into the bag, and started to snooze immediately. This boded well. Hopefully I was going to get a much needed good night's sleep. Drifting off ten minutes later, I heard distant laughter. At first I thought it was part of a dream but it got louder. I turned over, checking my watch: 9.35 p.m. The laughter was getting louder. I could make out kids' voices, boys and girls, screaming and shouting. They weren't only in the park but were fast approaching the clump of trees behind which I'd taken refuge. I sat up "boltright" and within a minute the tent was surrounded. I reckoned there were about fifteen of them and guessed their ages were between twelve and seventeen. They must've been from nearby housing estates, bored on this summer evening, looking for something to do, when they'd spotted *me*. I wasn't frightened, as they were kids, but instead of getting bored and leaving they started daring each other to do things.

One of them said, "I wonder if there's anyone in there?"

"I bet it's some old ******* tramp! Let's pull it down and find out!"

Another said, "I'll do it for a pound."

As they became more confident I was aware that they were now right next to the tent, a foot away from me on the other side of the nylon. I felt someone twanging the guy ropes, laughing.

Another cackled, saying, "Has anyone got any ******* matches?"

A chill ran through me when I heard, "No, but I've got my ******* knife. Shall I slash it?"

I realised I had to nip this in the bud right away or things could get out of hand. I hadn't made a sound as yet. I didn't want to go mental and start shouting or ranting, neither did I want to get out and "reason" with them. I may never have got rid of them, or they might have turned nasty. The "mob mentality" could be dangerous if I wasn't careful. Instead I reached for the inner zip and pulled it down quickly, making a sudden rasping noise as if someone was about to rush out. With this there were high-pitched girls' squeals and I could sense them all running away in panic. All was quiet for a few minutes but I could hear them returning quietly, more curious than ever this time. It hadn't worked. I lay there silently, holding my shortened walking pole, feeling very scared and vulnerable now. The tent began vibrating again as they tugged and pulled at the guys, daring each other to go further. Before getting out to confront them I thought I'd try one more thing.

I lowered my voice and growled as scarily as I could: "Why don't you all p*** off!"

I sounded like the voice from *The Exorcist*, but they all screamed and ran away again. This time they didn't return, thank goodness. I still held my Leki pole, listening for any audible sign that they'd returned. I feared they might creep up on me and burn the tent down and attack me in the dark. It was 10.05 p.m. now but I remained awake till midnight. What a horrible experience it'd been. My mind kept straying to what might have happened. In a way I was very lucky with the outcome. I made a vow, however, that I'd never camp near a town or any habitation ever again. It'd be better to walk right through the night rather than go through this sort of thing again. I set the alarm for 7 a.m. as I wanted to get out of the park early in case.

Day 45: Wednesday 28 May

After a very uneasy night I awoke feeling wasted. Lying in the tent, I was aware that it wasn't a pleasant morning outside. It wasn't raining but I could sense it was dull and grey. When I opened the flap I was amazed to see I was surrounded again; not by kids, but by a thick fog! I'd heard about these sea mists but this was the first one I'd experienced. Visibility was about 5 yards. I began packing away in the damp air. The foot-high grass in which I'd pitched the tent was saturated, making things very unpleasant. Everything was going to be wet, thus heavier to carry. Why couldn't things be nice for a change? Presently a red setter came running up to me, full of the joys of spring, having a great time. I stopped packing to make a fuss of him when his owner appeared out of the mists on a path nearby.

She gave me a cheery, "Good Morning!" making me feel a whole lot better. We had a bit of banter. Smiling, she called over to me: "You can hardly see your hand in front of your face this morning, can you?"

"No, but it doesn't matter, cos I already know what my hand looks like."

I thought that was pretty damn good for 7.45 a.m. after a sleepless night.

I got a nice smile back and a friendly, "Cheerio! Good luck, then!"

I was so pleased when I was ready to leave at 8.30 a.m. I needed to walk quickly to warm myself up and get the damp out of my bones. By now more dog walkers had appeared. They were a friendly crowd, all bidding me good day and smiling. It warmed the cockles of my heart at least, if not the rest of my organs. It was hard finding the path again but I guessed it right. What a great start to the new day – I wasn't lost. My next destination was the lovely coastal town of Dawlish, but I feared it wouldn't look quite so lovely this morning. In fact I doubted I'd see Dawlish through the fog, apart from the pavement directly beneath my feet. I couldn't see the sea at all. I wasn't on the cliffs much (I think), but was mainly on roads or paths slightly inland. It felt quite surreal, walking without seeing where I was going. I didn't mind it, as it was a bit of a novelty, but wouldn't have fancied a whole day of it, plus there was always the worry that, without total concentration, I may walk over the edge of a cliff. At 9.30 a.m. I descended and followed the main A 379 into Dawlish joining the early morning "rush hour" traffic of about half a dozen cars. The ornamental gardens to my left, known as The Lawn, were still shrouded in fog. Not a soul was in sight as I passed them. It all looked very spooky, especially as I'd seen the town bathed in sunshine on previous visits.

It's difficult to describe Dawlish apart from saying that it's quite Dawlish-ish! In more clement weather the small town has a quiet, relaxing feel to it. I remember it being charming and atmospheric, with its elegant, Regency, Georgian, and Victorian buildings. Dawlish was once the haunt of such literary giants as Charles Dickens and Jane Austen. Old Dickens used the town as the birthplace of his Nicholas Nickleby character. Normally, when you can see it, The Lawn is a beautiful public park with an avenue of mature chestnut trees, and stunningly colourful flowerbeds, accented by exotic cacti, tropical plants, and tall palms. Ducks and wildfowl live by the river and streams. It's a lovely sight, perfect for holidaying families, but not today in the dense murk. At night, a myriad of coloured lights running along the length of the water courses are switched on, giving the town a fairyland-style appearance. It's definitely one of my favourite Devon towns. The strangest thing about Dawlish is the way the mainline trains run along the edge of the main beach where the railway station is located. The station is a fine period piece and an attraction in its own right. You don't see many stations on beaches, do you? As I stood there looking, Brunel's famous railway line was immediately to my right. This amazing feat of engineering hugs the coast for several miles here, providing "in yer face" spectacular sea views for its passengers, as it winds around – and sometimes through – the headlands, by way of purpose-built tunnels, laboriously drilled out with great difficulty 150 years ago.

In need of early morning sustenance I made straight for the Signal Café at the station in the heart of the town. Someone told me it was good and they weren't wrong. Inside it was a no-messing, old-fashioned café with a no-messing, old-fashioned menu. I selected the no-messing "Mega Breakfast". No namby-pamby muesli here. I loved it here in the cosy warmth. There was only one other customer who appeared to be a regular. We exchanged a few friendly words, mainly about the fog. The breakfast certainly was "Mega" all right. I could hardly finish it, but ensured I did, washing it down with two pint-mugs of tea, the second of which was complimentary. No stupid litres in here. What a bargain for £4.95 and about ten times bigger than any full English I'd had on this trip. The only problem was leaving, mainly because I didn't want to. What I did fancy doing was crawling into a comfortable bed and flaking out for the entire day, to make up for the hateful, listless night I'd spent in the tent. Unfortunately though, this would have to remain a fantasy. I needed to press on and cross the estuary of the Exe by ferry from Starcross. I'd be walking the ancient Jurassic Coast World Heritage Site for the final 100 miles, from Exmouth to The Old Harry Rocks beyond Swanage. This would be a huge psychological barrier for me, as I'd be on the last leg of my epic journey. So after a quick wash and shave in the station gents', I reluctantly shouldered my pack again, said thanks and goodbye to the nice waitress, and wandered back out into the fog. The next forty-five minutes was most unusual. I walked on the top of the sea wall in the fog, with the sea 15 feet below me to my right, Brunel's railway line 6 feet to my left, with the cliffs of Langstone Rocks hovering above. I enjoyed it greatly, possibly because it was very flat. A few other people were about but apart from a few hellos I didn't stop to chat, being hell-bent on getting to the ferry as soon as possible.

Approaching Dawlish Warren with its nature reserves I spotted a crowd of people staring at a huge black and wavy sculpture. This most peculiar dynamic structure featured a series of fifty or so 12-foot-high "peaks", occupying an oval area of ground some 40 yards long and 20 yards wide. I felt compelled to investigate further. After joining the throng, I tried to reason out what it was. I got chatting to a local chap taking multiple photographs of it.

Intrigued, I asked him, "Who's it by and what's its significance? It's very Hurst, Emin, or Gormley, but much, much larger, isn't it?"

He gave me the oddest look and said, "Come again?"

I elaborated: "Maybe it represents man's eternal socio-ecological struggle with his own black depressions with regard to now unstoppable and inevitable climate change; also his psuedo-nihilistically challenged ego, which thereby deters him in his psycho-metabolical quest to reach the lofty peaks of secular propriety, as implied in Freud's writings, thus leading to flawed unfulfillment in sedentary motion, perhaps?"

He quickly replied: "I don't think so, mate, it's the remains of the fun fair. It burnt down three days ago. I'm taking pictures for the local paper."

I felt like a proper Charlie and had to pretend that I'd been joking, but everyone knew really. Not wanting to hang around to be ridiculed, I ran off inland with my tail between my legs in search of the ferry point. There didn't appear too much else of interest around to gawp at anyway, though Dawlish Warren is one of the few natural sand spits in the world. It's home to a wide range of rare, exciting wildlife and plants, but I couldn't be bothered to look. Once you've seen one sand spit you've seen 'em all, ain't yer? I came to a small parade of shops where I asked a local woman about buses to Starcross. Otherwise it meant 3 miles of dangerous main road walking, which the guidebook strongly advised against. In the local newsagents I bought a mint Feast. I needed this as I hadn't had a pudding after my Mega Breakfast. I like a desert after breakfast, as it seems only right and proper. I caught the bus that took me due north up the western side of the estuary. This was quite wide, which I found rather distressing, doubting I could swim that far when the ferry sank with me on it in about an hour's time. I was dropped off on the side of the main road by the ferry point, which could be reached by way of a small jetty which had a good old wooden hut on its tip. Nobody else was around, so I settled down to wait, donning my camo fleece as it was quite breezy by the water. The fog was not quite as thick now. I could make out the coast a mile away on the opposite side and hoped I'd get there in one piece.

Before long a few other passengers turned up. We chatted to pass the time. After ten minutes a uniformed captain arrived. We all walked in single file to board the craft via a dodgy-looking gangplank, on which I stopped briefly to take a picture of the medium-sized blue and white boat, named *My Queen*. As I came to board I realised I'd taken a picture of the wrong boat. Ours was at the other end of the stupid T-shaped gangplank! Still, they looked virtually identical, so who cares? I sat on the open back of the boat for the twenty-minute trip, chatting with an elderly couple and their grandchildren, who were on holiday from Birmingham. Once the ferry embarked the old boy went inside the empty cabin beside us and sat alone.

His wife, who was reminiscent of a Brummie version of Cilla Black, looked at me, pulled a sad face, and said, "He's terrified of boats. He always thinks they're going to sink. It's ridiculous but that's the way he is, the old fool."

Thinking on my feet I answered confidently: "*No*, really? That's ridiculous! The big girl's blouse! Fancy being afraid of something like that! Anybody would think we were on the *Titanic*, or something."

Yeah, anybody like *me*, for example. The funny thing was, this chap's terror was making me feel stronger. Maybe it was because I'd done about a dozen crossings and was beginning to feel like a bit of an old seadog.

When he looked back at us with fear in his eyes I gave him the old thumbs up, mouthing, "Only ten minutes to go." If he'd been sitting next to me I'd probably have said, "Just you stick with me and you'll be all right, son." As we pulled into the harbour at Exmouth, he emerged smiling from the cabin. I gave him a pat on the back saying, "Nothing to it, is there?"

I felt quite confident now and was looking forward to the next ferry already, until I realised there weren't any more. I'd done the last one, just as I was getting used to them – typical! The quaint little gift shops and cafés around the harbour were bustling with tourists as I passed by. Lo and behold, the sun was trying to push its way through the fog. Things were looking good. Reaching the coast, I glanced back, observing that the entrance to the estuary of the River Exe behind me was almost closed off by the sand spit of Dawlish Warren on the opposite shore, from whence I'd come, leaving a tiny gap of a few hundred yards across for river traffic.

There was no reason to visit the town centre, so I wandered eastwards through the small streets to get back on track asap. I had trouble finding the SW Coast Path again. This was ridiculous. All I had to do was walk for 100 yards down a straight road and it would be there, but that seemed beyond my capabilities. A nice uniformed lady on a bicycle stopped next to me for some reason. Before she could escape I commandeered her and asked if she knew where the path was.

"That's it there," she said, pointing at a large sign nearby, stating: "The South West Coast Path", complete with direction arrow! I pretended I'd come from the opposite direction so had only seen the back of it. Leading me by the arm, she said, "It's written on the back too. See?"

I was hoisted with my own petard and not for the first time. I mumbled something about the fog obscuring it, which was a bit silly as the fog had gone now. I said thanks and goodbye feeling like a complete fool before setting off along the road that ran along the sea front. Walking along the flat promenade was most pleasant in the slightly misty sunshine, with visitors now venturing on to the beach to enjoy themselves. At lunchtime I passed some beach huts, whose doors were open, thus allowing the aroma of frying bacon to be wafted out to my nostrils, making me feel peckish again. After half an hour I stopped at a large kiosk for a rest and a large double-coned ice cream. It was fantastic as I lounged on a bench looking out to sea. When I'd covered all 3 miles of the promenade and reached the end of the beach I climbed up steeply through the mists and came out on the top in brilliant sunshine. This had been worth waiting for. I looked at my watch: 2 p.m. It seemed an eternity since I'd packed away in thick fog in the dodgy Teignmouth park. I was now in a different world. I'd have to leave the coast briefly at Straight Point, as access was blocked, owing to the active firing ranges on the peninsula. The diversion took me through a massive caravan park, one of several in this area. Seeing that the big clubhouse was open I couldn't resist going in for a pint. I was boiling from the tough ascent, so I downed a Worthington's. After a quick chat to the lone barman I set off once more. My objective – Budleigh Salterton. Whilst pulling on the pack outside, three loutish lads of about eighteen went past me. I got the feeling they were going to try and take the Mickey. As I was feeling quite brave, before they got the chance I gave them "the old King Leer", at the sight of which they thought better of it, fell silent, looked at the ground, and went into the bar. I felt quite tough for a couple of minutes. I continued though the caravan park where, to my surprise, many of the owners were sitting inside their pristine statics watching TV or reading newspapers. It seemed like an odd way to spend a holiday. You could easily do those things at home but "there's nowt as queer as folk", as the old saying goes.

After finally leaving the huge site behind there was some more grassy climbing. I paused at the top to look back over the view, which was most eerie. In the foreground were the small yellow gorse flowers, with the huge caravan park a mile below. Beyond that a long, flat strip of pure white "cotton wool" sea fog, which was still invading the entire Exe estuary to a height of roughly 150 feet above. Beyond that I could see the cliff tops near Dawlish and Teignmouth. A photograph was definitely called for. By teatime I could see the town of Budleigh Salterton a mile ahead along the straight coastline. I soon descended to walk along the shingle beach with its rows of beach huts and a scattering of small boats. Beyond them at the far end were some trees and the funny-shaped promontory of Otterton Ledge. I ambled lazily among the sightseers on the pebble beach, taking it all in, before speaking to a woman and her son, collecting coins for an ME charity by getting the more generous members of the public to place their spare change on top of the seawall forming neat, regular rows. It looked very impressive, stretching for 30 or 40 feet. There must've been a fair amount of "poundage" there too. I added a few extra coins whilst taking care not to get too carried away.

I mentioned the painting *The Boyhood of Raleigh*, which I knew was painted somewhere on this beach, by artist John Everett Millais in 1871. Raleigh himself didn't pose for the painting though, having already been dead for about 250 years. The woman immediately confirmed that it was painted there whilst pointing at a spot some 5 yards away. Wow! I went over to the spot and picked up one of the actual stones that Raleigh must have stood upon all those years ago. The stone was quite flat, so I presumed he must've been pretty fat and heavy as a boy. The scene depicted in the famous picture came to epitomise the culture of heroic Imperialism in late Victorian Britain and in British popular culture too, up to the mid-twentieth century. It shows a wide-eyed young Sir Walter Raleigh and his brother sitting on the beach here, listening to a story of life on the high seas, narrated by an old seadog as he pointed out the sea. The painting was influenced by an essay written by James Anthony Froude on 'England's Forgotten Worthies', which described the lives of Elizabethan seafarers. It was also probably inspired by a contemporary biography of Raleigh that Millais had read. I used to have a copy myself that I picked up from a market or jumble sale. Millions of coloured prints were around at one time, gracing many a living room wall over the decades.

I felt quite uplifted by this experience and decided to pop inland, do the town, and get a cream tea while the going was good. I'd noticed the striking red cliffs along the way since Exmouth and, to my surprise, read that these were the oldest rocks of all, dating from the Triassic period. Although 250,000,000 years old, they didn't look that old to me, especially as they seemed to be in much better nick than the Jurassic ones I'd seen on a previous holiday around the Charmouth area. These had been all mouldy-looking, horrid and crumbly, yet were supposedly a mere 150,000,000 years old. I reckoned the geologists had got it the wrong way round and one day, when I wasn't so busy, I'd prove it. Somebody had said earlier that there were radioactive nodules containing vanadium and uranium in the red marl at Littleham Cove, so I'd given that bit of coast an extremely wide berth when passing by earlier. You've got to watch yourself when it comes to these rocks. I wouldn't trust them as far as I could throw them.

Apart from old Sir Wally, born at nearby Hayes Barton, other notable folk associated with Budleigh Salterton include broadcaster Sue Lawley, Sally McNally – puppeteer of good old Muffin the Mule – and actress Belinda Lee, born there in 1935. It's also the home of the fictional character Giles Wemmbley-Hogg, portrayed by Marcus Brigstocke in the radio programme. In the song 'Now I Know (where I'm going) Our Kid' by the parody group The Shirehorses, Budleigh Salterton is cited incorrectly as being on the road to Scotland. Its comedy-sounding name has been mentioned in *Monty Python*, *Black Adder*, and other comedies. On *Top Gear*, Jeremy Clarkson suggested it should be the name of a chap who drives a Bentley Continental GT.

The main street was only 50 yards away, swarming with pleasant retired people. I couldn't be bothered to walk its length, especially after spotting The Butler's Pantry, a delightful old-fashioned tea shop with lace curtains and hopefully a few weary bulstrodes asleep on chairs. I was escorted to an empty table amid a flurry of friendly hellos and good afternoons from other customers, as I attempted to squeeze between them with my pack without decapitating anybody. I always found that most people were very good about this sort of thing, never complaining about the mayhem and disruption I caused. The cream tea was superb. I read a brochure about Budleigh Salterton as I supped my sixth cup of tea. I wished I could have stayed longer but as usual it was too early to stop. Besides, I was hell-bent on reaching Sidmouth by tonight. After leaving I found myself outside the tourist information office. I pushed open the door, went in, asked the two lovely ladies if they knew which hotel in town was used by Terence Rattigan when he wrote his famous play, *French without Tears*. Narrowing their eyes, it became apparent that they didn't have a clue. They were slightly embarrassed with this bureau supposedly being the font of knowledge for all things local. They started looking at their own brochures and booklets but found nothing. They were most apologetic for not being able to answer my question.

One of them said meekly, "I didn't realise that *French without Tears* was written in Budleigh Salterton."

I assured her that it was, but I too was baffled, and said without thinking, "You'd think that something as important as that would be common knowledge around here, wouldn't you?"

This remark unintentionally rubbed salt into their wounds. After the ladies offered more sincere apologies I left and went into Spar to stock up for the evening, buying orange juice, two pork pies, and three Müller "coot fromers". Once out of town I needed to make an inland diversion of roughly 2 miles and walk around the nature reserve in order to cross the River Otter by a small bridge. It made a pleasant change from the coast and was nice seeing all the birds, which didn't fly off when they saw me, despite being rare! After crossing the little wooden bridge I turned back south for the coast and rejoined it only 100 yards or so from where I'd left it forty-five minutes earlier. After travelling north-east for a while I saw the horrific sight of the aptly-named "High Peak" 4 or 5 miles ahead. At nearly 500 feet I didn't like the look of it and for about the millionth time so far, thought, Why *me*? Walking on, my mind drifted back to the incident in the tourist information bureau. Whilst pondering why the ladies hadn't known the *French without Tears* story it hit me like a bombshell: Rattigan did *not* write it in Budleigh Salterton but in a hotel back in bloody Heybrook Bay near Plymouth, which I'd passed through a couple of weeks ago! I knew at the time that somebody famous had written something there, but couldn't remember who or what until now! Those poor ladies! I'd misled them horribly – *idiot*! Too late to apologise now, and too humiliating if I admitted my mistake to them. Best let sleeping Rattigans lie. I might send an anonymous card to them and sign it Victor Pinnywhistle or Claude Sheepfunnel. There was some beautiful walking that evening as I sauntered through Ladram Bay with its striking offshore red stacks of rock. I considered looking for the camp site there, but soon decided not to waste the wonderful evening by stopping too soon. There was at least another hour's walking yet that'd take me through and beyond Sidmouth. By then I'd feel most satisfied with my efforts for the day.

As I neared High Peak, the path was broad, flat, and grassy, with fantastic views past the red and green bulk of High Peak to Sidmouth directly ahead, which lay above sea level, bordered by rich, deep-red cliffs on both sides, sloping down towards the town. These cliffs, though very lofty, had a softer look to them now as I approached the ancient Jurassic coast. By the time I'd toiled up High Peak I realised its bark was worse than its bite. I wouldn't say it was easy, but after traipsing through thick mud and steep woodland, the views from the top were very rewarding. I could see for many miles inland, over the unspoilt rolling green Devonshire countryside. Its hills, woodlands, meadows, and distant villages reminded me of Herefordshire. I'd just one more major ascent to tackle before reaching Sidmouth, namely Peak Hill, which was virtually the same height as High Peak. From its summit I could see down over the town, which was bathed in a pale gold and red evening glow, with thick white wisps of sea mist floating between the cliffs beyond Sidmouth. I loved this place. It couldn't look much better than this in any light. Once on the edge of the town I passed through its wealthy, leafy suburbs with their splendid Victorian houses, hotels, and churches. Sidmouth appeared in the Domesday Book as Sedemuda.

Like many other towns on the South Coast, it was initially a small fishing village. They had no imagination in the old days, did they? Had nobody thought of jet-skiing, hang-gliding, or plain old-fashioned speed boating? Though attempts were made to construct a harbour here, none succeeded. A lack of shelter in the bay prevented the town from growing as a port, which let's face it, made a pleasant change from everywhere else along the coast. Sidmouth remained a small village until the fashion for coastal resorts grew during the eighteenth and nineteenth centuries. The town became a fashionable resort for the gentry. Now the town's many fine Georgian and Regency villas and mansions are mostly hotels.

Although it'd gone 8 p.m. a few people were still strolling about on the lengthy straight promenade whilst others leaned on the railings looking out to sea. The shadows were lengthening and the low drifting mists ahead added a ghostly quality to the cliffs as they washed in over the lower ground in between them, leaving their tops exposed. I pushed on to the end of the prom. After stepping over the titchy River Sid (Vicious), which was less 2 feet wide here, I began the ascent of Salcombe Hill, through sloping green meadows bordered by hedges that would take me out of Sidmouth. Above me the cliff top was heavily wooded. Before reaching the trees I came to a lovely area that'd recently been mown. Although it was steep I found a flat bit and, looking back over Sidmouth, realised this was the perfect camping spot, potentially the best of the whole trip. My shadow was at least 20 feet long as I pitched the tent 3 yards below the tree line beside a handy wooden bench. The light was still beautiful though it was beginning to turn to dusk. I was aware of a fit-looking lady jogger who said hi as she ran past me and up in to the trees. I sat in the tent porch and put the kettle on. I needed a couple of pints of slop to rehydrate myself. I turned round to look at the view back over Sidmouth, spread out in the valley below. Well it had been the last time I looked, however, everything had changed over a mere five minutes. The pure white sea mists had quickly rolled in and veiled the town completely whilst I'd been preoccupied with my tent and kettle. It was a stunning sight. Sidmouth had been there one minute and vanished the next! The entire valley below was filled with a translucent white cloud with only the clear summits of the lofty High Peak and Peak Hill visible as they rose up through the flat thick layer. I felt like I was watching it from a plane. The camera came out again. I had to capture this incredible sight. As I did so the lady jogger reappeared from the trees and stopped beside my tent.

Pointing at the amazing phenomena, she said, "Wow, I've lived here for years, but it's the first time I've ever seen anything like that!"

We both sat on the bench, gazing at it in stunned silence for a few moments, before she asked about my journey. We had a good ten-minute chat. I gave her some tea in my horrid folding plastic cup, which she seemed to enjoy nonetheless, before setting off down the hill. It was nice to be able to share that special moment with someone who appreciated it as much as I did. It'd been one of the best sights so far. As I sat finishing my tea, the sea mists cleared as quickly as they'd arrived, exposing Sidmouth again, and all was back to normal. The light was failing now. I climbed into the bag at 9.45 p.m. I was weary but within five minutes I had to get out of the bag, feeling far too hot. I unzipped it fully and laid it over me like a duvet. At least I could stick my arms and legs out to control my body temperature. I slept fairly quickly but woke several times during the night mainly because I was still far too hot. Summer was on the way and about time too. A superb day after another difficult start.

Day 46: Thursday 29 May

I'd set the Timex for 7.15 a.m. and by the time it went off the sun was already rising. I packed slowly as the temperature rose and afterwards sat on the bench to eat my breakfast. The view over Sidmouth was still great but so different to the previous evening, with no sign of any mists today, it being too hot. I walked into the trees at 9.10 a.m. I was grateful for their shade. This was going to be a sweltering day, thus hardly ideal for walking the "severe" terrain that the guidebook had warned me about. As I hadn't bothered to stop in Sidmouth I was getting low on water again, especially after the large amounts of tea I'd drunk last night. I felt concerned about getting a refill somewhere. Unfortunately there was nowhere en route until Branscombe. I'd have to eke out the remaining pint for as long as possible. The sun rose and the heat became stifling, without the usual cool breeze. I climbed and descended at least four monster cliffs including Dunscombe, Weston, and Coxe's, sipping small amounts water regularly rather than guzzling it down like I really wanted to. In the deep valleys between the cliffs there was usually a stream and at each one I stopped to soak my Tilley hat, fill it up with the water, and plonk it onto my bonce. I was tempted to drink the cool liquid too, but decided to only do that if things got really desperate. I didn't fancy cholera again today. If nobody was in sight I also removed my top and shorts and soaked them before wringing them out and replacing them. Despite this, they were still drying out within half an hour in the noonday sun. I was so thankful when I got to the shade of the Sea Shanty tearooms at Branscombe in time for lunch. Not being able to face a full English in the blazing heat I ordered a prawn salad, two large cakes, a pot of Earl Grey tea (never in a month of Sundays, vile muck), and loads of iced water. At £10 it was quite pricey but I didn't really have any choice apart from walking inland where I'd probably have died of heatstroke whilst attempting to save £1.50. I hung around in the café for as long as possible, dreading the inevitable climb ahead to Seaton – that's Seaton-Devon, as opposed to Seaton-Cornwall – where I'd almost got into that punch up. After ninety minutes of skiving I got my water bladders refilled, adding around 10 lbs. to my pack. I attacked the hills slower after that, as I was carrying over 50 lbs. I made a mental note to get this down lower as it was plain stupid. The hills, although still grim, were not as bad as the earlier ones and I made progress, slowly but surely. Once round Beer Head I saw the town of Seaton across the bay, about 3 miles away. For the first time I was approaching some white chalk cliffs, interspersed with the familiar red

ones. The colour contrast was most unexpected and unusual. I came down
to the village of Beer where I immediately ran into the Anchor Inn and
ordered a pint of cider. I didn't want to do the predictable thing. I downed it
in one and then, still not wishing to do the predictable thing, asked the
barman for a pint of ale, stating adamantly that I definitely did not want to
order something beginning with "B" and ending in "R" with two "Es" in
between. He gave me Greene King, which did have two "Es" in the middle.
I've always liked it, but I think he thought I was a bit strange for being so
pedantic about such a trivial matter. I stuck to my guns, knowing I'd be able
to hold my head up proudly in the future. I'd stand out above other mortals
as: "The only man who did *not* order a beer in Beer"! In retrospect I was
forced to admit I may have been making a mountain out of a beer hill.

Feeling light-headed I somehow got chatting to a boring, ugly, female
Canadian backpacker. I felt myself dozing off as she moaned on about this
and that. Only *I* am allowed to moan about everything, I mused to myself.
She wasn't doing the Coast Path so, after a couple of minutes, I could hardly
be bothered to pass the time of day with her. Being Canadian, she made me
think about Janet, though nothing else about her did. Janet was a cute,
bubbly lady, full of energy and fun. This woman was miserable and
negative. In fact she reminded me very much of *me*! There were a few jovial
locals in the pub. One bloke with long white hair – à la Gandalf – seemed
to be some kind of folk poet, making everyone laugh. I made my excuses
and left Beer by climbing through a playground area with hanging ropes
and ethnic-type swings and things that tourists were enjoying.

After an easier cliff I came down to Seaton in the unbearable heat. It
was apparent that, although a pleasant enough place, Seaton was not nearly
as upmarket as Sidmouth. There were more fish and chip shops, takeaways,
"Kiss Me Quick, bucket and spade" style of tacky gift shops, but I still
enjoyed strolling around it before hitting the large central Co-Op for more
supplies. I rather overdid it though, buying far more than needed and far
more than I could comfortably carry. I got three more "court frooners", as I
was having a bit of a craze on them, two chicken and ham pies for the price
of one, a Scotch egg, a heavy pot of potato salad, a large carton of Tropicana
orange juice, some Eccles cakes, and a whole heap of chocolate bars. It
must've weighed a good a good 8 lbs. I'd have to eat at least half of it before
leaving Seaton. As I was stuffing it all into my already bloated pack outside,
a great punky-looking girl with red and black hair, dressed in a fashionable
green and black outfit, smiled, giving me a wave and a friendly hi as she
walked by with her dog. I really liked Seaton now, but kicked myself later
for not asking her if I could kip in the kennel with her doggie tonight. I set
off back towards the coast where I'd have to stop to eat some of the food
before carrying on even though I wasn't particularly hungry. My plan was
thwarted when I spotted a nice-looking fish and chip shop near the front.
Being crippled by the weight of the pack after five minutes, I decided to take
it off and sit inside the restaurant for a fish supper! It was an impulsive

thing to do. Although the plaice, chips, and peas were good, I really wished I'd thought it through first. Apart from not being hungry it'd cost £6.50 and I'd still have to carry all the supplies, as I couldn't possibly eat anything else on top of the meal. I'd bungled badly again. As I walked, stooping forward in pain, I totted up, figuring I must've spent over £20 in all today. I'd have to half that amount and live frugally from henceforth on a bread and water diet. I decided to have a quick rest on the sea front to let my supper go down before continuing.

It was 6 p.m. as I crossed the River Axe via the bridge. To my left were Seaton and District Electric Tramway and beyond it was the large flat nature reserve with its ponds, long grasses, and funny-looking birds. The path veered inland as it began to climb. I crossed another golf course, where several golfers were making the most of the good weather, which was about bearable now, as the intense heat was going out of the sun. I was coast bound again, aware that I was about to reach the start of the mystical, famous section known as "The Undercliff". I felt apprehensive about venturing into this long nature reserve, as there was no escape route for about 8 miles should something go wrong. When I arrived it was 6.30 p.m. Absolutely typical; there couldn't have been a worse time to arrive. It was too early to camp yet too late to begin the traverse. It'd be 10.30 p.m. and dark before I'd emerge from the other end near Lyme Regis (or "Slime Penis" as some people prefer). Unwilling to camp so early, I plunged undaunted into the heavily-forested Undercliff, deciding I'd have to play it by ear when darkness descended.

This section of the East Devon and Dorset coastline had been prone to land slips for thousands of years. The most recent, largest, and spectacular landslip occurred at Dowlands Cliffs between Axmouth and Lyme Regis over the Christmas period of 1839, when over a period of forty-eight hours, roughly 16 acres of land, or 8 million tons of rock, split off from the cliffs and slid towards the sea. This opened a chasm three-quarters of mile long, 120 yards wide, and between 30 to 45 yards deep. The movement of so much rock forced up a section of the seabed, about a mile long and 12 yards high to form a reef running parallel with the shore, enclosing a pool or bay, which at one point was suggested as a harbour for the Royal Navy. This reef has long since been washed away by the sea and the raw steep sides of the chasm have been further eroded by the weather and smaller landslips to form the landscape visible today. The cliff tops are 100-150 yards above sea level with the landslip sharply dipping down to 20 yards above sea level forming a landscape sheltered from the worst of the weather, benefiting from its own microclimate.

It was very quiet as I crept along in wonderment, noticing signs of the giant landslip everywhere. The path ahead was crossed with cracks in the ground. Huge rocks appeared to be sliding slowly towards the sea whilst the serpentine path twisted and turned side to side, sometimes up, sometimes down, all within a landscape that'd become densely overgrown. It was like walking through a mini jungle with much of the sunlight being blocked out by the tall trees and thick vegetation, causing me to constantly look at my watch to remind myself that it wasn't getting dark yet. I got the occasional glimpse of sea to my right, and to my left occasional glimpses of the cliffs towering high above. The path was often slippery, wet, and rough going. On a couple of occasions I skidded on the mud, almost sliding down into deep pools of black, horrid water, managing to grasp a tree or something in the nick of time. It was a close thing and very scary. There were various varieties of plants and trees too, with dense ash woodland and hazel coppice mixed with stunted trees covered in wild clematis or Old Man's Beard to impenetrable scrub. The foliage of the ash woodland allowed light to reach the ground below, so that primroses, orchids, and many other wildflowers, together with a huge number of insects, including biting ones, had found a natural home protected by the microclimate of the Undercliff. It was definitely the weirdest place I'd ever walked in my whole life but it did have a particular charm and, needless to say, I didn't see a single soul. I was alone with nature and it was terrific.

Despite the difficult nature of the walking I soon got into some sort of rhythm and made very good time. It was like playing a children's game, using my agility and almost running down a slope to give myself the momentum to run up the next one. I was enjoying myself in there. The only real problem was the lack of anywhere to pitch a tent. It occurred to me that I hadn't been subjected to my terrible Nasty Notemares for ages, at which point they started up as if on cue. I carried on while trying, with little success, to block out the moronic wailing bagpipey melodies. Once I'd got 'em they were usually there to stay until I stopped walking. By 9 p.m. I could hardly see the path, thus it was almost pitch black inside the Undercliff. At one point I heard a dog barking to my left – or was it a wolf? Oooh, er! This led me to believe there may be a house nearby, though I could see nothing. There was also a strange brick-built windowless hut about 30 yards away, which looked like it might belong to the water board or something, but how and why was it built here? I considered investigating further or trying to pitch somewhere near it, but it didn't look too inviting. In fact it looked downright spooky, so I hurried on looking for richer pickings. I calculated that I'd been in the Undercliff for around two hours, meaning I'd still have almost two hours more to go before getting out if it. This wasn't feasible tonight, so I felt a bit desperate, having not yet seen one decent place to pitch so far.

After another ten minutes I rounded a corner in the ever darkening gloom to be confronted by the sight of a massive tree off the path. I couldn't tell what it was in the blackness, but discerned a circular flat patch all around it, in which no vegetation had been able to thrive. My luck was in. This wasn't ideal but it'd have to do. I threw off the pack and hurriedly pitched the tent, which wasn't easy in the inky blackness. Whilst doing so I became aware of a gentle whirring sound becoming louder and closer. The hairs on the back of my neck stood up. I grabbed my pole, knowing someone or something was approaching fast. It appeared from out of the undergrowth, going like the clappers of doom, scaring me half to death. A second later I realised it was a lad of about fifteen riding a bicycle. His feet and the pedals were a blur. He wore a look of abject terror on his face as he roared past me without uttering a sound before disappearing into the trees again. What the hell was he doing in there? Where had he come from and where was he going? Surely he couldn't have been aiming for Seaton at this time of night? After a few minutes I concluded that it must've been the ghost of a boy who'd died a horrific death in the Undercliff, perhaps by falling into it whilst cycling on the cliffs above in the 1920s! I shuddered at the thought, but it sure made my imagination run wild in this black eerie wilderness. A man could go crazy here. I got into the bag where I felt much safer and started to doze. Before long I awoke with a start, thinking I could hear distant voices. Sitting up, I craned my neck to listen. Oh my God! There were voices and they were getting closer. Having been desperate I'd pitched about 3 feet from the path, so whoever was coming wouldn't miss me and would probably trip over my guy ropes in the dark. I prayed it wouldn't be another load of dodgy kids. I lay still, clutching the pole to my chest, as they approached the tent. It sounded like two or three blokes chatting quite cheerily, not sounding too frightening, thank goodness. They were almost upon me before they noticed the tent, when they fell silent, obviously surprised at seeing it bang in front of them in the gloom.

As they passed by one of them joked, "Hey, Bob, wasn't it round here where that bloke got eaten by a bear one night last year?"

It was meant for my ears though, not Bob's.

Bob said, "Oh yes, but the other twelve were killed by wolves and witches."

I thought it best not to respond, as I didn't know what sort of blokes I was dealing with. I wanted to stay alive for as long as possible. They didn't sound at all like walkers but more like locals walking to the pub, obviously unfazed by being in the middle of the eerie Undercliff at night. Maybe there was another way in and out after all, which only the locals knew about. This would account for the ghost cyclist too. The sound of their voices faded as they walked on towards Lyme Regis. I lay there relieved, hoping nobody else would disturb me. Seemingly these woods were swarming with hoards of people now it was dark. Oh no, what if was another dogging site? I'd certainly be in for a rough night if it was. You can take that any way you like! I settled down again but it took an hour to get off to sleep. I kept imagining all sorts of sounds and unpleasant things going on around me. I was drained and exhausted from all the effort I'd made today, but felt on edge at the same time. Finally I slept, but was awoken sometime around 2 a.m. by something huge grubbing around outside the tent. I prayed it wasn't a bear. Logically it had to be a badger or a fox but when you're out there alone in a strange dark jungle it could as easily be a werewolf, a sabre-toothed tiger, a crocodile, a massive poisonous serpent, or a pile of doggers!

I called out: "Go away! Shoo! Shoo! Go on, get lost!"

Let's face it, that wasn't going to deter some gigantic wild creature who had homed in on my pheromones, about to help itself to a huge portion of them! There was no way I was going to confront whatever lurked outside, so I pulled the bag up over my head and hoped for the best.

Day 47: Friday 30 May

The next time I woke up I was boiling hot and it was morning. The sun's blazing rays were piercing the foliage in fine shafts, warming the nylon of the tent. The Undercliff was alive with birdsong but luckily I couldn't hear any ominous roaring or bellowing anywhere in the vicinity. I felt exhausted and didn't feel like I could do another tough day in the heat. On the other hand I couldn't stay here either. It wasn't exactly the kind of place in which to have a day off. As I packed away feeling very rough I had a nasty attack of hay fever. I sneezed hard about thirty times, which drained me of the little bit of energy I'd left, making me feel faint and feverish. My heart sank because this could stop me dead in my tracks if it got really bad. I've suffered with hay fever since I was eighteen, but normally it began around mid/late June, not the beginning of it. I'd considered this whilst planning the walk and had intended to be home before mid-June to be on the safe side. I was now about five days from my target. Surely it wasn't going to end like this – bloody hay fever!

I left at 8.30 a.m. after checking my camping spot thoroughly. I walked much slower today knowing I needed to pace myself. I also had some lower back pain caused by running with the heavy pack the previous evening. To my amazement, after less than half an hour I walked out of the landslip, into a green meadow with Lyme Regis a stone's throw away. I could hardly believe it as I realised it'd only taken me two and a half hours to walk through the Undercliff when it should've been four. Admittedly I'd been motoring last night, but I also must've been much fitter than I thought, despite not feeling fit that morning. I came to the outskirts of Lyme Regis by 9.15 a.m. feeling like death on skis and sneezing like a Trojan. I sought sanctuary under some trees in a small park overlooking the famous "Cobb"; an ancient stone wall or pier that jutted out into the sea in a kind of triangular circle (I know what I mean), protecting the harbour from violent storms. There were many small boats in rows, safely moored inside it on this humid morning. Nobody else was about, so I sat on a bench and ate the remainder of my food from yesterday before it went off, even though I wasn't hungry. It felt fantastic to think that I was now firmly in Dorset. Hooray, my final county! Even so, I felt ill and miserable, not fancying doing anything but sleeping. But in this sorry state the intrepid explorer and adventurer within me spurred me into action again. I felt quite "Shacklonic" – like Ernest Shackleton – when he went in search of the North West

Passage or somewhere in 1914. I know I was merely going in search of The Lyme Regis Passage, but I bet old Ernie-boy would've had trouble finding that too like I did later on.

Once in the bustling town centre the heat was so stifling that I had to stop for another rest, despite only walking for ten minutes. To try cheering myself up I bought a huge double ice cream cone and sat on a circular bench where I was hemmed in on both sides by tourists and little kids. Everyone was having a great time in the sun except me. I felt suicidal, wondering how the hell I was going to get through the day. The ice cream had also failed to cheer me up, making me more depressed, as it meant I'd wasted yet another two quid after vowing yesterday to control my outrageous spending. £20 was outrageous to me at that time.

After getting my water bladders topped up at the ice cream parlour, I reluctantly pulled on the pack before slowly heading out of town in the 90-degree heat. I was walking at the speed of a sluggish snail, heading inland, following a diversion sign, as there'd been a serious rock fall. The coast path had been blocked off by the council. Away from the coast it was hotter without the slightest trace of breeze. I crossed several open fields where I could feel the noonday sun burning into the back of my neck, arms, and legs. Occasionally I passed through a bit of woodland where I stopped to rest, drinking water plentifully from my hose. I was having bouts of hay fever every half-hour. I felt stupid for not buying some pills while I had chance in Lyme Regis. My next objective was Charmouth and then, a few miles beyond that ... well, I didn't want to think about it, mainly because it was the highest cliff on the entire south coast – namely the dreaded Golden Cap! – measuring roughly 627.10034 feet and every one was upwards. My back was hurting more now. I hit a very low point, but that old Scott-Shackleton ethic would not let me pack it in no matter what. I wondered what it was that kept driving me on when it would be so easy to catch a train home. I could be lying in my own bed in a couple of hours if I chose but I couldn't do it. In pain I soldiered on through the blistering heat until I came to a road that took me down into Charmouth.

I walked the last half-mile with a bloke named Jim who lived in the Canary Islands but was on a walking holiday in Dorset. He cheered me up considerably when he constantly moaned about everything that was wrong with his life. He was especially peeved about his ex-wife getting all of his money, leaving him broke, twitter, and bisted! This made me very pleased that I'd never taken the plunge and got myself a wife, though I'd been engaged three times in the 1960s and '70s. It was the done thing back then. I didn't want to get stuck with Jim for too long, so when I spotted a fossil shop I pretended I really loved fossils and was going in to look at some. He immediately said he loved them too so would join me. Oh no! I looked at my watch a bit too obviously and told him I was late, so would have to skip the fossil shop after all. He said he was also a little late so would carry on walking with me. In the end I turned sharp left up a side street without speaking and hid round a corner until he'd gone. When I looked back he was 100 yards away peering into shops and alleys, obviously wondering where I'd gone. I crept into a Spar supermarket to give him time to move on. Whilst chatting to the pleasant girl behind the counter, Jim stuck his head around the door.

"Oh there you are! I thought I'd lost you for a while."

I rolled my eyes for the benefit of the girl and told him I wasn't walking anywhere now, as I was about to have lunch with her.

In my desperation to get rid of him I implicated her by saying, "We're going to that restaurant, aren't we? The one round the corner?"

Without dropping a stitch she improvised brilliantly: "Oh yes, the table for *two* is booked for 2 o'clock and it's five to now."

Jim looked sad but thankfully said, "Well I'll be off. Have you got a phone number I could have so we could keep in touch?"

"No, I haven't got a phone. I'm never at home anyway. In fact I'm between flats at the moment, living out on the old trail so to speak, ha, ha!"

He finally left, disgruntled. I thanked the girl profusely for her help. I bought more supplies before carefully making my way to the beach whilst keeping my eyes peeled for old Jim.

I chuckled to myself as I imagined him thinking, That bloke must be the most incredible Casanova. He'd only been in that Spar shop two minutes and he'd got a date with that pretty girl and a table booked. How the hell did an ugly sod like him manage that?

Charmouth beach was packed with sun-drenched revellers, not to mention fossil hunters, as I arrived by its two old buildings, one of which I intended to visit. Apart from the beach café with the museum upstairs – more fossils I expect – there was one other small lock up shop – Rock Follies – a women's clothing shop. It was this place where I was heading, as I knew the lady owner from the huge Gloucester car boot sale. Her name was Jack (Jacqui) and she was quite a character. In fairness, she'd been friendlier with my business partner, as they both specialised in retro clothing, but she knew me too. As I hadn't seen her for a year or two it'd be nice to say hello again, but a sign on the door told me she was closed for lunch. This didn't matter, as it'd give me time to write some dog-eared postcards that I'd been carrying for a week. I sat in the shade under the metal staircase that led up to the museum writing out my cards. Somehow I acquired a lovely little woofer, a kind of terrier, whose owners wanted to visit the museum, which was a "no dogs allowed" deal. I looked after Robbie for them. He was good company and no trouble. I was quite sad when they came to collect him twenty minutes later. I wrote cards to my friends Sally Bundy and Donna Cooke, also Roger Foreman, and Mum and Dad. I eventually gave up as it was too hot to continue writing. I looked down the coastline towards the terrifying vastness of Golden Cap. Its cap, I concede, was a bit golden. I shuddered at the thought of having to tackle it later today, as apart from the climb, the shimmering heat would be unbearable.

There wouldn't be any shelter up there, plus I still felt feverish and as tired as hell. As I stared up at it I renamed the mountain "Golden Crap"!

I ambled over to Jack's now open shop at 2.05 p.m. She didn't recognise me at first, owing to my new guise of a slim, fit, tanned backpacker. I hadn't been to Gloucester boot for ages, so she didn't know about my change of size, image, or direction, or about me leaving the shop. She looked well, though had been through a severe illness since I'd last seen her. Her shop, currently full of girls and women milling about, poring over the racks of cool clothes, looked good too. We chatted for half an hour and she bought me a cooling Tangle Twister ice lolly. I reminded her of the time at Gloucester boot when she'd taken a shine to a horrible gnarled tree trunk on a stall with a "sold" sticker on it. The vendor had probably found it lying in a ditch on his way to the boot. Not to be thwarted, she'd hung around until the buyer returned to collect it and somehow managed to haggle it off him, much to the disgust of her disinterested husband, who not only had to pay for the pointless monstrosity, but had great difficulty in wedging it into their car before driving to Dorset. I took some photos of Jack smiling with some of her girl helpers. She took one of me looking exhausted in my wild green shorts, which were now thankfully fading. At 3 p.m. it was time to leave. I waved to Jack and trudged off in the direction of *Hell*. Prior to that there was another inland detour before I could return to the coast briefly to begin the vile ascent.

As Golden Crap loomed ever larger ahead I realised that the temperature had dropped a little with a slight cooling breeze proving most welcome at a time like this. I was climbing gently when I spotted a family on the path in front of me. I developed a sly plan to use them as pacemakers like Bannister had done with Chattaway and Brasher when he'd run the first four-minute mile in 1954. I hung back, letting them set the pace. Before long we were halfway to the summit and I wasn't out of breath – a stroke of pure genius. This plan continued right to the top and it worked. I got the feeling that like High Peak, Golden Crap's bark had been worse than its bite.

Once on the top I chatted to the lovely family asking if they'd like a permanent job as pacemakers as they were great at it. Following this there was much mirth and merriment before we shook hands and said our goodbyes. They were descending by the same route whereas I was carrying on over more high cliffs. I'd done the worst one but its two or three henchmen still lay ahead and no doubt they'd be awkward. The strange thing was that after I'd beaten the "Old Crap" I started feeling okay for the first time today. It may have been that psychological barrier thing again, plus it was a bit cooler, combined with me always feeling better towards late afternoon and evening. My hay fever had subsided and I hadn't had one bout since Charmouth. By 5 p.m. I'd done the majority of the tough stuff. From another lofty peak I could see right down to Seatown, another small coastal village. Picking my way down the steep slope I overtook several more friendly walkers. When I was half a mile from Seatown I heard a distant whirring sound and upon rounding a bend saw a large rescue helicopter hovering at a hideous angle, its rotors roaring, very low above the edge of the cliffs beyond the village, being watched by crowds of people who'd climbed up for a better view. Two walkers were standing watching. We wondered if somebody had fallen over the edge and some kind of brave rescue was being attempted. It gave us a feeling of apprehension, fearing that people were in trouble. We wandered down the hillside to the small beach to try finding out more. I went straight into the classy beach café that doubled as a post office and local shop and got my fifth ice cream of the day. So much for curbing my spending. I asked the elderly lady behind the counter if she knew what was happening out on the cliffs.

She smiled and said, "Don't worry, it's an exercise. They do it regularly along the coast here."

I felt much better on hearing this news and relaxed again. I chatted to her and bought some sandwiches and pies for the evening session before making my way towards the crowds and the 'copter. By the time I was almost there the noisy machine turned on its heels and flew out to sea. The crowds began dispersing too. They were all coming downhill as I was going up. I felt obliged to nod to everyone who took the trouble to say hello to me – all 200 of the swines! After they'd passed me I stopped for a rest, fearing my neck could be broken from all the pointless polite nodding. Why hadn't I donned my James Dean-style cool shades from the pound shop and ignored the lot of them? I tweaked my head and neck around checking to see if they still worked. It appeared that I'd been fortunate and no permanent damage had been done. A nice lady saw me and began laughing.

I called over: "It's all right for you! I've been through a hell-mare of nonsensical nodding!"

We had a laugh and chat about her holiday as I leaned on my pole. After parting company I was delighted by the progress I'd made, especially considering the inauspicious start to the long day. I climbed another tough hill – Thorncombe Beacon – and began thinking about camping earlier, feeling in need of a more comfortable night. It struck me that I'd been given the phone number of a pub in Seatown by its landlord who'd been a customer at my Hereford shop last year. He was a good bloke. When I mentioned my proposed trip he'd told me to ring him when I arrived at Seatown and he'd "see me all right". *Why oh why* had I not brought his number with me? Worse than that, I couldn't remember the name of the pub or its whereabouts, other than that it was somewhere around the Seatown area! I hated myself and started kicking at my left leg whilst trying to stay upright. I'd probably let a golden opportunity slip away – but not a Golden Cap. I might have had a bed for free plus all the free beer I could drink. Of course, when I got home I found the slip of paper he'd given me with The Anchor Inn, Seatown, plus the phone number written on it. I chewed it up and swallowed it in disgust.

During another descent I came to a homely-looking little camp site off the path. After checking with a few satisfied campers I was directed to a hut where I could enquire about camping. Unfortunately it was locked up. The boss had left so that was that. I could never risk camping without knowing how much it was going to cost. I could easily be stung with a bill for 100 quid in the morning if the owners took a dislike to me. I was quite upset, as it meant I'd now have another long climb ahead to reach the next campsite at Eype, which was visible at the very top of another grimbold hill. (That word simply crept in, I couldn't help it.) I'd already mentally rejected the idea of this climb tonight when I'd arrived at the pleasant campsite, but now I'd no option but to un-mentally un-reject the same idea and bloody well do it! Wild camping was out of the question, as lots of tourists from both campsites were wandering about on the cliffs, plus I wanted to feel secure tonight. I needed to sleep soundly, have a good shower, and wash my clothes properly instead of rinsing them in streams every couple of hours. I began the final push of the day. Although knackered, it made sense to get it done tonight, ensuring that first thing tomorrow I'd be *descending* to West Bay.

It was 8 p.m. when I reached the top where a maze of tents of every shape, size, and colour were pitched as far as the eye could see. I stumbled over to the nearest one and asked the campers, who were lighting a barbecue, where the reception area was, only to be horrified to learn it was about half a mile inland! I couldn't bear the thought of walking one more step, but I'd have to or risk carrying on downhill to the village of West Bay, which could be dodgy camping-wise. They also told me they were paying £14.95 for the whole weekend and this was for a family of four. At least the price seemed reasonable. After a fifteen-minute search, asking numerous campers along the way, I found the campsite office and pushed open the door. Inside it was very professional-looking and state of the art with rows of computers positioned along the lengthy counter. Only one uniformed member of staff was on duty; a smart elderly, slightly aloof woman, who asked if she could help me. I asked how much it cost for a single backpacker for one night.

She punched the information into her computer, looked at the screen, and glanced up, saying cheerfully, "That'll be £14.95, please. How would you like to pay?"

Shocked to core, I blurted out: "I wouldn't like to pay at all! You've got to be joking! I told you I'm a single backpacker with a 6 by 3 foot tent and only want to stay for one night. I can't possibly pay more than £5."

She repeated haughtily that £14.95 was the "standard rate", and more or less told me I could take it or leave it. I tried reasoning with her, imploring her to forget about the damn computer screen, and use plain simple common sense instead. I told her about the family of four who were paying £14.95 for the whole weekend but it was to no avail. I got the feeling she was enjoying the situation, watching me squirm and plead.

She kept repeating smugly, "£14.95 is our standard rate otherwise I'm afraid I can't help you."

I disliked her intensely and I'm sure the feeling was mutual. This was a real body blow at this time of night. What the hell was I going to do? It'd be dark in three-quarters of an hour. Realising I was banging my head against a stuck-up brick wall I shuffled out of the office demoralised and headed straight into the campsite bar next door. I sat alone supping a miserable pint of expensive beer trying to decide what to do next. I may have to make a last minute dash down the hill and pray I'd find a secluded spot to camp before I reached West Bay. Realistically, there was little chance of that. I downed the remainder of my pint and decided to have one last try with the snooty "Madame Jobsworth". As I stood up I became aware that my belly was aching again, no doubt from that pricey pint. Back in the office she'd now been joined by a younger man sitting doing some paperwork at the back. He didn't look up when I stated my case, but the answer from her was the same as before.

"It says £14.95 on the screen so I'm afraid there's nothing more I can do."

For God's sake change the bloody record woman! I walked towards the door for a second time. Once outside, with all hope now evaporated, I began to walk the half-mile back to the coast, when I heard a voice calling out.

"Excuse me, sir! Excuse me!" I looked round to see the chap from the office. He was definitely talking to me. He went on: "I'm the campsite manager and couldn't help overhearing what you were saying. I agree with you. £14.95 is extortionate for a single backpacker. What do you normally pay on campsites?" I told him it had varied between £1.50 and £7.50. Smiling, he replied, "How does £6.00 sound? We've got very good facilities here."

I grabbed his hand and shook it vigorously, saying "Thank goodness someone's got some common sense around here!"

His logical approach was further reinforced when he added, "By trying to charge you £15 nobody wins. You'd walk away and we'd make nothing. We'd simply have an empty patch of grass instead. I'd rather get £6 than nothing for that patch of grass." What a sensible man. We returned to the office to sort it out. I really loved it in there this time. He turned to Madame Jobsworth and said calmly, "This chap's staying. I'll sort it out now. He'll be paying £6. Some common sense is called for in these instances."

Hoisted with her own petard, which was a much higher petard than the lower petard I'd been hoisted with back in Exmouth over that signpost! She was now forced to step away from the computer without uttering a word, but with a look of total shock on her face; her authority completely undermined in front of the bloke she'd treated with such contempt. Now the boot was on the other foot and the cows had truly come home to roost. It was wonderful! I'm not a huge gloater normally, but on this occasion I did have a lovely little gloat. I paid up the six quid after we'd filled in the necessary form, and insult was no doubt added to injury when the manager began treating me with great respect in front of her.

"Have a lovely stay, Mr Watts, and best of luck with the rest of your amazing walk. If you fancy a pint later I'll be in the bar around 10 o'clock; my treat. Might see you later, then. Sorry for the mix up."

We shook hands again as she looked on horrified. As I walked off I would've given my right arm to have been another fly on that office wall to see if she'd been further reprimanded or not. I must say that if I'd been him I'd definitely have sacked her on the spot! A little drastic perhaps on reflection but hopefully she'd been brought down a peg or two and would think twice about how she treated backpackers in the future. I was so happy that I had another quick expensive pint to celebrate my good fortune before rushing back towards the coast to camp before it got too dark. As I was pitching the tent the dying rays of the sun cast a peaceful red shimmer all around the quiet tents as well as the sea in the opposite direction. Four smart-looking campers strolled towards me, smiling. Turned out they were two forty-something couples, one from Kent, one from Northamptonshire. They were going out for a meal in West Bay. We joked and laughed for ten minutes. One guy introduced himself as "Tuppenny". I laughed, asking where that had come from.

Apparently, when he was born, he was so tiny that a relative said, "He's no bigger than a tuppenny piece."

The nickname stuck from that moment. I said it was brilliant, but was there ever such a thing as a tuppenny piece in those days? None of us knew but we chortled anyway. They asked me to go into West Bay with them and eat but understood when I said I was worn out. Besides, I wasn't about to fork out another thirty quid on a posh meal and I wouldn't expect them to pay for me. After they'd gone I lay in the tent watching the red glow fade to grey on the seaward horizon, eating my sandwiches with a normal-sized Snickers for afters, and a pint of 50 per cent water, 50 per cent orange juice. Thinking about Tuppenny and Snickers bars made me come up with another interesting riddle, namely: would a fun-sized Snickers still be a fun-sized Snickers to a fun-sized giant? I think it would, because a fun-sized giant is probably the same size as a slightly bigger than normal human being, so if the fun-sized Snickers is still about fun-sized to the slightly bigger than normal human being, logically it must also be about fun-sized to the fun-sized giant, who's marginally bigger than a slightly bigger than normal human. Riddle solved! Admittingly it could be a close-run thing, depending on his actual height. If it transpired that he happened to be a marginally taller fun-sized giant than average, he'd immediately qualify for a normal-sized Snickers instead! I'd be able to sleep easier now I'd solved that one. I was out within five minutes.

Day 48: Saturday 31 May

The Timex went off at 7 a.m. I'd set it early to beat the mad rush for the showers. I ain't no mug. You've got to plan well ahead on these campsites that hold thousands of campers. It was the best night I'd had for ages and was able to make the 40-yard dash to the immaculate shower block easily, where I got a free cubicle and stepped under the jets. I rapidly stepped out again. The water was practically boiling! Whether it was a clever ploy on behalf of the campsite to save hot water or not I'll never know but it was impossible to stand under that shower for more than one second at a time. There were no controls to alter the temperature, so I was stuck with it. I did find a fabulous way to do my laundry, which involved throwing it onto the shower floor, pouring shampoo all over it, and "treading" it as if it were a mound of grapes. This way the water was about bearable as long as I kept my upper body away from the jets by twisting and turning when necessary. I picked up the sodden, soapy articles and scrubbed myself all over with them before repeating the process over and over again. I shaved in the cubicle sink, dried myself off with my tiny "miracle towel" whilst letting the shower jets rinse the remainder of the shampoo out of the clothes. I went back to the tent well-scrubbed, carrying all my damp laundry. As it was looking like another scorcher I knew it'd dry quickly. I put my hat, top, socks, and shorts on wet and tied the other stuff to the back of my pack. I was ready to leave by 10 a.m. I chatted briefly with Gary from Cambridge, and William, who'd got an amazing semi-circular tent which totally mesmerised me, as it was reminiscent of a World War II Nissan hut. I loved it but it would've looked better with a massive World War II tank standing beside it, possibly with a posing James Blunt too.

Back on the coast path I got my first sight of West Bay a mile below. Although it was a hot morning there were already white mists swirling in from the sea making everything beyond the town hazy. The pack was lighter today, as I'd jettisoned the vast quantity of water I'd been carrying recently, knowing I'd be able to find it more easily in the frequent coastal settlements ahead. Heading down the long green hill, into the small town, it was time for breakfast. West Bay has always been used to serve the larger town of Bridport a mile or so inland. It has a great little harbour, beach, and a multitude of cafés, restaurants, and shops. This Saturday morning it was bustling with activity, with tourists and locals going about their business with gusto. Near the harbour I found a little row of kiosks providing all types of takeaway food. I approached the gaudiest-looking one and ordered a lamb roll, which sounded weird and creepy because lambs probably do roll when they're still alive and kicking in a field. It was excellent, so I went back and ordered a spicy chicken burger and a cold "fruit" drink, which sadly turned out to be a mistake. The drink was called a "Slaker" and was full of sickly, sugary saccharin, thus almost undrinkable. But at 80p. I was going to force it down somehow, though there was no chance of it "slaking" my thirst. The one plus point was the handy plastic bottle it came in. I really liked the shape of it and, being virtually weightless, I decided I'd hang on to it in case one of my bladders got a puncture. I've still got that same bottle five years on.

All was well with the world as I sat in the sunshine eating my breakfast. I'd less than a week to go, though couldn't predict the exact day that I'd arrive at South Haven Point. I began wondering what the finish would be like and how I might feel when it was all over, but another swig of the vile Slaker brought me back to earth with a thud. It was time to stop pondering and get on with the task in hand. I stood up, took one look at the almost vertical East Cliff, promptly ordered another mug of tea, and sat down again. The tea was about strong enough to get rid of the acrid aftertaste of the Slaker. Whether it was an optical illusion or not I couldn't tell, but the worrying East Cliff now looked, from where I was sitting, very much like the North face of the Eiger. Could it really be that steep? Twenty minutes later when I was halfway up it I realised that it could. When I paused to rest it was like standing on a central rung of a 300-foot ladder. If I overbalanced I'd fall down the precipice to the foot of that ladder and West Bay! To make things worse I'd climbed into thick fog. Visibility was almost nil. Why hadn't I taken a day off in the lovely West Bay? I could've caught a bus into Bridport and everything. Now here I was back on my head again. You must've heard that joke about Hell, when the Devil says the punchline: "Right, tea break over! Back on your heads."

I pulled myself up, often having to use my hands on the near vertical terrain, and reached the top ten minutes later. I glanced at my watch, barely able to make out the face in the fog. I think it was midday! My stomach ache from the previous day had returned slightly – that grim Slaker – and my lower back was still playing up, but luckily the old "yellow fever" was not present today. Can you get hay fever in thick fog, or would the large, damp wisps prevent the pollen from going up your nose? I recalled that I'd never once suffered from hay fever whilst in Texas, possibly because the grains of pollen there were so big that they wouldn't fit up my nose. On the top it was probably flat, but as I couldn't see more than 10 feet in front of my face, I couldn't be sure. Well, it makes sense to me. All I did know was that it was horribly dangerous and as I was walking up one particular slope, about to step over the ridge at the top, I realised there was absolutely nothing there but thin air – it was the cliff edge, a section of which had fallen away some time in the recent past! I managed to stop in the nick of time otherwise it would've been curtains for poor old Overend, and I don't mean nice floral Laura Ashley ones either.

After I'd "felt" some more ups and downs and made a useless detour through a drab caravan site I glimpsed Burton Bradstock through the swirling mists about half a mile inland. Seeing no point in visiting it in these unpleasant conditions, I trudged on. Without being able to pinpoint my exact position I found myself at sea level again, walking on pebbles with a high shingle beach to my right, behind which I presume were the hidden waters of Burton Mere with the sea beyond them. To my left there was now practically no visibility, which was great news, as apparently there was some sort of nudist beach somewhere around here according to the book, and we all know those places are always teeming with dodgy-looking blokes, yet there's never a woman in sight. I could just about make out what appeared to be grassy fields sloping gently upwards. The whole area looked like it may be a nature reserve, which would've been ironic as I couldn't hear one single sound, not a breath of wind, no birdsong, not a whisper, as I stood silent without breathing, listening for any audible signs of life. There weren't any. It was like being in a vacuum. The only sound I heard was my heart beating. It was too silent for the Notemares. It was what I imagined it would be like on the planet Pluto, not Dorset! It was eerie and chilly, with thick grey swirling ghostly mists, completely barren of all forms of life, a bit like my living room except there're mice there. It was an unforgiving desolate place. I felt a shiver run right through me. Maybe the world had ended and I was the last human being left alive. That's what it felt like. I hated it and didn't want to be there another minute. My aim was to get the hell out of there asap, so I began walking much faster. It struck me that on a beautiful summer day it could possibly become a kind of paradise, with beautiful birds and little animals running amuck everywhere, enjoying themselves like there was no tomorrow but not today. Where were they and what were they doing?

After half an hour of unpleasant walking the mists cleared slightly. I saw two people sitting on a bench about 400 yards ahead. I wasn't the only one alive after all. As I got within 50 yards of them they got up, without looking in my direction, and carried on ahead, leaving the roughly-hewn bench vacant for me. I plonked myself down without removing the pack in case I was forced to make a quick getaway, should a phantom nudist appear, or worse still a real one. Five minutes later I was back on the path, heading for West Bexington with the weather improving every minute. The welcoming beach café was the first thing I spotted. It was the *only* thing I spotted, apart from a couple of nearby bungalows. It was fantastic to be back in the land of the living after one of the weirdest stretches I'd hiked. I walked through the small garden and into the café. It looked pretty good with plates of cakes and goodies on display. I stood there for a minute before a woman emerged from the back room. To my astonishment she looked and dressed exactly like Hinge and Bracket; same hair too. You could have knocked me down with a feather duster. She only looked like one of them, but not having studied their work in great depth as yet, I didn't know which one. I'd need to go online when I got home to find out. Could it be Hinge, or was it the enigmatic Bracket? I once had a signed Hinge and Bracket LP on sale in my shop for 50p. It lay there undisturbed for fourteen years before I finally gave it to an old tramp for Christmas, along with a signed Don Estelle LP and a moth-eaten Teddy boy jacket, thus making him the coolest tramp in Herefordshire.

Having already had a large breakfast I bought the two biggest cakes on sale and sat outside under a parasol with a pot of tea for seven as I was exceedingly thirsty. As the sun's rays pierced the remains of the fog I had a nasty bout of hay fever. I couldn't win. Nevertheless, once it was over I felt much better than in the morning, with no more back pain or belly ache. I returned my tray to the café, said goodbye to Hacket (or Bringe), and left along a narrow gravely path bound for Abbotsbury. The shale was slide-y and horrid. I didn't fancy it at all, so when I saw a woman walking behind me I slowed right down, allowing her to catch up so I could ask if this gravel went all the way to Abbotsbury. This nice local woman told me it did, but pointed out an inland route that she insisted would be much easier. I thanked her but noticed that the shale didn't seem to be deterring her as she set off along the path that I was about to leave. I made my way half a mile inland and uphill (of course), turned right for a while, left, right again, before stopping, throwing off the pack, and ranting at top volume. I was lost again. If only I could get my hands round that nice local woman's neck! After the rant was over I pulled on the pack again, stumbling around like a blind man. I had another violent bout of hay fever, using my miracle towel as a handkerchief to catch my watery sneezes. I staggered up to a lone farmhouse that seemed to be right in the middle of the fields. A sign outside read: "Labour in Vain", the name of the farm. If I hadn't been so furious I would've appreciated this far more.

Instead I stared at it and mumbled miserably, "Yeah, I know what you mean, mate."

In the farmyard a chap was lying on the ground repairing a large lawnmower. When he saw me I tried as hard as possible to behave like a normal person but don't think it fooled him for one minute. As it happened though, I couldn't have picked a better chap. Apart from being practical and technical he also knew every inch of the surrounding area. His name was Nigel, which seemed a bit of a strange name for a farmer, but who cares, as long as he knew the way? He told me to hang on while he went inside, only to reappear seconds later clutching an OS map. In the meantime I'd spotted an old beaten-up bike jacket hanging from a peg inside a nearby shed, but about managed to refrain from asking him if he was a member of that notorious and dangerous motorcycle gang known as the "Hells Nigels", as he most likely wouldn't have appreciated the awful pun.

Pointing at the map, he said, "Look, you're here and you need to be here."

It all looked so simple on the map. Pity I hadn't bothered using any. I was sure that if I had I would've saved myself a lot of mental anguish and physical pain, not to mention many the lost miles. It seemed I needed to retrace my steps to the horrid shale path and walk it after all.

When I expressed my concern about this he said, "Don't worry, there's only about 100 yards of shale before it turns to grass. The rest of the path is dead easy."

If this was true why hadn't the nice local woman told me? Must throat her! We shook hands before I went back the way I'd come. I'd wasted almost an hour by the time I'd returned to the path. I hurried along with my old plates sinking into the shale as I slid about, but sure enough Nigel had been right. I soon stepped onto soft but firm grass. It was easy from here onwards, no thanks to that nice local woman – must neck her! By the time I reached the start of Chesil Beach I was knackered and it was getting much hotter too. When I saw another beach café I ran inside to cool off. I ate my first ever Maxibon ice cream. This peculiar kind of affair was on a stick, sort of chocolaty and square, with funny biscuity stuff in it. I made a note of the name for Wretcher Fewforence again in case he fancied one later. I filled both my bladders and the little Slaker bottle too, as I'd be climbing soon in the blazing afternoon sun. I found some of the posh-est and largest sandwiches I'd ever seen, lurking at the back of the food fridge, reduced to below *quarter* price! I picked out as many as I could carry, including exotic fillings like lobster, prawns, crab, and avocados. "I'll 'ave two cardos if it's all the same to you, guv!"

Which reminds me, when I played in a band in Italy during the 1960s we took a roadie with us from deepest, darkest Herefordshire who, until then, had hardly ever travelled beyond Much Cowarne. Whilst sitting with him in a café in Bologna it became apparent that he'd led a very sheltered life.

When I asked the waiter for a cappuccino, he chimed in with, "Make that two cups o' chino, master!" Several days later in another café I ordered cannelloni and he bamboozled another waiter by exclaiming, "Make that two cans o' loni, master!"

Anyway, back to the present. The crux of the matter was that I bought a massive pile of the posh natty sandwiches for four quid. Some purists – a better word may be "tossers" – insist on walking every agonising stony step of the 10-mile-long Chesil Beach itself, so they could say they'd done every single inch of the coast, but I'd no wish to go through any more unnecessary pain simply to become a coast-path martyr. Besides, it'd make a pleasant change to view the whole coastline from the gentle grassy hills that lay a mile inland, while also walking parallel to Chesil Beach rather than on it. After leaving the shade of the swanky bijou café, I began climbing inland towards the town of Abbotsbury, although the path would bypass it. I could see the picturesque St Catherine's Chapel standing out on the bare hill to my left. Legend has it that in around AD 600 St Augustine sent out his priests to convert the heathen English from paganism to Christianity. He also suggested that it'd be better to make use of some of the existing temples as the people would be more likely to worship at familiar sites. In other words they'd feel more at home in them. The early Christian missionaries would naturally try choosing a patron saint that continued, as closely as possible, the pagan dedication of the temple. St Catherine's chapel was probably one of these. Her chapels are often situated high on hills too, perhaps as a reference to Mount Sinai. It's possible that the Romans suggested the name "Katerina" (the pure one) to the Celts, and they recognised the new goddess in an old one, hence the new saint became known as St Catherine. The chapel itself was built on a definite platform that could've been made originally for the pagan worship, but the existing chapel was built later in the expansionist 1300s. Wessex first became Christian around 800 so it seems unlikely that a pagan temple could still be active 500 years after the conversion of Wessex to Christianity.

Today's building presumably replaced an earlier Christian structure. I passed by within half a mile of it as it gleamed golden in the mid-afternoon sun; a beautiful, impressive site. From above I looked down over the famous Abbotsbury Swannery with Chesil Beach and the sea as its backdrop. This has also been in existence since medieval times, established by Benedictine monks, who built a monastery at Abbotsbury during the 1040s. The monks farmed the swans to produce food for their lavish banquets, but St Peter's monastery was destroyed in 1539 during the dissolution. Some of the ruins are still visible around St Nicholas Church in the village. Since that time the Swannery has been under the stewardship of the Ilchester Estates. Apparently the swan feathers themselves played a massive role in England's cultural development, as it was from these, hardened in hot sand, that quill pens were cut. The old saying goes, "No swans, no Shakespeare," which might be a bit far-fetched cos he could've used a Biro if the worst had come to the worst.

At the highest point I joined a ridge and walked eastwards along it with spectacular views down across the countryside in all directions. To the south, beyond the fields and woodlands, also running west to east, lay the long, narrow Fleet Lagoon. Immediately south of that is the constant low cream-coloured line of Chesil Beach, which acts as a natural seawall, maintaining the Fleet Lagoon's fresh water status against all the odds. It was good to see some old sheep grazing too. I hadn't seen many on the trip. There'd been far more cattle and ponies. There have been many shipwrecks along the Chesil Beach, where treacherous currents and a strong undertow have caused the loss of many lives over the years. Some of the shipwrecks would initially have had survivors, but few of them would've been strong enough to fight and survive against the strength of nature. The village of Fleet, Chesil Beach, and the Fleet lagoon, were all made famous by the 1898 smuggling novel *Moonfleet*, by J. Meade Faulkner. A violent storm in 1824 caused severe flooding and extensive damage to property in the in the area, destroying many buildings in the village of Fleet itself, and destroyed the Esplanade at Weymouth.

Considering I was some distance from the coast I found my way comparatively easily. Mind you, my direction of travel was predetermined by my simply keeping an eye on the coastline, ensuring I was parallel to it at all times. The inland walking in this "green and pollen-t land" had a downside. I began having nasty bouts of hay fever every fifteen minutes or so. Sometimes the bouts were so bad that I had to remove the pack and lie down in the shade. My eyes were itchy-red whilst my stinging nose streamed like a tap. The fever itself was like having the flu, and I don't mean "man-flu" either. At one point I saw family crossing the path ahead of me, so I hid rather than face them in my awful state. If we'd met and they'd had the impertinence to say, "Bless you!" I would've undoubtedly "throated" and "necked" the lot of them. I hate idiots who glibly and benignly utter those stupid words in answer to every single agonising sneeze, thinking they're being both amusing and considerate. Well I've got news for them: you're *not*, you b******s! I'd love to see them get really bad hay fever for five minutes. They'd never say "Bless you!" to any real sufferer again. Pork fever *pigs*, the lot of 'em!

After more high field walking, the path, after bypassing the wild-sounding village of Langton Herring, made its way down to the banks of Fleet lagoon and rather frustratingly proceeded to follow every single meander on its northern edge when it could've easily missed out half of the more boring ones. The one consolation was that I got a good close-up view of life on the Fleet, namely the variety of birds and the fishermen sitting in boats. I wondered what they were fishing for. Obviously not cod, bass, mullet, haddock, or any salt water fishes unless they'd somehow sneaked over the shale of Chesil Beach in the night in search of a better freshwater life. It was a peaceful little place and I enjoyed it immensely, as I tended to enjoy most of the more quirky places along the way. It was around 7 p.m. when I started to wonder about camping earlier tonight, as the bouts of bubonic plague had taken their toll, making me feel peeky and tired. I'd already passed several handwritten signs pointing inland, stating stuff like, "Campsite 1 Mile", which I'd ignored, as there was no way I was walking uphill for a mile and back again the next morning. I'd rather jab my own eyes out with a red-hot bodkin.

I'd calculated that Ferrybridge was roughly 8 miles away along the winding, meandering Fleet. I probably wouldn't get there tonight, nor did I want to, as it was on the edge of an urban area, adjacent to Weymouth, the likes of which I now intended to avoid like the proverbial bubonic. I was thinking about where I might pitch when, rounding a corner, there was a lovely-looking campsite on the path. That was it for the day. I wasn't walking another inch. By that I meant I wasn't walking another 100 yards because by the time I'd been to the office, booked in, got my pitch, had a quick look around, been to the gents', I'd probably have walked another 70 yards. The first port of call was the campsite office/shop where I checked in for six notes before buying two cans of beer for later. I chatted to the young chap as he prepared to close the office for the night. He pointed out a green phone box from which I'd be able to call my parents later. I got some change before going to pitch the tent. With an onsite bar with a restaurant open until 11 p.m., I reckoned I'd made a good decision. I found my little pitch about 40 yards from the bar and 20 yards from the nearest tent. 40 yards in another direction though half a dozen kids were playing football on an empty patch of grass. When they saw me pitching my tent they immediately stopped and ran over to me, shouting.

"Hey, Mister! What are you doing? Why are you walking? Why have you got a rucksack?"

My heart sank. I was too tired to answer their inane questions. Their ages ranged from about nine to thirteen. They were okay if somewhat annoying, so I did my best to remain civil. After all, I was a kid myself once – or was I?

One of them asked, "What would you do if someone tried to steal your gear, Mister?"

I impulsively replied, "They'd be dead before they got 5 yards."

"Have you got a gun in that rucksack, then?"

I replied with my tongue firmly in my cheek: "Knives, guns, hand grenades, bazookas, rockets, you name it; I've got it in there."

When I looked up after pushing in another tent peg they weren't smiling. Not knowing much about kids I hadn't realised that they'd take my words at face value, but I didn't bother to elaborate or enlighten them. I thought that if they, or any of their older mates, got any silly ideas in the night they'd think twice about doing anything.

They all spoke simultaneously: "Can we see them, Mister? Show them to us! Go on! Please, Mister!"

The old saying, "Oh, what a tangled web we weave!" sprang to mind, but I wriggled out of question by saying, "I can't, because they're, err, err, they're sewn into the lining in the bottom of the pack."

Brilliant, though I say so myself! They were disappointed with that reply, possibly smelling a rat, and after a few more daft questions, one by one they lost interest in me and ran away to resume their kick-about, all except for the youngest lad, who showed no sign of leaving whatsoever. After five minutes he was still grilling me with questions.

"Were you in the war, Mister? Are you in the SAS, Mister?"

He was a decent enough lad but I was fed up and very tired, but at the same time I didn't really want to tell a nine-year-old to **** off. I also didn't want to be seen talking to a child on my own with nobody else around. It's not the done thing nowadays. Times have changed. Some people might have put two and two together and got the wrong idea.

I started dropping hints like, "Look at all your mates. They'll be needing you on the football pitch. Your mum and dad'll be wondering where you are, won't they?"

"Nah, they won't care. I'd rather stay and talk to you. Can I get inside the tent and look at all your knives?"

Oh God *no*! Why *me*?

I said firmly, "*No you can't*! Now go find your parents like a good boy. I've got to go make some important phone calls."

He looked a bit hurt but I had to nip this in the bud. I was extremely relieved when he finally ran off. I continued unpacking my sleeping bag and other gear in peace. Five minutes later he was back, smiling, pushing something towards me.

"I've bought you an ice cream from the shop, Mister."

Oh Christ, no! He was only trying to be kind but I told him, while trying to remain calm, that I didn't want an ice cream. I didn't want anything. Please leave me alone. This of course hurt his feelings again.

"I only wanted you to be my friend, Mister."

Pointing, I said, "Look, you've got loads of nice friends over there. I'm a boring old bloke. I'm eighty-nine now. You go have a nice time with them."

I couldn't believe he'd latched onto me like this. I presumed he must've been quite a neglected child, or maybe he was simply intrigued by my camouflage pack, the "pretend" knives and guns, and the sense of adventure of it all. I finally convinced him to go and give the ice cream to his brother.

I imagined him animatedly telling his parents, "I met this scruffy old man over there. I nearly went into his tent. He's got loads of knives and guns and things in there. I got him a big ice cream. I'm going to go back and get in his tent with him later."

I could visualise his father turning purple, getting a campsite lynch mob together, and stringing me up from the nearest tree for being some kind of pervert. How the hell did I get into this situation? All I did was try to be civil to a bunch of kids. Once I'd got set up I decided to zip up the tent and not return to it until it was time to sleep when the bar closed.

I headed to the phone box, put a pound coin in the slot, and dialled Mum and Dad's number. Dad answered but when I spoke he couldn't hear my voice. I kept pressing the buttons but it was no use. Eventually I cut him off. The pound coin was lost of course. Campsite belly *pigs!* I tried again with a 20p coin and the same thing happened. The phone was obviously f*****! When I told the bartender he shrugged, telling me I'd have to wait until the shop opened in the morning to get my money back. As I was already in there I ordered a pint and after looking at the menu, a portion of scampi and chips too. The barman said that the scampi would take about fifteen minutes, so instead of sitting waiting I decided to get my mobile and ring Mum and Dad quickly in case they had been worried when I'd failed to get through earlier. This entailed going back to the tent and getting the phone out of my Tupperware box where I'd safely stashed it. Trouble was, it wasn't there. I rummaged high and low, tipping everything onto my airbed, searching every pocket on my pack – nothing. I flew into a panic. Had I lost it or maybe chucked it away with some rubbish? Had those kids stolen it? No, I'd only left the tent for ten minutes. The kids were okay anyway. I continued ripping at things, throwing stuff about. I whimpered quietly to myself but was unable to rant at full volume for fear of drawing attention to myself. The young lad might hear me and come back. When fifteen minutes had elapsed I realised my meal would be ready. I left everything where I'd slung it, zipped up the tent, and ran back to the bar where my cold scampi was waiting for me on the table.

I told the barman I'd lost my mobile but he was unconcerned, simply saying, "Your meal's gone cold."

I ate the cold food like a zombie without tasting one single mouthful. All I could think about was the missing phone. It wasn't a pay-as-you-go either, so if someone had got hold of it I could possibly get a bill for thousands of pounds when I got home. This was already hard enough to stomach but it occurred to me that, while searching, I hadn't seen my tiny Sony radio either. I wondered what else might have gone missing. This could be the tip of the iceberg and it was turning into a major catastrophe. I only realised that I'd eaten a meal when I noticed the empty plate in front of me. I stood up and walked grimly back to the tent, determined to carry on searching, though by now I guessed it would be in vain. The anger was gone, being replaced by a kind of melancholy, as I slowly moved the gear around without really looking at it. Finally, dejected, I lay down, forced to accept that the phone, the radio, and God knows what else, would never be seen again. Suddenly I jumped up excitedly, grabbed at my cooking pot, and after ripping the lid off saw the phone and the radio lying safely inside, still wrapped in their plastic ziplock bags! I was ecstatic, over that old proverbial moon. I'd moved them from the Tupperware box a couple of weeks ago to make room for some extra chocolate bars but had forgotten all about it. Overjoyed, this called for some sort of celebration. So, after a quick cheery call to my folks, I set off to the bar for a couple of pints. The barman remained his usual passive self.

When I told him the brilliant news he merely grunted, "Right."

There were a few families sitting around having meals but it was a rather subdued atmosphere with nobody I could get chatting to (or bother), so the evening was a bit of an anti-climax. At 10 p.m. I decided to call it a day and retire. I felt quite drunk as I got into the tent. My belly was twinging again. Nothing bad, but it was still not back to normal. After falling asleep immediately I was woken up by the sound of laughter at midnight. This continued as I lay in the dark, quietly willing them to belt up. I felt thirsty; probably dehydration from the pints I'd drunk earlier. It occurred to me that I still had two cans of beer that I'd bought in the shop the previous evening, so I decided to drink them now. By doing so I'd be killing two birds with one stone. First, I didn't want to carry them with me in the morning, and secondly they'd quench my thirst now, hopefully making me tired enough to sleep through the cackling and chatter. I pulled the ring off the first can and downed half of it in one. It tasted good so I drank the rest a little slower, feeling a bit bloated. I didn't really fancy the second can but had to use it up or leave it behind in the morning. After that I didn't feel too good at all. The beer felt very cold inside me and my stomach cramps worsened. I slept very badly.

Day 49: Sunday 1 June

I managed a bit more troubled sleep before admitting defeat at 5.30 a.m. after waking to hot sun and birdsong. I made the decision to shower and get out of the place before the hordes were up and about, especially that kid, who'd probably be full of energy and could be more of a nuisance in the morning. In the shower block there was one solitary cleaner at work so I was able to get on with everything without delay. I did the lot in half an hour and was packed and ready to leave by 7.00 a.m., thus forfeiting the £1.20 I'd lost in the thieving green phone box. I crept quietly out of the campsite and was back walking on the edge of the Fleet lagoon before any of the other campers had stirred. I felt distinctly queasy this morning, but kept going anyway, aiming for Ferrybridge and the fascinating Isle of Portland. The sneezing part of the hay fever didn't seem as bad but I was sweating and felt slightly faint as I followed the increasing twists and turns of the path along the lagoon's edge. I couldn't help thinking that if I'd been able to walk in a straight line I'd only have to cover about one-third of the distance, which was frustrating, especially as I felt so rough. The sun vanished and the weather turned grey, humid, and ominous. Thunder could be on the way. I rested every half-hour or so, lying on my back in the grass for five minutes each time. Pulling the pack back on was agony with me feeling so weak. This was definitely the roughest I'd felt during the trip. I wondered if I should pitch the tent somewhere and sleep. This would also stop me from getting soaked if there was a thunderstorm, but something inside made me carry on, thinking I may find a B & B at Ferrybridge, even though it was only 9.30 a.m.

This part of the Fleet was not so nice, though that could've been down to the miserable weather. I passed several drab caravan sites along the way but finally saw the conurbation of Ferrybridge a mile ahead. Once there, all I wanted to do was get out of it. It was a most unprepossessing place, so I kept walking until I hit the main road, which was the sole route south across the bridge, onto the Isle of Portland. Not wishing to walk the narrow exposed bridge of land, I found a bus stop and waited for the next ride. Being a Sunday morning I wasn't sure if there'd be a bus until I was joined by two local old ladies who assured me there'd be one in ten minutes.

They reminded me of Harry Enfield's old comedy sketch ladies, as when I asked them about bus stops, they answered, "Ooooohh, young man! You wanna get orf at the Royal Victoria, doesn't he, Flo?"

Flo put in her two pennyworth: "Oh yes he does, don't you, young man? You wanna get orf there at the Royal Vic, doesn't he, Mabel?"

"Ooooohh yes! That's right, Flo. You get orf there, young man, and you won't go far wrong. Ooooooh, when I was your age, young man!"

They were both falling over backwards to help me. I got the impression, without wishing to sound arrogant, that this little episode may have been the most exciting thing that'd happened to them all week!

The bus took me the mile across the narrow causeway. I alighted at the Royal Victoria Arms Hotel. As the bus pulled away I saw the old ladies waving to me through the window.

They were mouthing, "Ooooooh, that's it, young man! You'll be all right now. Oooooh, you are a one! When we were your age!"

I chuckled to myself as I crossed the road, thinking, I bet they're only about ten years older than me. I walked slowly through a small harbour near West Bay and Chiswell where some surfers and tourists were hanging around on the quayside. Some nodded, saying good morning. I nodded back but felt too ill to exchange pleasantries. I could see the steep cliff that I'd have to climb in five minutes. Puffing and panting through some houses, I was quarter of the way there. I flopped breathless onto a conveniently placed bench. As I sat there trying to get my breath, it occurred to me that I needn't have set foot on the Isle of Portland, as it's never been officially declared part of the South West Coast Path. I could've bypassed the island and gone straight into Weymouth without cheating, thus having a perfectly clear conscience. But what the hell? I wanted to walk it and get a feel of the place anyway, as I'd driven here twice before on brief visits. Apart from all the ailments that I was suffering, I was now aching all over too. My whole body was hurting. So was my brain, as the vile Notemares were back! With a supreme effort I made it to the top, but fell down on the grass, sweating and in agony. I lay without moving, wondering if I was capable of carrying on or whether I'd now be forced to pack it in. I got my breath back before resuming and heading south on the cliff tops through the bare area known as West Weare. It began to rain lightly but there were no signs of any thunderstorms. The sea to the west looked quite rough as I looked back over the length of Chesil Beach. I didn't put on the waterproofs as I couldn't be bothered and was too hot. I'd have to endure getting damp whilst walking through some old quarries and workings.

There are two prisons on Portland: HMP the Verne and HMYOI Portland. The harbour contains Britain's only prison ship, HMP *Weare*. There are old facilities on Portland that have been converted for the use of the coastguards and Search and Rescue teams. One of the most intriguing stories for me is the fear amongst the local population of the word "rabbits". Rabbits have been associated with bad luck for centuries on Portland and the use of the name is still taboo, with the creatures often being referred to as "underground mutton", "long-eared furry things", or "bunnies" instead. This fear is believed to have come from quarry workers who'd sometimes see rabbits emerging from their burrows immediately before a rock fall, and blame them for increasing the risk of dangerous or deadly landslides. There have been cave-ins and in one instance a man died when his crane toppled on weak ground above the burrows. If a rabbit was seen in a quarry, the workers would pack up and go home for the day, until the safety of that area had been checked. Today, older Portland residents are often offended or become silent at the mention of rabbits. Also on the downside it seems a real shame that poor old Chas and Dave will never be able to play a gig on Portland! Most houses retain the yellow-grey colour of the stone, giving Portland's settlements a different character to that of the mainland. The Isle has a vast range of rare plants, flora, and fauna. Portland Sea Lavender can be found on the higher sea cliffs and it's one of the UK's rarest plants. The many varieties of wild flowers and grasses also provide an excellent habitat for numerous species of butterfly. Rare visitors to the surrounding seas include dolphins, seals, and basking sharks. The southernmost tip of the Isle is known as "Portland Bill", which is comprised of a narrow promontory of Portland stone and houses the main lighthouse, which became computer-controlled in 1996. Two much earlier lighthouses stand further inland, one of which is now an important observatory used by ornithologists, providing records of bird migration and accommodation for visitors. Thomas Hardy features in this potted history as his 'Isle of Slingers' was based on Portland. Hardy was so impressed with the Isle that he named Portland the "Gibraltar of the north". I wouldn't wish to get into an argument with Hardy but surely that's a bit like saying Skegness is the San Tropez of the north. The Isle was also the main setting of *The Well-Beloved* and was featured in *The Trumpet-Major* too.

The drizzle ceased as I trudged on with the belly ache still bugging me. I felt sure it was those cans of beer that had exascipated the problem. I passed some grim-looking high-rise council blocks a few hundred yards inland, which looked quite incongruous on this little island with their long lines of laundry flapping about on the balconies. Later on, arriving at the top of a ridge, I could see Portland Bill half a mile below, with its red and white lighthouse standing guard, as well as one of my favourite cafés, The Lobster Pot. The toilet block at the end of the sizeable car park would definitely be my first priority once I got there. I hurried down the hill and straight into the gents', emerging minutes later feeling slightly better but still quite delicate in the belly department. It was 11.30 a.m. before I got inside the old "Pot" and it was pretty full. I reckoned there were fifty or so "Potters" squeezed inside. Most of them appeared to be locals who shared my fondness for the 1930s' Lyon's-style tea shop. The atmosphere was friendly with much chattering and laughter. A waitress dressed in black ushered me to the only available table which happened to be the one where I'd sat many years before. This time the chair opposite me was empty, causing a quick pang of loneliness, as my former dear friend and business partner Berto Griffiths (Roberta) was missing today. Strangely though, I never felt lonely out on the cliffs or in the wilds when I truly was alone.

Scanning the old-fashioned menu, I realised I wasn't very hungry, owing my dicky tummy. It also made sense not to overdo the food today and treat my stomach with a bit of respect. I ordered a pot of tea and a bowl of minestrone with a bread roll. When it arrived I took my time but managed to consume it all, before pouring my tea into a floral bone china cup (and saucer) with the use of a silver-plated strainer – none of those newfangled, gimmicky teabag things here. That's what I call pure *class*! I sat alone amid the pleasant chitchat, gazing through the window, out to the grey-green sea where small boats and various other craft passed by every so often. The twists and turns of life are so strange, I thought, before rising to leave – very profound. The elderly couple on the next table, who'd been nodding and smiling at me throughout my soup, now called gently across to me.

"Thank you very much. It was lovely to meet you."

"Likewise, I'm sure," I replied, despite the fact we'd not met nor conversed until now.

They were really nice and for some reason or another they'd obviously taken a shine to me, in sharp contrast to the effect I seem to have the majority of people who see me. We all nodded and smiled again before I left, kind of dragging the pack awkwardly behind me about an inch from the floor, as there wasn't enough room to shoulder it inside the full café without killing someone. As I paid the bill in the tiny lobby, I saw all the cheap and tacky souvenirs behind the counter, realising I'd bought most of the same items last time I was in here cos I do like all that kind of seaside kitsch. Once outside I pulled on the mighty pack and set off on the coast path around the eastern side of the isle. It was very rugged and stony, apart from being very "Portland-y" too. Although there was still no sunshine the sky was now a sort of neon white, causing everything in sight to hurt my eyes, forcing me to squint white stone, white path, white sky, white flowers, white sea – well bits of it were white. There was a nasty glare bouncing off everything. It became so unbearable that I was forced to stop and take off the pack again to search for my cool Pound Shop shades, which I'd hardly worn yet. I'd buried them somewhere deep inside the pack and, typically, couldn't remember where. When I did find them minutes later there was a big crack in one of the lenses, thereby rendering them most uncool, but luckily still functional. I'd have to put up with looking like a nerd. So what's new? I still felt a bit off-colour, but before I could get the pack on again, a couple in their mid-thirties came round the corner and stopped for a chat. Their names were Stuart and Angela. They were fantastic. They were special needs teachers from Chard in Somerset, out having a day at the seaside. We chatted and laughed about walking and lots of other things. I was crying with laughter at one point and could hardly contain myself. It was a good job I'd taken off the pack or I may have rolled over the edge in a fit of wild guffawing. After twenty minutes it was time to say goodbye, which I always hated doing when I'd met particularly lovely people, but the day was slipping by. We all needed to get the baby washed and get on our way. As we were shaking hands we realised that the sun had come out and it'd become a beautiful afternoon, so we shook hands more vigorously, as if in appreciation of the lucky sunshine.

As I continued I realised that everything had changed in the last hour. Before The Lobster Pot I was feeling exhausted, ill, and so down that I was beginning to have serious doubts again about finishing the walk. Now, over an hour later, I felt on top of the world. The food and ambience of the café had done me good. That wonderful couple had really cheered me up, so much so, that on a scale of 10 I'd gone from a 1 to a 9 and three-quarters. I also noticed my belly was completely better now, with no twinges. I couldn't understand how or why. On top of all that I didn't feel tired or feverish. Apart from being teachers, had Stuart and Angela been faith healers too? If the two of you ever get to read this I want to say thank you so much for that precious twenty minutes of your lives because you saved mine. I can never tell you how much good it did me though I am trying. I bet you're great teachers too. Freshly invigorated, I bounced along the path, whistling and humming, mostly 'She's Been Talking' by the Mutton Birds. What a *great* song! I only wished I'd written the bugger. I would've done if only old Don McGlashon hadn't beaten me to it. It's not fair. Anyway, I was so bloody happy that I forgot to check the guidebook and before I knew what'd happened, I was utterly lost again, but for once I didn't give a damn. I was high up on the cliffs but could clearly see several people walking a low level path near the shoreline. I got the feeling that I should be down there too. The dilemma was that if I was able to scramble down to join the path, I'd have to climb back up again if the path ascended which, with my luck, it was bound to. I reasoned that sooner or later the paths would merge and become one as the cliffs "evened out". Unfortunately this never happened. I found myself veering inland, missing out on walking the east coast of Portland and a whole corner of the Isle. Never mind, it wasn't compulsory. I passed a massive collection of strange-looking buildings on my left, surrounded by solid high security fencing, allowing only glimpses of their roofs. At first I thought they may be related to the quarrying industry but later realised they were probably prison buildings.

Half an hour later I walked down the sunny main street of Fortuneswell and straight into a small supermarket to get a much needed ice cream. I grabbed Magnum and a Summer Fruits Oasis drink. The friendly lady on the till tried charging me £1.10 for the Magnum, immediately causing an argument to break out. With everyone behind me being forced to wait, I dragged the lady over to the freezer, pointing out the price list to her. Magnums were 80p.

She replied, "Those prices are two years out of date. They're £1.10 now."

I wasn't happy with this and started on about the Trades Description Act. After all, we were talking about the not inconsiderable sum of 30 whole pence here. I was laughing and it paid off.

Smiling, she said, "Oh go on, I'll let you off this time!"

This was probably to get rid of me so she could serve the number of irate customers in the growing queue. Outside I leaned on a post and ate my bargain Magnum on this lazy Sunday afternoon. Apart from the customers who came and went it was quiet in Fortuneswell. It kind of reminded me of the old mining town of Cinderford in the Forest of Dean, not far from where I lived. A nice-looking girl came out of the supermarket, smiling, and said hello as she passed me. She walked 30 yards down the road before turning into a gate. I preferred her as a girl though. She gave me another friendly smile before going into her house. Straight away I thought, Can she be of any use to me? I know that sounds selfish and mercenary, but this is what had been happening gradually throughout the walk with the phrase, "You can't look a gift horse in the mouth", constantly springing to mind and fast becoming my new backpacking dictum. I'd never dream of thinking this way if I was at home, but now I was living on my wits outdoors. If anyone happened to show me the slightest bit of kindness or friendliness I'd want to seize the opportunity, hoping it'd lead somewhere useful, usually regarding camping, shelter, food, water, washing, or finding my way. I'd met a huge amount of people who'd helped me on the journey and I was still hoping to find a few more yet.

This girl had gone inside and I thought it might be carrying things a too far if I were to knock on her door and say, "Excuse me, I noticed that you said 'Hello', so do you mind if I come in and have a bath and wash a pile of laundry in your sink?" Or words to that effect.

With my luck the door would probably be opened by her massive irate boyfriend instead, who was bound to be 7 feet tall, as hard as nails, and furious that he was now missing *Match of the Day*. He'd give me a bunch of fives followed by a punch up the bracket before sending me packing with my tail between my legs. As a result of this train of thought I didn't knock on her door, but instead went and drew £100 from the cash machine outside the shop and hotfooted it down the hill, heading for the Royal Victoria Arms Hotel. It was 3.15 p.m. but there was no sign of the old ladies this time as I sat near the Royal Vic to wait for the bus into Weymouth. The bus took me back through Ferrybridge where a dozen people got on. Four of them were sixteen-year-old lads wearing hoodies who went straight to back of the single decker and began larking about. As more people got on along the route the lads' behaviour became worse and worse. When they realised they could get away with it they started swearing, cursing loudly and aggressively, trying to outdo one another.

It made me feel quiet depressed as in the old days someone (possibly me) would've said something like, "Now come on, lads. Please quieten down, you're upsetting everyone."

Probably looking sheepish, they would've quietened down, but not anymore. These days they were more likely to pull a knife and use it. A very sad indictment of today's society. So I sat there feeling like a coward, putting up with the offensive row through gritted teeth, as did the other passengers and the driver. Fortunately, there were only three minutes to go to the terminus. I guess if it'd been longer, one or more of us would've cracked and torn into them no matter what the consequences might be. All the same it was a relief to get off the bus and walk away from the situation. I walked around the modern marina that formed part of the Inner Harbour and was crowded with yachts and all kinds of small craft. Crossing a bridge, I stopped and looked at several large fish cruising below the water's surface. They were grey mullet. NB: do *not* ever order *grey* mullet in a restaurant, as they are notorious for hanging around by sewage outlets where they tend to feed. *Red* mullet are fine, so unless you happen to be colour-blind you'll be okay. If you're not okay you'll soon know about it.

I found my way onto the recently constructed promenade, which was beautiful, and not what I'd expected at all. I thought it'd all be a bit rundown like poor old Ilfragloom and Weston-Un-Super-Mare, both of which I love, but no, this was modern and stylish, but still retaining a certain old-fashioned charm. After a quick look round I decided to carry on in the direction of Osmington Mills, but as I walked along the prom I had another thought. With about two days to go it'd make good sense to make the final stage as easy as possible by posting home everything but the absolute basics. However, as it was a Sunday afternoon, there'd be no post offices open. I resolved to try and find a B & B even though it was early, to sort out my gear and relax. I also felt I deserved a bit of pampering after the supreme effort I'd made today, despite feeling so rough to begin with.

Apart from all this I desperately needed to buy some hay fever tablets, as this would be my last chance before setting off into the wilds, until Swanage, and "the fever" could still be a real threat if it came on badly. I found a phone box on the prom and pulled out the guidebook, which was very dog-eared by now. I got no reply from the first couple of B & Bs, but when I rang a third one a pleasant-sounding lady answered. She'd got a room for £20. We chatted for a few minutes and she gave me directions – it was back the way I'd come on the bus! After telling her I'd get there before 5 p.m., I rang Mum and Dad to tell them I was okay and where I was. My sister and her ex, Mark, were round having Sunday tea, so I chatted to everyone in turn for a good half-hour. We were all in a jovial mood. Being in no great hurry, I called my mates Rick and DR – David MacDonald – who, although related to former Prime Minister Ramsey MacDonald, is nothing much like him apart from looking identical and having the same personality, that is. It's *true*! Neither of them could believe I'd made it this far and were very encouraging.

Afterwards I retraced my steps back through the town, past the marina again, saying hello to the same grey mullet who rudely ignored me, and found the bus station near Debenham's, where I had a fifteen-minute wait for a bus to take me to the Rodwell district of Weymouth. About ten of us were waiting quietly in the warm sunshine with no sign of any trouble. The journey only took ten minutes. I stepped off the bus onto Rodwell Road, finding myself in a pleasant suburban area. I crossed the road and soon located The Double Three, which got its name from being Number 33. The door was answered by the lovely lady I'd spoken to on the phone – Miss K. Amos. We got on well instantly. She invited me inside, telling me her name was Kathy, and that I could choose whichever room I wanted. I was the only guest tonight. Slightly puzzled, I asked if Weymouth was always this quiet in June.

Kathy replied, "Oh no, it's very busy, but I don't open until mid-June."

When I asked why she'd allowed me to stay she said I'd sounded like a really nice bloke – wow! That made a change – and that she'd felt sorry for me. Also, the rooms were almost ready, so it wasn't much trouble finishing them off. I thought she was extremely kind to do all that for me. On the phone I'd told her I hadn't felt well that day, which may have helped persuade her. Interestingly, people didn't seem to loathe me as much when I wasn't visible to them. It seemed to be the look of me that infuriated them the most. She showed me three rooms, from which I chose the smallest one on the quieter side of the house, painted pale green. It had a TV, kettle, sink, and the bathroom was next door. It was all mine – wonderful!

Back downstairs I chatted to Kathy about walking, Weymouth, and the like, before doing my laundry in the bathroom, and sorting out the pack contents for the umpteenth time. I was totally ruthless now, removing my stove, small gas cylinder, mermal thug and kettle, apart from virtually all of my clothing and gadgets, keeping only the absolute basics. I considered losing the tent, sleeping bag and mattress, but would've been totally committed to B & B'ing, which could prove costly should the weather hold me up again. Following some deliberation I retained them. I reckoned I'd reduced the overall weight by another 6 or 7 lbs. I'd only be carrying about 40 lbs. when fully laden, so a bit better than the 60 lbs. I'd started with.

With all the work done I lay on the bed, relaxing in front of the box. I was so glad I'd decided to stay in Weymouth. I was most impressed by the firm pillows and wondered where the hell you could buy them. All mine at home were thin measly affairs that couldn't support a mouse's head yet alone my weighty bonce. By 8 p.m. I felt peckish, but not wanting to get dressed and go out in search of food, I unwrapped the posh sandwiches from the previous morning. Although it seemed an eternity since buying them near Abbotsbury, they still looked fine if somewhat squashed. I put them to my nose. They smelled fine, so I thought, Waste not want not, and tucked into them. They were very tasty. I washed them down with several cups of tea and two giant-sized Snickers, which would definitely be too much for two dwarfs, before writing up the journal with the telly in the background. It was only then that the panic set in. Nothing was wrong, but my mind started wondering about the sandwiches before becoming obsessed with them. Were they really still okay? They'd been in the pack for thirty-two hours and the weather had been mostly hot. They were also past their sell by date when I bought them, hence the "less than one-quarter price" tag. On top of this the sandwiches contained *salmon* in a special sauce with cucumber, *lobster* thermidore, *prawns* with avocado, and finally *duck* with orange sauce, all of them a sure-fire recipe for salmonella food poisoning! All this on top of a dodgy stomach. What would happen if I died in the night? Not much really. I felt fine but would it last or would I collapse writhing in agony and fall unconscious? I kept feeling my stomach, pushing and prodding at it for any unusual signs. Still unable to convince myself that I would last the night, I got my felt tip pen and a sheet of A4 paper and scribbled a note, which read:

Hi, Kathy, sorry to bother you, but if you happen to find me in a coma today please tell the ambulance men that I've eaten the following sandwiches: lobster, prawn, salmon, and duck. They may have gone off. Help! Help! Help! Overend. PS: SOS too!

I placed the "anti-suicide note" on the coffee table, which I pulled across to the door where nobody could miss it. Realising I could do no more I got into bed, still pushing and prodding, but all seemed fine.

Day 50: Monday 2 June

The next thing I knew the Timex alarm sounded at 7 a.m. I'd slept right through and felt wonderful for the first time for three weeks. I prodded my belly and it was still there. I sprang out of bed and into the bathroom. I spotted an iron and a board on the landing so ironed my freshly-laundered black shorts, which already looked ten years old, worn and faded from the battering they'd taken from the weather during the two weeks I'd owned them. I was downstairs eating my tasty full English by 8.30 a.m. All signs of the dicky tummy were thankfully gone. I reasoned that the salmonella in the posh sandwiches must've killed off the E-coli bugs that I'd probably caught from drinking those cold beers the other night before keeling over themselves after the immense struggle. Having said that, biology was never my strongest subject at school. The food was served by a nice chap, who appeared to be Kathy's partner, although I didn't pry.

Afterwards I cadged a couple of dustbin bags off him to place my excess baggage in before posting it home. I said goodbye to Kathy and her partner before finding out that the fantastic pillows came from Ikea. I would've nicked one but it would've completely filled the rucksack, forcing me to leave its entire contents behind to make room for it, which might have looked a bit suspicious! Apart from that my gear had cost around £1,000. I'd expect to be able to buy more than one pillow with that amount of cash. I'd never nick anything anyway, as I'm far too honest. I walked off briskly down the hill in the warm sunshine towards Weymouth. No buses for me today as I felt fantastic. At the marina the grey mullet waved frantically to me this time. Their fins churned up the surface of the water as I was now a familiar sight to them. I found Lloyds chemists and bought some Zirtec hay fever tablets. Pharmacist "Greek George" assured me they were non-drowsy. He was a great guy and began asking me about the walk, seeming fascinated by it. I'd already told him a couple of funny stories when I realised that all of the dozen customers plus three staff members were all listening and smiling too, causing me to feel slightly embarrassed. I don't like deliberately drawing attention to myself. I'd hate to come across as a bighead or a know-all. They were a nice crowd though and they all wished me luck for the remainder of my journey before I left for the nearby King Street post office. I found a small supermarket next door and cadged a medium-sized cardboard box –would it be a fun-sized cardboard box to a tallish giant? Outside on the street I shoved the dustbin bags of redundant gear inside the box and taped it up securely before posting home it at a cost of £6. I must've spent around £30 on postage alone but felt it was money well spent, making the walking much easier, putting less strain on my back. I popped a hay fever tablet and walked along the sunny prom again, out of Weymouth, heading north-east on this gorgeous morning. I felt extremely fit climbing up to the cliff tops again. Somewhere high above Bowleaze Cove I discovered a car boot sale! It was the last thing anyone would expect to see up here. There were more sellers than buyers. It'd probably started early so all the punters had been and gone. The sellers looked dejected as I wandered between stalls, as by now they were clutching at straws. I saw a lot of good stuff going cheap. If I'd still had my shop I could've cleaned up and bought sizeable pile of stock. On one stall stood a small, beautiful roll-top desk. I couldn't help mentally calculating that it would've been worth around £150 in my ex-shop. I lifted the price ticket and saw the asking price was a reasonable £100. The pleasant lady said as it was late I could have it for £75.

The old canny dealer still deep inside me said, "Thanks, much appreciated, but could you make it 50 quid, seeing as it's *me*?"

"£65 is the best I can do."

A super deal, I thought, but pulling out my cash I remembered I was on a serious backpacking trip on the cliffs in the middle of nowhere, carrying a large rucksack. What the hell was I thinking! I would've needed a van to get it home. Besides, I didn't have a shop anymore in which to dispose of it. I apologised to the lady for being a buffoon.

She laughed and said, "I was wondering how you were going to carry it."

She gave me a phone number in case I changed my mind when I got home. I thanked her and did the rest of the stalls. This was a really pleasant little boot, so far removed from the rowdy cut-throat boot at Gloucester, which was full of hard-bitten ruthless dealers. I'd seen numerous punch-ups there too, almost being involved in a few myself. I'd visited it twice a week for twelve years with hardly a break, all in search of stock. God knows how I'd done it for that long. The nicknames of the different areas of the infamous Gloucester car boot sale struck fear into the heart. Nicknames such as "Death Alley", "Suicide Corner", "Shark Bite Street", and "Reeler's Dough". The latter being my own Freudian & Spoonereristic corruption of the more boring "Dealers Row". Yet if I felt particularly playful I'd sometimes refer to it as "Roller's Dee" instead!

Strolling round, I found a box of new identical Matthew Sweet CDs on one stall priced 50p. each. The poor seller said he hadn't sold one and I could have the lot for an Uncle Ivor (a fiver). Thirty-one were in the box, but I couldn't carry them. I also kept reminding myself that I no longer had a shop. I'd only jacked it in four months ago and old habits die hard! I could've sold them for more than a tenner each, although it would've taken around a year to do that. Matthew Sweet, for the uninitiated, is a respected and sought-after leader and exponent of the 1990s US-based genre of music known as "Power Pop". As the name suggests the music sounds like 1960s melodic guitar pop but far more attacking and meaty. It's fab too. I bought one CD for myself and for "old same's tike". Leaving behind loads of bike jackets for a pound or two each, plus numerous other goodies, I set off over the cliffs. Next stop Osmington Mills.

Now well and truly on the most "modern" part of the Jurassic Coast I was walking on Cretaceous limestone cliffs, some of which were a mere 40,000,000 years old. I worried that they may crumble and collapse under my feet, being so recently formed! It was hard work in the heat and the terrain was by no means a doddle either. Around the Osmington Bay area I passed a funny-looking conglomeration of old buildings, appearing like some sort of ancient Borstal-style establishment. Whilst thinking about all the strange buildings that I'd seen adorning the coastline since Minehead, a hefty blonde backpacker, aged about thirty-five, appeared walking slowly towards me. Overlooking Weymouth we stopped for a chat about 30 yards from the weird old chalets. Her name was Carla and she was from Ramsgate. She was walking from Dover to Land's End for charity but was feeling exhausted and down. Amazingly, when I pointed at the odd buildings, she said that she'd stayed there in the 1970s when it was an Outward Bound camp for teenagers. This nice gutsy lady had walked around 200 miles, but now confided that she couldn't carry on much further, as she was missing her husband, her kids, and her dogs very much after three lonely weeks on the trail. She asked me how far it was to Land's End. I tried softening the blow by fibbing.

"It's a couple of hundred miles or so. About the same distance as you've done since Dover, so you're probably past the halfway stage now." It was more like 340. Instead of cheering her up, this news did the complete opposite. She started crying, saying she couldn't carry on. I put my arm around her shoulder and said, "Don't worry, it doesn't matter. You've done brilliantly already. 200 miles is no mean feat for anybody."

I thought to myself – in sympathy, not in a cruel way – that for a woman her size, 200 miles is a bleedin' miracle. It's true, she'd done exceptionally well. She blurted out that she was going to pack it in when she got to Weymouth, but the thing that upset her most was that she'd already collected the charity money in anticipation of finishing the walk. Now she wouldn't be able to face all the sponsors and her friends back home. I felt sorry for her, as she was a genuine person, but this kind of trip requires steely single-mindedness and the will to succeed at all costs. Nothing must be allowed to stand in the way of your goal as I'd learned myself over the past six weeks. It's easy for me to say this, as the difference between us was that she had a family who were dependent on her, and she on them, and they all missed each other terribly, whereas I was a single bloke who was comfortable with his own company – especially when ranting – and was walking to get away from people. Both he, and I, loved the solitude and the freedom, so it was a different ball game! I did miss my parents and sister, nephews and friends, but speaking to them every so often helped a lot. I didn't need to be with them. I tried cheering her up by acting the fool and she seemed a bit better by the time we parted company. I turned and waved to her before she disappeared down the hill.

Walking on, I was so glad I hadn't put myself in the stressful situation of doing my walk for charity. The pressure would've been enormous. Although I don't think I would've wilted under it, I may have driven myself on to the point of collapse because there would've been no way I could return home without succeeding no matter what, be it flu, pneumonia, agonising back pain, a broken bone, feet hanging off, or falling over a cliff. I'd walk until I dropped. I'm that type of person. If I say I'm going to do something I bloody well *do* it at all costs! Stubborn as hell, that's me, sometimes foolishly so.

The coastal views were stunning this afternoon, both over Weymouth and the Isle of Portland. In the other direction, past the chalk cliffs towards St Aldhelm's Head, the sea was a rich dazzling shade of ultramarine. The weather couldn't have been better. All was looking good for the end of the walk, which I guessed was a couple of days away, but I never liked speculating too much.

I arrived at Osmington Mills where I'd been looking forward to a pint in another of the more well-known coastal pubs, The Smugglers. This was another large thirteenth-century character inn situated in the most stunning location of any pub so far. After getting my pint I sat at a table outside to sip it, admiring the magnificent seascape spread out before me. The pub nestles down below the surrounding cottages and houses in its own little valley, an idyllic spot with a stream running down to the sea. The pub was once the home of the leader of the most notorious gang of smugglers in the area during the eighteenth and nineteenth centuries, namely Emmanuel Charles. The Charles family intermarried with the Seaward and Champ families who were also involved in smuggling activities. Emmanuel Charles was running the pub, alongside his smuggling, during the 1790s, but he also found time to make some additions to the building. A related family, also involved in smuggling, took over the running of the pub around 1840. Ann Champ was the first known of the family to run the pub. She was the landlady according to the 1841 census. By 1848 she'd passed it on to her son James Champ when the pub was known as the Crown. At some time it changed its name to the Picnic Inn before becoming the Smugglers Inn, as it is today. Perhaps Osmington's most famous visitor was the painter John Constable. He was a good friend of the Archdeacon John Fisher, rector of Osmington. Constable spent many holidays at the Vicarage. During his time here he painted many of his famous paintings including some of the village, Osmington Mills, Weymouth Bay, and Portland Bill. His best known painting of the area is *Weymouth Bay*, now hanging in the National Gallery, although it's actually a painting of Bowleaze Cove. I wondered if he painted the nice little car boot sale too.

It was busy on this sweltering Monday lunchtime. I guessed most tourists had made a beeline for the place, but as yet I wasn't hungry. If I had been I'd certainly have lost my appetite after seeing the prices on the menu! I decided not to hang around too long, so after getting my water bottles topped up by the chatty Aussie barmaid I lifted on the pack, which no doubt would've felt as light as a feather were it not for the entire gallon of water that I was now carrying. This is one of the main drawbacks of hot weather walking. I'd only been walking for forty minutes when I came to Ringstead Bay, which happened to have a great-looking beach café. Though I'd only covered 2 miles since The Smugglers, in this heat I wasn't going to miss out on an ice cream and another rest. I kicked myself for carrying the 8 lb. gallon of water when it hadn't been necessary after all. I still wasn't particularly hungry so apart from an ice lolly I bought an Oasis Citrus Fruits drink and a packet of good old-fashioned Eccles cakes for later. The pleasant lady and I got chatting about other old-fashioned sweets and cakes. I was careful not to bring up the subject of Snickers bars and their various sizes. Eventually we got on the subject of another blast from the past, which I immediately felt a strong craving for, but despite my pleading, the lovely lady didn't have any and hadn't seen them for years. What I was referring to, and now coveted was "Pontefract Cakes", those flat, round, chewy pieces of liquorice about the size of a £2 coin. I hadn't seen them since I was a lad. Where had they been for the last fifty years? Does anyone eat them in the twenty-first century and are they still produced? I must find out. I hoped this sudden craving didn't mean I was pregnant.

Being the only punter I sat down at a table to rest, wondering if a Pontefract Cake could possibly act as an emergency discus for a tiny midget, when a large woman of around sixty-five hobbled over on a Zimmer frame and asked if she could sit down. This was a bit strange considering half a dozen tables were empty, but I said it would be fine. She proceeded, in a thick Dorset dialect, to tell me about all her illnesses and operation, putting me off my Tangle Twister. Although I tried changing the subject, she wasn't going to be sidetracked.

"... then I had to have me gizzard removed and they thought I'd got gangrene in both me feet but it turned out to be an inverted heart so I'd another operation, me kidneys both went purple and yellow and had to come out ..." Two walkers arrived. They smiled and waved at me before going to the counter. The woman carried on: "My son's picking me up soon if I don't drop dead in the next five minutes, that is. I've got a terrible pain in me left arm now, and all up the front of me back too."

She continued in a woeful minor key. I'd had enough and decided to make a bolt for it.

I got up and said, "I hope you don't mind but some friends have arrived and it would be impolite for me to ignore them."

The poor lady replied with a sad, "Oh goodbye, you go off and enjoy yourself. I don't suppose I'll be around much longer but it's been lovely talking to you."

If that was "lovely" I dreaded to think what the alternative might have been. I walked over to the counter where I got chatting to the new arrivals. The first thing I asked them was whether they had any Pontefract Cakes. The chap immediately burst out laughing while the girl, aged about nineteen, stared at me blankly. We got chatting and it turned out they were father and daughter from Kent. They were walking the coast from South Haven Point to Exmouth with the intention of visiting his son who was at college there. The girl, named Jessie, was incredibly good-looking, along with being a lovely girl. She went straight to Number 1 in my "Most Attractive Woman of the Trip" charts and remained there for the duration. Her dad, whose name I didn't catch, was a really nice guy and it was fun chatting to them. Behind us, the old woman's son came to collect her. As he gently began escorting her back to his car, she tutted impatiently, shook him off, and strode speedily ahead, leaving him to carry her Zimmer frame and handbag! We laughed at the scenario after they'd left.

On the table in front of us was a huge water bottle, which must've weighed about 15 lbs. I asked who the unfortunate one was that had to carry it.

The dad pointed at Jessie, saying, "She does. It weighs nothing to her. She leaves me behind on the hills. I can't keep up with her."

It didn't really surprise me, as Jessie looked fit in every sense of the word. She was wearing sunglasses, but being fair-skinned she'd caught the sun quite badly on her bare arms and legs. She needed to rub some sun cream on pretty soon or she'd be in trouble. I would've gladly volunteered for the job but thought it best to keep quiet, as we were having such a good time. I didn't want them to think that I was a Murty Old Dan. On a more serious note they told me that the military firing ranges had closed last night for six weeks of manoeuvres. These ranges stretched along the coast for 8 miles between Lulworth Cove and Kimmeridge and inland too. They'd been lucky, as a soldier gave them permission to go through at the very last minute. Oh dear, I'd worried about this for some time but hadn't been aware of the actual closing date until now. It was going to be too late for me, leaving no option but to take a lengthy, awkward inland diversion. If only I hadn't chatted to quite so many people along the way and arrived here *one* day earlier I'd have been in time. Pork loin *pigs*, the army! You're all real *porky*! All right, very brave too, but still *porky*.

All too soon it was time to move on. We shook hands and went our separate ways. It was sad to think I'd never see them again. I often felt like this at partings. After another climb I was approaching an undulating 5-mile stretch of spectacular white cliff walking with a grassy path beneath my feet. It was terrific as I came first to White Nothe, Bat's Head and Swyre

Head, and finally the most amazing of the lot, Durdle Dor, the impressive large limestone arch that juts out dramatically into the sea. In these conditions it looked surreal. It consists of craggy white limestone, translucent with its light dusting of green moss, contrasting sharply with the ultramarine blue of the sea behind it. I took some photos as I stood rooted to the spot by the natural splendour of it. If it had been 9 p.m. I would've pitched the tent exactly where I was but it was far too early. After a drink of water and a quick breather I walked on. Quite a few picnicking families were on the sandy beaches below so I stayed on the top all the way. While I was resting at the bottom of one valley some white wispy sea mist came unexpectedly rolling in. Through it I spotted a small figure silhouetted against the sky on top of the cliff I'd descended. Watching, I saw a young man wearing camo army clothing jogging down the hill towards me. How could he do that in this heat?

Running past me, he smiled and said, "And now for the difficult bit!"

He was right, as I watched him run to the top the next cliff. He must've been in good shape to do that. The mist rolled out as quickly as it'd appeared. As I marched on towards Lulworth Cove I found myself singing 'Der-derr-derr-d-durrr, I wish that I was Jessie's Girl', the old Rick Springfield classic I'd always loved. It was a good example of early power pop, now having a new significance for me … sort of. I didn't wish that I was Jessie's *girl* so I'd to change the words to Jessie's *bloke*, which didn't sound right. I contented myself by simply humming the chorus with gusto instead, with a bit of air-mixed-with-walking-pole guitar thrown in for good measure doing the riff, romantic old fool that I was.

By 6.30 p.m. I descended the final hill, reaching the beautiful Lulworth Cove, which was surprisingly deserted. I guess all the tourists had returned to their lodgings for a meal. I found a café that was closing and persuaded them to flog me some leftover cheese and pickle, and chicken salad sandwiches, some of which I ate on the edge of the cove before deciding to get as far inland as I could, leaving less distance to cover tomorrow. Before beginning the inland trudge I went into the village pub to have a cool pint and a half-hour break. I could afford to take my time a bit more now that the evenings were getting longer. On the wall was a large map of the area showing my proposed route, the coast path, and the military firing ranges, which were much larger than anticipated. I tried studying the map and made a mental note of the difficult bits, but it was quite confusing. By missing out the coast I'd also be missing out the old lost village of Tyneham, which was requisitioned by the army in World War II for military use and never returned to the locals afterwards, despite promises that it would be. Some of the old buildings, including Tyneham church, still exist and can be visited by the public when the ranges are not in use. Pork tanks! There hadn't been too many disappointments so far but this was quite a blow, as I'd really looked forward to seeing what still remained of this village.

It was quiet but nice in the pub. I began to relax and feel weary so asked the landlord about B & Bs in case I couldn't get out of the village through sheer fatigue. He told me there were a few up the lane where I was heading but they may not be cheap. After a Herculean effort I pulled myself to my feet and staggered through the door. The pack had never felt heavier. It was a pleasant sunny evening though as I set off inland past the small chocolate-boxy cottages. One displayed a sign that read: "B & B £35." Feeling shattered, I thought about knocking, but common sense prevailed. I walked on, telling myself not to think about it. It's a fabulous evening. What could be better than sleeping under the stars tonight? Well, a luxurious en suite room with all the trimmings for a fiver would possibly be better. I walked the main road uphill for 2 miles. It skirted the perimeter of the military danger area, fenced off to my right, before turning right onto the B3070. I'd just remembered this from the map on the pub wall. I kept sticking to the road, passing Lulworth Castle, before nipping into a nearby pub to ask about camping.

The land where Lulworth Castle now stands was first acquired by Thomas Howard, son of the second Duke of Norfolk by him marrying one of the last of the de Newburgh family. Also acquired at this time was land at the Bindon Abbey Estate. In 1575 Queen Elizabeth made him Viscount Bindon. In the same year Thomas built a country house on the site of Bindon Abbey. He held high office at the time, including that of Vice Admiral of Dorset, and defender of the Dorset coast against smuggling and piracy. Thomas Howard was succeeded in 1582 by Henry, a nasty man who associated with pirates. He also ill-treated his wife. In the same year Henry's aunt died, leaving him the rest of the abbey estates. When the horrid Henry died, his nice brother Thomas inherited and re-established the de Newburgh deer park and built the Castle as a hunting lodge to host hunting parties for the King. Over the years, the castle has had numerous uses, occupants, and has had a colourful history. A number of significant events transpired at the Castle, like the devastating fire of 1929.

The pub was another one of those rural ones where everything goes silent when a stranger walks in, like in the film *High Noon*. The landlord was friendly enough though he couldn't help me at all. His customers, however, were gawping at me like vacant cows standing in a line at a five-bar gate. As I let the door close slowly behind me I could hear sniggering starting up.

Someone said, "Stupid f****** b******!"

I thought exactly the same about them too. I pressed on, walking north-east, hoping to find a nice spot for the tent well away from the road. I still hadn't seen anywhere suitable when I came to an open road barrier. Red signs were everywhere, displaying frightening statements like, "Danger Military", "Restricted Area", "Live Ammunition", and "Beware! Unexploded Bombs". I was unsure which way to go, as there were a few smaller roads going off at tangents to the main one. I worried that I may have already gone wrong somewhere after the pub. From here onwards the land on both sides was fenced off, thus only allowing passage along the road itself. This was terrible news for me, as if I continued I'd be trapped on the road with no obvious escape routes or camping spots, apart from on the tarmac road surface itself. Despite this I really had no option but to proceed. I thought hard, trying to decide on the best course of action. I remembered that old saying, "He who hesitates is lost", but as I took a step forward I thought about that other old saying, "Look before you leap"! Confused, my body took control and walked ahead under its own steam as my brain went into meltdown.

Entering the danger area I found myself muttering things like, "He who hesitates has a silver lining", "Too many cooks save nine", and "A stitch in time spoils the broth while the sun shines."

Next time I looked at my watch it was nearly 9 p.m. The shadows were lengthening and there was still no visible end to the restricted area. The road had become straight with high barbed wire fences on both sides and narrow verges. The occasional car flew by at high speed going where I hadn't got a clue. It was times like this when I wished I'd got a map. Though I'd just about managed on the coast without one, this inland walking was a different matter altogether. Panicking as twilight approached, I began running along the dead straight thoroughfare for all I was worth, yelping a bit, bordering on the verge of a tantrum. I couldn't spare the time or energy to have a proper raging one, so it'd have to wait until I'd found somewhere to camp and cheered myself up with a nice cup of tea, before treating myself to a tantrum! At the point of desperation I came to two tiny lay-bys, one on each side of the 15-foot-wide road. A 3-foot-wide grass verge was against the high fence about 6 feet from the road. I threw off the pack and fell down to get my breath before attempting to pitch the tent. As I lay there an expensive-looking red and white motorbike came roaring along the road at over 100 mph. It couldn't have been more than 4 feet from me as it raced by. This was going to be a scary night. A minute later it reappeared from the other direction. This time the guy pulled into the layby opposite and took out a mobile phone. Before he had time to switch it on I was asking him if he knew how far it was to the end of the restricted area.

Pointing, he replied, "It's up the road, 300 yards away by those trees. It ends there."

Thanking him profusely and extremely rapidly, I grabbed the pack and ran like the Devil up the road with the bewildered motorcyclist still watching me. As I ran I thought, If he's lying I'll swing for him, providing I can catch him. He was true to his word though. Sure enough, I came to an identical barrier and a load more warning signs, but this time I was leaving the restricted area. It was a great feeling to get out of there, but I still had to find somewhere quickly. I turned right into the first quiet-looking lane that crossed the main road and saw a sign stating, "Holme Lane". This was a tremendous relief. I hadn't gone wrong after all. This was where I was supposed to be. Much happier now, I hurried along with about fifteen minutes of twilight left. I came to a scattering of cottages and saw a bloke gardening by torchlight in the gloom. I asked if he knew anywhere I might be able to camp, such as his garden, but despite my obvious hinting he was about as much use as a cardboard hammer. He kept telling me that there was a campsite 4 miles away whilst pointing in the opposite direction! I tried explaining that this would entail me walking 4 miles in the wrong direction tonight and the same distance back in the morning. Besides that, it'd be pitch dark in ten minutes, but it didn't sink in. The man was obviously a fool.

He starting shaking his head glumly as I peppered him with quick-fire questions like, "What's the name of the village we're in now? How many beans make five?" He couldn't answer anything and crumbled uselessly in front of me.

Realising I wasn't going to get any sense out of him, and not wishing to appear like a Nazi interrogator any longer, I ran off pell-mell down the lane shouting, "Thanks for nothing, squire!"

I felt sorry for the poor bloke in retrospect and I hope I didn't spoil his otherwise peaceful evening too much. After all, the poor old devil couldn't help being thick. After a couple of hundred yards I spotted an overgrown field gateway to my left the 30 foot grassy track came off the lane swung round behind a high hedge parallel to it, making it quite secluded. It was very overgrown, meaning it hadn't been used by vehicles for some time. This was to be my home for the night. If I shouted loudly enough the poor old gardening chap would've heard me. I pitched the tent in the blackness hoping that nobody would see me and move me on. Suddenly I started itching, especially my bare arms and legs and around my exposed neck and temples. Midges! This was my first night away from the coast so I hadn't had to endure this awful kind of onslaught before. I tried to pitch as quickly as possible, but it all went wrong in the heat of the moment. It took forever before I was able to clamber inside and zip up the "no-see-um" midge-proof mesh door. I lit a small piece of my green insect repellent coil in case any of the little sods had got in with me. They'd already taken a few thousand chunks out of me during the ten minutes it took to pitch. My temples were throbbing with large itchy bumps forming on the delicate skin there. Not having any antihistamine cream with me, I took another Zirtec tablet, which would kill two birds with one stone – or two midges at least. I massaged some Avon Woodland Fresh skin lotion, or "Fred-land Whoosh" as I prefer to call it, into the worst affected areas. Woodland Fresh also acts as an insect repellent but I hadn't had enough time to locate it prior to being bitten. Apparently it was used in the Scottish Highlands by Mel Gibson and the entire cast of *Braveheart*. It's also a favourite among the angling fraternity and the SAS, as it contains no harmful chemicals such as Deet. Good old Greek George! I hadn't had one single bout of fever since I'd taken that Zirtec tab in Weymouth this morning. I was in the bag at 9.30

p.m. and lay in the dark, not using any artificial light for fear of prowlers, eating the remainder of my sandwiches with diluted orange juice. I must've dropped off around 10 p.m. but awoke on numerous occasions, feeling itchy and feverish, either sweating or freezing cold.

Day 51: Tuesday 3 June

I awoke – feeling bloody terrible, possibly the worst I'd felt *ever* – at 7.30 a.m. to the sound of the Timex. I groaned in misery as I turned over in the bag, realising I couldn't afford the luxury of a lie-in this close to the village. When I unzipped the tent flap I groaned. The sky was grey with darker rain clouds looming. I began scratching almost immediately so popped another Zirtec tab to ease the continual itching of the bites. It took me forever to pack away. I kept getting it all wrong, having to begin again. As I did so I wondered what horrors might lay ahead today. I reckoned there was about 20 miles to go until I reached Swanage. If I were to get there tonight that meant today would potentially be the penultimate day, leaving only 8 more miles to go before South Haven Point for the following morning: the *end*!

Although on paper, or in this case in my head, it was good news, that 20 miles may as well have been 200 with the way I felt. At that moment it seemed impossible. I should've felt ecstatic but instead felt grim, bedraggled, and stony-faced as I left, aiming for the coast at Kimmeridge. A total contrast to the previous morning when I'd left Weymouth in the sunshine, feeling great and full of the joys of spring. I turned right onto Dorey Farm bridleway before a railway bridge and followed the rough track across open ground towards some woods, not really knowing if it was correct. I needed a map now I was away from the coast. I found a sort of tumbledown garage-cum-workshop in the middle of nowhere. The guys inside, although surprised to see a live human, were helpful and said I was on the right path for the strangely-named Creech Road. A mile further down the track I came to a lone farmhouse, which may or not have been Dorey Farm. I never found out. I decided to ask again and maybe get some water at the same time. As I came to the gate I was greeted by two angry farm dogs who ran towards me, barking fiercely, baring their teeth. Luckily they stopped about 15 feet from me, guarding their patch. I called out but received no reply. I decided to risk getting bitten or killed and went into the farmyard. The dogs backed away. I knocked loudly on the door. Nothing. Nobody was home. How could they all be out on a Tuesday bloody morning? The dogs had thankfully calmed down a bit now. One of them came over to have his old head patted. I called across to the younger one who was still staring, snarling, and bristling with rage.

"Look, yer fool! *He* knows I'm no threat, so what's the matter with *you*, you silly boy?"

He momentarily quietened down but once I walked away, into the woods, he started up again, ensuring he saw me off properly. Once in the dense woodland my heart sank. Surely this couldn't be right. There wasn't a proper path to stick to. I kept going all the same, but panic started setting in. As I went deeper and deeper into the woods I began shouting for help at the top of my voice, in the faint hope that a woodsman, gamekeeper, or topless model may hear me and come to my rescue. The yelling became even more panic-stricken, especially after sinking up to my knees in a marsh, but it wasn't a Jodie Marsh! I feared I'd never get out of that jungle alive, but fifteen minutes later, still shrieking at top volume, I came out into a clearing where, right in front of me, stood a large half-built house with six large builders standing in a row, trowels in their hands, looking nervously in my direction. They'd heard me approaching for quite a while. This time it was too late to pretend that someone else was responsible for the baleful racket. Caught red-handed, I couldn't be bothered to lie by saying something inane about the wildlife sounding wonderful today.

Instead I simply blurted out despairingly, "Does anyone know where the **** Creech Road is?"

Obviously relieved that I hadn't pulled out an M16 and gunned them all down, the leader said, "Yeah it's over there, mate, just 30 yards away."

I replied very meekly: "Oh right. Thanks."

I couldn't believe my eyes when I saw a sign five seconds later that read, "Creech Road". I'd been right all along but unfortunately hadn't had the courage of my own convictions. Turning right and walking down hateful Creech Road, I couldn't have blamed those builders if they'd decided to have a good laugh at my expense, but I heard nothing. They were obviously a pleasant bunch of blokes, different from that horrid crowd in the pub last night who'd disrespected me for no reason.

There was light drizzle as I trudged the many ups and downs of the tree lined wooded road. The pack was really hurting, particularly my shoulders. I was exhausted and as miserable as sin. I guessed I was walking south at last as I passed the stately pile known as "Creech House". The firing ranges were on my right again, but I'd no idea how long it'd be before I'd hit the coast at Kimmeridge Bay. The road went forever up until I came out near a huge layby, boasting a viewpoint on the top of the Purbeck Ridge. I looked over a large rural valley with more hills on the opposite side, all of which I'd have to traverse before reaching the coast. It was only 10.30 a.m. and I was wiped out already. The drizzle had eased and at least the next bit was downhill. I gamely attempted to speed up a bit when heading in the direction of that famous landmark Corfe Castle, which I never glimpsed.

Before the final climb the path passed through the farmyard at Steeple Leaze Farm. Here I encountered the farmer who allowed me to fill my bottle from the outdoor tap. Once again the water tasted fantastic. Several old caravans were parked in one field, half hidden behind a hedge. I wondered if I should ask the farmer if I could sleep inside one of them for a few hours, as I could barely keep my eyes open. The water woke me up for a while as I splashed it onto my face before setting off uphill to the top of the ridge. When I reached the top I could see Kimmeridge Bay and the coast a mile or so below but saw no obvious way of getting there. There didn't seem to be any direct route. I slumped into another fit of depression. I picked my way down with the aid of the guidebook, but the book was confusing. It listed complex "alternative routes" that seemed to constantly intertwine. In the end I didn't know if I was coming or going. I walked in every direction possible but still couldn't find a way through to the coast. I was nearing rock-bottom when I spotted an elderly couple and grabbed them before they vanished. They were most helpful though I couldn't hide my general grumpiness from them. They still patiently directed me down a track that would take me to Kimmeridge. They said a café was open in the village, giving me a fresh glimmer of hope. I needed a hot meal. I hadn't had one since breakfast at the Double Three the previous morning. Eventually I found the village, went straight to the café, only to find it closed. The village, which had about as much life in it as fossilised dodo, was devoid of any signs of human activity. What else could anyone expect in any tiny place like this on a drizzly Tuesday morning?

A bit further down the road I found a grocers where, in the absence of any hot food, I bought myself a pike paw (change it round yourself. I'm too tired), a ram hole (and again), two shortbread biscuits, and an Oasis drink. After eating some of it outside whilst studying the guidebook I went back in again and bought another roll and a pile of chocko bars as it looked like I'd be passing no further habitation on the coast path to Swanage. There'd be no hot meal or a warming cup of tea for me today. Serving in the shop was a huge ugly lummox of a bloke with a personality the exact opposite, but he still managed to annoy me without it all the same. Obviously not a real shopkeeper, he was about 6 feet 11, weighing 40 stone, with milk-bottle glasses, and he knew absolutely *nothing*. He made the torchlight gardener from last night look like Albert Einstein. He didn't know any prices for the items I'd bought. I had to point out his own price tickets to him. This really baffled him. I also had to do the adding up, as after five minutes of trying, he hadn't made any progress. I asked if he'd lived in the area long.

He said, "Yes, all my life."

I made the big mistake of asking, "In that case can you tell me how far it is to Swanage by way of the coast path?"

The farmer had told me this morning it was 10-12 miles by road, so I'd a rough idea it must be somewhere in between 15 and 20 miles via the coast.

His reply, however, was, "I think it's about 2 miles."

All his life? All his bloody life and he knew *nothing*! F*** *all*! I left in disgust. After having a quick wash in the village gents' I set off in search of the elusive coast path. Although I could see the choppy grey sea a mile away, I still got lost six times before finally arriving at 1 p.m. in Kimmeridge Bay, in an evil mood. The only person in sight was a uniformed coastguard-type chap who told me that the forecast wasn't good.

I groaned, speaking angrily, as if it were all his fault: "This is hell! I'm sick of this damn walk and I hate this place too! What a dump!"

He didn't say much but reckon he thought I was a bit weird. As I began the inevitable climb it started raining again, but I'd spotted a sort of "Leaning Tower of Kimmeridge" at the top of Hen Cliff. I figured that if could get up there without getting soaked to the skin I'd be able to shelter in it. I toiled away at the 300-foot incline as the rain got heavier. When I arrived at the top, the stupid derelict tower was fenced off with a big sign that read: "Keep Out! Building in Danger of Collapse". I blamed the fool who built the faulty thing in the first place. The tower looked like it was about to collapse into the sea, which, though I hated the thing for being fenced off, would be a sad end for it. I've learned since that the tower was saved by dismantling it and "re-mantling" it 80 feet further inland where it'll be let as a holiday home to recoup some of the huge costs of the operation.

Anyway, with no place to shelter from the rain I almost went berserk, but controlled myself, as I needed all my strength. I felt done in by this time. I hurried along the cliff edge through the rain without seeing another soul, praying it was a long shower, but to my dismay I found myself wading through chest-high long grasses upon which grew numerous chest-high nasty flowers. Their pollen was coming off all over my clothing and filling the air around me. I couldn't prevent breathing in the clouds of yellow dust. I was simmering with rage. After a couple of minutes I was yellow from head to toe. The rain started pelting down, mixing with the pollen, forming a beige-brown sticky sludge that became glued to me, forming a vile one-piece bodysuit. Being drenched through it was also pointless trying to put the waterproofs on. This is *not* what walking is all about, I told myself, and myself agreed. To add to this, the out-of-control Nasty Notemares invaded my brain, making all rational thought impossible. The swirling Celtic cacophony made me feel giddy. Where was Andy Stewart when I needed saving from the bagpipes? Being Scottish he would've known how to stop them. It'd been a pig of a day, with virtually everything going wrong, like rowing the *Titanic* through a sea of giant-sized Snickers bars and tall dwarfs. It was probably the worst day of the whole trip and it was getting worse by the minute. I finally snapped when a gust of wind lifted my soaking Tilley hat clean off my head and deposited it 20 yards away in taller pollen-y grass. After retrieving the offending article and getting more sludge all over me I ran to the edge of the cliff and screamed at the top of my voice whilst frantically waving my arms out to sea.

"You ****** ********! You all think you can get me, don't you? Well I'm here to tell you that you f****** well *cant*! You're all a bunch of b******, the lot of yer! I hate yer f****** guts and that thick lummox from the shop too! You won't get me! I'm too f****** smart for f***** scum like you! Ha, ha, ha, ha! I'll be in ******* Swanage tonight, but you won't! You'll never get the better of *me*, so why don't you all f*** off big-time! Ha, ha, ha, ha!"

I was cackling like a fruitcake the whole time. It was a loud rant and by far the longest and most articulate one. I felt great letting it all burst out unfettered. It was most cathartic, I must say! Once it was out of my system I walked on refreshed. I wondered later how a psychiatrist might have viewed this.

Anyway, I hadn't gone 10 yards, and the Devil can strike me down if I'm lying, when I saw, cowering on her knees in the long grass, a frail-looking girl of about twenty, with her frail ginger hair tied back in a frail bun, and a *very* pale frail face. This didn't surprise me one bit after the verbal tirade she'd been forced to witness at close range. She appeared to be some kind of student, judging by the clipboard lying on the ground, while she clutched a jam jar in one hand and some sort of spatula in the other. As she looked up at me with terror in her eyes, I smiled faintly, still twitching, and asked her idiotically if she was collecting butterflies. How the hell could anyone collect butterflies with a spatula in a gale? Maybe they could smear it with superglue and wave it wildly about, hoping for the best. I felt more stupid after asking this but what else could I have said? Without giving anything away she simply nodded her head as she slowly edged further back into the long grass to get away from me. I couldn't think of anything else constructive to say that might ease the situation.

I muttered, "See you, then," and walked past her.

I imagined her thinking to herself, Not if I see you first, you psycho! I must admit I felt embarrassed, but unable to turn back time, I'd have to live with it.

If she'd known what sort of day I'd been having she might possibly have said, "Good on yer, son! Better out than in."

I couldn't imagine her saying anything like that though, as she was far too frail. It began raining heavily but I didn't really care anymore. "They" were not going to stop me from getting to the end now, no matter what manner of rubbish "they" threw at me. Already wet through, I rummaged for the waterproofs and put on them over my dripping clothing. Talk about horses and stable doors. The terrain was as "severe" as any I'd covered and the rain made everything more slippery and difficult. The Notemares were back with a vengeance, putting the rat-flavoured icing on the hideous, poisonous, inedible, and unpalatable cake! At one point I felt so weary that I began looking for a sheltered spot to try and pitch the tent so I could kill myself in peace once inside it. Such was the state of the sodden ground, I feared I'd lose my concentration and slip over the edge of the vertical cliffs, and tumble to my death on the rocks below. Bring it on! This wasn't the normal kind of weariness that I'd become accustomed to. This was a real leaden heaviness. It felt like I was on some kind of strong drug. I realised that I *was*! It was those damn Zirtec tablets! I'd taken three tablets in the twenty-four hours since buying them. I'm afraid "good old" Greek George was wrong. The accumulative affect *had* made me drowsy – drunkenly drowsy – but it'd taken several hours to kick in. When I realised this it gave me some comfort, as there was now a very good reason why I felt like death. I managed to stay awake somehow. I think the cold wind helped by blasting icy sea spray into my face every five seconds.

I passed above Chapman's Pool, which, in more clement weather, would've been beautiful from a walking perspective, but it was impossible to appreciate today. I gritted my teeth and carried on, having to divert frustratingly inland to avoid dangerous sections of coast before turning due south at last for St Aldhelm's Head, also known as St Alban's Head – take your pick. After what seemed like an eternity I arrived there and headed straight for the ancient chapel, situated on its tip, shrouded in sea mists. Apart from wanting to look inside it I also wanted to get out of the weather for a while. I'm sure old St Aldhelm (or St Alban) wouldn't have minded if he'd been in, though I would've had to ask him which of his two similar and confusing names was the real one in order to avoid any future confusion!

The chapel, at around 20 feet square, is in the parish of Worth Matravers. The architecture is Norman in style. There's an interesting legend associated with it, saying that in 1140 a bride and groom were sailing around the headland, watched by the bride's father, when a storm arose. The boat capsized and both were drowned. The devastated father is said to have built the chapel in their memory. A light was always kept burning to warn other seafarers. Whether this story is true or not, most authorities accept that this vaulted building was some kind of chantry. After falling into ruin the chapel was restored in the nineteenth century, after which it re-opened in 1874. Inside the square chapel it was rather gloomy, but there was a simple peace and beauty about the place. If it'd been 9 in the evening I would've had no qualms about kipping down for the night. I sat on a wooden pew for several minutes rest and reflection before leaving the chapel for the cliffs once more.

I met with a pleasant couple who were around my own age. They had a beautiful Border collie that was football mad! At first the dog sat quietly at our feet as we chatted but the woman soon illustrated the point by saying "David Beckham" in the dog's direction. He sprang to his feet and faced us, barking excitedly. It was fantastic! He soon sat down again but the moment anyone said "David Beckham", no matter how quietly, he was up again, barking. First a pipe-smoking doggie, now a football-mad pooch. What next? The funny little episode lifted my spirits as I set off again.

After half an hour I encountered an upper-class lady with her son of about thirty-five. When I asked if they knew of any cafés near the path, the lady looked horrified, answering haughtily.

"No, thank you very much. We locals don't want any nasty establishments spoiling our beautiful coastline."

I couldn't resist ribbing her by saying, "I agree, but it would be nice to have the occasional one, maybe every quarter mile or so; nothing ostentatious. Perhaps a chain of small tastefully-built MacDonald's on the cliff tops. It would be nice for all the holidaymakers, especially their kids wouldn't it?"

Her severe expression said it all, while her son smiled knowingly. I got the feeling he quite liked seeing his rather superior mother lightly teased. There was no more rain but I couldn't believe the severity of the terrain. I thought Dorset would be easy and gentle. In some places I was scrambling up almost vertical slopes, using my hands to hang on to the ground and pull myself up. It was more akin to rock climbing than walking and was extremely energy-sapping.

As I was walking through a valley towards one such perpendicular cliff I looked up and saw a strange-looking man standing on the top facing me. He appeared to be furtively watching something to his left and hadn't noticed me. I thought he may be a birdwatcher, as he seemed to quickly duck and dive behind rocks, before emerging seconds later, resuming looking furtively to his left. As I got closer, however, I spotted two female walkers about 30 yards away in the direction he was looking. I don't know why but there was something very shifty about him. I half wondered if he was stalking them. When I got nearer and began climbing towards him, he looked down and saw me. Judging by his body language I could tell he wasn't happy. I saw the women a few hundred yards away. I felt relieved, as they seemed to be out of any potential danger. With them gone, his gaze seemed to focus on me. His staring made me uneasy. I felt his eyes boring into the top of head. I'd no choice but to keep on climbing, as I could see no alternative "path" up the cliff face. When I was about 30 feet from the top he turned and vanished. It was with great apprehension that I pulled myself over the edge in case he was hiding with the intent of committing some wicked act, possibly with an axe.

There was a deeply-rutted forestry track on the top, running in a northerly direction inland along the partially wooded cliff, but I couldn't see anyone lurking. I gingerly made my way along the track towards the next section of path. I heard the loud roaring sound of an engine and turned in time to see a beaten-up Land Rover racing towards me from out of nowhere. I flung myself off the track in the nick of time. It sped by bouncing wildly up and down over the bumps. I managed to glimpse the maniac driver. It was the same guy going hell for leather. Whether it was a coincidence or whether he'd deliberately aimed for me I'll never know, but it was a very unnerving experience. I was glad to get back to open ground and to the proper coast path again. I kept a look out but never saw him again.

A mile further on I saw four smiling guys walking towards me equipped with all the appropriate wet weather gear. I told them they were the first people I'd spoken to for six hours. We chatted about the area. They said Swanage was about 6 miles away. Although the news cheered me up slightly, it still meant I'd over two hours to go. It was almost impossible to average 3 mph on this kind of torturous terrain in these conditions. The guys, on the other hand, were almost at the end of their day walk, so were about to head inland to the pub. They asked if I fancied a pint. I did but when I found out it was a mile uphill I declined. To my dismay they said the pub was the famous Square and Compass at Worth Matravers, one of the three "must visit" pubs along the SW Coast Path. I'd already done the others, namely the Tinners arms at Zennor and the Smugglers at Osmington Mills, but I'm afraid this one was beyond me now. All I could focus on was getting to Swanage and getting into a bed – not my tent, but a bed; any bed! I'd have to come back another time and visit the Square and Compass. We all shook hands and I watched them set off up the gentle incline towards Worth Matravers and a heavenly pint –lucky sods.

It was back to the grindstone for me. Although I no longer felt at death's door, I certainly wasn't myself. I was Napoleon. Whichever way I looked at the situation I had to admit that these remaining 6 miles would be gruelling and horrific. They proved far worse than that. Zombie-like, I trudged and stumbled onwards up down, up down, up down, with the ascents and descents getting ever steeper. I was staggered by this. Dorset was supposed to be easier not harder. At one point, exhausted yet again, I stopped and leaned heavily on my pole. I peered down to the sea, thinking something funny going on. Either the cliffs were getting higher or the sea was getting lower. I felt for the all the walkers who'd decided to do the SW Coast Path the other way round, starting at Swanage, thinking it'd be a more gentle start. I'd say these cliffs were tougher than their corresponding counterparts around the Minehead area where I'd started.

I tried singing songs to take away the pain but with my mind and body being numb it was hard to think of anything else. Eventually I came to a series of steps that, as mentioned before, are the pits when it comes to ascents, requiring massive reserves of energy to climb. There must've been three or four sets of them. In one ascent alone I counted a crippling 204 steps. Amazingly, I only had to rest once at about step number 100. If this had been six weeks ago, I would've stopped at least twenty times, i.e. every ten steps. In spite of everything that was dogging my progress, I must've been incredibly fit to be able to do this, giving me fresh heart.

I met an elderly walker who'd started from South Haven Point the previous morning. He was finding the going tough and was already thinking about packing it in! He'd had trouble with wet quicksand near Studland and had kept sinking into it. I didn't like the sound of that. I'd be there tomorrow. It was 6 p.m. when I passed Dancing Ledge and Blacker's Hole from where I could see a lighthouse with its regularly intermittent flashing beam a mile ahead of me. It gave me a warm comforting feeling, as it must've done for many seafarers during its lifetime. I was running out of steam after walking over 20 of the toughest miles of the journey. With the Notemares easing, I removed the pack and sat down beside the lighthouse for a well-earned rest. The sky looked more promising now that it didn't really matter anymore! I'd only got 2 more miles to walk. After five minutes I rose and carried on.

I met two Aussie walkers and we had a quick chat. Immediately afterwards I met another two. To cap it all another four Aussies appeared. Where were they all coming from? I reasoned that Swanage must be where the tunnel directly from Adelaide comes out. I passed near the famous Tilly Whim caves. They'd have to wait till next time. I soon came to Durlston Head where I swung a left before climbing past the signs for Durlston Country Park. I was slightly concerned now, unsure if I'd have to walk miles of bays or inlets before arriving at Swanage itself. I stopped two identically cloned old ladies with white perms and glasses (why do they all do it?), who I saw walking nearby. I gently interrogated them about cafés, directions, and B & Bs. The former were all closed except for the town of Swanage but they came up with the name of a B & B for me, run by one of their friends. I jotted the name and number down, thanked them, and made for Swanage, which they told me wasn't going to be difficult to find. They were as good as their word and as I rounded the side of a green suburban hill I got my first view, across a park, of Swanage below. It looked beautiful. The sun was shining on it too! I walked down a long road of smart terraced Georgian and Victorian houses in the newly arrived evening sunshine and into the town centre. I was starving but first I'd more important fish to fry. I went into a phone box, took the guidebook out, and flicked through the B & B section for probably the last time. I tried a couple of sixteen quidders first but got no reply. An eighteen quidder was also full up, so I was forced to move right up the price scale to twenty whole quid! A nice-sounding lady answered. She'd got a vacancy. I booked the room and asked for directions. Imagine my dismay when she told me she was situated near Durlston Head from where I'd just walked! I was gutted and couldn't face walking right back up that long hill.

The disappointment obviously showed in my voice, as she immediately said, "Do you want me to come and collect you in the car? You can give me a pound extra for petrol if that's okay with you?"

I couldn't complain at £1, so said, "Brilliant! Thank you."

I had a bit of a brainwave and asked her to give me an hour so I could have a hot meal in Swanage by way of celebration. She agreed. Looking round for a suitable meeting place, I spotted the nearby Purbeck Arms Hotel, and said I'd be outside on the pavement at 8 p.m. I called Mum and Dad who were amazed at my rapid progress over the last few days. I told them I could possibly be home the following evening, though I hardly dared believe it. All done and dusted, I went in search of sustenance, but after 2 whole yards was worn out again, so I ended up in the Purbeck Arms Hotel. I had the place all to myself and ordered roast beef with all the trimmings, banoffee pie with cream, and a pint of bitter. Whilst waiting for it to arrive, I reflected on the day's walking, which I'd say had definitely been in the Top 3 of my "most difficult day" charts. I was so glad it was over at last. I'd now walked 622 miles but still had another 8 to go in the morning. Believe it or not, I still wasn't confident that I'd be able to make it, such was the state of my mental and physical exhaustion. The meal was good, but halfway through an old familiar tune emanated from the TV in the corner. I immediately thought, Oh no! Please not *that!*" It was the theme from bloody *Emmerdale Farm*! During the past six weeks I'd managed to escape from almost all the bad TV habits that I'd acquired over the years. I hadn't missed the programmes one bit, but now here they were being shoved right in my weather-beaten face. I asked the barman if I could switch it off and he said okay. Truth be known, I lost interest in *Emmerdale Farm* when Kathy emigrated to Australia years ago.

I had another celebratory pint before going outside to wait for my ride. As I stood there I began nodding off and had to keep shaking my head to keep awake. At 8 on the dot a car pulled up. A lady leaned over, opening the passenger door. I got in and liked her straight away. Her name was Jane. She was younger than me and had a shock of really wild hair that I couldn't help complementing her on. She said she lived in a smart block of flats and if we saw anyone on the way in I must pretend to be a friend of hers, and definitely *not* a walker at all costs. She explained that the other residents didn't like the idea of loads of unfamiliar people continually coming and going. They'd been complaining about it at residents' association meetings, maintaining that it was also against the rules. Jane was probably going to leave Dorset soon. She needed to raise some cash, so was flaunting these rules by advertising in the SW Coast Path guidebook. It made me feel slightly uncomfortable, but I had to go along with it and hope for the best. The only thing that concerned me was that I may end up on the street and have to start looking again if a row broke out. When we arrived minutes later I could see what she meant. It was a fine art deco block of flats, quite upmarket. As we made our way up the stairs to her flat we of course bumped into two residents coming out of their flats.

Jane addressed them confidently saying, "Hello, this is a very good friend of mine who'll be staying over. His name is, erm, erm, erm ..." Her voice petered out pathetically.

Being quick on the uptake, I stepped in and politely said to them, "It's Overend, pleased to meet you. You must excuse my friend, erm, erm ..."

She stepped to save *me* this time: "It's Jane."

"Yeah, that's it! *Jane's* had a long day and we haven't seen each other for ages, have we, erm, *Jane?*"

I don't think we fooled anyone. Apart from me carrying a massive wet camo rucksack, a camo shoulder bag, and a fully extended walking pole, I was unshaven, scruffy, covered in yellow-y brown pollen-y sludge and mud I doubted they would've believed anyone would visit an old friend in this bedraggled state. They were civil but I got the feeling that the issue probably along with several more similar ones, would be raised at the next residents' meeting. Poor old Jane. The flat was lovely inside, quite large spread out over one floor. It also had fine sea views from most of the rooms After depositing my gear in my spacious en suite room, at Jane's invitation

I went and sat on the living room sofa while she proceeded to open a bottle of red wine and put on some relaxing music. It was warm in the room and after a glass or two I felt myself dropping off again, despite the interesting conversation. She told me quite a bit about Swanage. She also knew the coast path pretty well being a jogger herself and extremely fit as a result. When I told her about the awful stepped cliffs she grimaced.

When I specifically mentioned the one with 204 steps she said, "That's the one we call 'The Beast'!"

I laughed as it was such a fitting description of the nightmare cliff. We chatted about music, literature, maritime history, fun-sized Snickers bars, and eventually I told her I'd been slightly disappointed at being too tired to visit the Square and Compass at Worth Matravers on the way. As she opened another bottle of wine she told me we could go up there if I was up to it. It wasn't far away by taxi and there'd probably be live music on. Unfortunately I wasn't up to it and could barely keep my eyes open. I declined her kind offer, which was a real drag. I managed to hang on for a while but by 10.30 p.m., with red wine still flowing, adding to my weariness, I was forced to knock it on the head and turn in. It'd been a lovely relaxing evening. Jane was great company too.

As I got up to say goodnight she placed her hand on my arm and said warmly, "Is there anything I can do to help you sleep?"

I wasn't quite sure how to take this, so smiled and said, "No, not really. I'm almost out on my feet already."

As I climbed into the comfortable double bed I wondered what she'd had in mind to help me sleep and whether or not I was looking a gift horse in the mouth. Or had I merely got the wrong end of the riding crop? But surely she hadn't meant cocoa? Before I could dwell on it though I was out for the count.

Day 52: Wednesday 4 June, THE FINAL DAY

I awoke to the appetising aroma of frying bacon that I presumed was going to be mine. It was 7.50 a.m. and I'd slept right through. As a result, I felt great for the first time since Minehead! Not to add any insult to any injury whatsoever, when I flung back "the Lionels", the sunlight came pouring in and it was a beautiful summer's morning. Wow, what a result! I was so grateful. I'd been dreading having to finish the walk off in depressing rain and gales. For the last couple of days I'd toyed with the idea of staying in Swanage an extra night, if the weather had been atrocious, to give myself some chance of finishing in the sun. Of course, this could have been very hit and miss and it would've cost me at least another £30-£40, which I couldn't afford, but all was looking good now. Apart from that I also had a strange feeling of excitement and anticipation, knowing I'd reach the end today, barring a disaster! After showering and washing the pollen-y mess out of my clothes I sauntered down for breakfast at 9 a.m. – a far more civilised hour than I'd been used to at other B & Bs. The food was delicious. Jane had really pushed the boat out by going out while I was still asleep to buy fresh mushrooms. The previous evening she'd asked me if I minded not having mushrooms as she hadn't got any. I'd told her I wasn't fussy and not to worry about it. But no, she'd decided I was going to have my mushrooms at all costs, so she'd made the effort to go and get them. It was beyond the call of duty in my eyes. What a lovely gesture from a lovely lady! We chatted over breakfast and she said an estate agent was coming round to value the flat. Would I mind pretending to be a friend again, rather than a paying guest? It was no skin off my already peeling nose. When he arrived I went into "friend" mode, which entailed me hiding my rucksack in the wardrobe and swanning around her Swanage flat doing anything I fancied without asking for permission, making it look authentic. I slobbed out on the sofa with my feet up on that coffee table, flicking round the channels nonchalantly, before you could say "Nescafe Gold Blend". I may have overdone it slightly, as he seemed to think we were an item. After he'd gone Jane was quite cheerful, as he'd told her that her flat was worth about £50,000 more than she'd thought.

I said, "How about giving me 25,000 grand seeing as you've made a profit and we'll both be happy!"

After drinking half a dozen more coffees and chatting for another half-hour it was time to say goodbye, which was very sad, with much hugging going on. I sort of wished it had rained after all so I could've had a pleasant day off looking around Swanage, and maybe make it to the Square and Compass too, but I couldn't afford to waste the glorious weather. At one point Jane offered to drive to South Haven point with my rucksack to save me carrying it, and wait for me to arrive, but I said that after 622 miles I wouldn't feel right without it on the final leg. How stupid can one man be? I took a bit of video of us saying goodbye. At 11.30 a.m. I walked out of the door, almost forgetting to pay in the "moat of the heament", and back downhill again into Swanage. It'd been a delightful stay. I liked the smart little town greatly and resolved to return sometime in the future and check it out properly. In the meantime I picked up a couple of leaflets and sat on a bench reading in the sun for ten minutes. I still felt good so didn't take a Zirtec tablet. I'd rather risk getting the fever than feeling like a zombie at the finish line. I wanted to be 100 per cent for that so I could savour the moment. I still wasn't convinced I'd get there, as anything could happen during those remaining miles. When I got to the beach I bought a few last-minute postcards before walking out to Peveril Point, back along the coast, past several old buildings, sheds, and the old Victorian pier before turning north along the prom and out of the town, making a mental note to return and do the place properly one day.

Once past the built-up area I was on the long sandy beach with low cliffs. Jane told me to look out for the wooden steps that would lead me back up onto the coast path, but as I walked past all the groynes I couldn't see any way up off the beach. After a mile or so the familiar panic of being lost began setting in. Before flipping my lid though, I spotted the old flight of steps ahead and breathed a sigh of relief, not wanting anything to go wrong today of all days. Up the steps and a right turn brought me on the grassy coast path again aiming first for Ballard Point. I climbed easily now, despite the long ascent, pausing only to look back over Swanage Bay and take a couple of pictures before continuing up to Ballard Cliff Ballard Down. The views were beautiful looking out to sea.

I was feeling very cheerful now, knowing that virtually all the climbing was over. Above me and to my left was a low ridge about 50 yards away, so I walked up to the top of it to see what was the other side. The views from the top took my breath away more so than those from Start Point. The main reason for this was that from my elevated position I could see the lot. As I looked down the green slope to the north I could see the full sweep of Studland Bay, with its golden dunes and beach shimmering in the midday sun, with the dazzling blue sea to the east. At the end of that beautiful golden sandy curve, 4 miles away, I could clearly discern South Haven Point, my final destination, with the spit of land known as Sandbanks almost touching it. I felt a strong wave of emotion well-up inside me as I stared, almost in disbelief, at the most welcome sight I'd ever seen in my life; the sight I'd been waiting to see for seven weeks. It was now within my reach. The End!

I looked to the north-east and saw the famous old chalk stacks known as "Old Harry" less than half a mile away down the slope. Beyond them, across the bay, was the resort of Bournemouth and the low cliffs of Hengistbury Head. Further round again, Milford-on-Sea and finally, looming out of the sunshine, the Needles and the fabulous Isle of Wight. It's believed that Old Harry and his "wife" were once connected to The Needles on the Isle of Wight. They also form the eastern end of the Jurassic Coast World Heritage Site, which is the Cretaceous bit. The Old Harry stacks are chalk with some bands of flint that have been gradually reduced over the centuries. Some of the earlier stacks having fallen while new ones have been formed by the breaching of narrow isthmuses. Poor Old Harry's original "wife" crumbled into the sea in 1896, so he's got a new one for the present. Legend has it that the Devil had a sleep on the rocks, which led to the old euphemism of the Devil being called "Old Harry". That Devil certainly crops up a lot all the way round the SW Coast Path, but I never saw him once, thank God! Another possible source of the name is that the rocks were named after a famous Poole pirate Harry Paye, who used to stash his contraband nearby.

As I walked down towards Old Harry looking at the distant coastline ahead, it felt odd to think that I wouldn't be walking it. I'd got so used to looking ahead to the next range of cliffs, wondering what would be in store for me when I got there, but now I wasn't going to be climbing them. I felt kind of sad in a way, which was daft, as I'd dreaded and hated every single climb of the walk. Several people began appearing, wandering about on the grass above the stacks. They were mostly tourists or hikers sightseeing on this glorious day. As I strode in their direction, some of them hello to me, others asked if I was walking the SW Coast Path. I confirmed I was.

Before I knew it they were calling out to each other: "Hey! This guy's walked the whole of the South West Coast Path and is about to finish!"

A small crowd gathered round me, slapping me on the back, all wanting to shake my hand. It was a real surprise. I was quite moved, taken aback by their enthusiasm and genuine sincerity. It was like being a minor celebrity, basking in the glory, and for a while I had a bunch of about twenty people walking beside me, asking questions, offering encouragement. I felt like The Pied Piper except my faithful followers were affable human beings and thankfully not scary rodents. It was a special impromptu moment and couldn't have been any more magical or beautiful if the whole thing had been orchestrated. We reached the beach at Studland together where there was a café and pub. Despite numerous invitations to buy me a pint, I told everyone I had to press on, being anxious to finish. As I said goodbye to the assembled throng, a spontaneous round of applause broke out, bringing a lump to my eye and a tear to my throat!

It also prompted me to say, "Hang on, folks, I haven't made it yet. Don't forget the old proverb, 'There's many a slip 'twixt cup and lip'."

Everyone laughed as I waved goodbye, setting off to cries of, "You'll do it, no problem! You're as good as there already!" and other shouts of encouragement. One comment was rather more ominous though. Someone called: "You'd better watch your back near those dunes or you'll be sorry."

I thought of the old gentleman from yesterday who sunk into the quicksand, so I presumed that the statement must've referred to that particular danger. In the sheer joy of it all I'd forgotten I still had about 3 miles to go, so I was alone with my thoughts again. I hurried along the beach on the harder damp sand near the water's edge to avoid sinking in. There was a 3-foot-wide strip of it where the tide was going out. What a bit of luck, as struggling through energy-sapping soft sand in this heat would've been a real downer at this stage. The end of the curve was now visible. I could feel the excitement building. It should take about half an hour from here. I noticed dunes were appearing to my left about 40 yards away. Looking over to them, squinting, I discerned some figures appearing to be naked. Needless to say they were all men! I stopped to check the guidebook. This was the notorious Studland Naturist Beach. I'd heard about it, but it'd slipped from my memory. I hoped it wasn't going to spoil the end of the walk. My worst thoughts were confirmed when I came to a sign that read: "Naturists may be seen beyond this point". I thought the wording was most odd. It suggested that the general public were in a privileged position by being generously allowed to view the said naturists as if they were animals in an enclosure. I'd hardly passed the sign when I noticed that both the sand dunes and beach were swarming with them. I'd no choice but to step over a load of naked old blokes who were lolling about, literally letting it all hang out before my eyes! It's strange how there're never any women around. One guy was posing so blatantly on the path that I had to walk in the sea to pass without brushing against the big brinzely bronzer! Afterwards I was irritated to find my boots and socks were soaked. I tried putting my shades on but hadn't realised that they'd make everything more visible by reducing the glare, so I quickly removed them, preferring to be blinded by the sunlight than seeing anything horrid or dangly! I couldn't imagine what sort of people would want to flaunt themselves in front of total strangers in this manner.

I guess their argument would be: "We're all the same. There's nothing to be ashamed of."

They may well be right but surely a public footpath is not the place to do it. After all, we don't all necessarily want it shoved right down our throats! Once past the danger area I realised what that chap must've meant when he'd said about watching my back near the dunes! At least I was getting closer to the end by the time I'd passed the naturists. With only ten minutes to go my heart started beating faster and my left foot began hurting badly. What if I collapsed now? What if I had a heart attack and died before reaching the finish? What if a freak wave lifted me up and carried me out to sea and I'm never seen again? What if that thug from the Seaton café is waiting for me at the finishing line and shoots me before I can cross it? Maybe I was destined to fail at the last minute like old "Snot of the Antartic!" Anyway, the list of horrific "What ifs?" grew and grew during that last 10 minutes, though I knew most of them were improbable. The trouble was, if something awful did happen now, the gruelling seven weeks would've all been in vain. No way could I do the whole thing again – *ever*.

Groaning, I looked up at the sky as I hurried on, praying aloud: "Please don't let me die now. After half a mile more I'll gladly drop down dead, I promise. Let me be found with a smile on my face clutching the finishing post. Ten more minutes! *Please!*"

Before I knew it I was at the end, but where was the 10-foot-high finishing post; that lovely intricate piece of metalwork consisting of a mast and ship's sail and the ornate floor compass I was looking for? Where were they? I couldn't see them anywhere. I spun round in a complete circle searching for it before realising I wasn't at the end after all, but had come to a bend in the bloody coastline! Looking in the distance I saw the large ferry that travels between South Haven Point and Sandbanks. I still had another half-mile to go! Shoulder of pork *pigs*! They'd fooled me again! Gutted, I turned north-west, having to go through the anguish all over again, still not believing I was ever going to get there alive. I was practically running round the edge of Shell Bay towards the ferry whilst praying my old ticker would hold out. There was only 100 yards to go; 50; 20; 10; 5; 2; 1. I lunged forward, grabbing the beautiful shining blue finishing post with both hands, kissing it, hanging on to it for dear life, almost breaking down, unable to prevent tears of joy from welling up in my eyes and running down my face. I ran through the whole gamut of emotions in a few seconds. Apart from the obvious joy and delight there was also the massive overwhelming sense of relief that I'd done it. I'd succeeded. Nothing could take that success away from me now. *Nothing* and *nobody*. In that moment I really didn't care if I dropped dead or not! It'd been the greatest challenge of my life and by succeeding I immediately felt like a far stronger person. I'd never be weak again. I knew that all the confidence that'd drained away over the previous twelve years of hardships and setbacks was now fully restored. I felt I could achieve anything now! At the same time there were also waves of tremendous melancholy because my wondrous adventure was now at an end. Things would never be the quite the same again. This was a turning point. I could *never* go back to my dull old life after this, where each day had merged into the next in a monotonous blur as life drifted aimlessly by. I'd have to make every day count from now on. I stood alone, still desperately clinging onto the sign, staring at the sand beneath my feet. Mixed thoughts and waves of emotion still washed through and over me.

I was brought back to earth by a friendly voice: "You made it okay, then?"

I turned round to see two smiling couples standing on the road nearby. They'd been among the lovely people who'd walked alongside me an hour ago prior to Studland doing "The Pied Piper Stroll". They took turns shaking my hand vigorously, congratulating me, before I commandeered them to take a few photos by the finishing post. We said our goodbyes and then, still in a state of euphoria, I picked up the rucksack, which miraculously seemed weightless now, and strolled onto the large chain-driven ferry for the hundred-yard crossing. I didn't give a damn if it sank either! My local Herefordshire newspaper would've probably read something like: "Local man drowns after completing the South West Coast Path walk" – the operative word being "completing", so I'd die a happy man!

I'd be able to hold my head high at the gates as St Peter asked: "And what have you done in your life, me old mucker?"

"I've completed the South West Coast Path walk, mate, so you stick that down on my CV for a start. Is there anywhere round here where I can get a pot of tea for thirty-one and a load of giant fun-sized Snickers bars?"

THE JOURNEY HOME

The crossing took all of two minutes and I stepped onto the Sandbanks peninsular at 2 p.m. and went straight into a nearby café for a snack, trying to work out how I was going to get home; something that'd never crossed my mind until now. As I ate my pasty and chips, plus one raw tomato, my thoughts turned to the week ahead. It was going to be so strange being at home again with everything at my fingertips. On the trail all of the normal priorities had gone out of the window. All that concerned me was where I was going to get my next food and water, where I was going to sleep that night, how I was going to avoid getting lost, staying safe, washing, and what the weather was going to be like. Apart from these six simple things nothing else had really mattered. I'd never had to think about household bills, terrorism and tragic news stories, politics, nuisance calls, *Emmerdale Farm*, religion, the media, *Big Brother*, greed, junk mail, PC problems, running a car, tidying up, gardening, working, though this journey was far tougher than any work I'd ever done. Although I'd watched a little TV, I could easily do without it now. The list was endless, but this journey had altered my whole perspective on life without me realising it until this moment of reflection.

All I really needed in life I'd just carried on my back. Everything else was superfluous. There was a kind of beauty in the simplicity of it all. I felt I'd never be materialistic in the future, realising I'd been happier this last seven weeks with virtually no possessions at all. All of these thoughts had brought on another feeling that I wasn't too familiar with: contentment. All right, I'd had the odd tantrum (276) when I'd managed to get lost, but looking back it all seemed quite funny, as I always found my way again fairly quickly. I'd mostly seen the better side of human nature and met some wonderful, kind people, 99.9 per cent of whom were great, apart from the odd pillock or two, but they'd made the whole thing more diverse and interesting. I felt my life had been enriched and rejuvenated by the whole experience. I'd have to ask Canadian Janet if she felt the same way too. Despite all the hardships along the way, I'd felt wild, free, and – strangely – completely ageless. I could've easily been twenty-five years old again! I'd lost 2 stone in weight, was tanned, and was also the fittest I'd ever been by far. I'd hardly had a day's illness, apart from the general weariness. That stomach ache was only caused by forcing down those cold beers.

It was 2.30 p.m. when I paid up and left, caught a bus into Poole and a train to Gloucester, which broke down of course! This caused me to miss my connection at Bristol. I got a feeling of déjà vu. Two trains in thirty years and they'd both let me down! After a couple of frantic phone calls I was able to arrange for my parents to pick me up at Gloucester Station at 9 p.m. and I was able to enjoy the rest of the journey. The evening was golden and beautiful.

The atmosphere on the train was wonderful with everyone chatting like long lost friends, no doubt pulled together by the "wartime spirit" that had invaded us all when the train had broken down, leaving us stuck for an hour. At least we had a great view, overlooking the beautiful river near Bradford-on-Avon. It was dusk when we finally pulled into Gloucester station. There was an emotional and wonderful reunion with my lovely Mum and Dad. They'd avidly followed my every step all the way, almost living the trip with me, keeping my spirits up over the phone when I'd been down, keeping notes and tracking my movements with various maps, which was a damn sight more than I'd done! We called briefly at my house to ensure it was still there. We continued to the family home where Dad had made some great "Welcome Home" signs and got some champagne in for the celebration. Despite the length of my day and my parents being in their eighties, we stayed up for most of the night, chatting about what they'd been doing, and with me relating some of the funnier stories that sprang to mind. There'd be many more stories to come over the next few weeks. I confessed that before leaving for the trip I'd written them a "Goodbye" letter, which I'd left on my desk at home should anything awful happen to me. A bit melodramatic maybe, but such had been my level of concern. When they asked if I'd be doing any more walks I roared with laughter.

"What, and go through *that* again? No fear, never, not for all the tea in China or the rest of the world!"

I'd only intended doing this as a one-off. I wasn't interested in putting myself through anymore unnecessary torture, but as the days rolled by and the lovely memories came flooding back, and the grimmer ones receded, I began wondering. After all, I'd got all the equipment.

And Clive Parkinson's words kept reverberating inside my head: "You'll probably find that walking will get into your blood if you manage to finish this one."

After a month's rest and relaxation at home I realised that he'd hit the nail on the head. I'd got itchy feet but what about all that crippling weight? No, surely I couldn't endure that again? The crowning glory came when, a couple of weeks later, Dad presented me with a book he'd bought for me, called *Ultralight Backpacking*. I read it from cover to cover in two days. It changed everything. If only Dad had found that damn book three months earlier! After this new discovery I could no longer rule out another backpacking trip. I'm sure I'll still hate walking, but maybe not quite as much, *if* there is a next time!

THE END

EPILOGUE

I t's now the 13th May 2013 as I'm typing this update - it's my 66th birthday today and 10 years since I did this monumental walk. The first of many as it turned out - despite everything I said. It's been a very eventful 10 years during which I've experienced many highs and lows, more than in all of the other decades of my life put together.

Immediately after the walk I was offered some part time work with a music company in Hereford helping local artistes to further their careers. Along with all my production work it was very rewarding to be able to put something back after my own long, yet spasmodic career within music. This in turn led to more part time music work with several organisations, which I enjoyed immensely for 3 years until I decided to take things easier and concentrate on my walking again - which actually meant I did NOT take things easier at all!

Sadly, in 2006 my dad passed away at the age of 85 but I'm lucky enough to still have my mum around. She is a wonderful, talented & lively lady of 92 - but looks and acts 30 years younger than that. She's as sharp as a tack. And people cannot believe it when they find out her actual age. She's a great role model and example for people of all ages. My mum, sister Jane, and I have become even closer over the years and I'm indebted to them both for being there for me 111% (at least) through the hardest period in my life.

My walking has continued every summer. I had decided to tackle all of the National Trails of Great Britain, and so commenced upon this gargantuan task in 2004 - albeit slowly at first, but increasing in numbers of trails per year as my confidence, experience, and fitness levels grew. I became an "Ultralight Backpacker" reducing my total pack weight from 55 lbs to just 20lbs in total, which made the long distance walking so much easier. I just wish I could have done it on the South West Coast Path but I'd never even heard of it back then sadly.

In 2009 I walked 3 of the Scottish National trails and then played a series of 5 successful sold out reunion shows at Hammersmith Apollo with my band Mott The Hoople. This came up unexpectedly and was a lot of fun if somewhat terrifying as we hadn't played together since 1972 - that's 37 years! Personally, I had not set foot on any stage at all for 31 years - funnily enough it all came flooding back once I got up there though - fortunately!

Then, after being a single man for many years I met a beautiful lady and we had 18 months of fantastic fun, laughter, and walking together before we were struck by unforeseeable tragedy. Sadly, our relationship did not survive this and we went our separate ways. Eventually, I was able to set about my arduous task again - to finish walking all of the National Trails. I also embarked upon some more musical adventures in 2012, which took me into territories I'd never visited before.

I did the one remaining Scottish National Trail - "The Southern Upland Way" in 2012, and at the time of writing I'm planning to walk my final National Trail of the 19 that currently exist - "Glyndwr's Way" in mid Wales.

However, no other walk has ever been as difficult and gruelling as the SWCP, not even Land's End to John o' Groats. It was a very steep learning curve, especially for a novice like me, and even now all these years later, it still seems like madness that I even decided to go for it. It's even crazier that I didn't give up and come home after the first few days in hell! Afterwards, I did feel quite proud of myself for enduring the abject misery for 7 weeks, thus managing to complete all of it.

Back to the present: Mott The Hoople will be playing another series of concerts in November 2013 culminating in a show at the London O2. After that I plan to return to Scotland, tour in my motor home and also walk as many of the Scottish Isles and "wild places" as is humanly possible in whatever time I have left, and possibly write about them. I also haven't ruled out doing some more musical projects. So the future is looking busier than ever!

Many other things have happened too, but if I'm not careful I'll be writing another book!

WALKS in order since 2003:

1. The South West Coast Path
2. The Ridgeway
3. Offa's Dyke Path
4. The Pembrokeshire Coast Path
5. The Thames Path
6. The South Downs Way
7. Hadrian's Wall Path & Saints Way (Cornwall)
8. The North Downs Way
9. Peddar's Way & The Norfolk Coast Path
10. The Cotswold Way - as part of Land's End to John O'Groats incorporating The Heart of England Way, The Limestone Way & sections of other well known trails.
11. The Pennine Way - also as part of Land's End to John O'Groats
12. The West Highland Way
13. The Great Glen Way
14. The Speyside Way
15. The York Wolds Way & Tabular Hills Walk

16. The Cleveland Way
17. Hadrians's Wall again - not solo this time.
18. The Southern Upland Way proceeded by The Oxford Canal.

All walks were done solo and in one go. Land's End to John o' Groats was done in 2008 - 1259 miles in total on a central route.

The toughest of all were The South West Coast Path and The Southern Upland Way, which was walked in horrendous conditions throughout.

Equipment list, April 2003

Tracpac Airjet 65 litre camo rucksack & plastic liner; Vango Micra 100 tent (blue); Snugpak Softie 3 Merlin sleeping bag (red); camo shoulder bag; 1960s Hawkins leather walking boots (£3 and rubbish); lightweight sandals; camo groundsheet; Tilley hat; Leki pole; army fleece; camo long sleeve shirt; 2 cycling tops - polyester; 1 black coolmax top; green army trousers; desert camo trousers; wild green/black Bermuda shorts; wild Hawaiian shirt for evening wear; Berghaus Extreme Paclite rain jacket; green rain overtrousers; 4 pairs socks; baseball cap; fleece hat; Coleman pocket stove & small gas cylinder; frying pan; aluminium pot; kettle; folding knife; knife sharpener; whistle; can opener; Nisis dv2 camera & 2 CF cards; batteries; mobile phone; tiny Sony radio & headphones; emergency blanket; kitchen roll;1 x ill-fated yellow folding bucket; 2 x 20 foot ropes; para-cord; 2 small travel towels; razors; flannel; shave oil; liquid soap; shampoo; tiny deodorant; after shave; sun cream; insect repellent; anti-histamine cream; foot lotion; plasters; tiny brolly; 2 water bladders & hose; credit cards; phone card; cash; small journal & pens; SWCP guide book; 1 small map of the entire SW Peninsular; paracetamol; Ibuprofen; Ibuleve gel; 3 Guardian lights (2 white &1 red); credit card-torch; 2 spectacles; shades; thermal mug/lid; emergency food - cuppa soups; noodles; nuts; protein bars; tea bags; coffee; 6 tiny "café style" milk cartons;

Bought en route: Scarob multi tool-Falmouth £5.99; black wicking top - Falmouth £14; Berghaus Explorer boots-sale Falmouth £59; black shorts - Torquay £6; gas; Compede, blister spray; plasters; Zirtec hay fever pills; green Minack baseball cap-Porthcurno £7; 1 Matthew Sweet CD at a cliff top car boot sale outside Weymouth - 50p!

2013, 10 years on: Everything has been replaced with ultra-light gear. The only 2 items I've retained from the above list are my fantastic Tilley hat, still going strong, and the same butterfly knife sharpener - which has never been used - as YET! I still carry as many items but now it's all pared down to save weight and space. As a result my pack now weighs 18lbs (without water) instead of 60lbs; and I use a 26 or 30 litre pack instead of a 65 litre one. I would love to include a current list so everyone could compare them and see the difference. However, nobody would actually be able to gauge the difference unless they were to try and shoulder the 2 packs - then they certainly would!

ACKNOWLEDGEMENTS

Peter Purnell, Jerry Bloom at *Wymer UK*, Keith Smith - Editor *Two Miles From Heaven* - the MTH fan club magazine, and without whom this book would never have been written, Charlie Hall, Jonathon Manning (the former Editor of *Country Walking* magazine), Phil Syphe, Dale Griffin aka Buffin, for his loyal friendship and constant encouragement throughout my life - & Jean Smith, Shirley Purnell & Christine at *Angel Air Records*, Ben and James Johnstone (my talented nephews), Rick & Sarah Battersby, David & Mary MacDonald, my all-time favourite band - The Contrast from Peterborough, The Mutton Birds, Eels, Outdoor Warehouse Windermere, Ultralight Outdoor Gear - Teesside, Terra Nova Tents, Montane Outdoor Clothing, Inov8 Roclite Footwear and Rucksacks, Golite Gear, Julia Bradbury, Mark Bower, Phil, Michelle & Carla Hendriks, Moshe Julia, Bettina & Nicholas Hanlon, Tim Johnstone, Darcey Bussell, Angie & Howard Copping, Nick Stevens, Guy Stevens, Stan Tippins, Verden Allen, Ian Hunter, Mick Ralphs, Martin Chambers, Morgan Fisher, Ariel Bender, Blue Weaver, Mick Bolton, Ritchie Anderson & Phil John, Mick Hince aka "Booster", Kris Needs, Mick Jones, Brian May, Joe Elliot, Doc Mellor, Trevor & Dawn Berry, Andrew Pritchard and Rosie, Allan Ricketts & Yvonne, John "Screw" Farr, Cath & Nick Farr, Michael Hardingham, Angie, Leah, Rufus, Duncan and Jake McBain - and the Reid family from Stevenston, Maria Jannelli, Jenny Morgan, Pamela Chuck- aka Wookie, Carole Bruce aka "Boo Boo 2" (the smaller & least important of the 2 Boo Boos), Diana Reading & family, Helen Turner, Roberta aka "Berto", Megan, Bob, & Jamie Griffiths, Jacqueline Crilley, Dr. Laura MacFarlane, Ian Thelkeld, Unkie Wubble aka Peter Bates, Andy & Sue Middleton, Peter & Roz Daniels in Devon, Richard and Roe in Hatherleigh, Derek Langley, Steve Watten, Dales View Pete & Gail the border collie in Youlgreave, Dawn & Peter Robertson for their hospitality, Silly Boy Wonniamson, Natalie Tokered, they bleddy Soilents, Mr. Frizz, Mould & Betty, Softy Brooks, Fred Fishpool, Sally Bundy & Donna Cooke, Geoff Diprose, Richard Butler Estate Agents - Ross-on-Wye, Penny Smith, Jo Blythe - Central Weather, all my friends in Scotland and the isles, The Mambo Sons & Tom Guerra, The Phantoms, Warren Zevon, Richard Thompson, Chris Wood, The Cardiacs, The Monks, The West Coast Pop Art Experimental Band, and all the great, and even the "not so great" Bed & Breakfasts and establishments that took me in, and, of course, all of the great characters I met or who helped me en route, and who made the walk and this book possible... and, of course, all the ones that may have slipped my mind too !

THANKS TO YOU ALL

ABOUT THE AUTHOR

Born "Peter Overend Watts" in Yardley, Birmingham on 13th May 1947 to Ron and Joan Watts. Ron was an engineer/lecturer and his mother Joan, a noted miniaturist - being a member of The Royal Miniature Society. Overend attended Church Road Primary School and then Eastbourne House, Acocks Green, before the family, which now included a baby sister, Jane, moved to Worthing, Sussex in 1957, where his father took up a post as an engineering lecturer at Worthing Technical College. Overend attended Maybridge County Primary School followed by Worthing High School for boys before the family relocated to Ross-on-Wye Herefordshire in 1960 where his father became a Head of Department at Cinderford Technical College.

In Herefordshire, Overend attended Ross Grammar School where at 12 years of age music soon became his priority. After playing in local semi-pro pop/rock bands he left his job as a trainee architect, turned professional, and toured Germany in 1964 in the wake of the Beatles. Long trips to Germany and Italy followed where he had some degree of success with The Doc Thomas Group before returning to England in 1969, taking a job as a Christmas postman before becoming a founder member of Mott The Hoople, along with other Doc Thomas Group musicians including Mick Ralphs and Buffin (Dale Griffin).

From 1969 to 1979 Overend recorded and toured extensively with Mott The Hoople, Mott, and British Lions before shunning the limelight and turning his hand to record producing, gentlemen's hairdressing (briefly!), and dealing in antiques - even taking a stall for a time at the famous Portobello Road street market. Despite several chart successes with his productions he opened an antique/record/retro shop in Chiswick, West London in 1985, opting for a quieter life. At this point, however, most of his spare time was spent in the pursuit of large carp and he became a well-known figure on the gravel pits around the London area, where he always used luminous pink carp rods, so his mates, and the carp, could locate him easily! In 1989 he finally left London behind and returned to Herefordshire to be nearer to his family and concentrate on his carp fishing - becoming a water bailiff at the legendary Redmire Pool, and live an even more peaceful life in general. A highlight of his fishing "career" was in 1993 when he managed to capture the legendary mirror carp "Raspberry" from Redmire. The fish was 61 years old at the time and continued to thrive until the ripe old age of 71 after his brief encounter with Overend.

After a few years of doing the antique fairs and auctions he concentrated on recycling and painting furniture and restoring antiques before opening a large "retro" department store in Hereford, which proved popular with customers from all over Great Britain, and also attracted many international customers too, with it's specialist clothing, unusual antiquities, instruments, and rare music. However, 10 years on with the rise of the Internet, the business began to decline - so, as they say - "If you can't stand the heat get out of the frying pan and into the fire". In other words, after 10 years he had tired of it so it was time to move on again.

After leaving the retro store in February 2003, by way a of a change, Overend then attempted the SW Coast Path National Trail. Since 2003 he has earned a living doing various jobs including helping local musicians/bands through various local organisations, also recording them at his home studio, along with some schools projects. He has also sold antiques online and written articles for various publications on music and latterly on backpacking and walking. Since backpacking the South West Coast Path, Overend has also completed all of the other national trails including The Ridgeway, Offa's Dyke, The Pembrokeshire Coast Path, The Thames Path, The South Downs Way, Hadrian's Wall (3 times), The Saint's Way, The North Downs Way, Peddar's Way & Norfolk Coast Path, The West Highland Way, The Great Glen Way & The Speyside Way, The York Wolds Way, The Tabular Hills Walk, The Cleveland Way, The Oxford canal, The Southern Upland Way, Glyndwr's Way, & Wainright's Coast to Coast. In 2008 he completed a marathon 1,250 mile walk from Land's End to John O'Groats in 63 days - incorporating The Cotswold Way, The Heart Of England Way, Staffordshire Way, Limestone Way, Pennine Way, Cheviots, Grampians and Cairngorms. He has also walked sections of many other trails, including The Two Moors Way, Gritstone Trail, Camel trail, and many others.

Now semi-retired he spends most of his spare time quietly in a former croft in the Scottish Isles, when not backpacking, fishing, or travelling in his motor home.